Presented by

Margaret Mendelson

American Nervousness, 1903

AMERICAN NERVOUSNESS, 1903

AN ANECDOTAL HISTORY

TOM LUTZ

CORNELL UNIVERSITY PRESS   Ithaca and London

To Martha, Jesse, Yarri, and Cody

Contents

Illustrations

Could a historiographer drive on his history, as a muleteer drives on his mule—straight forward;—for instance, from *Rome* all the way to *Loretto*, without ever once turning his head aside either to the right hand or to the left,—he might venture to foretell you to an hour when he should get to his journey's end;—but the thing is, morally speaking, impossible: For, if he is a man of the least spirit, he will have fifty deviations from a straight line to make with this or that party as he goes along, which he can no ways avoid. He will have views and prospects to himself perpetually soliciting his eye, which he can no more help standing still to look at than he can fly; he will, moreover, have various

Accounts to reconcile:

Anecdotes to pick up:

Inscriptions to make out:

Stories to weave in:

Traditions to sift:

Personages to call upon:

Panegyrics to paste up at this door:

Pasquinades at that:—All which both the man and the mule are quite exempt from. To sum up all; there are archives at every stage to be look'd into, and rolls, records, documents, and endless genealogies, which justice ever and anon calls him back to stay the reading of:— In short, there is no end of it . . .

—Laurence Sterne, *Tristram Shandy*

Preface

In this book I have constructed a historical laboratory, within which I have prepared a section, properly sliced and dyed, of a cultural complex—a disease called neurasthenia—at a specific historical "moment"—1903. I originally began to conduct this experiment in synchronic history as a way to resist the impulse to narrate, to resist foreclosure, but these resistances have been overcome by the conclusions I have been led to about the importance of "American nervousness" to the story of cultural change at the turn of the century.

The specific means by which a culture reproduces itself historically is a question this book attempts to provide with a local answer. One central argument is that the discourses and practices surrounding the idea of American nervousness lent themselves to plural interpretations and appropriations, and that such a set of discourses and practices made sense to and was important for a society coming to terms with itself as pluralistic. This growing sense of pluralism did not result in an efflorescence of democratic egalitarianism; it was based, in fact, in an insistence on difference and distinction. The denial of fluid boundaries among the constituent groups of American society in 1903 is striking: African Americans, labor unionists, immigrant communities, "brain-workers," and other groups argued to themselves and others that they were different and would remain so and that therefore they wanted their piece of the pie now. This political climate encouraged certain discourses at a national level which might be called economistic discourses, because of their economic rhetoric and logic and because they economically answered the needs of a wide variety of people in diverse circumstances. These were discourses capable of meaning many things to many people, and American nervousness was just such an economistic discourse. One of its functions was to address fears of economic upheaval and create the sense of (or the desire for) the economic "well-being" conducive to a consumption economy. The liminal nature of neurasthenia further ensured that it was available to individuals who were experiencing the disorienting effects of cultural and social change, and ensured that those individual and collective changes would in turn bear the stamp of their nervous origins. The economic, social, and cosmic chaos feared by late-Victorian elites became a temporary subjective state, to be replaced by assimilation to or withdrawal from the regulated economy of consumer appropriation. Throughout this period of rapid change, artists and intellectuals and other "experts" on subjectivity and morality produced advice and anecdotes for that group that identified itself as the middle class, and it is the advice and anecdotes of these artists, intellectuals, doctors, politicians, and other cultural workers which I examine here.

I incurred massive intellectual and personal debts in acquiring the ingredients for this strange brew. Richard Maddox, Kathleen Diffley, Scott Lankford, and Jay Fliegelman all read the manuscript with intelligence, insight, and good humor, working beyond the call of friendship. Kelly Hurley, David Halliburton, Mary Louise Pratt, Eric Solomon, Ian Watt, and Paul Young read large parts of the manuscript at various stages, and offered important advice. José Cuellar, François Lagarde, Wendy Griswold, William Veeder, David Long, Kenneth Warren, Mary Klages, Tom Dean, Bernice Hausman, James Hall, Janet Delwiche, Barbara Welch-Breder, Brooks Landon, Bruce Harvey, and Mort Sosna also read more or less of the manuscript and offered their advice or at least good will. Had I listened better to all this advice, as the saying goes, the book would have fewer faults.

I also thank Dr. Loco's Original Corrido Boogie Band, Jon Wilcox, Deborah Laycock, the Lincoln Garcia Band, Herman Rapaport, Ed Folsom, John Raeburn, the Blue Tunas, Juan-Felipe Herrera, Jonathan Arac, my students at Stanford University and the University of Iowa, and Norris Pope, Al Gelpi, Renato Rosaldo, Dennis Des Chenes, the memory of Jack Winkler, Ed Cohen, Maria Damon, Richard Nolan, John Sitter, Robert Keefe, Ernest Hofer, and Marie Brazil for various forms of support, encouragement, and sustenance, intellectual and otherwise, at steps along the way. I am grateful to the Stanford Humanities Center, the University of Iowa, the Project on the Rhetoric of Inquiry and the National Endowment for the Humanities for fellowships that made this project possible, and to Bernhard Kendler at Cornell University Press for his encouragement and the extremely helpful readers for the press, Glenn Altschuler and Philip Gura, for their advice. And many thanks to my editors Marilyn Sale and Patty Peltekos, and to Loretta Collins for her work on the index.

To Jesse, Yarri, and Cody Lutz I owe the paradoxical and over-determined debt incurred through the privilege of parenthood, to George and Carol Lutz that incurred as a son. To Martha Eisenberg I owe my sanity, health, and heart.

Tom Lutz

Iowa City, Iowa

American Nervousness, 1903

An Introduction
to Nervousness

In 1903, Frank Lloyd Wright designed his first major public building, the Larkin Administration Building in Buffalo, which he called "the first emphatic protestant in architecture"; Kate Douglas Wiggin's novel *Rebecca of Sunnybrook Farm* became one of the year's three best-selling books; and Elbert Hubbard, author and messianic leader of the Roycrofter's community in East Aurora, New York, said of his own divorce scandal: "Just how much discord is required in God's formula for a successful life, no one knows; but it must have a use, for it is always there."[1] How might the relations among these three apparently incommensurable events be described?

There is a geographical relation. Wright's building, Hubbard's community, and the setting Wiggin described in her novel all lie within a few hundred miles of each other, at the fringes of the cultural centers of the Northeast. There is an economic relation. In the novel, eleven-year-old Rebecca sells soap door-to-door to receive a premium, a parlor lamp she wishes to give to her poor neighbors. Elbert Hubbard, it turns out, made his fortune by devising a sales program in which people sold cases of soap in return for premiums, such as parlor lamps. Hubbard's company, his interest in which he sold so that he could retire to his community in East Aurora, was the Larkin Soap Company, whose administration building Wright designed. Rebecca's soap is the soap that made Hubbard's fortune and the money to pay Wright's fees.

And there is a cultural relation. Rebecca is a Larkin soap seller, but one with a social conscience; she sells soap not just for personal gain but to help her lampless neighbors. Her economic activity is only a story within the story of her emergent character. In her enthusiasm for her good-will project to bring a lamp to the poor, she is represented as having an inner light, a lamp inside, burning with good will. Her enthusiasm for doing the right thing keeps her "nervously excited," and her aunt worries that she will become sick, for she has one of "the souls by nature pitched too high, By suffering pitched too low."[2] At the turn of the century, nervous excitement was considered the first symptom of a progressive disease of the nerves, neurasthenia, which could end in nervous prostration, brain-collapse, insanity, or death. According to medical wisdom, this disease attacked only those with the most refined sensibility, and so Rebecca's nervousness, her high-pitched soul's ability for low suffering, is meant to be a mark of her uncommonness, of her extraordinary spirituality and sensitivity.

The signs of such uncommonness were surprisingly common, however, in 1903: nervousness marks the superiority, of one kind or another, of neurasthenic protagonists in stories by Mary Wilkins Freeman, Hamlin Garland, William Dean Howells, Frank Norris, Henry James, Theodore Dreiser, and many others. Ideas about pathologically low or high levels of nervous energy or nerve force are found in all disciplines of thought and all genres of writing and representation. Neurasthenia was introduced in the medical literature for the first time in 1869, but it became more and more common through the beginning of the century. By 1903, neurasthenic language and representations of neurasthenia were everywhere: in magazine articles, fiction, poetry, medical journals and books, in scholarly journals and newspaper articles, in political rhetoric and religious discourse, and in advertisements for spas, cures, nostrums, and myriad other products in newspapers, magazines, and mail-order catalogues. As this list suggests, neurasthenia was both elaborately defined discursively and elaborately useful rhetorically, and was both for sale and used as a sales incentive. Rebecca's nervousness (her high energy and her relation to higher things) and Rebecca's entrepreneurial salesmanship, in other words, are two signs of the same character.

Elbert Hubbard was also "neurasthenic" and also a consummate salesman: his nervousness got severe enough while he was a successful advertiser and salesman that it necessitated his early retirement, and his continued nervousness conditioned his subsequent literary production and practical philosophy, both of which were in turn shrewdly marketed in magazines and books. The relation between nervousness and economics can also be seen in the presumed link, in Hubbard's statement, between discord and the successful life: the question is not whether discord is necessary to the successful life, but how much discord is necessary. The statement has parallels in numerous texts in 1903 which link nervousness and success, nervousness and social mobility, as well as nervousness and divorce or any other disruption of the gender system.

Hubbard's practical understanding of that discord echoes the neurasthenic William James's pragmatic philosophy, and in particular James's idea of the pragmatic value of the distress of the "sick soul." The religious overtones of Hubbard's statement and James's philosophy were common to many representations of the disease, as nervousness was common to many representations of religious life. Frank Lloyd Wright argued that modern, powerful, pragmatic design should replace "this brain-sick masquerade we are wont to suppose art." His buildings, especially their medieval motifs and their atmospheres of aesthetic harmony, were meant to counteract some of the wear and tear of the modern world—the same wear and tear widely believed to be a cause of nervousness. And like Wright's medieval motifs, those of Henry Adams have a series of relations both to neurasthenic discourse and to religious ideas. Adams's own nervousness came to a climax in 1903, according to his autobiography, in his perception of the disintegration of the universe. For Hubbard, Wiggin, Adams, James, and Wright, nervousness had physical and metaphysical repercussions. And all five were aware of the pragmatic effect of neurasthenic environments, of what James called the "cash value" of discord.[3]

Nervous Characters

George M. Beard, M.D., the physician who became known as the father of neurasthenia, was also a neurasthenic and an entrepreneur. He and other neurologists developed a theory of mental and physical health and disease which depended on folk theories of bodily energy which were themselves expressly economic. People were assumed to have a certain amount of "nerve force" or nervous energy, which was subject to a strict bodily economy. When the supply of nerve force was too heavily taxed by the demands upon it, or when the available nerve force was not properly reinvested, nervous bankruptcy, or nervousness, was the result. Some spending of nervous energy—productive work and procreation are prime examples—was considered to be effectually a reinvestment, a reinvestment that led eventually, Beard said, to peace and "finer and spiritual things." Other ways of spending one's nerve force—the paradigmatic examples are masturbation, gambling, and other forms of illicit sexual or financial activity—constituted a waste, a drain on nerve force without any corresponding reinvestment. The idea of "dissipation" thus is based on a notion of dispersed rather than directed nerve force, spent without any possible return on the investment. Dissipation eventually led to "decadence," the death and decay of nerve centers in the individual, and the death and decay of civilization at the social level. The links between medical thinking and economics, and the links to morality, were constantly apparent to both doctors and patients. According to Beard and other neurologists, the end result of processes of dissipation, or of any unwise nervous investment, was a disease called neurasthenia, or "American nervousness." Conversely, if patients were sensitive and refined enough to begin with, neurasthenia could be brought on, regardless of their moral probity, by simple exposure to the hectic pace and excessive stimuli of modern life. The disease could thus be a sign of either moral laxity or extreme moral sensitivity.[4]

Neurasthenia was, then, most succinctly, a sign of modern life. *"American nervousness is the product of American civilization,"* Beard wrote proudly and emphatically in 1881 in one of the first full-length studies of neurasthenia. "The Greeks were certainly civilized, but they were not nervous, and in the Greek language there is no word for that term." Ancient cultures could not have experienced nervousness, Beard wrote, for while only civilized peoples can become neurasthenic, "civilization alone does not cause nervousness." Neurasthenia is, instead, the direct result of modernity. "The modern differ from the ancient civilizations mainly in these five elements— steam power, the periodical press, the telegraph, the sciences, and the mental activity of women," Beard explained. "When civilization, plus these five factors, invades any nation, it must carry nervousness and nervous disease along with it." Neurasthenia, literally "nerve weakness," had become epidemic in certain circles by the late nineteenth century, especially among leisure-class men and women, artists, and brain workers of various kinds, those most involved with "the modern." Henry Adams provided an odd echo to Beard's analysis when he complained in "The Virgin and the Dynamo" that steam power and the fact that women no longer served in the culture as sexual symbols had combined to break his "historical neck," a slightly more violent image of the disruption of the nervous system caused by cultural change.[5] But while Adams bemoaned the loss of the body of the Virgin, Beard reconstructed and celebrated the body as Dynamo, and the doctor as moral mechanic.

Every upper-class family was familiar with one or more of the many symptomatic forms of neurasthenia, such as nervous dyspepsia, insomnia, hysteria, hypochondria, asthma, sick-headache, skin

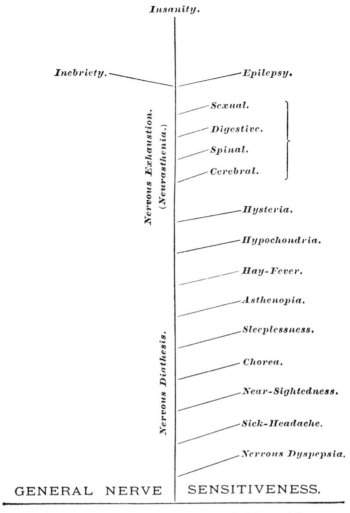

EVOLUTION OF NERVOUSNESS.

The tree of nervous illness, from George M. Beard's *American Nervousness* (1881).

rashes, hay fever, premature baldness, inebriety, hot and cold flashes, nervous exhaustion, brain-collapse, or forms of "elementary insanity."[6] It would be easy to read Beard's emphatic statement of the Americanness of neurasthenia as an indictment of American civilization, especially considering the horror with which other writers, often having been diagnosed as neurasthenic themselves, represented the disease. The narrator's growing insanity in Charlotte Perkins Gilman's story "The Yellow Wallpaper" (1892), Edna Pontellier's suicide in Kate Chopin's *The Awakening* (1899), Curtis Jadwin's breakdown in Frank Norris's *The Pit* (1903), Lily Barth's death at the end of Edith Wharton's *House of Mirth* (1905), Martin Eden's suicide in Jack London's autobiographical novel of the same name (1909), Eugene Witla's breakdown in Theodore Dreiser's *"Genius"* (1915)—these are some of the many explicit narrative representations of neurasthenia, and in these books neurasthenia is used to criticize, to excoriate aspects of modern society. "The Yellow Wallpaper" makes explicit links between woman's estate and ill health and further criticizes S. Weir Mitchell, who along with Beard was one of the major theorists of neurasthenia, its causes, and its cures. But Beard and Mitchell seem largely unaware of the possibility of such a critical project. Beard's statement is, in fact, a celebration of what he called "this distinguished malady," made both "necessary and possible in a new and productive country." Neurasthenia, Beard wrote in 1881, was "modern, and originally American; and no age, no country, and no form of civilization, not Greece, nor Rome, nor Spain, nor the Netherlands, in the days of their glory, possessed such maladies." Beard argued that neurasthenia was caused by the highest levels of civilization and that the epidemic of neurasthenia was proof that America was the highest civilization that had ever existed.[7]

Nervousness, according to Beard and many others, was therefore a mark of distinction, of class, of status, of refinement. Neurasthenia struck brain-workers but no other kind of laborer. It attacked those, such as artists and connoisseurs, with the most refined sensitivities. It affected only the more "advanced" races, especially the Anglo-Saxon. It affected only those of the more "advanced" religious persuasions, proof of which was that "no Catholic country is very nervous." Some people or peoples in other racial or social categories have been "moderately nervous," according to Beard, but only if they were at "stopping-places between the strength of the barbarian and the sensitiveness of the highly civilized." The disease became such a marker of status and social acceptability, in fact, that it could be coveted: the best thing about neurasthenia, according to William Marrs, M.D., in his *Confessions of a Neurasthenic* was that it allowed one to "move in neurasthenic circles." In medical, literary, and popular discourse, neurasthenia had class and racial implications and was closely allied to the discourses justifying dominant American culture, and Anglo-American high culture in particular. Beard expresses some typical late-Victorian fear of the possible degeneration of the handful of people who are the caretakers of a fragile civilization and argues that while those affected by the disease constitute a very small part of the culture as a whole, the rest of the population was as unrefined as it was healthy. Agreement with this view was widespread, as can be seen in the statements of the then-president of the Reading Railroad, Robert Baer. Baer is the man who exclaimed, during the anthracite coal strike of 1902, that "the rights and interests of the laboring man will be protected and cared for—not by the labor agitators, but by the Christian gentlemen to whom God has given control of the property rights of the country." In front of a congressional committee he countered charges that he was mistreating his immigrant laborers with a statement that links the possession of Anglo-American culture to the very ability to suffer: "They don't suffer," he said of the immigrant laborers he employed, "they don't even speak English."[8]

But although the population affected by neurasthenia was small, Beard saw neurasthenics as the caretakers of civilization and thus saw neurasthenia as having extremely important consequences. "The philosophic study of the several branches of sociology, politics, charities, history, education, shall never be even in the direction of scientific precision or completeness," he wrote in his preface to *American Nervousness* "until it shall have absorbed some, at least, of the suggestions of this problem of American Nervousness." Beard's belief in the scientific foundations and possibilities of his theories and his belief in the fragility of civilization and the directive force of elite brain-workers led him to overestimate the "philosophic" consequences of the disease. But it would be difficult to overestimate the cultural consequences of neurasthenia. Because the people who were central to the production and reproduction of the discourses and practices of "sociology, politics, charities, history, education" and other fields were very often themselves neurasthenic, and had a view of nervous energy and civilization very similar to Beard's, a study of turn-of-the-century American culture does, in fact, need to examine "the suggestions of this problem of American Nervousness."

Economic Plots

On January 1, 1903, the lead editorial in the *New York Times* was called "What the Year Will Bring Forth." "The great question in the year 1903," the editorial began, "is to be that of supply and demand." While it remained somewhat cautious, the editorial found the country at the beginning of the year to be under "conditions of high prosperity," which would continue if there were "profitable reinvestment" of the new wealth. The editors expressed some fear that rising wages might result in laborers spending on "mere luxuries or in improvident living," thus squandering the surplus and halting the growth. But if the new wealth being created was instead properly reinvested, the editors announced, "the doubters and the pessimists will have to wait some time yet for the fulfillment of their gloomy predictions." The idea of the improvidence of workers was widespread in 1903, perhaps the most influential example being Ray Stannard Baker's muckraking classic of antiunionism, "The Right to Work." The unions, according to Baker, through providing strike funds and demanding that miners who save help those who don't, are encouraging improvidence. Besides, some miners then take the free hams provided by the strike committee and trade them for beer. "Now that system is putting a premium on improvidence, and fining every man who has saved up any money."[9]

The editors at the *Times* were interested in telling the story with a moral different from Baker's, however, one about the possibilities for peace and prosperity. The matter of vital importance "to all the world," the *Times* editorial continued, "and of paramount interest to the great commercial nations," is the creation of "new safeguards against disturbance of the peace." One month earlier, British and German warships had blockaded Venezuela, bombarded its ports, and destroyed part of its navy after Venezuela defaulted on its large foreign debt and refused to submit the claims to arbitration. Although other editorials on the same page praised the peace and prosperity made possible by American military action in "our new colonial possession," the Philippines and championed the broadest possible interpretation of the Monroe Doctrine, explicitly justifying military intervention to protect American security and interests in Central and South America, the *Times* berated the military expedition by the British and Germans as a "miserable and sordid business." "The time has passed," the paper claimed, "for forays undertaken from such motives and conducted by such methods.... Peace is now the supreme interest of the world, not only for its material welfare, but for its advancement in finer and spiritual things."

Supply, demand, reinvestment, peace, spiritual advancement: the smooth weld between economic analysis and the highest cultural aspirations is familiar to students of American ideological formations—the Revolutionary and Civil War periods, for instance, could provide analogous series of terms, as could the 1950s; the 1980s can provide an identical series in the rhetoric of Ronald Reagan. Narrative in form, this series of terms, only some of which are drawn from economics, is structured as a highly moralized plot, and one contradicted by many of the economic theorists of the day.[10] Nevertheless it informed many, diverse discourses at the turn of the century in America. It is the plot of melodramas of high finance and of religious experience, of tales about sexual morality and worldly success, and of the informing narratives of interpersonal relationships, international affairs, consciousness, and social relations, as well as the plot of bodily illness and health, neurasthenia and its cures. The simplicity of this widely inclusive plot is a mark of its level of abstraction, and its ubiquity a mark of the hegemonic assent it managed to evoke. The actual narratives and discourses informed by this plot structure varied enormously, as they were variously motivated and as they were cut across by other social strictures and structures, by other contingencies of value. But they all share, besides their economism, some form of both conservatism and progressivism.

Progressivism and conservatism, as their names imply, are generalizations about political attitudes in terms of the relation of those attitudes to change. Turn-of-the-century writers claimed that theirs was a time of rapid, widespread, and significant change in almost all areas of social life, and historians later in the twentieth century have concurred. The years 1890 to 1910 in America saw, to give just a few random examples, the introduction of the safety bicycle, then the automobile, and then the airplane; an increase of 1500 percent in the number of telephones and 1000 percent in the number of commercial ice plants; the revolution in the physical sciences which followed the work of Planck, Einstein, and the Curies; a 50 percent rise in population, in part the result of the largest influx of immigrants in the country's history (13 million); the introduction and widespread distribution of motion pictures and the advent of modernism as an artistic movement; the most violent labor unrest in American history and the establishment of national labor unions; the "closing" of the continental frontier and the beginnings of overseas empire; the quadrupling of the number of married women in the work force; the incorporation of major industries and a vast increase in the governmental regulation of business and social life; the emergence of modern advertising and consumerism; a rise from an average of six hundred books of fiction published annually to an average of twenty-three hundred; a 100 percent increase in the number of cities with a population over one hundred thousand.[11] This very partial and heterogeneous list of changes only suggests the scope of social and cultural change in these years. Through all this change, for many communities and across many discursive fields, the economic plot provided what might be called one of the deep structures of hegemonic assent, a structure that could give the ring of truth to even the most crackpot political, managerial, scientific, medical, sociological, psychological, philosophical, or religious tracts and that functioned to naturalize a wide variety of diverse, often competing discourses.

Theodore Roosevelt, for instance, worried about "race suicide" in his articles and speeches. The limited supply of good women available to propagate the "better races" and the apparently unlimited supply of mothers in the "other races" was leading, Roosevelt argued, to the extinction of the "civilized" races. One of the main causes of this impending extinction, he wrote, was the fact that many of the best women in America chose to waste their time in careers instead of reinvesting their energies in the future by becoming mothers. If these women would instead decide to make the proper reinvestment and procreate, not only would race suicide be averted, but the "mighty civilizing races" would be able to "continue to export peace into the red wastes where the barbarian peoples of the world hold sway." Eventually that exported peace, Roosevelt claimed, would lead to the advancement from barbarian to civilized status for the entire world. In this story, the plot is based on an economy of American middle-class women's time and energy, in which a limited supply and overwhelming demands create the necessity for careful reinvestment. The reinvestment in propogating the race makes possible the enforcement of peace at home and the exporting of peace abroad. Since spiritual growth and economic growth are implicitly equated, the colonialist exportation of "peace" leads to the spiritual advancement of mankind. Colonialism—specifically America's relation with its new colonial possessions, territories conquered and occupied during the Spanish American War and its aftermath—is thereby justified with a very indirect method of accounting. And at the same time, in the same arguments, the civilizing mission of imperialism, in the form of military service, business activity, and bureaucratic management, offered prime models for the ideal work of men.[12]

Similar elaborations of the economic plot can be seen in the criticism of waste in the work of Frederick Taylor and Thorstein Veblen. In his first major article, "Shop Management" (1903), Frederick Taylor, the "father of scientific management," argued that the supply of time has too many demands put on it which are not in themselves reinvestments; time is wasted. When the supply of time is properly used, labor is reinvested, peace is established between labor and management, and human progress is ensured. Again the economic plot is elaborated within an economic context; again economistic understanding, through conservation, leads to progress. And again, the plot of supply, demand, reinvestment, peace, and spiritual advancement sets up a progressive economy of competing economic desires. Veblen, although he came to a prescriptive conclusion almost the opposite of Taylor's, made a parallel argument in his criticism of the wasteful spending, the "conspicuous consumption," of the wealthy in *Theory of the Leisure Class* (1899). Veblen saw an imbalance in supply and demand resulting in forms of spending by the higher classes (such as the purchase of otherwise useless status markers) which did not constitute a reinvestment. This wastefulness was slowing the pace of social evolution, Veblen argued, through maintaining the miserable conditions of the working class. Thus, according to Veblen, the competing economic desires fostered by the American economic system made impossible the fulfillment of the progressive economic plot for the majority of workers.[13]

In Taylor's version, the economic plot elided the question of the condition of the working class altogether. "Efficiency," Taylor's answer to the problem of supply and demand, does not deny the demands of labor; instead, in his specific deployment of the economic master plot, they are subsumed in, and subordinated to, a larger economic narrative, just as they were in the *Times* editorial.[14] As in Roosevelt's rhetoric, the economic plot provides a discursive beginning, middle, and end to central social conflicts. The competing claims of economic rivals (labor and management, leisure class and working class) could be profitably subsumed, explained, hierarchized, recast, and even ridiculed (depending on the teller) through recourse to what appeared to many to be the simple, persuasive, and pervasive logic of the relation of supply to spirit which the economic plot attributed to the progress of social life.

Neurasthenia was imbued with the logic of the economic plot. Beard's texts construct a neurasthenic logic from economic, political, moral, and medical discourses intertwined with the language of personal emotional experience, a cross-fertilization that can be seen elsewhere in the culture, as in emotion-words like "panic" and "depression" in economic discourse and in etiquette manuals that linked emotional restraint to financial success. George Horace Lorimer's best-selling *Letters from a Self-Made Merchant to His Son* (1902) is one of the clearest statements about the relation of the moral conservation of energy to business success directly in the Franklinian mode. Charles Eustace Merriman's parodic answer, *Letters from a Son to His Self-Made Father* (1903), relies for its humor on reversals of the same set of beliefs about economy and self-help. The son in Merriam's version is represented as spending as much of his father's self-made wealth as he can get his hands on, helping himself to the fruits of his father's economy despite the father's dyspeptic displeasure. Such neurasthenic representations had become so frequent by 1903 that in many cultural debates, as in debates about foreign policy or about the condition of the working class, the two sides more often argued about the bodily and energetical economics than about the political or financial economics involved.

Both Roosevelt the professional politician, for instance, and Taylor the professional manager argued from neurasthenic assumptions about bodily energy. Taylor's arguments about efficiency are frequently based on notions of the limited energy available in the bodies of industrial workers, and his notion of waste is most often that of a waste of the energy of human bodies. Improperly invested energy makes both workers and management sullen or "morbid," an important word in medical and moral discourse. Roosevelt's argument about race suicide is based on a notion of the differential bodily energy of men and women, of the civilized and the savage, and of upper and lower classes. As we will see, Roosevelt's rough-riding philosophy and his formulation of imperialist foreign policy were the direct result of his immersion in neurasthenic discourse and practice. The editors of the *Times* could make their argument about economic life, in fact, only to an audience steeped in neurasthenic understanding. The idea that the moral dissipation of the lower class might lead to a systemic breakdown receives its cultural force from an understanding of the relation of moral action to bodily condition, and specifically one that is differentiated by class. The image of economic "collapse," in relation to the stock market, is itself preceded culturally by the idea of brain-collapse, a name for nervous breakdown. The gloomy predictions of morbid pessimists, like the disturbance of the peace caused by bad investments, signify more clearly in the psychophysiological register of neurasthenia than in the statistical and theoretical register of economic theory.

Roosevelt, Taylor, Beard, and the editors of the *Times* depend on the same progressive, economistic logic, and their arguments and explanations are marked by a conservatism (especially as a desire to conserve energy and an abhorrence of waste) and an optimism, however guarded. These nervous professions and assumptions of progressive optimism are discursive hallmarks of an era of intense change, and the frequency of such statements marks as well the embattled context in which such optimism existed. So, also, does the anxious reiteration of claims to conservation—in the case of neurasthenia the conservation of nerve force, in Roosevelt's racism the saving of the "Anglo-Saxon race" (and in his arguments for the "conservation" of public land as well), and in Taylor's work the saving of money through the conservation of energy and the avoidance of waste. Roosevelt's warning about race suicide is finally optimistic; it is not so much the apocalyptic raving of a prophet of doom in the desert of the modern as it is a confident call to civic duty, fully expecting its answer, and fully expecting to have an influence on the trajectory of social change. But his optimism is nevertheless rhetorically situated in the context of possible apocalypse, imaged as an apocalypse for Roosevelt's class, an apocalypse of enervation and of economic change, an apocalypse that might bring on a systemic nervous breakdown.

History and Structure

These four examples of parallel rhetoric—the *Times* editorial, Roosevelt's warnings about race suicide, Taylor's efficiency theory, and Beard's discourse on nervousness—all rely on a basic economic understanding. This is not to imply, however, that American culture in 1903 is determined by an economic base, that economic forces are ultimately decisive, or that the symbolic order of the time is structured, simply, like the language of economics. Economic discourses are always at some distance from economic reality, however much they are shaped by economic desires and condition economic choices. The economic history of 1903, for instance, certainly does not follow the plot that informed these dominant strands of American culture. That year was the peak of a business cycle, and the prosperity alluded to by the *Times* editorial was real enough; the front page on the same day reported an announcement of a profit-sharing plan by U.S. Steel, a sign and effect of, and meant to be a further spur to, the widespread prosperity. But by the end of the year U.S. Steel was laying off some thousand workers in a cutback that marked the end of the boom. The boom did not end because workers improvidently wasted their minimal wages on mere luxuries, nor was it the result of large-scale disturbances of the peace by European powers. The prosperity, while it lasted, brought no measurable increase in peace or spiritual advancement. No matter how distant the economic plot became from economic reality, however, the discourses that relied on it continued to flourish. Even attempts to rewrite economics relied on the same plot and its understandings, as in the case of economist Simon N. Patten, one of the early popularizers of demand-side economics. Patten argued, in 1903, that surplus wealth increased energy and that the extra energy, when dissipated through consumption, stimulated production, created progressively more surplus energy, and led finally toward conditions for attaining the highest aspirations of society. Economists who rejected Patten (and other new demand-siders including Richard T. Ely) did so by attacking the reversal of supply and demand as a moral outrage.[15]

And the economic plot is not a language that captured the speaking voices of economists or consumers; the plot is a rarefied abstraction that itself represents an imaginary relation to whatever symbolic order existed in the nervous America of 1903. The identification of plots in discourse helps structure understanding, for both cultural actors and cultural historians. So do other generalized abstractions, such as "neurasthenia" itself, and given the diversity of symptom, syndrome, and treatment, neurasthenia was clearly as much an abstraction for turn-of-the-century doctors and patients as it has been for cultural historians. Because it borrows and refers to so many other important discourses, from religion to commerce, neurasthenia offers the historian what Michel Foucault would term a rich node of intersecting discourse. But while neurasthenia can help describe a significant cultural space, it does not therefore undergird the culture of 1903: it can simply function as a particularly helpful heuristic abstraction. As such, neurasthenia can illustrate what Marshall Sahlins would call the "structure of the conjuncture" of competing cultural processes and products in 1903, the conjuncture, for instance, of Wiggin's sentimentalism, Wright's medievalism, Hubbard's entrepreneurial ethos, Roosevelt's progressive and imperialist rhetoric, Taylor's notion of efficiency, the *Times's* analysis of economic health, Beard's celebration of civilization, Mitchell's lectures to women, and diverse other strands of American culture.[16]

Jackson Lears has argued that neurasthenia was a response of members of an elite group fearful of and opposed to modernity. Lears calls this fear and opposition antimodernism and sees cultural formations and movements such as medievalism, the arts and crafts movement, and neurasthenia as particular responses to what this elite group (and Lears) perceived as the "evasive banality" of modern culture.[17] Antimodernism, a kind of evasive banality in response to evasive banality, had the paradoxical effect of shoring up the cultural power of this group, whose nervousness was at least in part the result of a perception of lost power. Ironically, a nostalgia for their own lost cultural supremacy, as if infectiously, spread through American culture, and the intellectual authority of this group was to an extent reinstituted. But while this reading of neurasthenia helps explain the careers of such men as Henry Adams, it cannot account for the experience of the majority of turn-of-the-century neurasthenics. Neurasthenia and related discourses were not primarily evasive: they were constitutive discourses, were often part of and parallel to the "progressive" discourses of the era, and though they were adaptive they were not any more or less escapist than the other available forms of cultural explanation. Whatever neurasthenia was, it was not simply "evasive banality." Van Wyck Brooks's lethargy, Theodore Roosevelt's asthma, Edith Wharton's illness, Emma Goldman's depression, Mary Wilkins Freeman's insomnia, Theodore Dreiser's rashes, and Henry Adams's despair involve not only a series of very different symptoms but a series of different responses to cultural change, different attitudes toward cultural production, and different forms of cultural construction and criticism. There was not a single motivation for these different cultural discourses and practices, but a series of very different motivations, understandings, and practices that all made use of a single cultural discourse. Neurasthenia is less an ideological formation, in other words, than a multiaccented story, a story necessarily read differently from different social positions. Rather than being the source of a nearly universal cooptation, the heteroglossia of neurasthenic discourse (that is, its polysemic, overdetermined nature) accommodated both processes of cooptation and processes of contention, as well as processes that were not clearly either.

Arguments that resolve into narrative conclusions, based on a description of history as collective experience, can help provide an understanding of such large-scale historiographical concepts as the "rise of consumer society," the rise of the "therapeutic ethos" which replaced liberal notions of an autonomous self, the "incorporation" of America, the "revolt against formalism," the advent of the "modern," and the commodification of the body. But they necessarily gloss over significant differences, both within and among the various constituent groups of turn-of-the-century American society. Rather than provide a description of the generalizable experience of Americans, I analyze the significance of the different experiences and writings of a heterogeneous but circumscribed group of cultural producers. Their differences can be most easily represented in terms of the divergent ways in which they appropriated this one, generalizable discourse at one specific time.

Ironically, this synchronic approach does not "fix" time but makes it appear as indeterminate; synchronic study produces, oddly enough, historiographical diachrony. The narrative argument that the combined effects of increasing urbanization, rapid technological development, spreading secularization, and an increasingly interdependent market economy in the late nineteenth century resulted in a widespread feeling of unreality or "weightlessness" within the middle class, for instance, can be countered with numerous examples of writers complaining about excess gravity. Many local colorists describe the neurasthenic despondancy of their characters in terms of feeling weighted down, as in the stories of Mary Wilkins Freeman or Kate Chopin. Alice Brown, in *The Mannerings* (1903), which reviewers thought well illustrated the morbid types of New England character, locates the melancholy of her characters in the boredom of small town life. Her characters' desire for "life" is a desire for modern experience as represented by and in the city, a desire that is not antimodern but precisely promodern in its antitraditionalism, and a desire that seeks less gravity rather than more. Brown also connects the desire for intense experience not to the loss of Christian belief but to a nostalgia for the days of "the youth of the world, when gods walked with men," an image gleaned directly from German romanticism, as in Schiller's thesis on the naive and the sentimental.[18] In addition, ongoing secularization, another supposed cause of neurasthenic weightlessness, had no constant relation to either the relative weightlessness or weighted-down feeling of people in 1903 with as different attitudes toward secularization as those of Jack London, William James, Henry Adams, Theodore Dreiser, Samuel Clemens, George Santayana, or Josiah Royce. Some neurasthenics did bemoan the loss of authentic experience they assumed was known by generations of pioneers. But Beard and others argued, at the same time, that such pioneers were barely civilized and that the intensity they were capable of experiencing was a mark of their lack of civilization. He also argued that civilization, by sensitizing people to their own experience, made the containment of experience necessary.

Of the various cultural arguments advanced by philosophers, fiction writers, and physicians in 1903, then, some seem ahead of their time by forty years and some seem behind the times by as much. The attitudes of Schiller and Goethe coexist with those of Emma Goldman and Charles Eliot Norton, Hamlin Garland and Edgar Saltus, and all are as out of synch with the unfolding of any specific historical narrative as they are with one another. Beard's early texts on neurasthenia are particularly interesting in this regard since they seem to encompass almost all of the various views attributed to different times in the narrative histories of the disease. It is perhaps exactly this encyclopedic disregard for contradiction which led to his text's continued appeal and influence. At any rate, reducing Beard's text to a specific position in the available narratives of neurasthenia and ideological change, narratives that necessarily force historiographical clarity on a historically contentious period, is impossible because of the text's attitudinal inclusiveness. Neurasthenia as Beard described it allowed for a wide variety of different, sometimes opposing appropriations, only some of which might be persuasively linked to the historiographical functions it has recently exercised.

Neurasthenia offers a common horizon to the texts of 1903 because of its ubiquity, which was itself made possible by the disease's amorphous possibility. As William James suggested, "The literally present moment is a purely verbal supposition, not a position; the only present ever realised concretely being the 'passing moment' in which the dying rearward of time and its dawning future forever mix their lights."[19] There is no "moment" for us to pinpoint, whether we isolate a century, a decade, or a year. My "1903" is, to use James's words, a "purely verbal supposition." But this synchronic supposition has two significant advantages. The first is the nature of the historical specificity it allows, since, however artificial it may be, the very finite time period provides a way to determine how much what might look like historical change is actually cultural variation. Second, it can help make apparent the agency of individual subjects in the production, reception, and reproduction of culture: whatever the discursive, epistemic, or structural constraints involved, Kate Wiggin, Elbert Hubbard, and Frank Lloyd Wright (and Emma Goldman, and Henry James, and W. E. B. Du Bois) appropriated the discourses and practices of nervousness from very different motives, in very different combinations, and with very different consequences, both intended and unintended. What the synchronic approach offers is a way of determining the structure of such unlikely conjunctures. And whatever clarity this synchronic approach offers is perhaps augmented by the nature of neurasthenic discourse, which was itself, in part, an attempt to establish discursive clarity in the context of widespread contention.

1903

But why 1903? The year has a certain numerological joke value. Robert Benchley titled one of his books *After 1903—What?*, suggesting that life could hold no thrill or value after such a year. That year is never referred to in the book (although neurasthenia is)—the title itself is an isolated joke. A recent comic feature article in the *San Francisco Chronicle* outlined a series of fictitious California cults, among which were the pyramid sales cults, the sun-dried tomato cult, and the cult of 1903. True believers in this last cult feel that everything that happened in 1903 has sacred significance, and so they collect tokens, facts, books, references to the year. This apparently is funny.

But certainly I have not chosen the year simply for its joke value.

A very good argument could be made, in fact, despite Virginia Woolf's assertion that the modern world began one day in 1911, that the modern world began some day in 1903. That is the year the Wright brothers flew at Kitty Hawk and the year the Curies won the Nobel Prize for isolating radium; the year the United States created the Republic of Panama as a site for an interoceanic canal, put down a rebellion against American rule in the Philippines, and established naval stations in Cuba; the year Albert Einstein wrote his first professional paper. Ivan Pavlov began his experiments in conditioned response, Pablo Picasso painted *The Old Guitarist*, and the Bolsheviks and Mensheviks split; the year that saw the creation of federal police power and the first automobile cross the continent from New York to San Francisco; the year the first radio transmission of a human voice was sent between cities and the first global communications link was established with the laying of the Pacific cable; the year the first "feature" film, *The Great Train Robbery*, was produced and distributed and the New York subway system was under construction; the year in which Henry Ford organized the Ford Motor Company and King C. Gillette marketed the first safety razor with disposable blades; and the year in which the first baseball World Series was played and the teddy bear was invented. In other words, in many areas of science, technology, communication, politics, and culture, much of what we experience as central aspects of modern life made their debut in 1903. While I do not argue that 1903 represents the actual threshold of modernity, in many ways it is in the center of a series of changes from what we can generally and reductively call Victorian culture to that which we term modern. Nevertheless, however easy an argument about the significance of this year might be to construct, it would be a mistake to construe American culture in 1903 based on the idea of modernity. The year 1903 is awash in change, but despite all its entries in the record books, and however much it might legitimately be seen as a site of cultural origin, it is nonetheless dominated by cultural continuity. In cultural terms, as the prevalence of neurasthenia in 1903 demonstrates, the nineteenth century did not end in 1900, and the twentieth century was well under way.

The discourse of "nervousness," for instance, is quintessentially Victorian. It is defined by and helps to define ideas of gender, class, civilization, medicine, the person of the doctor, physiology, and psychology which are all more Victorian than they are modern. Nervousness had been a part of popular medical understanding in America since the late eighteenth century, but it was not part of official medical culture until the Civil War, when it received its medicalized, Latinized name and what physiological specificity it had. In the period between the Civil War and World War I, the medical and popular elaboration of neurasthenia allowed the medical discourse to override earlier forms of nervousness. Neurasthenia became then both a medical specialty and a central new cultural articulation of psychological, moral, physical, social, and economic understandings, especially understandings of psychological, social, and economic change. "Nervousness" in literary, academic, and journalistic discourses was most often used in explaining change in gender roles, change from one stage of life to another, change in financial circumstances, change in cultural values, change in marital status, change in social status, change in an individual's relation to institutions, or changes in the institutions to which an individual is related. The year 1903 was alive with such changes to be diagnosed or explained. Neurasthenia was the primary discourse available to mediate these transformations in 1903, and it was available in numerous forms and packages, from many sources, and advertised with numberless promises.

Signs of the Time

Roosevelt, Veblen, Goldman, Hubbard, Adams, Beard, and Mitchell all suffered, at one time or another, from the epidemic of neurasthenia among cultural producers. This is true of the other writers, academics, and artists that have been mentioned in passing so far: Wharton, London, Taylor, Dreiser, Santayana, Royce, Chopin, Gilman, Brooks, Eakins, Remington, Wister, Wiggin, Freeman, Brown, Norris, Garland, Saltus, and William and Henry James. The roster of other cultural workers who either had been diagnosed as neurasthenic, displayed the characteristic symptoms of neurasthenia, and/or relied heavily on neurasthenic themes and images in their writings and works could be extended to include Andy Adams, Brooks Adams, Jane Addams, James Lane Allen, Ambrose Bierce, John Burroughs, Willa Cather, Charles Chesnutt, Samuel Clemens, Francis Marion Crawford, Richard Harding Davis, Margaret Deland, W. E. B. Du Bois, Mary Baker Eddy, John Fox, Jr., G. Stanley Hall, Pauline Hopkins, William Dean Howells, Alice James, Sarah Orne Jewett, Mother Jones, Helen Keller, George Cabot Lodge, Brander Matthews, John Muir, Charles Eliot Norton, David Graham Phillips, Jacob Riis, John Singer Sargeant, Upton Sinclair, Lincoln Steffens, Gertrude Stein, Ida Tarbell, Booth Tarkington—the list could go on until it included the majority of well-known cultural producers of the time. How they appropriated neurasthenic discourse varied enormously because the motivations were so varied; it is these variations that are my focus. In the economy of representation and in the representation of the economy, in the lives of cultural producers and in the thematics of fiction, in philosophy, political discourse, and social commentary in 1903, neurasthenia was a central figure, a nearly universal trope for the individual's relation to cultural modernization. Neurasthenia itself was created out of strands of discourse on evolution and civilization, on gender, on science and technology, on ethical action, on religion, on sexuality, on health and disease, and on race, class, and art. After having been "neurasthenicized," some of these strands were then rewoven into new discourses, such as those of imperialism, pragmatism, and modernism, and thus the warp of Victorian culture and the woof of modernism form, in 1903, a mottled and uneven neurasthenic tapestry.

Because of its ubiquity in the discourses of change, neurasthenia can provide a model, I will argue, for the way such an overdetermined discourse functions in the management of cultural change in a pluralistic society, the way it functions as a "cultural space" in which individuals negotiate their personal relations to change, and at times their relations to stability. In Pierre Bourdieu's terms, neurasthenia creates systems of schemes for perception, appreciation, and practice for individuals, and these systems structure their dispositions and thereby condition their social actions and trajectories. Neurasthenia is thus a prime example of a discursive "space of social transformation."[20] The rest cure and the exercise cure can be seen as the enforcement of new practices specifically designed to create a temporary "life-style" for the patient which would, it was hoped, work backward and result in a restructuring of the patient's schemes of perception and finally effect an adaptation to the patient's evolving habitus. The rest cure for women and its enforced infantilization and isolation, usually in the home, and the exercise cure for men, with its rugged outdoor sports and other public activity, are clear indications that cure was designed in response not to a specific pathology but in response to ideas of a man's or woman's "place."

Beard, Mitchell, and other neurologists argued that social mobility was a prime cause of neurasthenia and suggested regimens that manipulated the way their patients lived and those patients' understanding of their own social trajectory. The class, race, and gender biases encoded in the neurasthenic diathesis demonstrate that socially constructed practices and positions determined who, how, and why one became diseased. The very different relations of individuals to those class, ethnic, and gender markers—which ranged from embrace to rejection, from subversion to reinforcement—and the contradictory meanings of these markers in individual cases (for instance, for an upper-middle-class, uneducated southern European female immigrant) demonstrate an accommodation of difference in neurasthenic theory, an understanding that something like an individual position and perceived trajectory does indeed intercede between social construction and individual practice. My argument here is that the available positions in the social structure, including economic positions, were understood by many doctors and patients in terms of a neurasthenic hierarchy of energy, will, and consequence which conditioned the habitus of the middle-class subject. Neurasthenic discourse was part of the objective condition of the patient (and therefore of the habitus, the system of schemes for cultural production, and the practices and works generated) and so could be used in its modification as well as its reproduction. The various forms of medical prescription and self-directed therapy, as they intervened at the level of practice, conditioned what Bourdieu calls the "classifying practices" of the life-style, which both marked and classified the subject's own position. It is in this process that we will be able to see the force of neurasthenic double-dealing in subjective and cultural transformation.

Victor Turner has made popular a reading of individual and social transformation in terms of a "ritual space," in which an individual is freed, at least for a moment, from normal social demands and expectations before being "reincorporated" into a social group, usually in a new social position. Arnold Van Gennep argued in 1908 that such rites have three distinct stages, "preliminal rites (rites of separation), liminal rites (rites of transition), and postliminal rites (rites of incorporation)." Liminal rites, according to Van Gennep, suspend normal social expectations and create an unstructured space in which individuals slough off old social positions in preparation for the new ones awarded in postliminal rites. Following Van Gennep's structural analysis, Turner argued that liminal rites involve the construction of a ritual space in which participants exist momentarily "betwixt and between successive lodgments in jural political systems." This liminal stage, which Turner claimed is not so much unstructured as it is a mirror structure, or antistructure, is the time during which both individuals and cultures construct new ways of seeing and being. Individuals who pass through this mirror structure emerge restructured, and thus neurasthenia, when considered as a liminal rite, is a disease that in its full etiology reconstructs subjectivity. Its mirror structure is evident in the cures, since women who are too active are put to bed, and men who are not active enough are given exercise. But the symptoms themselves are also mirrors, mirrors that display in exaggerated form both progressive and conservative dreams, fears, and controls. Women who were active were, in the convex mirror structure of the neurasthenic world view, exhausted. Men who were inactive were, when they came to inhabit the same antistructure, both enervated and effeminate. If, as James A. Boon has argued, all cultural description requires exaggeration, the exaggeration in neurasthenic description may be a sign of its function as cultural definition.[21]

Neither Turner nor Van Gennep derived their data or examples from American society. But using Turner's theories, Carroll Smith-Rosenberg studied the religious revivals of the Second Great Awakening as a "massive rite of passage marking the emergence of the American bourgeoisie." Smith-Rosenberg is careful to stress that she uses Turner's terms as metaphors, and she states that she desires to combine "anthropology's sensitivity to . . . symbolic languages, and history's awareness of heterogeneity, change, and conflict."[22] Turner himself has argued for the relation of liminal states (and "liminoid" cultural products) to conflict and change, but Smith-Rosenberg is right that Turner tends to maintain a monolithic notion of "society" unsuited to complex, pluralistic cultures. For example, she shows that since women's positions in the social structure determine their relation to ritual practice, women's relation to revivalism was different from men's. My study of the individual appropriations of neurasthenic discourse is in methodological terms an extension or elaboration of Smith-Rosenberg's concern for heterogeneity in the analysis of social structure and the discourses of antistructure. Neurasthenia is not so much a specific social rite of passage as a liminal discourse that was available to individuals involved in a broad variety of passages and changes, one that allowed for embracing or rejecting change, for reinforcing or transforming traditional roles, and for a wide range of possibilities in between. In other words, I concentrate on a dialectic of adaptation in which the liminal discourse of neurasthenia plays a central, active, but far from unitary role in the reconstruction of social norms. The neurasthenics I studied helped create a neurasthenic society and effectually fashioned a pluralist, expansionist world of consumer desire at the same time that they each refashioned, however unconsciously or unintentionally, their own life styles and subjectivities. Of the figures described in this book, many had experiences of neurasthenia which fit Turner's model neatly, but several had experiences considerably less ritualistic and transformative. Nonetheless, the plural appropriations of the disease made possible its cultural significance, and its cultural significance encouraged plural appropriations.

This plurality of cultural functions and the encouragement of appropriative possibility are made possible by the vast array of symptoms and syndromes related to the disease and by its discursive heterogeneity and semiotic vagrancy. "Semiology" was a term originally adopted by Ferdinand de Saussure from medical discourse, where it was synonymous with symptomatology, or the study of the signs of disease. From this Roland Barthes has argued for an analogous relation between medical semiology and current notions of semiotics, such as the arbitrariness of the sign. In doing so he points to one of the central problems for the kind of study I am conducting in what he calls "the dizzying reversibility between the signifier and the signified" in medical diagnosis: "The disease is defined as a concurrence of signs: but the concurrence of signs is oriented and fulfilled only within the name of the disease, there is an infinite circuit. The diagnostic reading, i.e., the reading of medical signs, seems to conclude by naming: the medical signified exists only when named." As a result, a strict definition of what exactly neurasthenia was (the disease became officially extinct in America with the publication of the third edition of the American Psychiatric Association's *Diagnostic and Statistical Manual* in 1980) is impossible. I therefore bracket questions of the relation of neurasthenia to diagnoses that may or may not have replaced it, the question of whether neurasthenia was "really" a mental or physical disease, and all other questions of the essential or material nature of neurasthenia as a disease, including the current attempts at a revival, in favor of a study of the rhetoric of the disease and the practices surrounding it.[23]

At the same time that the rhetoric of neurasthenia had particular functions for individuals in their negotiations of and personal relations to social transformation, neurasthenic language was widely used in general, abstract explanations of the nature and conditions of social life. These two functions are closely related, since the appeal of neurasthenia as a disease was in part the way in which it allowed patients to reexplain the world to themselves, and the appeal of neurasthenic discourse for social theorists and commentators was also the ease with which it was recognized as an explanation. This was true in Europe as well as America. While Saussure found a notion of the master code of cultural formation in the formation of symptoms, Freud argued that mental phenomena partook of the nature of symptoms that were interpretable within a system (a symptomatic language as Lacan would later read it) created by the individual's relation to society. Friedrich Nietzsche, who spent the last years of his life reading nothing but medical pamphlets, saw neurasthenia as emblematic of the internalized guilt, denial of the body, and glorification of powerlessness he found at the center of modern culture. Émile Durkheim studied neurasthenia and Max Weber was himself neurasthenic. While what Foucault refers to as the "abstract universality of disease" has been used as a general explanation of social life at least since Plato, at the turn of the century neurasthenia became especially attractive as an explanatory metaphor because of its ability to authoritatively encompass the multiple conjunctures experienced by cultural elites in a world of violent change. The discourse of neurasthenia provided, especially for intellectuals and artists charged with representing the consequences of subjectivity, a malleable and yet coherent structure of feeling amid and beyond what Henry Adams feared as the chaos of a "multiverse," the newly discovered pluralism of the universe. Neurasthenia was, as Beard and most other commentators agreed, a disease that was a sign of the times, and as such it makes sense that the uses to which it was put were at least as heterogeneous as they were discursively commensurate.[24]

What follows, then, is a study of neurasthenia as (to adopt Henry Adams's term) a "multiversal" disease. This should not be seen simply as an instance of Foucault's claim that discourses are discontinuous or of his argument that the appropriation of a particular discourse is a form of maintaining or appropriating power. Unlike Foucault in his writings on medicine, in which he outlines a historical shift in basic medical perception which then becomes appropriated as a discursive enforcement of normality, I will concentrate on the micropolitics of appropriation and the dispersion of power which ensues. Roger Chartier and Robert Weimann have recently argued that a reformulation of the notion of appropriation which goes beyond Foucault's should be, in Chartier's words, at "the centre of a cultural historical approach." This reformulation would "emphasize plural uses and diverse readings," Chartier writes, and would enable a "social history of various interpretations." Robert Weimann has suggested the same: "As against both the classic-romantic view of the text as the purely referential activity of some reflecting subject and the (seemingly opposite) view of the text as some autonomous locus of self-determining referentials or epistemes," Weimann offers "the concept of appropriation." He defines this in double terms: "Both the world in the book and the book in the world are *appropriated* through acts of intellectual acquisition and imaginative assimilation on the levels of writing as well as reading."[25]

Like Foucault, Chartier, and Weimann, I am interested in the discontinuities of plural appropriations. But whereas Chartier and Weimann are primarily concerned with appropriation as the space between textual representation and practices of interpretation, and

Foucault is interested in appropriation as the exercise of power, I am interested in a specific kind of discourse which encourages plural response, a kind of discourse which thrives precisely because it exaggerates and thereby leaves open the space between representation and practice, a discourse that encourages a refashioning of one's relation to a changing world, and one particularly suited to structuring a radical conjuncture. The word "appropriation" points to the economistic, individualistic, and pragmatic sense in which many neurasthenics acquired the preconditions, the condition, and the reconditionings of the neurasthenic course. The individual appropriations of neurasthenic discourse involved, in varying degrees, a specific imaginary relation to the value system of a particular time and class, an "accented" reading that made those values their own, and specific practices (regimens, writings) that contributed to the further delineation of the range of acceptable possibilities for change through social reproduction.[26] Therefore neurasthenic discourse always displayed, again in various combinations, both a sense of propriety and a proprietary sense, a sense of the appropriate and of the appropriative.

The figures examined in this book appropriated neurasthenia in discursive terms, as the pervasive use of neurasthenic themes, tones, and images in their texts demonstrates. They also acquired neurasthenia as a disease and therefore had both a subjective experience of neurasthenia and what Anthony Giddens would call a "practical consciousness" of the disease.[27] Their experiences can be analyzed in both personal and social terms. Neurasthenia could be caused, for instance, by indecision about one's life work or by idleness. But it could also be caused by overwork, and the cure was often a vacation dressed up as therapy. In either case, the disease was related to changing notions of work. Neurasthenia helped some newly upper-class Americans, swelling from the wealth created by industrialism and expansion, accept a leisure-class ethic at odds with the still-dominant work ethic. It suggested to others a redefinition of the social roles of upper-class men in ways that curtailed their leisure and created, among other things, a new sanction to work in the formerly "vulgar" world of business, finance, and industry and thereby profit from ongoing modernization. The specialization and professionalization of elite activity also created, along with new fields and new forms of cultural authority, a series of new roles for men and women. These new roles—including such phenomena as the appearance of the New Woman and the leisure-class wife and the increasing professionalization of medicine, academic work, journalism, art, politics, business, and literature—had widespread repercussions in American perceptions not only of class and privilege but also of the gender system and culture itself. Some neurasthenics retreated from these changes, while others were instrumental as cultural icons of the new modalities.

The individual appropriations of the disease at the level of practical and subjective consciousness had a variety of more or less unique personal motivations and personal outcomes, and in aggregate, or from another analytic perspective, they had a set of social causes and social effects. Individuals negotiated their relation to political economy by nervously reconstructing the economies of the self, as the culture moved from an ethic of production to an ethic of consumption.[28] And since the disease primarily struck "brain-workers," especially those brain-workers sensitive and refined enough to be working in literature, philosophy, and the like, the individual appropriations had cultural consequences beyond those felt by the neurasthenics themselves. As the producers of culture, these neurasthenics were looked to for advice on legitimacy, on the appropriate—they were charged with representing the values of subjectivity and the social space. As they recreated themselves through neurasthenic experience, they transformed and recreated hegemonic agreements about personal, social, and cultural value.

Anecdotal Histories

From 1903 as a field of inquiry I carved a territory of nervousness; from this territory I have further whittled a series of smaller fields: short biographies, or portraits, of the major cultural figures who, in almost all cases, were both neurasthenic and wrote about neurasthenic issues in characteristically neurasthenic terms, those writers and artists who had their experience formed by neurasthenia and helped to form or at least reform the discourses of nervousness themselves. The focus on individual appropriation and on a very short time period has resulted in what might be called an anecdotal history. In medical literature, anecdotal reports are sometimes published as notes, describing symptoms and courses that don't yet fit any known disease entity. The anecdotal reports presented here are not meant as evidence for the eventual construction of a disease entity, but the opposite: the disease has been deconstructed into anecdotal constituents. The anecdotes can be used for evidence for any number of larger narrative historical developments: here I will focus on just one, the way in which a discourse of the private body and self in need of attention structured the historical conjuncture of middle-class America in the early twentieth century, providing for the orderly reproduction and transformation of American culture in its most public forms.

The first section of the book, "Neurasthenic Economies," deals with the lives and writings of Theodore Dreiser, Theodore Roosevelt, William James, Hamlin Garland, and Edgar Saltus, the particular uses they each made of the discourse of neurasthenia, and the ways in which the discourse appeared in their writings. Their experience of neurasthenia involved both a variety of symptoms and a variety of changes (class, status, marital, professional, and geographical), and their writings invoke and respond to neurasthenic representations of disciplinary, political, literary, and philosophic changes. The second section will examine the work of Frank Norris, William Dean Howells, and Mary Wilkins Freeman, who along with William James, Samuel Clemens, and many others, wrote in 1903 on issues of nervousness, spiritualism, and the supernatural. In this section, I look at the metaphysical representation of neurasthenic issues, at the "Supernatural Naturalism" of the texts of these writers in 1903, and at the relation of these issues to changing notions of subjectivity. The third section, "Neurasthenic Representation and the Economy of Cultural Change," attempts to go beyond these themes in brief examinations of the work of Henry James, W. E. B. Du Bois, Edith Wharton, Charlotte Perkins Gilman, and a few others. In this section the relations among many disparate discourses—on socialism, on black Americans, on art and realism, on muckraking, and on the blues—are illuminated through the use of neurasthenia as a shared horizon, as are the relations of neurasthenia to disparate forms of cultural change.

Whether seen as a sign of refinement and position, as a form of cultural bootstrapping, as a space for social climbers, as a disease of the shabby gentility, as a mark of distinction, a sign of social deterioration, a fearful response to modernity, or a sign of old-fashioned values, it is clear that neurasthenia helped people negotiate the large-scale changes in culture and structure which radically changed the face of social life in America between the Civil War and World War I. The surprisingly different appropriations of the disease do not describe historical movement so much as they describe cultural heterogeneity, and, correspondingly, the fact and awareness of an increasingly pluralistic multiverse in 1903 is part of what created the role neurasthenia played. The anecdotal histories of these appropriations thus constitute a history of heterogeneity, change, and continuity.

The self-awareness of cultural pluralism and cultural change was clearest in relation to immigration, as thousands of immigrants from southern and eastern Europe arrived at Ellis Island and thousands of Asian immigrants arrived on the West Coast. This immigration made people nervous, for these undercivilized but "tired . . . huddled masses" posed, to many imaginations, an obvious threat to people made weak and martially deficient by overcivilization. Combined with decades of violent labor unrest, the middle class at times felt under siege, as Beard wrote in the 1880s: "All our civilization hangs by a thread; the activity and force of the very few make us what we are as a nation; and if, through degeneracy, the descendents of these few revert to the condition of their not very remote ancestors, all our haughty civilization will be wiped away." Some of the haughty few interpreted such warnings as a need to civilize the masses, so that Jane Addams, when she opened her settlement house in Chicago after years as a neurasthenic invalid, had as a prime ingredient in the routine for her inmates a course of reading in the classics of Anglo-American literature. Others, like Roosevelt, feared that overcivilization was sapping the strength of the civilized few, who therefore needed remedial training in barbaric violence and appropriation.[29]

The fear of overcivilization was often accompanied by fear of overwork and, especially, overproduction—a fear that the industrial machine was producing too much, too fast, and creating an economic miracle bound to end abruptly when there was no demand for the artificially high supply.[30] The fear of overproduction—from Norris's "wheat—wheat—wheat!" cascading out of train cars to bury freight agents to the muckrakers' fear of the enormity of the productive power of trusts—fueled the nervousness of America's middle-class and at the same time helped legitimize advertising and consumption. James's *Ambassadors*, for instance, clearly demonstrates (however much it problematizes) the belief that advertising was the "new force" that would replace nervousness and fend off the specter of oversupply. With the emerging acceptance of the principle of consumption, nervousness was reinterpreted as pure energy, and desire was reinterpreted as energizing rather than depleting. The easy answer to oversupply is overspending, and therefore the up-tempo sequel to the Age of Nervousness was the Jazz Age of the twenties, the cultural work for which was already under way in 1903.

Part of that cultural work was done by literary texts. The novel and the short story in particular provided models of neurasthenic adaptation for their readers, anecdotes of resistance and resolution, and guides to the changing etiquette of illness and healthy consumption. The explosion of magazine circulation (The *Ladies' Home Journal* advertised itself in 1903 as the "Magazine with a Million") and the emergence of the "best seller" are the two most obvious signs of a market for both anecdotes and advice about personal relations. Most of the text in these magazines consisted of short stories, serialized novels, and anecdotally based advice columns on fashion, home economics, health, and moral behavior, sandwiched between columns of advertising copy. Thus packaged, readers were encouraged to read all three—advice, advertisement, and fiction—with the acquisitive moralism recommended by many critics and practitioners of narrative art. F. Marion Crawford, himself a best-selling novelist, argued that what the reading public wanted was "to see before them characters whom they might really like to resemble, acting in scenes in which they themselves would like to take a part."[31] Although this describes only a fraction of Crawford's own voluminous output, it nonetheless expresses a major paradigm of reading: the fictional world consists of fantasy trajectories.

Two other popular genres—articles and photo essays of well-known businessmen and cultural producers, especially actors, actresses, and writers of fiction who were shown as having life-styles to be emulated, and exposés of the life of the undeserving poor—encouraged similar readings. The anecdotes of success and failure in fiction, which again and again represented neurasthenia as the cause and result of social mobility, were the most readily available of these various forms for the reader's interpolation. Fiction, long recognized as an arbiter of morals and manners, was a major forum for the articulation, dissemination, and elaboration of neurasthenic discourse, and most of the anecdotes that follow are drawn from the practice of fiction, especially fiction written by neurasthenic writers. After being temporarily consumed by disease, these writers, their characters, and their readers emerged prepared to consume, or at times prepared to resist, the new products and ideas of the twentieth century.

In *Illness as Metaphor*, Susan Sontag describes the "punitive and sentimental fantasies" and the "stereotypes of national character" surrounding the diseases of tuberculosis and cancer. Much of what I have to say about nervousness closely parallels her comments, in part because consumption and neurasthenia were thought to have similar causes, to demand similar cures, and to affect similar people (in fact it is often impossible to diagnose the characters in fiction as either neurasthenic or consumptive though they are clearly one or the other), and in part because they were often related to the same questions of national character. Sontag looks at the effects of metaphors of sickness in creating the experience of sick people and the uses to which those same metaphors can be put in other discourses, whether political, literary, or otherwise. Her stated intent is utopic, to help liberate disease from figuration—"My point is that illness is *not* a metaphor, and that the most truthful way of regarding illness . . . is one most purified of, and most resistant to metaphoric thinking"—a project that neither interests me nor seems possible, but like Sontag I am interested in the social and cultural uses of neurasthenic metaphors. As W. V. O. Quine suggested in another context: "There is mystery as to the literal content, if any, that this metaphorical material is meant to convey. And there is then a second-order mystery: Why the indirection? If the message is urgent and important as one supposes, why are we not given it straight in the first place?"[32]

The "indirection" of metaphors of illness is no different from that of any social signification. For instance, although we might be able to say some general things about polite lies, they can best be explained in terms of the particular social matrix of the individual telling the lie. Some generalizations about why people used neurasthenia are possible, such as that many women at the turn of the century did not feel able to approach their husbands directly about their desire to pursue a career or other interests, and for them the indirection of neurasthenia was a great help. But beyond such obvious uses, we must rely on the anecdotal evidence of the particular subjects described as or describing themselves as ill, the specific people resorting to the indirection of a pointedly metaphoric illness. Again, fictional texts offered a great variety of models for such indirection, as did the ethical, political, religious, and philosophical writers, who modeled the use of neurasthenic metaphors in arguments of all kinds. Like Elbert Hubbard of the Roycrofter's Community and Rebecca of Sunnybrook Farm, many of these writers used neurasthenia with the shrewdness of the turn-of-the-century entrepreneurial salesperson. From the looks of things, these writers were their own best customers, as the following anecdotal accounts of their neurasthenic lives will show.

PART I: NEURASTHENIC ECONOMIES

Sick Women and the Civilized Man

The various functions of neurasthenia in processes of cultural change can perhaps most easily be seen in relation to the gender system, since neurasthenia was a highly gendered discourse. Men and women became neurasthenic from different sets of causes, according to the medical theories, and the cures prescribed and the conception of health were gender-specific. The differentiated cures themselves required gender segregation: many "overly active" women were isolated in bedrooms to be taken care of by nurses, while many men feminized by the disease were sent out west to become men again. The discourse of neurasthenia, in both its assumptions about health and its analysis of the disease, provided legitimation for a traditional definition of femininity based on dependency and passivity. Women were susceptible to the disease because of their natural fragility and hypersensitivity; and the diagnoses and cures were based on these assumed weaknesses and on an explicit understanding that women's natural, healthy state differed not in kind, but only in degree, from their diseased state.[1] Women were not only naturally frail, some neurologists argued, but the greater level of education of the New Woman was destroying her health. She was engaged in brain work, and because of the limited amount of energy nature allotted women, the argument went, this brain work combined with their other duties could leave them in nervous bankruptcy. Both women and men had been alarmed for years at the number of women—sometimes estimated at half the female population—who were sickly

31

in America. As early as 1871, William Dean Howells wrote in *Suburban Sketches* that America sometimes "seems little better than a hospital for invalid women." Guidebooks for women often accepted sickness as a normal state, as implied in such titles as Joseph H. Greer's *Woman Know Thyself: Female Diseases, Their Prevention and Cure* (1902). S. Weir Mitchell, inventor of the Rest Cure and the physician mentioned in Charlotte Perkins Gilman's "Yellow Wallpaper," most succinctly summed up this view when he wrote, in *Doctor and Patient*, "He who does not know sick women does not know women."[2]

Neurasthenia weakens the subject's constitution, and the cures aimed at a reconstitution of the subject in terms of gender roles. In the Weir Mitchell Rest Cure, the most widely known treatment for women, the patient was prescribed bed rest for a month or longer, was not allowed visitors or permitted to read or write, and was spoon-fed a diet of milk by a nurse. Mitchell, in *Fat and Blood*, states clearly that he wanted to infantilize his patients, since they needed to turn their wills over to him for him to effect a cure.[3] His regimen of rest, quiet, and seclusion is also obviously related to notions of feminine decorum, the exclusion of women from public spheres, and obedience to paternal authority. In contrast to this infantilization and enforced debilitation, Theodore Roosevelt, Thomas Eakins, Frederic Remington, and Owen Wister were all sent to the Dakotas for rough-riding exercise cures (the latter two by Mitchell). Henry James was sent to hike in the Alps, and William James continued to prescribe vigorous mountain hikes for himself until he was in his sixties. Other men congregated at resort spas to play sports and to ride for exercise. Theodore Dreiser, for instance, tried two different exercise cures, one as a manual laborer and one at an elite spa where medicine ball and horsemanship were central therapies. A photograph of the spa where Dreiser took his cure shows the owner and director, the former champion wrestler and boxer William Muldoon, in a Rooseveltian pose on a white charger, with his patients lined up behind him like so many sickly Rough Riders. Elbert Hubbard, Senator Chauncey Depew, Elihu Root, and other notables all took Muldoon's "cure." Muldoon's technique of militaristic discipline, strict moral accountability, and incessant, rigorous exercise echoes Roosevelt's championing of the "strenuous life," his militarism (as enforced in part by his secretary of war, Elihu Root), and his private philosophy that constant, vigorous activity was the only way to stave off depression. It also echoes William James's late championing of martial vigor and, as we shall see, James's pragmatism itself.

Neurasthenia was considered a form of nervous exhaustion, and

John Singer Sargent. Portrait of S. Weir Mitchell (1903). Sargent's 1903 portrait of Theodore Roosevelt now hangs in the White House. (The Mutual Assurance Company Collection)

while women needed rest and quiet so that they might passively build up their reserves of nerve force, men needed actively and vigorously to build up theirs. Women became exhausted through too much exposure to the world, and so the rest cure, during which women were to center their thinking on their families, functioned to refit them for their basic social role. Neurasthenia in men made them unfit for a successful life in the world, and the survivalist, competitive, aggressive exercise cures can be seen as a way of refitting them in the basics of their available roles. Both cures were represented in terms of a return to traditional values of passive femininity and masculine activity, and in some cases, these cures did function as such a conservative return. In the context of an emerging discourse on the New Woman, for instance, a discourse advocating broader notions of acceptable roles for women, the retrofitting of the rest cure was reactionary. Mitchell refers explicitly to these developments, and to the place of neurasthenic treatment in correcting them: "The woman's desire to be on a level of competition with man and assume his duties is, I am sure, making mischief, for it is my belief that no length of generations of change in her education and modes of activity will ever really alter her characteristics. She is physiologically other than man. I am concerned here with her now as she is, only desiring to help her in my small way to be in wiser and more healthful fashion what I believe her Maker meant her to be."[4] The doctor's job was clear: to help women assume their God-appointed roles, so that they will be able to acquire and distribute the promised dividends of spiritual advancement.

But this is only one story. In the context of the rise of what Thorstein Veblen analyzed in the late 1890s as a leisure-class ethic and the concomitant role of the purely ornamental leisure-class wife, the rest cure can be seen as more than a simple return—as, instead, a kind of retraining. Mitchell was clear that the leisure class was his clientele: "I am reminded as I write that what I say applies and must apply chiefly to the leisure class; but in others there is a good deal of manual work done of necessity, and after all, the leisure class is one which is rapidly increasing in America, and which needs, especially among its new recruits, the very kind of advice I am now giving."[5] The leisure-class wife was a new role for many women and families, and the role seemed to fly in the face of the routine values of work, asceticism, and motherly and wifely duty. Its definition in terms of traditional values was so insufficient that medical intervention was often necessary to cure the confusion that resulted.

In addition, many women who were not leisure-class wives, and who could hardly be accused of reverting to traditional roles, used neurasthenia as a space for transformations not at all in keeping with the old notions of domestic passivity or the more modern notions of leisured consumption. Margaret A. Cleaves, for instance, was a successful doctor of nervous diseases who was afflicted by neurasthenia for years. In her autobiography she writes against the notion that women were more susceptible than men ("The complete exhaustion of supreme nerve centres as in this case rarely befalls a woman") and argued that it was only her work as a doctor that gave her what few moments of health she had. Her career was impeded by neurasthenia, but somehow made possible by it, since she used neurasthenia as a way to deny the gender-specificity of professional roles. Besides, as Cleaves wrote, "It is a recognized fact that the work of the world is largely done by neurasthenes." Edith Wharton also became neurasthenic at the liminal moments in her movement toward a professional career, and she also resisted the gendered reading of her disease. Like Samuel Clemens, another on-again, off-again neurasthenic, she dramatized her neurasthenic profession by writing in bed. And, perhaps furthest afield, Emma Goldman became neurasthenic in 1903 as an embattled anarchist and emerged at the end of the year as a cured socialist, without changing her basic notions about oppression based on sex and class. Although not at all in circumstances of their own choosing, some women managed to construct their own neurasthenic case histories in ways that effectively restructured their subjective relation to a neurasthenic habitus.[6]

At the turn of the century men's responses to neurasthenia also signaled changes of various kinds. The prevalence of neurasthenia in men was sometimes analyzed as an effect of the feminization of culture, and in the early 1880s Beard celebrated this feminization as an indication of the high degree of civilization America had achieved, manifested by the refinement and sensitivity of its cultured men. By the turn of the century, however, the feminized man had fallen out of fashion as a new entrepreneurial and militarist ethos arose, an ethos that was used to justify the elite pursuit of business success and the related political and economic changes involved in America's new success as an industrial and imperial power. The civilized man was being replaced as a middle-class hero by the civilizing man, by the man whose enterprise was expansion, and neurasthenia and its cures were available as forums for this replacement. American expansionist foreign policy is mirrored by the successful man's attempt to increase his bulk through vigorous muscle-building, conspicuous consumption of calories, or the making of "fat and blood" as prescribed by Mitchell. Thus a man's success in 1903 could often be measured by his girth. Diamond Jim Brady was renowned for his business success and his voracious appetite, which combined to swell his midsection to heroic proportions.

Roosevelt, like Brady, was constantly trying to expand, and Roosevelt's rhetoric, also expansive, clearly exemplifies a polemic for cultural change, a retraining, presented as a "return" to heroic, natural, and manly values. His cowboy machismo provides an image of how a traditionalist rhetoric was used to champion new norms and relations of power which were affecting all cultural systems, from diplomacy and business to "nature" and gender, and which were accompanied by changes in notions of duty and notions of success. In Edith Wharton's novel looking back to this period, *The Age of Innocence* (1920), the protagonist, a wealthy society man, specifically invokes Roosevelt as his role model in adapting to a reshaped culture. Roosevelt was self-consciously a model for the men of the upper classes, teaching them to take over and direct the enterprises that supported them, including entering the government, or "public service," as Wharton's figure does in a small way. The paternalism of Roosevelt's appeal (as the protagonist's wife says in Wharton's novel, "We all have our pet common people") made sense against the same understanding of role which informed the cures for neurasthenia, an understanding based on the family, on the moral value and necessity of duty and class distinction, and on the individual will as the basis of civilization. What marks Wharton's progressive protagonist as a nineteenth-century man, the badge of his anachronism, is his insistence on service rather than success. He lacks the neurasthenic understanding of his social duty as based on self-directed therapy and self-made success, and he lacks the mythic traditionalism of Roosevelt's invocation of the cowboy as healthy hero. In the end he renounces, as well, the expansive physicality of the age of experience.[7]

Not all civilized men made the transition to the civilizing mission. Hamlin Garland and Edgar Saltus—like Dreiser more interested in literary success than other cultural projects—maintained classic versions of the role of the civilized male, Garland as an adoptive Brahmin and Saltus as a Europhile decadent. These two roles required seemingly opposite but in fact overlapping attitudes toward sexuality, inebriety, speculation, and negativity, and toward literature and its practice. The lifespan of neurasthenia corresponds to the period of realism in American literature. This is far from accidental. The status of the individual, the sense of the importance of propriety, the nervous accommodation to social change, the contrapuntal representation of transformation and conformity, the importance of emotion as signifier, the insistence on the importance of social environments to the understanding of individual motivation and action, the reliance on a bracketed supernaturalism and a visualist positivism, the self-consciously adopted task of redrawing the boundaries of race, class, and gender for an elite audience, the gradual and partial expansion and democratization of that audience—all these things common to the discourse of neurasthenia and the discourse of literary realism (and to the civilizing mission) were shared and expressed in various ways by Dreiser, Saltus, and Garland, and seconded by James and Roosevelt. The various neurasthenic economies of gender, spirituality, and production shaped and were reshaped by writers and by public intellectuals at the turn of the century, and just as the ideology of female complaint was important to the structure of that neurasthenic conjuncture, so the actuality of male complaints was that ideology's informing antistructure, as these five men, in their different ways, exemplify.

1 Making It Big: Theodore Dreiser, Sex, and Success

Do you know that the main cause of unhappiness, ill-health, sickly children, and divorce is admitted by physicians and shown by court records to be ignorance of the laws of self and sex?
—Advertisement for *Sexology*, by Dr. William H. Walling, M.D.
(Puritan Publishing Company, 1903)

Millions of people always await the man with a real message.
—Advertisement for *Self and Sex* series, by Rev. Sylvanus Stall, D.D.
(Vir Publishing Company, 1903)

In February of 1903, Theodore Dreiser was down and out. Depressed, an insomniac, suffering from constipation, indigestion, skin irritations, and headaches, unable to write, separated from his wife, unemployed, with no income and no prospects—he was, by all reports, confused, anxious, and unhappy. Physicians in Philadelphia had diagnosed him as a neurasthenic, and over the course of the year he underwent several of the many available cures and regimens, including drugs, diets, homeopathy, and exercise, until he felt well enough, in January of 1904, to take an editorial position at the *New York Daily News*. There he began work on *An Amateur Laborer*, an autobiographical novel about the past year. The novel opens with the following epinician paragraph: "After a long battle I am once more the possessor of health. That necessary poise in which the mind and body reflect the pulsations of the infinite is mine. I am not overconscious. I trust I am not underso. All that is, now passes before me a rich, varied, and beautiful procession. I have fought the battle for the right to live and for the present, musing with stilled nerves and a serene gaze, I seem the victor." In this passage there are hints of many of the themes I will refer to, most important of which are the metaphors of battle and victory, transcendence, and the healthy possession of serenity.[1]

Based on what for the men in his culture were two prime, complexly interrelated arenas of victorious conquest, sexuality and the pursuit of financial success, Dreiser's transcendent, serene victory is a triumph of incorporation on an imperial scale: "all that is" passes before this newly constructed self in "beautiful procession." The "musing" philosopher of this passage makes some obvious claims to cultural authority (with his Emersonian ability to reflect the infinite), but Dreiser was much more concerned with social mobility, at least through 1903, than he was in cultural authority. Cultural authority was a sign of social status, and like neurasthenia itself, Dreiser wore its mantle as a prophecy of his future position. The mask of regal stoicism and philosophic detachment rhetorically denies or elides the ways in which Dreiser's neurasthenia was both a tactic in his career of conquest and a response to temporary setbacks in that career. The language of this opening paragraph, which implies a period of strife, strain, and confusion preceding the narrator's new-found serenity, contains the first of Dreiser's many attempts to represent his experience of neurasthenia as a significant, positive transformation. The projection of self as the hero of a battle of nerves acknowledges neurasthenia as a language of liminality, a language of personal transformation, and in this case as the acquisitive language of imperial selfhood.

Battle itself is associated with liminality in American culture, as in the work of Dreiser's contemporaries Stephen Crane, Jack London, and Frank Norris, and this association is one of the reasons the discourse of neurasthenia and martial discourses were so often intertwined. Like nervousness, which was both a topos and a painful emotional reality, battle was a trope that informed diverse discourses and rhetorics and was simultaneously an American reality. In 1903 American troops were still fighting in the Philippines, where an American military government was attempting to secure America's latest "possession" against widespread resistance. American warships cruised the seas off Panama in battle readiness as an American-fostered coup constructed the independence of Panama from Colombia and the possession of the Canal Zone for the United States. American bases were being built in Cuba and elsewhere as coaling and staging stations for the U.S. Navy. American troops were called in to break up the miner's strike in Cripple Creek, Colorado, and to patrol strike areas in Pennsylvania. Laborers clashed with police, militias, and private guards from West Virginia to Utah. This military activity spawned discursive justifications, resistances, and explanations in many forums, and in the hands of Roosevelt and others provided a series of metaphors which embraced all areas of political, social, and personal life. A rhetoric of conquest and battle, especially after the Spanish-American War and its heroes exploded onto the literary marketplace, appeared in descriptions of success in all other fields as well. Later in his life Dreiser would have things to say about militarism and political violence, but at the turn of the century his writings are a clear example of a militaristic discourse adopted without reference to its sources, in which battle was a simple metaphor for the road to success and individuation. There is no indication in any of his writing from or about 1903—including diaries, letters, memoirs, autobiographies, a dozen articles, and several autobiographical novels—that he was particularly aware of or worried about actual instances of imperialist expansion, militarization, or even, despite his continued attention to urban poverty, domestic labor violence.

He did describe, however, desires for the conquest of women and for a triumph on the literary stage. To describe those desires he employed a rhetoric compounded of militarism and medicine as similar to Roosevelt's in source and figure as it was different in motivation and effect. In Dreiser's rhetoric, the artist, like a commander reviewing troops, reviews "the rich, varied, and beautiful procession" of life. If the circumstances of colonial expansion elicited no response from Dreiser, the lessons of military expansion were not lost on him. In his novels and other writings, the battle for aesthetic expression, the battle for health, the battle for identity, and the battle of the sexes are all represented as forms of acquisitiveness. Like his appropriation of neurasthenic discourse, Dreiser's militarism was not so much a defense mechanism as a tactic, and both rhetorics aimed at a literary market, a market that bought reams of print, primarily journalistic, about Admiral Dewey and the other military heroes of the moment, and one that bought volume after volume of fiction about neurasthenic characters and their battles. These neurasthenic characters more often than not were represented as gifted, whatever setbacks they might be experiencing by nature and by the plot. Guy Wetmore Carryl's *Lieutenant Governor*, James Lane Allen's *Mettle of the Pasture*, Margaret Deland's *Dr. Lavender's People*, Hamilton Wright Mabie's *That Printer of Udell's*, Upton Sinclair's *Journal of Arthur Stirling*, David Graham Phillips' *Great God Success*, Alice Brown's *Mannerings* (all published in 1903), and novels by Howells, James, Norris, Garland, London, Freeman, Saltus, Wharton, and Wister all presented their readers with exceptional neurasthenics. These characters' struggles for moral and physical integrity tended to involve a search for a calling, a struggle for a rightful occupation or role, and this struggle was often figured as a military battle or campaign that ended in financial and social success. Dreiser adopted the rhetoric of martial violence in much the same way he incorporated neurasthenia and neurasthenic discourse, as part of a willfully constructed trajectory of acquisition and upward mobility modeled on those he had read about and, as a journalist, had himself written.

Dreiser was obsessed with success. He was born into a midwestern family beset by constant financial worries and forced relocations, and his background was similar to that of such protagonists as Carrie in *Sister Carrie* (1900) and Clyde Griffiths of *An American Tragedy* (1925). As was the case with these protagonists, financial and cultural insecurity combined with a desire for financial and social success created one of the most powerful contexts of his thought and activity. In the 1890s, as part of his own rise to success in journalism, he conducted a series of interviews with millionaires and robber barons for *Success Magazine*.[2] These men were much like Frank Cowperwood, the protagonist of Dreiser's epic trilogy of unscrupulous finance—*The Financier* (1912), *The Titan* (1914), *The Stoic* (1947)—based on the conspicuously successful career of transportation magnate and speculator C. T. Yerkes. "Those who interested me most," Dreiser wrote in his first autobiography, "were bankers, millionaires, artists, executives, leaders, the real rulers of the world."[3] By 1899, when he stopped doing free-lance journalism to begin his first novel, *Sister Carrie*, Dreiser himself had become extremely successful, getting paid up to two hundred dollars each for the forty-eight articles he published that year, eating at the best restaurants, dressing the part—a great homely dandy—and his decision to write novels was also a way to act the part. His move from writing newspaper and magazine articles to writing a novel represented not just a change in genre but a change of class, an entrepreneurial step up the ladder of success: it was a change from being a wage earner writing about the rich to being one of the bankers, millionaires, executives and artists himself. The inclusion of artists in his list shows how clearly Dreiser linked artistic success with arrival in a higher class.

Success Magazine was edited by Orison Swett Marden and dedicated to "Education, Enterprise, Enthusiasm, Energy, Economy, Self-respect, Self-reliance, Self-help, Self-culture, Self-control, Work, Sagacity, Honesty, Truth, and Courage." This list contains a set of values already central to American culture when Benjamin Franklin outlined them at the end of the eighteenth century: economy, self-help, self-control, work, and honesty. Marden combined these with a set of values propounded by Emerson in the middle of the nineteenth century, such as self-reliance, self-culture, sagacity, and truth. And finally Marden spiced the recipe with an admixture of turn-of-the-century variants of these terms: education, enterprise, enthusiasm, energy, and courage. When Max Weber, after a long neurasthenic crisis of his own, began writing *The Protestant Ethic and the Spirit of Capitalism* in 1903, he sought to codify the work ethic using the first set of terms, the Franklinian ethos, alone. Self-control, economy, and work were the secular hallmarks, Weber felt, of the Protestant notion of a person's "calling" and provided the cultural conditions for the development of capitalism. After his visit to America in 1904, he argued that whatever juncture capitalist culture had reached—and he was not sure what that was—Franklin's terms were no longer sufficient to explain its ideological or cultural foundation and effects. When he returned to Germany, he wrote the conclusion to his book, with its fearful passages about the "iron cage" of modern capitalist ideology and the rest of its halting, tentative conclusion, itself a kind of neurasthenic jeremiad. His conclusion reads like an early, murky version of Yeats's "Second Coming," evoking fear of some rough beast slouching toward St. Louis, for Weber saw the passing of the original ideological relation of religion to capitalism and worried about what would replace it. If he had read *Success*, he could have seen the Protestant notion of a calling being energetically replaced by the idea of success. The battle against sin and temptation had been replaced by a battle against illness (as it had in Weber's own case) and by a morally sanctioned battle for success.

Dreiser's own attitude was, in 1899, the confident and earnest one of *Success* magazine, and his only fear was a fear of failure. The success ethic elicited countervoices among socialists, anarchists, progressives, muckrakers, and other novelists. When the narrator asks, in Robert Herrick's 1905 novel *Memoirs of an American Citizen*, "Whatever was there to live for in Chicago . . . but Success?" readers were expected to feel the irony. Herrick's novel questions and offers a critique of the success-oriented life, as do such novels from 1903 as David Graham Phillips's *Master Rogue* and *Great God Success*, Alfred Henry Lewis's *Boss*, and Frank Norris's *The Pit*, but these were muckraking voices, whose sensational representations could easily be read as cautionary exceptions. The rapacious businessman who narrates his life in *The Master Rogue* is bothered by what he feels is a conscience, but the reader is meant to recognize, through the somewhat heavy-handed irony, that a "real" conscience is not at work, just a few momentary qualms. "Millionaire! In that word there was a magic balm for all the wounds to my pride and my then supersensitive conscience," the narrator remarks after one such qualm. Again with heavy irony, the narrator tells us in the first few pages that he would like the luxury of gentle feelings but cannot afford them, since "gentle feelings paralyze the conquering arm."[4] At times in Dreiser's novels we get an indictment similar to Herrick's or Phillips's, but even then he was a confessed believer in Marden's list of virtues, and was still in pursuit of success himself. While gentle feelings did occasionally paralyze his own conquering arm, much more often they did not.

An Amateur Laborer shows the ways in which being a neurasthenic provided a priori proof of gentle feelings and of the exercise of those gentle feelings at the same time that the condition explained "weary indifference" (156) as a physical pathology. Since indulgence in conscience was supposed to increase morbidity, neurasthenia could then provide a therapeutic rationale for an ethical moratorium. The narrator at one point, for instance, begins to think of "the crowded tenements, the sick babies, the people sweating under undue loads this very summer day and the women sewing, sewing, way late into the night," but these thoughts end in neurasthenic brooding, in "endless mazes of speculation" that are bad for his health (85). When he later looks at labor and oppression with a "gentle and melancholy eye," he immediately pulls himself up short with a reminder that "these speculations were not good for my mind nor profitable in themselves" (122). A successful cure required that he put aside depressing thoughts about social ills or the "petty local and social restraints" on the conquering arm.[5]

Bootstrap Conquests and Leisured Retreats

Perhaps the clearest view of the relation of success to neurasthenia and to notions of conquest can be seen in Brooks Adams's writings on civilization. Adams claims that wealth is stored energy, which can be transferred through military conquest or lost through martial "exhaustion," recapitulating the basic neurasthenic understanding of physical and social energy. For Adams, too, success is a value that needs no justification and inspires no criticism. "The criterion," he writes, "is success." Dreiser's writings display much less assurance and demonstrate the difficulty of pinning down such a seemingly simple criterion. Despite his many conquests, Dreiser did not, by the turn of the century, feel that he had arrived. Success, tied as it was for Dreiser both to Marden's list of virtues and to social status, was not calculable simply in monetary terms. Dreiser complained that though he was drawing a good salary, "from my stand point I am not succeeding." What exactly would constitute success for Dreiser he was unable to say, but it had to do with reputation ("In fact," writes Robert Elias, "he was more interested in the impression his reporting made than in what he reported") and finally with a status-based identity.[6] He wanted to be successful not so that he would be rich, but so he could be one of the rich. And so at least in part in response to the politics of subjectivity, he wrote a novel.

When *Sister Carrie* was published in 1900, it was condemned for flaunting genteel notions of propriety, especially sexual propriety, and when many bookstores refused to carry it, sales slowed to a trickle. Dreiser's publisher stopped promoting the novel and eventually offered to sell him the plates. His neurasthenic breakdown in 1903 is often attributed to his disappointment over the poor reception of *Sister Carrie* and the artistic self-questioning that resulted. But equally important was his failure to rise socially which this poor reception entailed. Instead of looking forward to a life with the millionaires and artists, he had to consider working again at the "hack" journalism he now disdained, to return from the leisure-class life of the novelist to the journalistic world of labor.

The autobiographical novel *An Amateur Laborer*, therefore, presents neurasthenic crisis and resolution as a heroic battle that takes place on the labor front. For the first three-quarters of the text the narrator/protagonist, a blocked writer who has been suffering from neurasthenia for three years and is therefore unable to work, slowly uses up what little money he has left and nervously worries about how he will ever make more. Even when he is down to his last couple of dollars, he cannot bring himself to look for work. When he tries to join a crowd lined up waiting for an employment office to open, he finds it "all very painful": "For the life of me I could not summon up sufficient courage to join that crowd. . . . Once I did go down absolutely determined to stop and take my place among them, but the keen conception of the difference between them and me which flared up in my mind as I approached drove me on by" (21). The narrator muses many times during his story about the differences and similarities between the rich and poor, between millionaires and laborers. Sometimes the discussion is standard social Darwinism; some are born more fit than others, some more fit for particular tasks, others more fit to be millionaires. The "battle" here, as the narrator says, is "unequal" (45). Sometimes the true value of a person makes him unfit for manual labor, no matter how fit he is as a thinker and poet (121, 172), and this fact leads the narrator to feel that life is unfair, that his sickness has cut him off from his rightful place. In accord with Beard's theories, the narrator assumes that his intelligence causes his nervousness. "It seemed to me as if my mind had been laid bare as if by a scalpel to mysteries of the universe," Dreiser writes, in a somewhat confused metaphor, "and that I was compelled to suffer, blood-raw, the agonies of its weight" (122). His refinement and sensibility have made him too sick to write and so have made it necessary for him to find some other work. But that same refinement and sensibility make any available employment impossible. He shrinks away from even applying for work, claiming to find the act and the other people in employment lines repulsive.

Still, the narrator presents himself as a man trying to become self-made. As Dreiser did, the narrator, now broke, hears of a railroad executive who patronizes the arts by giving temporary work to struggling artists. Using a variant of perhaps the most famous trope of Franklin's autobiography, the narrator describes himself at this point as down to his last loaf of bread, which, like Franklin's puffy roll, he wraps under his arm as he heads into the city to make his fortune. Fortified by this loaf and a letter of introduction from his publisher, he presents himself to the railroad executive as a neurasthenic literary man who needs strenuous exercise to calm his nerves, and he is hired as a laborer. The labor that was impossible when it meant he was becoming a laborer becomes possible if he accepts the role of a brain-worker in need of exercise. *An Amateur Laborer* describes the narrator's manual labor over what appears to be several weeks. Dreiser later wrote of his toil on the railroad as hourly, weekly, yearly, knowing no surcease ("Its grim insistence unrequited by anything save the meager wages wherewith it is paid") and a manuscript fragment makes the same reference to weeks, months, and years.[7] In fact, Dreiser did manual labor for one week. He then asked for and was given a clerical job and then a minor supervisory position. Two months later he was on a vacation before returning to journalism as an editor at the *Daily News*.

This self-imposed melodrama of bootstrap mobility cured the narrator as a similar one cured Dreiser. The exercise cure Dreiser had undertaken at Muldoon's retreat had been less effective, despite the fact that the very successful Muldoon—he was one of the most famous athletes of his day—ran his spa much like boot camp and emphasized martial vigor.[8] Muldoon's clients were in a temporary "retreat" from the battle, and his therapy assumed that supplies of nerve force and martial virtue needed restoring. Still, Dreiser's time at Muldoon's spa had only marginally and temporarily helped his condition (Muldoon himself claimed that this was because Dreiser remained at the spa for only one day) and functioned as only a marginal act of "recreation." His week of physical work, his "recreative career of labor" (113), was important not because it provided exercise, but because it provided an autobiographical explanation of class in terms of health. As it did for Hurstwood in *Sister Carrie*, downward mobility left Dreiser in a state of emotional and financial ruin. Because of the medical status of the exercise cure, manual labor was available as a therapeutic rather than a career option. Journalism and health then became possible as parts of a process of upward mobility. Journalism was impossible for him in 1903—he simply could not write—when he saw it as a step down from his career as a novelist; it was only possible

The Muldoon Hygienic Institute, where Dreiser, Elbert Hubbard, Elihu Root, Chauncey Depew, and others were treated for neurasthenia. (Photo from *Muldoon, The Solid Man of Sport*, by Edward Van Every. Copyright 1929 by Edward Van Every. Reprinted by permission of HarperCollins Publishers.)

when seen as a victory in his battle against disease and in his fight back up the social ladder. The title of Dreiser's autobiographical novel about 1903 glosses this distinction: it announces that he is not a laborer for the money.[9] The belief Dreiser had in his own social trajectory (as conditioned by his success as a journalist and his year as a novelist) did not easily coexist with the information about his actual social trajectory as reflected in such things as his minimal income and lack of recognition. "Oh the inexplicableness of it all," the narrator muses. "The shift, the change" (95). Neurasthenia provided a coherent explanation for his apparent failure without sacrificing his aspirations for or his belief in his ultimate success. From the depths of depression he looked up and saw that it was only "for want of a little money, and of health" that he "lacked recognition" (172). Role confusion and dissonant information about his social trajectory—two major destabilizing forces in the politics of the modern self—were resolved through the intervention of disease and the social form of the cure. Dreiser had lost a battle, but not the war. By remarshaling his energies to fight his disease, he would soon have a new victory to celebrate.

Women and Economics

This interpretation of Dreiser's neurasthenia as an answer to social dissonance resembles the theories of Beard and Mitchell in that it describes a social etiology related to roles and status. These doctors were also interested in a sexual etiology, and here we can see other ways in which neurasthenia provided individuals with liminal management of personal and social change. Beard's book following *American Nervousness* (1881) was *Sexual Neurasthenia*, first published in 1884, but revised and reissued in 1902. Beard's basic theory assumes that individuals start off with a certain level of nerve capital, and that if they spend this force faster than it can be replaced, the necessary result is an exhaustion of the supply. Beard believed that one way for the patient to replenish nerve force was to buy electric treatments (his treatise on the medical uses of electricity was reissued in 1903) that would send new currents coursing through the nervous system. Heidelberg Electric Belts, with genital attachments, were available through the Sears Roebuck catalogue, and Professor Chrystal's electric belts were sold in stores and through mail order. The ad in the Sears catalogue for the twelve-dollar belt promised a "wonderful cure for seminal or vital weakness, nervous debility or impotence, [which] stops almost immediately the unnatural waste or loss of vitality," and is "invaluable for all cases of female weakness." Chrystal's advertising pamphlet emphasized the curative properties of the belt for sexually related diseases: "electric belts with electric suspensory attachment for all diseases of the urinary organs such as *spermattorrhea, involuntary emissions, weakness of the sexual organs, loss of manhood, hanging down of the scrotum, inability to perform the duties pertaining to married life on account of nervous debility caused by early indiscretion, excessive sexuality, or occasioned by having at some time contracted a loathsome disease.*" The eighteen-dollar Heidelberg Electric Belt claimed to be "positively wonderful in its quick cure of all nervous and organic disorders arising from any cause, whether natural weakness, excesses, indiscretions, etc." The narrator of *An Amateur Laborer* is much less explicit, but Dreiser and his narrator were both clearly concerned about a "loss of manhood" due to "excesses" and "indiscretions."[10]

The belief that sexual activity drains people of their vital force has a long history in America, most clearly seen in the widely disseminated antimasturbation and hygienic literature for boys, and the neurologists and Dreiser accepted this view of a "spermatic economy." During his neurasthenic year Dreiser was convinced that his condition worsened after every sexual encounter. He wrote in his diary that on one occasion he was "foolish enough to indulge in copulation which put me back a number of days no doubt in my recovery" and, three weeks later: "Nervous condition rather worse this morning owing to a foolish hour of trifling with Mrs. D." The notion of sexual activity depleting the nerve force is itself economic and is expressed

The Heidelberg Electric Belt, from the Sears, Roebuck catalogue, 1903, one of the many available home therapy devices. (Courtesy Sears, Roebuck and Co.)

in economic metaphors: spending oneself too freely versus saving oneself, improper versus proper investment of vital energy, and the like. Clergymen as well as doctors preached this link. Henry Ward Beecher associated sloth in men with sexual licentiousness (though Beecher himself apparently combined licentiousness and cultural productivity) in the same way that the neurologists blamed depleted nervous energy on the same cause. And the doctors, like the clerics, claimed that sexual virtue paid off in both economic and spiritual terms. Clean living would bring both salvation and success.[11] In a fragment originally intended as part of *An Amateur Laborer*, Dreiser links the questions of brain work, income, status, and sexuality:

> I should say here that mine was a serious case of neurasthenia—or of nervous prostration. It had begun with the conclusion of a novel I had written three years before and which exhausted me greatly. It was enhanced by various physical indiscretions which it will serve no purpose to enumerate here and the general stress and worry incident to earning a living, as well as by moving into a neighborhood entirely unsuited to my nature. . . . on the East Side, facing the East River—the wretchedness of the poverty and the sight of the gloomy Blackwells Island on which were housed the sick, the criminal and the insane of the city had a most depressing effect on me. (127)

Sexual indulgence and a move into poverty combined to disease Dreiser. He had lost a hoped-for life of ease and was convinced that this loss was related to his "various physical indiscretions."

Other writers linked the discourses of economics and sexuality at the turn of the century as well. In 1899 Thorstein Veblen published his *Theory of the Leisure Class*, a comic classic in which he argues that private property originated with the practice of appropriating women as trophies of war, as symbols of the status of their owners. The purely ornamental wife of the leisure class, Veblen writes, especially if she is conspicuous about the amount of goods and services she consumes, functions in the same way. Veblen's representation of women's status as objects of appropriative desire and display was part of his general critique of American capitalism as barbaric appropriation. He analyzes sexuality and wealth as conquest: women and wealth were two ways in which the successful warrior displayed his success.[12] The mock-heroic tropes Veblen uses to make this metaphor both lurid and effective are derived from a combination of a prevalent social Darwinism in fiction, essays, and sociology, a very popular medievalism—middle-brow journals contained in almost every issue stories of knights and ladies and discourses on medieval art, while high-culture medievalism found its spokesperson in Henry Adams—and the war fever that surrounded the Spanish-American War and its representation in the press. Veblen's analysis was thus an omnidirectional critique of national culture.

In Dreiser's case, too, a link can be seen between a dream of wealth and a notion of masculine sexuality based on conquest. Throughout his life Dreiser was a compulsive philanderer, often having several mistresses at the same time. When women wrote praising his novels, he would write back asking for a picture and inviting them to please come visit. If these literary admirers accepted his invitation, Dreiser would attempt to seduce them. He then often put his new mistresses to work immediately as unpaid typists and editors, without whose substantial revisions—they sometimes needed to cut his notoriously verbose and ungrammatical manuscripts in half—Dreiser himself felt his work could not have been published. His lover-editors were emblems for him of his success with women; they at the same time made possible his literary success. In his novels Dreiser writes of the roles of wives and mistresses and their relation to economic realities and fantasies: in *Sister Carrie* and *Jennie Gerhardt* (1911) to the economic realities of wives and mistresses, but in his other novels to the economic fantasies of their husbands and masters.

Dreiser's particular conflation of gender roles and economics is related to changing perceptions of economic reality during the late nineteenth century, part of a general cultural response to a fundamental shift from a perceived economy of production to a perceived economy of consumption. Laurence Birken has shown the relations between the theories of the sexologists (in which group he includes Beard and Freud) and the "marginalist" economists (Simon Nelson Patten, Richard T. Ely, W. Stanley Jevons, Alfred Marshall, J. B. Clark, and others) who first argued that consumption rather than production was the driving force of economic activity.[13] These economists were already, in 1903, having some impact on popular middle-class culture, or vice versa; the lectures for Patten's 1907 *The New Basis of Civilization*, which made a big splash, were given in 1905, and Patten had published demand-side writings several years earlier, as in his *Heredity and Social Progress* (1903). Theories of neurasthenic sexuality could be used to support conservative notions of hoarding supply or to support the necessity, for a healthy economy, of spending. Like the muckrakers' nervousness about capital concentration and speculation, Dreiser's nervousness about sexual spending, status, and mobility was part of a general neurasthenic adaptation to the twentieth century.

For both Dreiser and the muckrakers this nervousness sometimes took the shape of a nervous exposé of social and economic change. At other times, as in Ida Tarbell's arguments about femininity in *The Business of Being a Woman* (1912) and in Jacob Riis's biography of Roosevelt (1902), a nervous endorsement of traditional values seemed to answer the same questions of propriety and prosperity. To this mix, Dreiser also brought a discourse of literary aesthetics, in particular the idea of the artist's compulsion toward beauty. This always became part of his self-portraits, as in the case of this self-description from *A Book about Myself* (1922):

> Aside from one eye (the right) which was turned slightly outward from the line of vision, and a set of upper teeth which because of their exceptional size were crowded and so stood out too much, I had no particular blemish except a general homeliness of feature. It was a source of worry to me all the time, because I imagined that it kept me from being interesting to women; which, apparently, was not true—not to all women at least. Spiritually I was what might be called a poetic melancholiac, crossed with a vivid materialistic lust of life.... [L]ove of beauty as such—feminine beauty, first and foremost, of course—was the dominating characteristic of all my moods.[14]

As a melancholy, materialistic lover of feminine beauty, Dreiser represents women triangulated by medical, fiduciary, and aesthetic concerns. As Walter Benn Michaels has argued, Dreiser links the protagonist Cowperwood's wife in *The Financier* to the settled, agrarian notion of value based on production (including the production of children) and links his mistress to the free-floating, gambling ethic of speculation and capital manipulation by which Cowperwood becomes fabulously rich.[15] Similar connections are apparent in Dreiser's autobiographical writings. The Mrs. D. of the diaries was a midwestern woman with whom Dreiser fell in love and became engaged when she represented economic security beyond his means at age eighteen. After he had moved to the city, become somewhat prosperous, begun speculating about a wealthy and artistic future, and transferred his desire to women in higher classes who were more aesthetically pleasing, he reluctantly married her anyway. While in the process of making that change, Dreiser was melancholy; he suffered from neurasthenia.

Dreiser's conflict between the fixed reality of his agrarian wife and his speculation in city mistresses found fictional form in the autobiographical novel *The "Genius,"* in which his thinly disguised protagonist, the artist-advertising executive Eugene Witla, attempts to complete his social climb by leaving his farm-girl wife to marry a debutante. When that plan is rejected by the debutante's family, the protagonist has a neurasthenic breakdown, datable by textual details (such as the construction of the New York subway system) to 1903, the year of Dreiser's breakdown. It is not clear, in *The "Genius,"* whether we are to assume that Witla's mistake is his social climbing or the sexual drive that led him to embrace his farm girl. The relation to the farm girl is based on lust and on agrarian security, while his relation to the debutante is based on "love of beauty" and on financial ambition. While Dreiser seems sometimes to suggest that lust is "productive" while ambition is "consumptive," he sometimes seems to suggest the opposite. It is perhaps this confusion in economic correlatives to sexual and financial moralities which has led critics to pan the novel. In any case, nervousness is the result of both lust and ambition, and neurasthenia the personal and cultural space of indecision, and finally change, in the protagonist's relation to sex and success. In *Sister Carrie*, Hurstwood's fatal mistake is that he separated love and economics: Dreiser represents this as impossible, as the high road to failure on both fronts. In *The "Genius"* the protagonist vacillates as well, and his speculative adventures result in neurasthenic disaster and the search for a cure.

In Veblen's analysis and in Dreiser's writings it is clear that the courting man is on an acquisitive foray, while the married man announces once and for all his status. In Dreiser's novels, in addition, the discontinuity between the courting and the married man is partially displaced onto the discontinuity between the characters of wife and mistress. While courting their mistresses Dreiser's characters are never neurasthenic. It is only when a relation with a mistress is broken that role confusion sets in. Neurasthenia then becomes a temporary option and marriage a temporary refuge, in sickness but not in health. In the neurasthenic imagination, marriage is the most economical forum for sexual spending, since marriage is a socially sanctioned investment, not a form of speculation. In the same way that money is "stored energy," as Dreiser writes in *Sister Carrie*, so is marriage: money in the bank and marriage form an intertwined system of clear values.

Neurasthenia, marriage, and sexuality, together with status and role confusion, form a cluster that appears in many novels of the period, such as *The House of Mirth*, *The Awakening*, and *Martin Eden*, novels in which neurasthenic confusion results in the death of the protagonist. In Edith Wharton's *House of Mirth* (1905), Lily Bart suffers financial and neurasthenic exhaustion leading to death when her role disappears with her advancing age; in Kate Chopin's

The Awakening (1899), Edna Pontelier's inability to decide between marriage and divorce ends in her suicide; in Jack London's *Martin Eden* (1909), Martin, unable to come to terms with a new social status, also commits suicide. In all three of these novels, the characters' moral commitments (commitments that are in each case tied to aesthetic issues) force their tragic resolutions. In *The "Genius,"* Dreiser's inability to force the moral issue results in a stoic, spiritualist resolution.

These novels of neurasthenic tragedy also represent the aesthetic sublimation of sexuality, and in them the relation between sex and aesthetics is often quite near the surface, as it is in *The "Genius."* Eugene Witla's sexual addiction is presented as an "addiction to beauty"; the desire for conquest which drives the artist-protagonist (and which drove Dreiser) is thereby aestheticized, and his sexual booty laid before the altar of art. He is drawn to seduce a debutante because as an artist he is helpless before "the lure of beauty" (550). When early in the novel Witla admires another artist, it is because "this man had virility and insight. . . . [T]hat was the kind of artist to be if you were going to be one" (51). Dreiser often excused his own exploitive sexual relations on the grounds of his artistic temperament, as a natural part of his sensitive, bohemian nature. Beard's causal explanation for neurasthenia, that it attacks those with the most refined sensibilities, is thus used by Dreiser to explain the activity that then explains, in turn, his sexual neurasthenia.

As Jürgen Habermas has written, this understanding is essentially modern. In modern culture, "interactions *within* the sphere of labor in one's calling are morally neutralized to the degree that communicative action can be detached from norms and values and switched over to the success-oriented pursuit of one's own interests," Habermas writes, explaining and extending Weber's analysis of the cultural consequences of changes in capitalist economies. "At the same time, success in one's calling is connected with the individual's redemptory fate in such a way that labor in one's calling, *taken as a whole*, is ethically charged and dramatized." Eugene Witla and Dreiser both at times allow themselves the entire sphere of their lives, since they are artists and the world is all raw material, as their sphere of labor, and thus all interactions are morally neutralized. But as Habermas goes on to say, the decentered understanding peculiar to modernity is the ability to "assume different basic attitudes toward elements of the same world."[16] Just as Weber's argument is itself more ethically charged and dramatized than Habermas's, for Dreiser and Witla this ability to assume different attitudes becomes a source of tremendous guilt. Their neurasthenia is a reaction to their own modernity, then, but rather than constituting a refusal and rejection of modernity, neurasthenia signals and makes possible an acceptance, however conflicted, of cultural change. In fact, in Dreiser's novel, and in the novels of Wharton, Chopin, and London, the possibility that art will allow the necessary freedoms of modernity is eventually rejected, and the place of art in romantic reorientations is filled by neurasthenia. Witla's art cannot save him, which is to say that it cannot afford him freedom of social movement, as neurasthenia eventually can. The failure of art as a liminal discourse is a standard complication in plots of neurasthenic transformation.

Some of the dialogue in *The "Genius"* is a verbatim transcription from the manuscript of *An Amateur Laborer*, and many of the events are rewritten using the same basic plot and characters. One of the fragments attached to the original manuscript of *An Amateur Laborer* describes a certain Miss Abbrechinna, the original of Carlotta in *The "Genius."* Miss Abbrechinna is beautiful and well known in the area to be very rich; she wears lavender silk with a long white plume in her hat and has a number of equipages. The narrator then finds out that she is lonely. This immediately interests him: "I thought of this as I sat on the porch that evening, viewing the flying and worked up a fine philosophic contrast between myself and her. Here was a woman who had money and health and was unhappy, and here I was without them, in the same state. . . . This lady with her wealth and her uncomfortable solitude had taken a very firm and interesting hold upon my imagination" (139–40). Health and wealth are equated, even if unhappiness doesn't necessarily follow. When the narrator realizes that this rich woman will probably never notice him, his description of his feelings changes, and he begins to talk about her solely in terms of her beauty and downplays her wealth. "I was not at all adverse to contemplating those things though I confess her beauty was the main object," he states. "Wealth had its charm. It provided the proper set, like the gold that holds the diamond" (141). Even in denying the importance of her wealth, he represents her as an index of wealth, as a diamond in the gold setting of her own possessions. The rich woman in *An Amateur Laborer*, like her counterparts in *The "Genius"* and *An American Tragedy*, promises immediate gratification— at least more immediate than the traditional women of his own class—and immediate status enhancement—or at least more immediate than somehow making a fortune himself. The amateur, in this kind of thinking, is on the road to what will become a classic American tragedy.

This similarity in the plots of novels from 1900, 1912, and 1925 suggests a continued desire for sex that is uninhibited by social stricture and consistently tied to financial and social success. This complex can be found in Dreiser's other writings as well, for instance in "Neurotic America and the Sex Impulse," in which Dreiser's critique of American sexual mores begins with attention to the profitability of representations of almost-illicit sexuality.[17] Changing mores about sexuality continually redrew the lines of the barely permissible, and when Dreiser gingerly overstepped those lines he found a healthy profit. When he went too far, his market failure brought on a case of neurasthenia attended by self-castigation for his own overspending. Sometimes quickly, sometimes slowly, as in 1903, Dreiser then nervously constructed new frontiers, a new homeland and colonies for his subjective designs.

The Prophet: Calculating Transgressions

Although he at times believed his strongest admirers and therefore felt that he had, starting with *Sister Carrie*, worked at creating a new literature, in the early years of the century Dreiser had little consciousness of himself as a radical innovator. He was looking for success. Brooks Adams's axiom was that "the manufacturer who is least bound by tradition is the man who, other things being equal, will succeed,"[18] and in this sense Dreiser was interested in manufacturing innovative novels. Alice Brown, in *The Mannerings* (1903), thematized the relation of fictional immorality to success when a small publisher reads the critical notices of his first book:

> "An immoral book, they call it, an immoral book! Dick, old man . . . we are made! An immoral book! By Jove! That sells it."
> "It's good for a thousand copies," said Richard indifferently.
> "Good for a thousand!" echoed Mannering excitedly. "Good for ten thousand! I'm the luckiest man in these United States."[19]

While Dreiser, too, was aware of the relation of scandal to marketability, he also felt that he was writing in the well-established, if still somewhat contested, realist tradition of William Dean Howells and Frank Norris, and indeed it was Norris who first read the manuscript of *Sister Carrie* and urged that it be published. Dreiser was therefore shocked to find that *Sister Carrie* was found too shocking to sell— he had seriously misread the reception his book would have.

Dreiser's miscalculation parallels that of Kate Chopin, who the year previous had published *The Awakening*, in which Edna Pontellier dies from a combination of sexual overspending and role confusion.

Edna's neurasthenic despair is connected, in a somewhat ambiguous description, either to a loss of desire or to its diffusion: "Despondency had come upon her there in the wakeful night, and had never lifted. There was no one thing in the world that she desired." The description of Edna's suicidal end matches standard description of the excitement of neurasthenic crisis followed by "exhaustion."[20] Like *Sister Carrie*, *The Awakening* caused a scandal because of the way it represented female sexual behavior. Chopin, who conducted a literary salon in St. Louis, and Dreiser, who wanted to be in similar circles in New York, confused the "advanced" understanding of these circles with the mores of the literary market as a whole.[21] While Chopin never wrote another novel, Dreiser tried and tried again. His second attempt, *An Amateur Laborer*, however, downplayed sexual themes, and in fact downplayed novelistic devices in general in favor of a more autobiographical genre.

The year 1903 saw the crest of a publishing boom in autobiographical texts from various walks of life. The *Independent* ran a first-person narrative portrait every two weeks as a regular feature: short autobiographies of a Corsican bootblack, a professor's wife, a Lithuanian stockyard worker, a labor leader, a miner. First-person, realistic, semiconfessional accounts such as *The Making of a Journalist* and *The Story of a Labor Agitator* were published, and *An Amateur Laborer* shows more generic similarities to these books than it does to *Sister Carrie*. Even closer are texts by writers who went undercover as workers to write first-person eyewitness accounts of the life of the working class. The most famous was Walter Wyckoff, a Princeton graduate whose two-volume *Workers* (1897, 1899) was hailed as the most important sociological document on what was known as the labor question. Others followed suit, writing participant-observation studies of workers in various fields. The 1903 volumes in this genre included Bessie and Marie Van Vorst's *The Woman Who Toils: Being the Experiences of Two Gentlewomen as Factory Girls*, Lillian Pettingill's *Toilers of the Home: The Record of a College Woman's Experience as a Domestic Servant*, and the most well known after Wyckoff's, Jack London's *People of the Abyss*. Wyckoff's descriptions of labor are somewhat more detailed and engaging than Dreiser's and his economic speculations less tangled in metaphysics. But his work at times sounds much like Dreiser's. Both go through a process of realizing the hierarchies and heterogeneity within what had seemed a "mass" of workers, both describe distortions in the sense of time when first trying to endure hard physical labor, and both speculate about the nature of supply and demand. Dreiser compares his work to that of undercover investigators, claiming his own as more authentic (*An Amateur Laborer*, 18).[22]

But *An Amateur Laborer* is less a description of labor than it is a delineation of the everyday life of the neurasthenic, and it embodies Dreiser's ambivalence about genre, about literary production in general, and, as the title suggests, about love, labor, and class. Mediating that ambivalence is the language of American nervousness, a language of the isolated body, and of battles and desires incorporated into the self. "I want love, I want health, I want individuality," the narrator finally exclaims (167). Dreiser's writings invert commonsense notions of the various forms of autobiographical writing. His diary is not the site of some kind of intimate immediacy and honesty; instead we find it the most censored version of his experience—his mistresses and his literary ambitions, for instance, are not mentioned. His first-person articles about his experiences tell a one-sided and largely unfactual story. The first-person autobiographical novel, *An Amateur Laborer*, is somewhat less guarded, in that the narrator has a girlfriend, but in this version he does not have a wife. The third-person autobiographical novel *The "Genius"* is less guarded still; it presents a more accurate account than the diaries do, but the emotional reality is still somewhat diminished and excused. In some ways it is only in the objective rendering of another's story in *An American Tragedy* (1925), Dreiser's final, most horrific conflation of sexuality and success, that the myriad interweavings of class and gender, of mobility and morality, and of ambition and desire are clearly represented. Fiction, not journalism or autobiography, was the primary arbiter of subjectivity.

In *An American Tragedy*, the upwardly mobile poor boy Clyde Griffiths plans the murder of his pregnant working-class girlfriend, Roberta, to protect his rise in business and social position, the essence and symbol of which is his frantic affair with a rich man's daughter. At this point Dreiser seems interested in representing the often tragic nature of American values. He spends over a hundred pages defending Clyde, leaving open the possibility that, though guilty in thought, Clyde is not guilty in deed. Dreiser indicts not Clyde but American values; instead of finding Clyde unequivocally guilty, culpability is displaced onto a sociological naturalism. Richard W. Dowell has argued that before 1903 Dreiser explained inequities of strength and weakness, sickness and health, wealth and poverty naturalistically, as part of nature's plan; after 1903, Dreiser's novels contain a cry for equity, a call to action.[23] What we can see, though, is Dreiser's increasing discomfort with naturalistic explanation accompanied by a continued reluctance to assess moral accountability. This is true even when the motivation behind the plot structure and the melodramatic highlighting of moral character, as in *The "Genius"* and *An American Tragedy*, lead in the direction of such accountability. Like naturalism, neurasthenia invigorated individualism by generalizing about and focusing attention on individual desire. While naturalism constructed motive force as "nature," neurasthenia constructed it as arising from both culture and the body. Like Freudianism, Dreiser's neurasthenic naturalism also appeals to both.

Dreiser's literary biographers see *An American Tragedy* as a triumph of his understanding of social forces, exactly the social forces that the rhetoric of neurasthenia had, for a time, allowed individuals to manage. Biographers less interested in ensuring Dreiser's literary reputation show that his life remained an American tragedy of self-destructive ambition and abusive sexuality. Always driven by uncontrolled desire to make it big and feeling that he never really succeeded, he suffered from loneliness and nervousness until the end of his life. Dreiser's work remained imbued with neurasthenic themes longer than that of many of his contemporaries in part because liminality was more a way of life for him than it was a stage. Dreiser's work has been compared to that of Durkheim, who also accepted neurasthenia as a fact of psychological and social life: in the works of both, individuals are seen as powerless to control the forces of social organization and behavioral deviance becomes the means for understanding this powerlessness. And there is a sense in which *An American Tragedy* does maintain, in ways the more autobiographical writings did not, the primacy of social forces. In *Suicide* (1897), Durkheim claims that "neurasthenia is a sort of elementary insanity" but that it is also "a much more widespread condition than insanity; it is even becoming progressively more general."[24] In telling Clyde Griffiths's story, based on a newspaper account he had read of a similar murder, Dreiser represents Griffiths's condition as so common that any newspaper might print a similar story, and as so normal that Griffiths's behavior is only accidentally deviant: the pregnancy is an accident, Roberta's death is an accident. The pregnancy and death are a tragedy, the rest is American.

The naturalism of *An American Tragedy*, the philosophic position that creates the necessity for the accidental nature of Roberta's death and of Clyde's fate, was out of date in 1925. Even two decades earlier in 1903, when Dreiser was writing *An Amateur Laborer*, naturalism was out of step with American high culture and American popular culture in a number of ways. American naturalists had learned from Émile Zola (who attributed his method to medical theory), but they owed more to Herbert Spencer, and it was Spencer whom Dreiser regarded as his philosophic teacher. Spencer died in 1903. Frank Norris, America's leading proponent of naturalism, died in 1902, and though a posthumous novel was published in 1903, it was not a naturalist novel. The culture was rife with debates on moral accountability, but the determinism of the naturalists was less and less often seen as a viable position within those debates. Naturalism in America had often centered on the bestial nature of human existence, as with Norris's beastly dentist McTeague, and by 1903 whatever naturalism remained in American social thought tended to describe only the animal-like existence of the lower classes. Jack London's *Call of the Wild* was one of the year's best sellers; significantly, this naturalist tract is about dogs. (Still, the dog-hero, Buck, has many of the standard marks of the recovering neurasthenic.) London's other books published in 1903 were *The Kempton-Wace Letters*, in which a strident young naturalist is made the fool, and *People of the Abyss*, a text more in tune with the reforming ethos of muckraking journalism than with the philosophic pessimism of naturalism. London himself repudiated his Spencerian past in 1903 in an article titled "How I Became a Socialist," and his socialism was a characteristically American mix of Marxian determinism and social reformism. It therefore represents a movement away from the deterministic sociology of naturalism toward a sociology of human agency. Another characteristic revisionist move was that of Lester Ward, who combined evolutionary science and romantic idealism in his *Pure Sociology* (1903), claiming that the agency working against natural determinism in human affairs was love and that love could then become the basis of "rational planning" and "social engineering." Albion Small, editor of the *American Journal of Sociology*, claimed that American sociology, unlike the sociology of Spencer, had a "deep loyal impulse of social service. Its whole animus is constructive, remedial and ameliorative."[25]

The study of Spencer's naturalism was part of an elite education, and the elite status of Spencer's thought made it attractive to Dreiser. But Dreiser was from the start more attracted to the metaphysical side of Spencer's writings than to the arguments about sociology or determinism—so that his own metaphysical musings tend to sound more Emersonian than Spencerian, like Spencer without a scientific or sociological imagination. In the last section of *The "Genius,"* after Eugene Witla has found solace in Christian Science, he remembers a long metaphysical passage from the last book Spencer published before his death, *Notes and Comments* (1902). Toward the end of his life Dreiser wrote his own quasi-mystical, quasi-scientific *Notes on Life* in an Emersonian style. As Laurence Hussman has argued, it is possible to see the spiritual, metaphysical side of Dreiser as the single most important constant of his career. That Dreiser's version of Spencerian metaphysics was tinged with the economism of neurasthenic discourse may be related to the fact that he discovered Spencer in 1893 and thus read him in the context of the famous Panic of that year, and may simply be a sign of the close relation Dreiser saw (as did William James and many others) between the liminal discourses of mysticism and neurasthenia. Dreiser later claimed that his neurasthenic crisis in 1903 was a case of being "sick spiritually."[26]

What also appealed to Dreiser as much as the content of Spencer's metaphysics was the elite role of priest that the discourse allowed its author. When Nietzsche called the reigning cultural elites "neurasthenic priests," his insult played off these groups' own aspirations toward becoming a secular clergy. As we shall see, many individuals and groups were competing in 1903 for such positions, Dreiser among them. While he was the editor of *Ev'ry Month*, his brother Paul Dresser's music magazine, Dreiser wrote a monthly column he signed "The Prophet," a name that has obvious religious connotations and homonymic economic associations; the use of such an editorial persona for a magazine dedicated to music publishing makes sense only in the context of a cultural free-for-all for such roles.

It was here that Dreiser first got to publish his Spencerian beliefs. In 1897 "The Prophet" had this to say of Spencer:

> He is a great father of knowledge, and his word is to be spread before all. . . . His is generalship of the mind—the great captaincy of learning and literature, the field-marshalship of the forces of reason. As Napoleon studied the military map of Europe, so Spencer studied the intellectual map of the world. . . . He ransacked with his army of learned subordinates the cities and valleys of dead-and-forgotten ages and caused them to yield up their story of life. . . . At the approach of his victorious mentality all living things bowed in vassalage, and he exacted the tribute of reason and meaning from all. "Wherefore are you?" and "what did you accomplish?" were his great field-pieces, and with these he thundered at the walls of ignorance and the city of darkness until they cracked and tottered, and finally yielded.

In figuring Spencer as Napoleon, Dreiser again displays a view of literary and philosophical success as conquest. The kind of martial metaphors often used in relation to class (class warfare, the war on poverty, Coxey's Army) and to religion ("Onward Christian Soldiers," the Salvation Army) are here put into service to describe philosophical eminence. In describing Muldoon, Dreiser dressed him in a cowled dressing gown, which made him look "more like some great monk or fighting abbot of the medieval years than a trainer." In adopting a Spencerian world view, an Emersonian style, and a Muldoonian militancy of the body, Dreiser was garnering three allies in the battle for accomplishment and for his own "captaincy" in the field of literature. Ironically, Spencer himself, elsewhere in the same book Dreiser quotes at the end of *The "Genius" (Notes and Comments)*, rails against precisely this kind of thinking, against what he sees as the militarization of all aspects of life and culture, from the creation of regimented bureaucratic armies to such phenomena as the Salvation Army. This "re-barbarization" of culture, he writes, is leading all workers and employers into a condition of "semi-slavery," where people "show little respect for a civilizing culture."[27]

Very few Americans, even those who feared "barbarism," however, rejected militarism altogether, as will be clear in the cases of both the imperialist Theodore Roosevelt and the anti-imperialist William James, the subjects of the next chapter. In fact most Americans, including Roosevelt and James, had the opposite view of martial values, considering them necessary to civilization. Unlike Dreiser, however, Roosevelt and James appropriated neurasthenic discourse in ways that engaged rather than bracketed social issues and political and economic battles. Dreiser, more representative of the average neurasthenic patient than either Roosevelt or James, appropriated martial and neurasthenic discourses to construct a personal identity and achieve personal gratification, with no reference to social or political realities outside his own: the world was, he hoped, simply to become his oyster. Such a strategy, at least temporarily, worked. Although he was to have several other neurasthenic episodes, Dreiser at the end of 1903, back on the long march to literary success, overcame the ravages of sex long enough to announce, somewhat prematurely, his serene victory. "Did I not," asks the narrator of *An Amateur Laborer*, comparing himself to the rulers of the world, "sweep with my breadth of imagination realms of which they did not dream?" (172).

The process of coming to such a victory was one of inner battles, moral battles figured as a battle for health and a battle against past sexual losses. In accord with the neurasthenic economics of subjectivity, the refurbishing of one's nerve capital led not only to a whole "individuality" but to success, or at least the possibility of success, in the world, since one could begin to spend wisely the interest of that capital. In this sense Dreiser, more than the other figures I examine, comes close to a purely therapeutic use of neurasthenic discourse, one in which socially frustrated desire is revalidated and thereby cyclically reproduced. If Dreiser's success shows therapy to be a process of social integration through codifying one's alienation, it also shows neurasthenia to be an opportunistic disease, one that takes advantage of constitutional weakness wherever it might be found and thereby flourishes. Even with the gradual disappearance of neurasthenic discourse, the liminal mirror discourses of warfare and medicine—in the 1920s and 1930s Ernest Hemingway is again perhaps the best example; a more recent example would be William Burroughs—continued to help structure the relation of individuals to their changing culture. Dreiser moved quite easily into the psychological world of neuroses which replaced neurasthenia in the 1920s, into a world in which "cure" as a concept was all but abandoned, in which opportunistic disease continued to be a well-trod path to individuation, and in which imperialist expansion remained the model of a healthy economy, both national and personal.

2 The Big Stick and the Cash Value of Ideas: Theodore Roosevelt and William James

So much depends on not being nervous.
Jean Webster, *When Patty Went to College* (1903)

At first glance Theodore Roosevelt and William James would seem to have little to do with Dreiser and his troubled sexuality and desire for money, status, and success. In March of 1903, when Dreiser was down to his last thirty-two dollars, James was teaching Philosophy 3 at Harvard, the course that first outlined his philosophy in its fully developed and final form. Roosevelt was confident enough in his execution of the presidency that he left Washington for a celebrated and politically innovative two-month publicity and camping trip through the western states. Both James and Roosevelt had very much arrived. Their reputations were spotless in terms of Victorian sexual propriety and were international in their fields of endeavor, their financial and social positions were secure, and their youthful aspirations by and large had been met. As Roosevelt put it, "The great comfort is that . . . I am entirely aware that I have had a first-class run for my money, and that whatever comes I am ahead of the game."[1]

They nevertheless provide a series of counterpoints to Dreiser which illuminate the differential experiences of neurasthenic discourse and the different uses to which it was put. Like Beard and Spencer, Roosevelt feared a rebarbarization of culture (in Victorian, not Veblenian terms), and he believed that military build-up combined with militaristic discipline at home could not only keep civilized countries from degenerating but also would allow "the mighty civilizing races" to "export peace into the red wastes where the barbarian peoples of the world hold sway." Roosevelt headed out west for his original rough-riding experience in 1883, on the advice of his doctor for his asthmatic neurasthenia. His most famous dictum of foreign

63

policy—"Speak softly and carry a big stick"—is one of the many instances in which he relates a notion of conservation of energy in bodily terms to thought, military action, and, we might add, to sexuality. Roosevelt may have had more influence in popularizing the kind of militarism seen in Dreiser's rhetoric than any other one writer. William James, whose twin notions of the sick soul and of the cash value of ideas represent his involvement in the spiritualist and economic corollaries of neurasthenic discourse, also suffered, like Dreiser and Roosevelt, from neurasthenic reactions to role confusion. Despite his very public denunciation of imperialism, he addressed the question of militarism in a late essay. "We inherit the warlike type," he wrote in "The Moral Equivalent of War," and to its "contempt of softness" we owe "most of the capacities of heroism" of "the human race." James hoped to see the day that these energies would be in the service of peace, but he was as convinced as Roosevelt that the energies themselves were both martial and beneficial. Imperialist and anti-imperialist meet the apolitical novelist on the grounds of bodily energetics.[2]

In addition, Dreiser's adoption of quasi-mystical, quasi-scientific sermonizing as a genre for his final work and for the opening of the neurasthenic bildungsroman *An Amateur Laborer* was a characteristic response to pressures felt by many "brain workers" of the time. Related rhetorics were adopted by the other groups competing for the position of secular clergy in 1903, such as literary writers and critics, journalists of various stripes, economists, sociologists, natural scientists, and most important for our purposes here, politicians, medical doctors, and philosophers. S. Weir Mitchell, for example, thought of his writings on neurasthenia as "lay sermons," William James attempted to "win converts" to pragmatism, and Theodore Roosevelt considered the presidency a "bully pulpit." In *Questionable Shapes* (1903), Howells equates the work of William James and Josiah Royce with that of the natural scientist Nathaniel Shaler in their effects on ethics and metaphysics, and Santayana would write in *Character and Opinion in the United States* (1920) of the philosophers at Harvard at the turn of the century as clergymen without a church. At that time, the doctors, particularly the neurologists, and the philosophers were both elite specialists in the already elite fields of medicine and higher education, and both were promising to create new understandings of human psychology. Just as medical doctors had taken over the writing of ethical guidebooks for the middle class from the ministers, psychologists and idealist philosophers had usurped the positions of theologians in departments of philosophy.[3] Like the doctors, philosophers were expected to have both a technical and

ethical understanding of life, and like many politicians, their profession was one of reform.

Two of the most prominent lay preachers of 1903 were the incurable
neurasthenic William James, philosopher, and the cured neurasthenic Theodore Roosevelt, politician. James was the philosopher of
his time who took most seriously his responsibility to produce moral
philosophical tracts for the "public," and he dedicated much of his
writing to what he called "popular philosophy" for cultural elites and
to editorial writing on the ethical conduct of social life for more general audiences. Much of James's writing in 1903 was on public issues:
he wrote on the American military action in the Philippines, on the
lynching of blacks in the South, and on academic abuses.[4] Roosevelt,
too, wrote voluminously on the ethics of social life, and like Mitchell
and James saw his writings and speeches as lay sermons. Man's
mission on earth, he said, was, in three words, "work, fight, breed."
Roosevelt preached not just by word but by deed, for his strenuous
lifestyle was both an advertisement for himself and an advertisement
for his views: he worked, he fought, he bred. These practico-ethical
discourses demonstrate a community of interest and belief at the
bases of the two men's otherwise diametrically opposed political positions, personal styles, and cultural aspirations.

Roosevelt's life had many similarities with that of James: both began careers as naturalists, both were Harvard men, both came from
patrician families that traveled in the same circles and lived in similar
styles (in 1869, for instance, both the Roosevelt and James families
went to Europe.) Both felt a need to continue the work of their fathers,
James in explaining and justifying religious experience, Roosevelt in
becoming part of "good government." Both developed an ethic of public service, and both felt that this public service should entail, in part,
editorial writing for elite and middle-class journals. They made contributions to academic disciplines, James in psychology and philosophy, Roosevelt in history and natural science. Both were
neurasthenics, privileged practice over theory, and had a belief in
willed action as the means for resolving conflict and as the means for
curing their neurasthenia.[5]

The two men had, at the same time, opposite opinions on almost
all of the pressing issues in 1903: on epistemology, "civilization,"
race, religion, business, and foreign policy. Although James and Roosevelt came to feel a pressure felt by many of the men of their class
to take an active part in the reform movements of their day—as Frederic C. Howe put it in *The Confessions of a Reformer* (1925), "We felt
that the world had been wished onto our shoulders"—they came to
have very different notions of what that duty entailed. They also had

opposing religious philosophies. In *The Varieties of Religious Experience* (1902), James contrasted the "sick soul" of a metaphysics
like Dreiser's (and like his own) to "healthy-minded religion." "On
this view," James writes of the healthy-minded, "religion and science,
each verified in its own way from hour to hour and from life to life,
would be co-eternal."[6] Roosevelt, the cured neurasthenic, embodied
such healthy-minded religiosity in his strenuous materialism and his
uninhibited championing of his own brand of Victorian morality and
epistemology, which he had settled on at the end of his neurasthenic
episodes in the 1880s. James's chronic neurasthenia continued to
provide a space for radical reconceptions of religion, science, philosophy, psychology, and social life. In these two men's careers we can
see the malleability of neurasthenic discourse, the agency of that
discourse in managing individual relations to cultural change, and
the imprint such management thereby left on those cultural changes
themselves.

James's Sick Soul

Neurasthenia was a constant in James's life, and despite all the
announcements he made of his cure, he continued to have relapses,
with symptoms of insomnia, depression, vision problems, and writing blocks. These last were so severe that his *Principles of Psychology*
was not finished until ten years after he first promised the complete
manuscript to his publisher. As with Dreiser, many of James's neurasthenic crises were the result of role confusion, and as in Dreiser's
case, the cures were metaphors for the social significance of their
resolution. James's first claims of being cured came in 1873 when,
after several years of indecision about his career, he decided that he
would eventually become a psychologist rather than a naturalist,
physiologist, or medical doctor. Of the seven years between James's
return from Brazil with the Agassiz biological expedition up the Am-
azon and the beginning of his teaching anatomy and physiology at
Harvard, James spent two as a medical student and five in a "search
for health." James was at best ambivalent about a career as a physician, feeling it to be a job for a "tenth-rate man." He wrote his father
that he had been cured by "giving up the notion that all mental
disorder" necessarily had "a physical base."[7]

After marrying Alice Howe Gibbens in 1878, he claimed that his
marriage—a resolution of a primary role conflict and an assured and
sanctioned sexual outlet—is what saved him from "hopeless neurasthenia." In 1900 he wrote to a colleague that he was considering
retirement from teaching, promptly had a neurasthenic attack, and

went for the restful, retiring cure at the baths in Nauheim. The question that plagued him for years, and which always caused depression when it arose, was whether he was to be a psychologist or a philosopher, and if a philosopher whether he should make academic or "public" contributions. And whenever this conflict surfaced, after an unproductive neurasthenic period James threw himself into his work, produced contributions in one of those areas, and believed himself cured.[8] While these neurasthenic crises were caused by confusion about his role and status, James's situation is also, in a way, the opposite of Dreiser's. While Dreiser was worried about gainful employment, and dreamed about making a fortune and becoming successful, James at this point was financially ready to retire and wanted to spend his time writing rather than teaching. James had grown up in the upper class and remained upper class; Dreiser grew up poor and remained betwixt and between. Therefore while James continued to believe in the efficacy of exercise, he could afford, in all the ways Dreiser could not, a rest cure.

It is tempting to see James's original decision to work in psychology as again metaphorically related to his neurasthenia, but in the 1880s and 1890s neurasthenia was not a psychological category. The criminal anthropologists, sexologists, degeneracy theorists, medical psychiatrists, psychic researchers, sociologists, and social reformers all had developed theories of abnormal psychology and deviance, but much of what would now be called abnormal psychology and most of what was then known as morbid psychology were not actively part of psychology proper.[9] Neurasthenia was not discussed in psychology textbooks, not even in James's own. There are several reasons for its absence.

First, academic psychology was a new field in search of general laws of mental functioning, so that most researchers believed that the study of morbid psychology needed to await those laws. Since morbid psychology was considered a degenerate form of normal psychology, the normal needed to be codified before one could follow processes of degeneration. With Freud came the opposite approach: the idea that abnormal psychology is not a degenerate but an exaggerated form of the normal, and therefore the best place from which to abstract normal processes. James makes a similar argument in *The Varieties of Religious Experience* that normal mental experience is easier to see in its "exaggerations and perversions. . . . Insane conditions . . . play the part in mental anatomy which the scalpel and the microscope play in the anatomy of the body." Many American researchers were interested in abnormal mental states, but kept their own research at the status of a hobby, rarely integrating it into their regular work. On S. Weir Mitchell's advice, for instance, James experimented with mescal; although Mitchell never wrote, in his popular or his medical pieces, about his interest in hallucinogens, he was an active experimenter with psychotropic drugs, as was James. (James complained, however, that his experiment with mescal gave him nothing but the *katzenjammer*.) James attempted to integrate—most successfully in *The Varieties of Religious Experience*—his interest in the morbid and abnormal with his popular philosophy. Still, James was in the distinct minority in pressing for the importance of the study of morbid psychology and in seeing the abnormal as a window on the normal.[10]

Second, neurasthenia was considered primarily a physiological problem, thereby requiring medical, not psychological attention. Third, psychology was a subdiscipline of philosophy, which meant that the two divided a field which was itself in flux. One example of the changes in the field of philosophy in the later nineteenth century is that, whereas James taught his course on the relations of physiology to psychology in 1876 in the department of natural history, in 1877 President Charles William Eliot had it transferred to the philosophy department as a part of a thorough restructuring of the department and of the curriculum as a whole in response to evolution theory and other developments. American philosophy was being torn from its theological roots and transplanted into the soil of idealism; "mental science" was the adjunct discipline for local tests of the naturalistic bases of philosophic thought. (It was not, in fact, until 1934 that psychology became a separate department at Harvard.)[11]

In practical terms, this situation often meant that psychologists dealt with issues of low-order cognition, such as perception, while philosophers studied more complex issues of cognition, such as logic and ethics. In Mark Twain's "A Dog's Tale" (1903), for instance, white-gowned researchers first ask a "psychological" question about optics and then a "philosophical" question about instinct and reason in a dog's mental life. Mental disease, when not seen as purely physiological and therefore medical, was not considered a problem at the level of perception or reflex, but a problem at the level of morality or ethics. James in *The Principles of Psychology* continually apologizes for psychology's inability to take up "metaphysical" discussions, refusing to intrude into the field of philosophy proper and even promising in his preface not to do so. "All attempts to *explain* our phenomenally given thoughts as products of deeper lying entities (whether the latter be named 'Soul,' 'Transcendental Ego,' 'Ideas,'or 'Elementary Units of Consciousness') are metaphysical. This book consequently rejects both the associationist and spiritualist theories." Finally, then, the whole question of normality and abnormality ran into consensual problems, especially when supernatural "psychic" phenomena or religious experiences like trance or mysticism were at issue. Hence the joke that opens Twain's psychological, philosophical tale: "My father was a St. Bernard, my mother was a Collie, but I am a Presbyterian."[12]

Psychology was at the turn of the century the most active subdiscipline in philosophy departments: at Harvard, in 1903, five out of the six doctorates granted by the philosophy department were in psychology.[13] James's international reputation had helped put psychology, the field in which most of his students worked, at the center of Harvard's department, but by 1903 James had already moved from thinking of himself as a psychologist to thinking of himself as a "public philosopher." He wrote for middle-class journals and newspapers, and his books of essays were intended for this same public; hence the subtitle in *The Will to Believe, and Other Essays in Popular Philosophy* (1897). James's career, after *The Principles of Psychology* (1890), was devoted on the one hand to this public philosophy, to giving pragmatic answers, he hoped, to the question of why, as one major address put it, "Is Life Worth Living?" (1895), and on the other hand to making a significant contribution to academic philosophy proper, which he had not yet done. By "popular philosophy" James meant not philosophy for the masses but rather for a highly educated and elite audience of nonspecialists, precisely for those brain-workers most susceptible to sickness of soul and body.

The continuity of James's early psychology with his religious thought and his late philosophy lies in the relation of each to his own "morbidity," his own neurasthenic sickness. His ongoing experience with neurasthenia, and the epidemic around him, also influenced his determination to push morbid psychology more definitively into the field. In this he was following a pattern similar to that of the neurologists Beard and Mitchell, themselves neurasthenics, who had pushed for medical recognition of the disease. James's disclaimers of metaphysical thinking in *The Principles of Psychology* set the stage for *The Varieties of Religious Experience* and its project to examine religious experience without any "metaphysical" discussions and without any reference to theology and helped dispel the moral or ontological resistance to morbid psychology as a field of study. Spiritualism and morbid psychology were alike outside the pale of psychology and James wanted to bring them in. The topics that after Freud were seen as areas of psychological investigation—from thought transference to the interpretation of dreams to hypnosis to mysticism to notions of individual and collective unconsciousnesses—were known in America only as subjects of "psychical re-search," a field that concentrated on scientific examination of spiritualism.

The titles of James's eight Lowell Lectures in 1896—"Abnormal Mental States," "Dreams and Hypnotism," "Hysteria," "Automatisms," "Demoniacal Possession," "Witchcraft," "Degeneration," and "Genius"—show the relation of James's construction of abnormal psychology to spiritualism and to later theories such as those of Freud. James claims in the second volume of *Principles* that "the fundamental *facts* of consciousness have been, on the whole, more accurately reported by the spiritualistic writers" than by the empiricists. When a textbook on psychology by the noted British psychical researcher and psychologist F. H. Myers was published posthumously in 1903, James reviewed it, expressing strong regrets that it did not include any of the material on "subliminal" topics which Myers was famous for publishing in the *Journal of the Society for Psychical Research* and elsewhere. James and Myers each served a term as president of the Society for Psychical Research, James in 1894–95 and Myers in 1899–1900. The society was dedicated to the scientific study of psychic phenomena, from hallucination to dowsing rods, and James in his presidential address applauded the society's "humanizing mission" in the face of what he saw as the mechanical rationalism stultifying academic science. In his posthumous review James claimed that Myers's work in this area was the wave of the future: "Psychologists as a rule have counted him out from their profession . . . [but] I seriously believe that the general problem of the subliminal, as Myers propounds it, promises to be one of the *great* problems, possibly even the greatest problem, of psychology."[14]

It was this "greatest problem of psychology" which James was considering in *The Varieties of Religious Experience*, published at the end of 1902 and widely reviewed and discussed in 1903. The book demonstrates how James's personal relation to sickness, his belief in his social obligations, and his academic work in both psychology and philosophy are connected; it dismisses theology and religious philosophy and defends and justifies personal religious experience. The book has been called an act of "filial piety," the redeeming of a pledge made at his father's death to understand the "meaning and value" of religion in his father's sense. His father, Henry James, Sr., had written *Moralism and Christianity* (1850), *The Nature of Evil* (1855), *Christianity the Logic of Creation* (1857), *The Secret of Swedenborg, Being an Elucidation of His Doctrine of the Divine Natural Humanity* (1869), *Society the Redeemed Form of Man, and the Earnest of God's Omnipotence in Human Nature* (1879), and other books. The titles alone provide a comparison and contrast to his son's views; William James might have agreed to the first half of the title of the last listed book, if restated, but the second half is in an untranslatable language.[15]

James saw faith as pragmatically necessary for a healthy society, and his text as a spiritual, but secular, homily. Psychology should justify religious experience, and though whenever possible philosophy should replace religion, when this is impossible, religious experience can at least replace nervousness. "In point of fact," James wrote, "the religious are often neurotic." The "healthy-minded" religion of people like Roosevelt, James admits, is a fine "religious solution": "But it breaks down impotently as soon as melancholy comes; and even though one be quite free from melancholy one's self, there is no doubt that healthy-mindedness is inadequate as a philosophical doctrine, because the evil facts which it refuses positively to account for are a genuine portion of reality; and they may after all be the best key to life's significance, and possibly the only openers of our eyes to the deepest levels of truth." This "melancholy" (an anachronism that gives a historical patina to neurasthenic despair) is a necessary ingredient to all religions, for in his briefest summation James writes that the two parts common to all religions are:

1. An uneasiness; and
2. Its solution.
1. The uneasiness, reduced to its simplest term, is a sense that there is *something wrong with us* as we naturally stand.
2. The solution is a sense that *we are saved from the wrongness*...

The structure of this model (sense what is wrong and be saved) is identical to that of Christian reform: see the evil and you will be forced to correct it. It is also identical to the model of the leading muckraking journalists of 1903. According to Lincoln Steffens, Jacob Riis, Ida Tarbell, and Ray Stannard Baker, the truth of our society, which the healthy-minded politicians refused to see, was one of poverty and corruption. The mission of the muckrakers was to create in their readers the nervousness and melancholy that would, in turn, lead to cultural salvation and societal cure. It is also, thus far, similar to the tradition of the jeremiad, as outlined by Sacvan Bercovitch and Perry Miller. But in James's further formulations, the model follows that of neurasthenic cures, in which one needed to become sick, of course, in order to get cured, and in which the awareness that "something is wrong with us"—that is that we are not just morally lax but have

a medically curable condition—leads in the end to "solution or salvation," a new "centre of energy," a "zest," and finally a new purpose,
an "earnestness and heroism."[16]

As it was for Roosevelt, then, for James the cure for neurasthenia
and for the "sick soul" was constituted as zest, earnestness, and
heroism. Unlike Roosevelt, however, James does not believe that
"black care," or neurasthenic depression, is to be avoided; it is to be
embraced as part of a process of moving toward health and as a
necessary part of understanding. James wrote his own spiritual autobiography in a now famous passage of "The Sick Soul," and there
the link to his own neurasthenia is even clearer. He introduces the
passage as a work originally written in French by a writer who "was
evidently in a bad nervous condition at the time of which he writes."
He then gives what he says is a free translation:

> Whilst in this state of philosophic pessimism and general depression
> of spirits about my prospects, I went one evening into a dressing-
> room in the twilight to procure some article that was there; when
> suddenly there fell upon me without any warning, just as if it came
> out of the darkness, a horrible fear of my own existence. Simulta-
> neously there arose in my mind the image of an epileptic patient
> whom I had seen in the asylum, a black haired youth with greenish
> skin, entirely idiotic, who used to sit all day on the benches, or rather
> shelves along the wall, with his knees drawn up against his chin,
> and the coarse gray undershirt, which was his only garment, drawn
> over them inclosing his entire figure. . . . This image and my fear
> entered into a species of combination with each other. *That shape
> am I,* I felt, potentially. Nothing that I possess can defend me against
> that fate, if the hour for it should strike for me as it struck for him.
> There was such a horror of him, and such a perception of my own
> merely momentary discrepancy from him, that . . . although the im-
> mediate feelings passed away, the experience has made me sympa-
> thetic with the morbid feelings of others ever since. . . . I remember
> wondering how other people could live, how I myself had ever lived,
> so unconscious of that pit of insecurity beneath the surface of life.
> (160–61)

This passage is a narrative representation of the relation between
anxiety about one's social trajectory and neurasthenia. The "depression of spirits" is due to "insecurity" about his "prospects." The passage refers to an event in the early 1870s, when James was having
trouble finishing his medical studies.[17] The "depression of spirits
about . . . prospects" and the "philosophic pessimism" with which the

passage opens are two sides of the same coin, for out of the neurasthenic depressions of the late 1860s and early 1870s, James emerged
with a new career and a new philosophy. He gave up forever his plans
for a medical career, a "trade" for "a tenth-rate man," and in 1872
was given a somewhat more prestigious position as a lecturer at
Harvard. He formed the Metaphysical Club, merging his status ambitions and philosophical ambitions, for it was to be "composed of
none but the topmost cream [socially if not financially] of Boston
manhood." "Philosophy interested well-to-do professional men,"
Bruce Kucklick notes of the founding of the club, and we might add
that philosophy, like novel writing, appealed to men who wanted to
be well-to-do professional men, whether they were or not.[18] James,
because his father had depleted a good deal of the family fortune, did
not feel that he could live without further income. In addition, with
the rise of the newly wealthy industrial bourgeoisie, the young men
of Boston society perceived a downward social trajectory for themselves, and professional academic work, especially in philosophy, was
one way of mitigating that decline. Always a climber, Dreiser, after
he had secured a place as a novelist, next decided to become a philosopher, the role he assigned himself when speculating on the nature
of the human will. James's activity and context were similar, but he
came up with a very different philosophy: a rejection of philosophical
pessimism through a reconstructed notion of free will.

    The link between James's philosophical and spiritual crises are
evident in his diary and notebook writings as early as 1870:

> Today I about touched bottom, and perceive plainly that I must face
> the choice with open eyes: shall I *frankly* throw the moral business
> overboard, as one unsuited to my innate aptitudes, or shall I follow
> it, and it alone, making everything else merely stuff for it?

> Can any one with full knowledge and sincerely ever bring one's self
> so to sympathize with the total process of the universe as heartily
> to assent to the evil that seems inherent in its details? Is the mind
> so purely fluid and plastic? If so, optimism is possible.

> I think yesterday was a crisis in my life. I finished the first part of
> Renouvier's second *Essais* and see no reason why his definition of
> free will—"the sustaining of a thought *because I choose to* when I
> might have other thoughts"—need be the definition of an illusion.
> At any rate, I will assume for the present—until next year—that it
> is no illusion. My first act of free will shall be to believe in free will.[19]

Not only are his philosophical conclusions represented as the answers to personal crises, but the crises are represented as similar to
those of his spiritual crisis, when, once again, he "touched bottom"
and was faced with the question of evil and of the "pit of insecurity
beneath the surface of life." His "solution or salvation" was the concept of will, which would be at the center of his moral philosophy
from then on. The concept of the will as he received it from Charles
Renouvier was already a psychological rather than an ethical definition—it is the effect of a willer on the stream of consciousness—
and in using it to defeat his own philosophical pessimism he was
also to defeat his indecision, at least temporarily, about his "prospects" in the "moral business."

The epileptic youth James describes is an image of advanced nervousness, as is clear from Beard's chart of the tree of nervous diseases,
showing epilepsy to be one step short of pure insanity. In seeing his
own potentiality in the patient, James denies that his socioeconomic
position—"nothing that I possess can defend me"—can maintain his
nervousness indefinitely. James's problem of settling on a profession
was that they all smacked of trade or business, a problem for a man
from a family that since his grandfather's time, according to his
brother Henry, was "never in a single case, I think, for two generations, guilty of a stroke of 'business.' "[20] Henry and William both had
to face the possibility of becoming thus guilty, and both had neurasthenic reactions to the prospect. A healthy soul, Henry explains,
was born with "a bottle or two of champagne to his credit," while the
sick soul is born sober; perhaps the most sobering fact being that
the sick soul has lived a life that created the desire but not the means
for that bottle or two of champagne in his cellar.[21] In communities,
such as working-class communities, where no such expectations existed for the cellar, neurasthenia was extremely rare.

James largely accepted and reiterated the neurasthenic discourse,
then, but he did so in a somewhat idiosyncratic manner, based on
particular personal and professional imperatives. In "The Energies
of Men" (1906), James argues for a more psychological, less physiological understanding of psychic energy.[22] Everyone has a certain
amount of natural resources, he wrote, and everyone knows the feeling of being only half-awake, of being cut off from those resources.
"In some persons this sense of being cut off from their rightful resources is extreme," he writes, "and we then get the formidable neurasthenic and psychasthenic conditions, with life grown into one
tissue of impossibilities, that so many medical books describe" (12).
The problems of personal "energy-budgets," as he calls them, are not
so much the result of different birthrights, as it were, as they are the

result of being somehow artificially cut off from a full budget. James, like his brother Henry, felt that he was somehow cut off from his rightful resources as well. His family resources were not ample enough for him to continue the life to which he had grown accustomed, unless he supplemented them with a profession. His solution was pragmatic, and his explanation of it in later years, as he looked at the question of neurasthenia through the eyes of his own success, was in terms of the value of psychology and philosophy rather than medicine.

In "The Energies of Men," James rejects, along with the physiological explanation of neurasthenia, the medical solutions to it. If we learn to expend more energy, James claims, we can build up new reserves faster, for "the busiest man needs no more hours of rest than the idler" (7). Not only is the sum of energy based on psychological attitudes rather than physiology, but the fear of wasting energy is also misplaced. James suggests, again using an economic metaphor, that "spending," even overspending, can be a good thing. "There is no doubt that to some men sprees and excesses of almost any kind are medicinal, temporarily at any rate, in spite of what the moralists and doctors say" (24). James's economic analysis is related to his creation of a psychology consistent with consumer capitalism; disregarding the standard neurasthenic discourse's understanding of an economy based on capital saving, James was a pioneer in understanding the need for a change in subjectivity as a "new basis for civilization," as Simon Nelson Patten was contemporaneously describing it.[23] And in his insistence on the centrality of the individual will, James anticipates twentieth-century theories of the subject centered in the notion of desire. Unlike Weber, who after his trip to America in 1904 wrote with great fear of the changes—which he clearly did not yet understand—occasioned by the transition to consumer capitalism, James saw the changes as positive, and argues that psychology can help people adjust to the new order. The function of neurasthenia as a space for personal change which I described in relation to Dreiser and which describes James's adaptation to the changing circumstances of his own life, James elaborates in "The Energies of Men" into an explanation for cultural change.

In "The Gospel of Relaxation" (1899), James argues that the rest cure was an "immense mistake."[24] Breakdowns are not the result of overwork or overstrain of physical resources, but simply the effects of "bad habits" of thought and attitude. Again the "application of psychology to practical life," this time with the help of sociology, can provide an alternative to nervousness (143). What primarily needs to be relaxed, James concludes, is our Puritan conscience. Like Weber in *The Protestant Ethic*, James sees that the cloak of the Puritan relation to work and goods has become an "iron cage," but James offers his "healthy-minded" therapeutics as an escape. And he offers it as an alternative to traditional religion, medicine, and the various therapeutic cults that partook of both. This then is the second economic corollary of James's economic argument. Having decided on psychology and philosophy rather than medicine, James did his best to fight for his discipline's ascendency in the competition for cultural authority. His arguments are presented, not only "despite what the moralists and doctors say," but in contradiction to what they say. The moralists, with whom James includes the mind curists, Christian Scientists, and other sects, are healthy-minded, James says, *and* they are therapeutically worthwhile, in fact they are almost as valuable as psychology. These movements, he writes in "The Energies of Men," incur "the natural enmity of medical politicians, and of the whole trades-union wing of that profession" (36), and thus James represents the tenth-rate profession as using labor-class strategies to fend off competition. Psychology, though, is the discipline that can explain the way all other therapies work, and, more important, psychology can offer the same rewards as religion to those who are too educated to believe in religious systems as such, and the same results as medicine for those convinced by arguments like James's of the quackery of medical therapeutics (37). And in a classic neurasthenic strategy, James implies that psychology is a higher-class field than medicine, a more "refined" science.

In *The Varieties of Religious Experience*, although one of its main aims is a justification of neurasthenic soul-searching, some counterneurasthenic attitudes are also evident. At least one reviewer of *Varieties* found that while James studied the abnormal, he did not champion it, and that if he justified religious experience, he did not, finally, condone it for itself but for its secondary effects. More important, wrote this reviewer, James saw the perniciousness of asceticism.[25] The reviewer is astute in seeing the disciplinarian function within James's very broad sympathies. In an age of increasing consumerism, ascetic lives are pernicious. Religion is important and useful primarily because it is a form of understanding very much like that of psychology and philosophy; its only problem, in fact, is that it is not as advanced as these human sciences. James himself may have had religious experiences, but they led him into profitable and socially useful work. James argued in several places that ideas have "cash value," and his ideas had cash value in the way of royalties, lecture appointments, and faculty positions. His individual profit could be imitated, he believed, and have national repercussions.

In "The Energies of Men" (also published under the title "The Powers of Men"), James argues for the significance of his version of the nervous economy and thereby for the social significance of philosophy:

> If my reader will put together these two conceptions, first, that few
> men live at their maximum of energy, and second, that anyone may
> be in vital equilibrium at very different rates of energizing, he will
> find, I think, that a very pretty practical problem of national economy,
> as well as of individual ethics, opens upon his view. In rough terms,
> we may say that a man who energizes below his normal maximum
> fails by just so much to profit by his chance at life; and that a nation
> filled with such men is inferior to a nation run at higher pressure.
> The problem is, then, how can men be trained up to their most useful
> pitch of energy? (7–8)

Unlike Weber, who feared a capitalist world that had abandoned the notions of duty, calling, and asceticism and had nothing to offer in its place except dissolute utilitarianism, James offers an energetic utilitarianism similar to Frederick Taylor's, an ethical profit, and the superiority that comes from nationalism. In these three hopeful concerns James has met Roosevelt, whom he refers to in the same essay, while discussing the "dynamogenic" effects of moral action on those who undertake it: "We are witnessing here in America to-day the dynamogenic effect of a very exalted political office," James wrote without explicitly naming Roosevelt, "upon the energies of an individual who had already manifested a healthy amount of energy before the office came" (15–16). James's appropriation of neurasthenic discourse resulted in a disciplinarian attack on the perniciousness of the neurasthenic and a championing of the correlated notions of superiority, profit, and utilitarianism; ending in the same place by a different path, Roosevelt's personal attack on the perniciousness of neurasthenia resulted in an appropriation of neurasthenic discourse and of the same correlated notions of national superiority, ethical profit, and energetic utilitarianism.

Naturalists, Nationalism, and the Big Stick of Patriarchy

Roosevelt had no quarrel with religious experience, and no desire that anything should replace religion. He had a very conventional piety and went to church regularly. According to his valet, he had a "sentimental liking for the old-fashioned hymns and old-fashioned religion. . . . I once heard him say that the man who didn't read the Bible was a fool." Rather than believe that philosophy should replace religion, he thought that action should replace philosophy. He had little of James's speculative curiosity, just as James had little of Roosevelt's taxonomic curiosity. Roosevelt had little, too, of James's habit of indecision. Although Roosevelt's asthma, stomach trouble, and insomnia plagued him throughout his life, after his 1883 trip he never talked of a cure, only of building himself up, a process he thought of as constantly necessary and only as beneficial as it was strenuous. The story of his childhood later became one of the most well-known and enduring myths of the American presidents, for decades as well known as Washington's cherry-tree integrity and Lincoln's log-cabin autodidacticism. Through constant strenuous exercise he transformed himself from a sickly, asthmatic boy into a Harvard pugilist and sportsman. He combined frenetic physical training with serious academic pursuits, avid hobbies, and a social whirl, all creating a hectic pace he kept up throughout his adult life. "Black care," he wrote in one of his books about the West, "rarely sits behind a rider whose pace is fast enough," and Roosevelt's pace was always fast. Roosevelt graduated from Harvard in 1880 and then, after several attacks of *cholera morbus*, went on an extended hunting trip—"I think it will build me up," he wrote his sister—and came back after putting 203 "items" into his game bag. Later in 1880 he married. In 1881 he went to law school, wrote the bulk of *The Naval War of 1812*, and climbed the Matterhorn and several other Alpine peaks. In 1882 he entered the New York State Assembly and managed to play ninety-one games of tennis in a single day. In 1883 he was elected speaker of the Assembly, made his first trip to the Dakota Territory, invested in a cattle ranch, and shot his first buffalo. As Howells would later say, "He is so strenuous I am faint thinking of him. No man over forty has the force to meet him without nervous prostration."[26]

The pace of those few years and the activities themselves are characteristic: Roosevelt would continue to push frenetically for success in politics, shoot game and live the strenuous outdoor life whenever possible, get sick and build himself up, find and accept challenges to his physical prowess and endurance, collect specimens, write about war, and travel extensively for the rest of his life. He managed to fit all of these activities, for instance, into his schedule along with his presidential responsibilities in 1903. John Burroughs, in writing about his camping trip with Roosevelt in 1903, apologizes for taking so long in producing his account (it was published in 1907). "The President himself," he wrote in ironic admiration, "having the absolute leisure and peace of the White House, wrote his account of the trip nearly two years ago!"[27] Roosevelt's search for health, his interest in natural science, his hunting and ranching, his warrior ethos, his political ambitions, and his patriotism formed, in his thinking and writing, an integrated whole, a political philosophy. He was first and foremost a "brain-worker." As in the case of Dreiser's career and James's pragmatism, not only was Roosevelt's political philosophy significantly influenced by the experience of neurasthenic symptoms, but his decisions about himself and his culture, too, followed the logic of neurasthenic cure.

Roosevelt's trips to the Dakotas in the 1880s were meant to have two effects: they were to help cure his asthma and other neurasthenic symptoms, and they were to reverse his original political image as a "Young Squirt," a "Punkin-Lily," and a "Jane Dandy" which haunted his first years as a legislator in New York in the 1880s. He arrived on the floor of the Assembly for the first time on the day of Oscar Wilde's arrival in America in 1882, his hair parted in the middle, sporting a single eyeglass with a gold chain, a cutaway coat with tails that almost reached his shoes, "a gold-headed cane in one hand, a silk hat in the other," according to one reporter, walking "in the bent over fashion that was the style with the young men of the day," his trousers "as tight as a tailor could make them," and speaking in a high-pitched voice with an exaggerated aristocratic accent. He immediately picked up one of the many effeminizing epithets he was awarded in those years, the *New York Sun* and the *New York Star* both referring to him as our own "Oscar Wilde." That characterization was at least partially responsible for his defeat in his 1884 election.[28]

Roosevelt's trip west was one of many attempts to attain a state of manliness, an attempt to exorcise through exercise his effeminizing sickness, and at the same time an attempt to masculinize and thereby strengthen his political position. Roosevelt's well-known championing of the strenuous life, an idea more than any other associated with his political persona, stems directly from the gender-based notions of cure for neurasthenia which he and the other creators of the myth of the cowboy—neurasthenic rough riders Owen Wister and Frederic Remington, for instance—had accepted wholesale.

These men, too, were cured of effete ailments by western exercise. Wister was sent to Wyoming by S. Weir Mitchell, who had earlier prescribed cures for both of Wister's parents and delivered Wister. Wister's first novel was written in collaboration with Mitchell's son Langdon, and his neurasthenic breakdown followed the polite but firm rejection, by William Dean Howells, of the first novel he tried to have published. Wister knew Roosevelt and dined several times at the White House during 1903; his book *The Virginian* (1902) is dedicated to the then-president. In 1903 *The Virginian*, the novel generally considered to have created the Western as a genre, continued to be one of the best-selling novels of the year, and its strong, quiet hero embodies the Rooseveltian dictum to quietly carry a big stick. After *The Virginian*, Wister was considered such a hot property that he commanded ten cents a word for his work. In an interesting reversal of doctor and patient, Wister wrote to his mother, "I really think Weir Mitchell would be sick if he heard anybody he knew in Philadelphia got 10 cents a word."

Frederic Remington was perhaps America's best-known and highest paid magazine and book illustrator as a result of his western themes: cowboys alternately breaking broncs and relaxing in the great outdoors. Like Wister and Roosevelt, he was an elite easterner whose first trip west was for treatment of his neurasthenia. Just as James's response to "occupational frustration" led him to professionalism, these men also responded to social fluidity and a changing culture by engaging in professional activity that cured their neurasthenia and that, like the study of philosophy, had an aura of leisure. The fictional Virginian's life, alternating between strenuous exertion on the ranch and a quiet placidity, was exactly what the West supposedly offered eastern health-seekers. When David Graham Phillips interviewed Wister in 1903, he was impressively healthy, and although he didn't have the vulgar muscles of the barbell lifter, Phillips reports, he had "real strength, strength of sinew," both physically and mentally. Roosevelt himself learned to speak more softly, to work more strenuously, and to wield the weapons of the West during his time on the ranches. He left New York a "shrill eunuch," as he was called by the press, and came back fit and masculinized. And thus from nervousness and its cure was born the rough-riding ethos Roosevelt would translate into a vigorous and imperialist foreign policy.[29]

The life of a ranchman, Roosevelt said, was akin to that of the southern planter, and both, we might add, are akin to that of the colonizer. Roosevelt explicitly related the fitness that results from the strenuous life to people's fitness to rule themselves.[30] "Such fitness," Roosevelt wrote, "is not a God-given natural right, but comes to a race only through the slow growth of centuries, and then only to those races which possess an immense reserve fund of strength, common sense, and morality."[31] The idea that the "backward" and "savage" races were evolutionary atavisms that needed the stewardship of the advanced races while they developed toward civilization is obviously not new with Roosevelt. But the idea that these races lacked a "great reserve fund of strength," while in itself as old as notions of heroism, is, when combined with evolutionary notions of

Frederic Remington. *His First Lesson,* an original painting for *Collier's,* 1903. An eastern dude transfers his nervousness to his mount. (Courtesy Amon Carter Museum, Fort Worth, Texas)

civilization and expansionist policy, part of a new complex, which demanded that one speak in a civilized way but, like a powerful barbarian, carry a big club. Roosevelt agreed with Brooks Adams and other writers that the civilized races were becoming soft, flabby, and feminized; he railed against "the ideas of the peace-at-any-price theorists, . . . the timid and scholarly men in whom refinement and culture have been developed at the expense of the virile qualities." He insisted on a strenuous and "manly" foreign policy and termed the anti-imperialist critics of his "big stick" foreign policies, in a metaphor that both continues the phallic imagery and turns earlier criticisms of himself against his own critics, a "small body of shrill eunuchs." He feared the "grave signs of deterioration in the English-speaking peoples," such as that evidenced by the "lack of fighting edge" of British soldiers in South Africa. The cure for such deterioration, like the cure for neurasthenia, he wrote, was the exercise of strength and the cultivation of manliness. Neurasthenia effeminized men, and since effeminized men lacked the fighting edge, neurasthenic cultures were doomed. To be neurasthenic was to run against the nationalist project as Roosevelt saw it.[32]

Roosevelt's ideas about masculinity and about race had their counterparts in his understanding of women's roles. "The first requisite in a healthy race is that a woman should be willing and able to bear children just as men must be willing and able to work and fight." Over the course of his life Roosevelt became increasingly concerned with the possibility of "race suicide." The upper classes tended to produce fewer children than the lower classes, and the civilized countries less than the undercivilized countries, and these well-publicized phenomena prompted Roosevelt to write regularly in upper-class journals warning nonbreeding couples of the dangers of what amounted to an explicitly classist Malthusianism. In doing so, he countered the emerging discourse about the New Woman, which advocated a broader notion of acceptable roles for women, especially in the professions. He wrote that a woman's greatest career and most significant social contribution has always been and would always be her role as mother. Men who were inactive were degenerate instances of the naturally active male, and women who were too active outside their home were degenerate precisely because they were not progenitive. In a presidential address in February 1903, Roosevelt claimed that anyone who hesitated to have children was "a criminal against the race . . . the object of contemptuous abhorrence by healthy people." For an elite woman selfishly to pursue a career instead of producing offspring was tantamount to committing suicide, race suicide.[33]

Roosevelt adopted the term "race suicide" from sociologist Edward A. Ross, a University of Wisconsin professor who was a strong advocate of restrictive immigration policies—he favored total exclusion of Orientals, for instance—and other federal policies that would help maintain the dominance of the "advanced" races. Roosevelt's understanding of other races as inferior made possible a paternalistic foreign policy, including the creation of the protectorship of the Philippines. Just as nervousness and its cures followed opposite paths for men and women, the civilizing mission as Roosevelt understood it collapsed several conflicting interpretations of what it meant to be civilized and what it meant to be savage. As in the theories of neurasthenia, women and the inferior races were defined in terms of a lack (the women lacked strength and the savage lacked civilization) and in terms of a surplus (women were too sensitive and thus easily overwhelmed and the savages were too wild and violent and thus possibly overwhelming). Thus, Roosevelt concluded, women and the inferior races needed protection from evil and from their own uncontrolled propensities, and this protection needed to be oppressive, or at least repressive. As the journalist Finley Peter Dunne's character, the Irish bartender Mr. Dooley, said while addressing the Filipinos in a parody of the Rooseveltian position, "[We Americans] propose for to learn ye the uses of liberty . . . ye miserable, childish-minded apes." Dunne goes on to show the contradiction in the notion of protection: "We'll treat you the way a father should treat his children if we have to break every bone in your bodies."[34]

But gender and race can coalesce into new formations—as can be seen in the function of rape in American racist culture, for instance— and so at times the protection of the savage and the protection of women come to be in direct conflict. As Marlow says in Conrad's *Heart of Darkness*, as justification for lying about Kurtz's colonial activities to Kurtz's fiancée, "the women . . . are out of it—should be out of it." Civilized women had hearts of pure light, and it is men's responsibility to see that they remain unsullied by the nasty male business of running the world. George Beard in *American Nervousness* illustrated why women "should be out of it" with an interesting fable, or bit of amateur ethnography, about the difference between savage and civilized women:

> Woman in the savage state is not delicate, sensitive or weak. . . . The weakness of woman is all modern, and it is pre-eminently American. Among the Indians the girls, like the boys, are brought up to toil and out-door life. . . . So different are the squaws from the tender and beautiful women of the white races, that they seem to belong to another order of creatures. The young wife of an Indian, having quarreled one day with her husband, seized him by both ears and the hair, as he was raising his hand to strike her, threw him on the ground, as one would throw a child, and raising his head with her hands, beat it upon the hard ground until he begged for his life. (184–85)

For Beard this fable illustrates why American women become neurasthenic while the stronger women of the inferior races do not, and there is some reason to agree with him, if not with his celebration of the neurasthenic condition. For his male readership, the anecdote also signaled whose cultural values should be adopted in a cross-cultural encounter: the choice is "beat or be beaten." Neurasthenia and "the weakness of women" are both "modern and pre-eminently American," and both, according to Beard, are good things. The weakness of women, nerve weakness, and the threat of the savage were three of the pillars on which brain-workers were constructing the greatness of an expanding America.

James, Roosevelt, and Peirce

In 1903, Charles Sanders Peirce, at James's instigation, was giving a series of lectures at Harvard on the subject of pragmatism, and Peirce's philosophy can provide a ground for comparison of the conclusions of James and Roosevelt.[35] James championed Peirce, felt a tremendous intellectual debt to him, and sought academic appointments for him throughout his life. James was responsible for popularizing the term "pragmatism," but he always gave credit for the basic pragmatist ideas to Peirce. Although James, Peirce, and Roosevelt all espoused some form of pragmatism, Roosevelt's thinking was closer to that of Peirce than it was to James's, and the difference is significant. James's final philosophic position was an extension of pragmatism he termed "radical empiricism." a relativist philosophy that was anathema to the common-sense realism of Roosevelt. Peirce's philosophy is now seen as the precursor of modern semiotics, and his ideas therefore have a currency among contemporary intellectuals which the ideas of James and Roosevelt simply do not. In some ways, however, Peirce was profoundly conservative, and like Roosevelt's, his social thought was thoroughly Victorian, especially in comparison with James's relative modernity.

Peirce himself, in his 1903 lectures at Harvard, and more explicitly again in 1905, denied responsibility for James's pragmatism and eventually felt called upon to distance himself from the word itself: "At present, the word begins to be met with occasionally in the literary journals, where it gets abused in the merciless way that words have to expect when they fall into literary clutches." He renamed his own views "pragmaticism," a name, he hoped, that was "ugly enough to be safe from kidnappers." But although Peirce considered James one of these abusive kidnappers, in the large and varied intellectual movement known as pragmatism, James's views, and not Peirce's, were finally most influential. Ralph Barton Perry, James's biographer and a philosopher at Harvard, concluded succinctly that "it would be correct, and just to all parties, to say that the modern movement known as pragmatism is largely the result of James's misunderstanding of Peirce."[36]

The competing theories of pragmatism, like theories of nervousness, were motivated by cultural contentions and anxieties well-removed from the theories' ostensible professional purposes. Both medicine and epistemology were enmeshed in cultural debates about science, the soul, meaning, and value. For Peirce pragmatism was a way of determining meaning, for James a means for determining truth; these formulations have led to an impression of Peirce as a modern relativist and James as a searcher after the Victorian Absolute or at least its replacement. In fact, although James saw pragmatism as a means for determining "truth," he believed that truth was relative, subjective, and at best intersubjective. Peirce saw pragmatism as a tool for analyzing meaning, not primarily of philosophical or everyday statements, but of scientific statements. His faith in the possibilities of science led him to see pragmatism's ability to analyze meaning as a tool in the service of science, especially science's gradual discovery and codification of the real, up to and including the reality of God.

In his axiomatic definition of pragmatism, Peirce states that the meaning of a conception is determined by its consequences: "In order to ascertain the meaning of an intellectual conception one should consider what practical consequences might conceivably result by necessity from the truth of that conception; and the sum of these consequences will constitute the entire meaning of the conception" (*Collected Papers* 5:89). But the meaning of an intellectual conception, and therefore its consequences, were important for Peirce only if they advanced scientific knowledge. Peirce never confused conceptions with the real but thought that conceptions were more or less true based on their relation to the real, and that this relation could be examined in terms of the conception's consequences. Conceptions were hypotheses that could be verified through experimentation; correspondingly, hypotheses were conceptions whose meaning was derived through experimentation. He argued that pragmatism was therefore thoroughly scientific; it was an importation of the scientific world view into philosophy which made logic and philosophy more useful to scientific inquiry.

For James, pragmatism asks a different question, unrelated to the question of science: " 'Grant an idea or belief to be true,' it says, 'what concrete difference will its being true make in any one's actual life?' " Ideas have "cash value": some are better than others, more true than others, because some are more efficacious than others, more useful, more profitable. The economic metaphors place James's thought in the economistic vein of neurasthenic thinking. In any case, such an understanding needs no belief in the real as such; truth resides not in a real that precedes conception but in the particular (real) consequences of acting on a conception. Actions, which are based on conceptions of what is real, have actual consequences, and these consequences *are* the truth of the conceptions. James's pragmatism, therefore, is radically relativist. "Common sense is *better* for one sphere of life, science for another, philosophic criticism for a third," James wrote, "but whether either be *truer* absolutely, Heaven only knows."[37]

Although Peirce's philosophy was directed toward scientific inquiry, he was committed to a realist epistemology that was in the process of being abandoned by the scientific community. In 1903, while he was defending his notion of pragmatism against that of James in the lectures at Harvard, Albert Einstein was publishing preliminary papers toward his first theory of relativity, a theory that would make James's approach more useful than Peirce's for conceptualizing the scientific project. Also in 1903, Henri Poincaré in France published *Science and Hypothesis*, which laid the foundations for what would become a science of chaos. Bertrand Russell in England published his *Principles of Mathematics* relativizing the basic language of science, mathematics. Henry Adams was realizing that the universe Victorian science attempted to define had been destroyed by science itself and had been replaced by a "multiverse." Like Einstein's and Adams's, James's epistemology was modern in ways that Peirce's simply was not. James had what would later be described as the quintessentially modern, decentered understanding of the world, one that allowed that different basic conceptions of the real have equal truth status. Since James made no distinction between experience and reality, he concluded that people's experience was their reality. "Thoughts in the concrete are made of the same stuff as things are. ... To be radical, an empiricism must neither admit into its constructions any element that is not directly experienced, nor exclude any element that is directly experienced." James's theory, based as it is on experience, allows for the relativity and the reality both of observation and of hypotheses, while Peirce's philosophy insists on a reality preexisting observation and unaffected by it. While James was in tune with the methodological understanding of the new physics, then, Peirce remained working within the epistemology of Victorian science.[38]

Roosevelt's epistemological and ontological commitments were also Victorian. His range of reference was encyclopedic—he would surprise dinner guests with his ability to enter enthusiastically into conversations first about boring tunnels through the Alps, then about the currency experiments of Frederick II of Hohenstaufen, and then about jiujitsu and Paderewski.[39] But for Roosevelt the taxonomist these areas of knowledge were categories of a real, classifiable universe. Unlike James, who entirely abandoned his early interest in natural science, Roosevelt continued to be an active naturalist and remained a consultant for the Smithsonian Institution for much of his adult life, specializing in taxonomy and the identification of species. James could not remain interested in taxonomic science even during his first year of teaching anatomy and physiology at Harvard, and he told his students to study the textbooks for these subjects on their own, since he would be discussing "more general" issues, which often meant the variable relations of physiology to psychology.[40]

All three of these men tied their epistemologies to ethics, and again Peirce and Roosevelt opted for a Victorian and James for a modern solution. Perry sums up the differences between Peirce and James:

> For Peirce a conception has meaning only so far as it expresses and promotes the idea of a well-ordered life. It is a habit reflecting the stability and uniformity of things; and its formation is at once an adaptation to this stability and uniformity and a participation in its growth. With James, on the other hand, the significance of a conception lies in its leading into the field of particulars and adapting the agent to the exigencies that arise therein. . . . For Peirce the good lies in coherence, order, coalescence, unity; for James in the individuality, variety, and satisfaction of concrete interests.[41]

Well-ordered, stable, uniform growth versus the adaptive exigencies of individual interest: James's pragmatic ethics are modern in the sense that they, too, are decentered, individualized rather than general, and developed and modifiable in interaction rather than created by and faithful to principle. Multiple and exchangeable, they are the ethics of pluralism, the ethics of consumer capitalism. Peirce's ethics are traditional, based on a notion of their own preexistent truth, and allow for adaptation only in terms of a progressive refinement in the service of the "well-ordered life." Roosevelt, too, argued for the public nature of truth, for stability and progress, and for order. While James argued that individuals and cultures created their own truths, Roosevelt, like Peirce, argued for conceptions of the truth whose meaning could be judged by their consequences. In Roosevelt's case this meant, for instance, that men of the ruling class should be manly and that women of privilege should bear children. The consequences of the truth of this conception can be expressed in positive terms—when men are manly and women bear children it means the preservation of their race—or in negative terms—if men are not manly and women do not bear children the result is race suicide.[42] Peirce and Roosevelt rejected the neurasthenic view, that the world was a place both overwhelming and degenerative, in favor of an assertion of order. The confirmed neurasthenics Adams and James sought meaning in a finally incomprehensible existence, a finally unknowable, chaotic universe.

James and Roosevelt both had a great fund of social ability, which, although developed by the social training of the same elite group, was of two very different sorts. Both men were noted for their ability to interact with a wide variety of people. James's ability was chameleon-like, and he wrote in *Principles* that "a man has as many social selves as there are individuals who recognize him" (1:294). When he was with young people, for example, he felt and acted young, to the point of severely damaging his heart while hiking too far and too fast, at the age of fifty-seven, with a group of young people. To be a social chameleon was in keeping with James's notion of a pluralistic universe—a notion whose truth he saw confirmed by the plural society he experienced. Roosevelt, on the other hand, had a different manner with his butler than he did with his guests, but all noted the integrity of his character. He maintained a stable and consistent presentation of self and had an inclusive, ordered, hierarchical understanding of his social duties. James was conscious of having a developing and changeable personality and Roosevelt conscious of his own unchanging, developed character, and in this difference they represent the twentieth-century and nineteenth-century options for selfhood. Roosevelt, who strenuously rejected disease, thereby avoided what he called the "black care" of self-doubt, while James's willingness to embrace sickness provided a liminal universe of pragmatic change.[43]

Peirce was a difficult man, with very few of the social graces, and this, more than the incomprehensibility with which his dense and active genius was met, made it hard for him to find regular academic work. James described Peirce to F. C. S. Schiller, for instance, as "a hopeless crank and failure in many ways." James tried repeatedly to keep Peirce in paying work, and in urging appointments he needed to argue that the intellectual excitement Peirce would bring to a campus would outweigh his "personal uncomfortableness" and "disagreeableness." By this James meant the nervousness Peirce elicited rather than any nervousness Peirce felt. Although it did not change the irascible and pugilistic tone of his regular letters to James, Peirce did take time out to thank him for the 1903 appointment at Harvard: "You are of all my friends the one who illustrates *pragmatism* in its most needful forms," he wrote. "You are a jewel of pragmatism." Peirce's healthy-minded belief in science kept the difficulties he had finding teaching and publishing opportunities from finding neurasthenic expression or resolution.[44]

Roosevelt and James, on the other hand, published widely and were writing, in the 1890s, to the same general audience. They published in some of the same journals and had a "popular" audience that consisted of a group of highly educated and intellectually active members of their upper-class social world. Peirce wrote quite a bit of hack work to make ends meet, but the highly technical papers that he saw as his real contributions to human knowledge were often too specialized for even the most specialized journals in the field, and his lectures too obscure for the graduate students and faculty of the Harvard philosophy department. James continually urged Peirce to pitch his writing at a wider audience and wrote that he and Josiah Royce agreed that at Harvard "there are only three men who could possibly follow your graphs and relatives." In discussing an upcoming lecture series, James wrote: "Now be a good boy and think a more popular plan out. I don't want the audience to dwindle to three or four, and I don't see how one can help that on the program you propose." Peirce accepted James's criticism but wrote back that he really could not understand the desire for nontechnical lectures. "I am not puritan enough to understand the pleasure of these chins on 'topics of vitally important character.' The audience had better go home and say their prayers, I am thinking."[45]

Peirce's rejection of popular "chins" was among other things a rejection of the role of lay clergyman enthusiastically adopted by Roosevelt and James. It was also a rejection of the neurasthenic description of the culture as sick, as in need of therapy, in a reversal of the way that Roosevelt's acceptance of the role of priest, despite his strenuous healthy-mindedness, shows his acceptance of the neurasthenic understanding of the world. Roosevelt's sermons, like his exemplary life-style, were directed toward cure.[46] In the religious language of his letter to James, then, at exactly the time that James was developing his justification of religious experience, Peirce was touching on a sensitive nerve of both James's and of neurasthenic culture as a whole.

Peirce found only one "concept of God" to be valid, the reality behind the representations of the Absolute presented by Confucius, "Gautama Boodha," Socrates, and other thinkers. Peirce's God is the God of philosophical contemplation of the "physical-psychical universe," and he claims that although God cannot be known, He can be inferred from the concept of God. The kind of experience that James wanted to validate in *The Varieties of Religious Experience* Peirce finds to be delusion, and the kind of quasi-religious observance he parodies in his letter he held in contempt. Religion was something Peirce and Roosevelt didn't question, but simply pragmatically accepted. "What," Peirce asked in 1903, "is the end of an explanatory hypothesis? Its end is . . . to lead to the avoidance of all surprise and to the establishment of a habit of positive expectation that shall not be disappointed."[47] The healthy-minded religion of Peirce and Roosevelt was just such an explanatory hypothesis, minimizing nervous expectation, disappointment, and surprise and, as the doctors treating neurasthenia also would suggest, helping to create positive habits. Roosevelt and James managed—in part because of their deployment of a neurasthenic discourse which managed to meld aspects of science and religion by medicalizing spiritual anxiety—to find the wide educated audience and cultural authority that eluded Peirce until half a century after his death. Roosevelt adopted a healthy-minded missionary zeal as the religious concomittent of his categorical reaction to neurasthenic "black care." Religion for James, on the other hand, remained a mystery to be solved, a legacy to come to terms with, and a scene of personal doubt and nervousness.

Imperial Selves

John Burroughs, like Roosevelt a well-known naturalist and nature writer, claimed in 1907 that much of Roosevelt's work as a taxonomist had the "double interest" of "showing one phase of his radical Americanism, while it exhibits him as a thoroughgoing naturalist."[48] Roosevelt continually insisted on the hardiness of North American animals compared to the degenerative species of Europe and Asia. Taxonomic thinking was for Roosevelt a form of hierarchical thinking, and Burroughs is right to see Roosevelt as a thoroughgoing naturalist: when this hierarchical, taxonomic naturalism was applied to social relations, it led not only to Roosevelt's ideas about racial inferiority, race suicide, and patriarchal usurpation, but to many other policy decisions.

The immigration act of 1903 limited the immigration of not only "inferior" races but of people with "inferior" intellects, such as idiots and anarchists, showing the sure slide from biological racism to political intolerance. Roosevelt's 1903 trip to Yosemite to meet John Muir ("the bulliest day of my life") helped publicize Roosevelt's ideas about a national park system, ideas based on a hierarchical taxonomy of land use and of the allocation of resources. In *Our National Parks* (1902), Muir wrote that the parks were primarily visited by "nerve-shaken" brain-workers from the city and that the "retreat into the wilderness" afforded by these parks was designed in specific response to the neurasthenic wear and tear of modern life. Muir and other naturalists often earned a living by acting as guides to wealthy health-

Theodore Roosevelt and John Muir at Yosemite, 1903. Both men were icons of healthy-minded nervousness. (Courtesy the Bancroft Library)

seekers, and thus they effected both a classification and a gentrifi-
cation of the wilderness environment, one of the many Victorian con-
flations of classification and class. The Coal Strike Commission,
appointed by Roosevelt to report on the anthracite coalminers' strike,
in their report of 1903 made a detailed sociological assessment of the
miners' lives, one of the early instances of social science (like Roosevelt's naturalism, a taxonomic, hierarchical, and quantitative form
of social science) used for policy decisions. The report clearly saw
social evolution within classes, not movement between them, and
analyzed workers and owners as two different species, species whose
conflict could be managed but not eliminated. The *Independent*, in
an article on Roosevelt's western tour, made explicit the relation between this kind of "classification," policy, and morality in the Coal
Strike Commission's report: "Their report was made just before the
Senate adjourned at the special session; and no Government document of recent years marks a more important piece of work better
done, and there is none which teaches sounder social morality to our
people."[49]

Roosevelt and the *Independent* approved of the morality of the
commission's report for several reasons. The report explained the
poverty of immigrant laborers and their unfit living conditions as a
matter of choice on the part of the immigrants, and advocated a
combination of cooperation between classes and competition within
classes as the answer to the social problem. The various criticisms
of capitalist competition which fueled the socialists' political plat-
forms and the muckrakers' exposé articles were alike in that they
were, for Roosevelt, a symptom of neurasthenic worry rather than a
cure for it, and this worry was exactly what the commission's report
was meant to dispell. One of the problems the report identified was
a lack of competition rather than too much competition, and this
was both politically expedient, since antitrust sentiment was widespread, and rhetorically expedient, since it provided a language to
condemn antiunionism as another means, like combination, of in-
hibiting competition. Roosevelt a few years later argued that socialism
was itself a symptom of neurasthenia: "Social conditions ... have
tended to produce a very unhealthy condition of excitement and ir-
ritation in the popular mind, which shows itself in part in the enormous increase in the socialistic propoganda." This connection
between radical left politics and overexcitability is to be found in
fiction, economic writings, and editorial comment throughout this
period. Roosevelt in his neurasthenic reading of socialism specifically
mentions David Graham Phillips, as perhaps a socialist, perhaps a
sensationalist, and it is Phillips's critique of the "conquering arm"

in such novels as *The Master Rogue* that Roosevelt's own rhetoric is meant to rebut. While the neurasthenic cast of Roosevelt's Darwinian thinking led him to equate civilization and bodily degeneration, he also saw a connection between political innovation and unhealthy excitement, and the fear of the strong and healthy masses was accompanied by a view of political unrest as something instigated by Phillips and other middle-class authors. The lower classes may have been physically fit, but they were not fit to govern or even to conceive of governing themselves.[50]

Nationalist naturalism relied primarily on ideas of social evolution—the Colombians, Roosevelt felt, were a "corrupt Pithecoid community," and blacks were "only just emerging from a condition of life which our ancestors left behind them in the dim years before history dawned"—and the natural inferiority of other national and ethnic groups justified not only increased social regulation at home but the big-stick policy abroad. In dealing with the Philippines, Roosevelt wrote to Rudyard Kipling, "I have first [to deal with] the jack-fools who seriously think that any group of pirates and head-hunters needs nothing but independence in order that it may be turned forthwith into a dark-hued New England town meeting."[51] Roosevelt's views had the support of the medical community (as we have seen in the case of Beard) and a large portion of the academic community, including David Starr Jordan, president of Stanford University, and the nationally known professors Edward A. Ross and John R. Commons of the University of Wisconsin, and he managed to garner the support of the American electorate for these ideas as well. Neurasthenia, and its particular encoding of race, class, and gender, was not only a corollary of theories of social evolution, it was a more widespread and assimilated discourse. It is this discourse that connects Roosevelt's own physical activity, for which he was renowned, with his social-evolutionary domestic and foreign policies.

Roosevelt's particular embodiment of neurasthenic discourse has enormous influence. As Arthur M. Schlesinger, Jr., has said, "Roosevelt transfixed the imagination of the American middle class as did no other figure at the time."[52] The prosecution of the Northern Securities Company, the settlement of the coal strike, the Pure Food and Drug Act, the creation of federal police power with the creation of the Interstate Commerce Commission, the regulation of railroads, the reclamation of millions of acres of land as government reserves all resulted in greatly increased state power, the flip side of his discourse of strenuous individualism. His example in entering politics, as Edith Wharton and others make clear, provided a model of public service for elite men. Through Roosevelt's example the "civilized man" became the "civilizing man," and this at exactly the time that the civilizing mission reached its heat in the "scramble for Africa" on the part of the European powers and in America's own overseas expansion. Roosevelt equated American indecisiveness about becoming a great military and economic world power with cowardice and with the moral laxity and flaccid, overcivilized inactivity of leisured elites, and he offered a single answer to both problems: replace morbid self-reflection with action, preferably military action. From the Spanish-American War to the invasions of Granada and Panama in the 1980's this kind of thinking has received wide support.

Oddly enough, William James came to a similar conclusion, despite James's well-documented negative opinion of Roosevelt and his policies. While Roosevelt was vice-president in 1900, for instance, James declared that Roosevelt was "still in the *Sturm und Drang* period of early adolescence." James was not alone in his criticism of Roosevelt's strenuousness. Henry Adams castigated politicians for whom "action was the highest stimulant" and who seemed to believe that their "energies were greater, the less they wasted on thought." Tarbell, in her autobiography, remembered seeing Roosevelt while she was interviewing General Nelson Miles after the declaration of war against Spain in 1898: "Everybody was at his post, everybody except Theodore Roosevelt, Assistant Secretary of the Navy. He tore up and down the wide marble halls of the War and Navy Building—'like a boy on roller skates,' a disgusted observer growled." Since Roosevelt was organizing the Rough Riders for an army regiment, Tarbell thought it only "polite" that he resign his post in the navy. "I remember this because it shocked me more than anything else I was noting. What chance had government in peace or war if men did not stay on their jobs?" James wrote that the acquisition of the Philippines was "the most incredible, unbelievable piece of sneak-thief turpitude that any nation had ever practiced" and believed that Roosevelt was in effect guilty of "murdering another culture." His rejection of strenuous militarism went well beyond personal distaste for Roosevelt. To F. C. S. Schiller James wrote, in 1902, "God damn the U.S. for its vile conduct in the Philippines."[53]

But despite the fact that James was a pacifist and an ardent and active anti-imperialist, his final statement on these issues argued that a culture could simply not survive and progress without the martial spirit. In "The Moral Equivalent of War," given as an address at Stanford in 1906, James argued that the virtues of "intrepidity, contempt of softness, surrender of private interest, obedience to command" and the like were necessary to social progress. "We inherit the warlike type," he wrote, "and for most of the capacities of heroism

that the human race is full of we have to thank this cruel history."
James hoped to see the day that these energies would be turned to
entirely peaceful ends, but he was as convinced as Roosevelt that the
energies themselves were both martial and beneficial.[54]

James had thirteen years earlier published the theoretical ground-
work for an imperialist conception of the self and consciousness, a
conception not, in the final analysis, very different from the one represented by Dreiser. A *"man's Self is the sum total of all that he CAN
call his,"* James wrote in *The Principles of Psychology,* and because
of the "instinctive impulse" that "drives us to collect property," our
empirical self is made up of many parts. The self possesses not only
feelings, clothes, family, material possessions, and reputation, but
all of "the individuals who recognize him": friends, for instance, "club
companions," masters, employees (291–95). The "spiritual self" is
the "Self of selves" and thereby owns them (296–301). The fundamental act of consciousness itself is "appropriation," James believed,
which changes only in relation to changes in our "powers, bodily and
mental" (371). Only the desire for or against appropriation deter-
mines what in our experience we subsume to ourselves and what we
do not, which we calculate based on a person's or object's cash value.
At the same time, James insisted on the unity of consciousness,
offering ten different proofs against the unconscious (162–76). The
Self, finally is one, the world of its desire multitudinous: if we want
it, we possess it, it is ours, and we are the sum of our possessions.

Theodore Roosevelt's escape from despondancy took a different approach to the unitary self, in the same way that his confidence in the
"appropriative right" led him to projects other than the construction
of a philosophical psychology. Roosevelt, like James, thought that
martial energies would eventually be in the service of peace. Just as
peace was the final goal of a cure from nervousness, so Roosevelt
planned to "continue to export peace" to the various "barbarian"
populations. Roosevelt considered pacifists "the timid and short-
sighted apostles of ease and of slothful avoidance of duty," since the
only acceptable peace was the peace of righteousness, which inevi-
tably entailed righteous action, not inaction.[55] Still, the civilizing
mission's final goal was peace, and this in two ways: it would bring
peace at home by curing nervousness through the exercise of martial
virtues, and it would erase savagery and thereby bring peace to the
rest of the world. The rough-riding, big-stick ethos was part of reorganization of American culture which included, and was often articulated in terms of, a retraining of men and women in proper gender
roles, and Roosevelt's speeches and writings provided his audience
with an education in the correct, gender-specific distribution of the

A POSSIBLE CUSTOMER.

PANAMA—"Those are mighty fine lookin' clothes he sells."

"Uncle Sam in Panama," cartoon from *Literary Digest,* 1903. The Panamanians were theoretically less likely to be nervous than Americans.

chores involved in working, fighting, and breeding. Military and other colonial action can then further divide the knowledge of men from the knowledge of women, through the use of the same set of justifications, figured in terms of health and its relation to gender. As *The Heart of Darkness* shows, the end of the colonizing mission has part of its object at home, where "the Intended" is left "out of it" because she should be out of it—that is, in fact, what is intended.

Just as the understanding of the relation of nerve force to neurasthenia and to gender could result in two notions of cure as diametrically opposed as rest and exercise, Roosevelt and James represent positions that at the level of public discourse seem opposed, even though both are based on the same kind of economistic thinking and finally lead their proponents to embrace nearly identical cultural programs. The permissive, relativistic, and humanistic understanding of James and the disciplined, ethnocentric, and authoritarian understanding of Roosevelt have characterized twentieth-century debates about everything from child-rearing to foreign policy. Both positions assume that there is a limited supply of energy in each nervous system and each group; that the cosmic context of human life is incomprehensible but important; that the possibility of human progress is real but endangered; that the choices faced by individuals and groups are analogous to, in fact almost identical to, a choice between sickness and health; that all these tensions make people nervous; that nervousness needs to be combated by individual and collective acts of will; and that the essence of willful activity is appropriative.

Roosevelt and James did "what philosophers are in the habit of doing," according to Nietzsche; they "adopted a *popular prejudice* and exaggerated it," and it is more the form of the exaggeration than the prejudice that accounts for their difference. In Percival Pollard's *Lingo Dan: A Novel* (1903), the con artist Lingo Dan, passing himself off as a minister (he has tied up the real minister in the parsonage), gives a sermon on hypocrisy while waiting to rob the church: "New doctrines come and go; men prate of new religion and new science," Dan preaches, "the traders on the world's trend-to-believe make bargains in the market place." The reference to James's notion of the will to believe is probably pointed. Later, Dan reads the work of a pragmatist philosopher and then hits on an idea for a new scam. When the scam works, he sends the philosopher a twenty-dollar bill, with a thank-you note signed "Dan, Practrician." The two pragmatic patricians, James and Roosevelt, managed to construct in their different fields a moral discourse of appropriative desire, in both cases based on an economy of sickness and health. As Henry Adams, his "historical neck" broken, wrote to his brother Brooks, the neurasthenic theorizer of imperial success, "Progress is Economy!"[56]

James, in his speech on May 25, 1903, celebrating the Emerson centenary in Concord, praised Emerson's contribution to cultural progress, especially his insistence on the "sovereignty of the living individual." James claimed Emerson as the intellectual father of the imperial self and argued that the "indefeasible right to be exactly what one is ... spreads itself, in Emerson's way of thinking, from persons to things and to times and places." Emerson had also written, in what can seem a prophecy of Rooseveltian strenuousness, that "a good deal of our politics is physiological."[57] And so, we might add, is a good deal of the psychology and, it seems, the ethics and philosophy of 1903. Anti-imperialism and imperialism, the fight against racism and the fight against race suicide, the cash value of ideas and the cash value of the big stick: for each man the pair of opposed views rests on the same foundation. Each is a willed decision, based on an ethical economy not in itself still Victorian any more than it is yet modern, as each man attempts a pragmatic response to his understanding of the lives of vast numbers of human beings and of his own responsibility toward those vast numbers, as he and the other elite brain workers watch the world move from one nervous century into the next. Roosevelt's influence on the office of the presidency and on the conduct of politics in general and James's continued importance to academic philosophy and humanistic inquiry in America are the conventional marks of their significance to American culture. But official endorsement of reform racism and the use of military and police force to assure corporate gain are also part of Roosevelt's legacy, and the relativist endorsement of imperialist adventurism and of intellectual classism part of James's. Their personal rites of passage, however diametrically opposed, their very different appropriations of neurasthenic discourse, their opposing constructions of imperialist selfhood, represent the poles and substance of the neurasthenic patrimony of modern American culture.

3 Hamlin Garland's Despair and Edgar Saltus's Disenchantment

We're all sick with the disease of our century! We're too self-conscious;
we're too analytical; we're too bookish!
                                    —Arthur Stringer, "The Professor of Greek:
                                    How He Found Hellenes Again" (1903)

Hamlin Garland and Edgar Saltus, like James and Roosevelt, seem
radically opposed in their literary and philosophical predilections.
Garland, the staunchly conservative midwesterner-turned-Brahmin,
helped maintain a genteel tradition in American letters into the late
1930s with his series of wistful, lettristic memoirs of the "middle
border," fleshing out the admirably lean nostalgia of his early, successful collection of stories, *Main-Travelled Roads*. But while Garland seemed to take the public William Dean Howells as his role model,
Saltus took Edgar Allan Poe. A celebrated debauchee who wrote irony-
and absinthe-soaked stories of terror, corruption, and paranoia, Saltus was Garland's antirealist, anticonventional opposite number. In
the works of both, neurasthenia appears as theme, subject, plot,
figure, and mood. In neurasthenia these writers meet, and in their
use of neurasthenia they immediately again diverge, demonstrating
the flexibility of the liminal discourse of neurasthenia as it structured
the politics, the processes, and the representations of subjectivity in
1903.

Hamlin Garland's *Hesper* (1903) is an account of a neurasthenic
young man, Louis Rupert, his sister Ann, and their travel to the West
in search of a cure. The novel represents a classic encounter of eastern
sophistication and disease with western health and values. Like
Frank Norris's heroines to be discussed in the next chapter, Ann
finds love and in the process her true feminine nature and role, while
her brother (like Roosevelt, Wister, and Remington) is masculinized
and cured by his exposure to western life and its manly role models.
Louis and Ann head to the home of their cousins, the Barnetts, who,

with a community of other health seekers originally from the East, constitute the financial center and high society of their Colorado town. Since the Barnetts own both a ranch and large interests in the mining industry in the nearby mountains, Louis and Ann get a tour of the economic and social possibilities of the American West at the turn of the century. Louis finds health and Ann finds love through the good offices of the hero, Raymond, who is Barnett's ranch foreman until he leaves to become an independent miner. Raymond then plays a role as mediator in the violent dispute between miners and the mine owners, a dispute that provides the climax of the novel: a labor war breaks out, the U.S. cavalry arrives, Raymond coincidentally strikes it rich, marries Ann, and everyone lives happily ever after.

A large number of health seekers came to Colorado and the Southwest in 1903. The area was a common setting for magazine fiction, and the social scene and landscape were familiar to magazine readers from illustrated, full-page advertisements for resorts and rail tours— of the six full pages of travel ads in the June 1903 *Cosmopolitan*, for instance, four and one-half pages advertised trips to Colorado.[1] O. Henry's "The Pimienta Pancakes" in the December *McClure's*, is a light farce set in Colorado, a somewhat anemic version of the southwestern tall tale. The narrator battles for the affections of one Miss Willella Learight, who is "stopping at Pimienta Crossing for her health, which was very good, and for the climate, which was forty per cent. hotter than Palestine." But he is outwitted by his rival and is thereby shown up as a naive provincial, however witty and wise in his own quaint way.

Garland's story, on the other hand, is entirely serious and its donnée has autobiographical overtones. Like Louis, Garland felt that he had been weakened and effeminized by his intellectual and artistic endeavors as a young man. In a passage of his autobiography reminiscent of Louis's experiences, Garland describes his own neurasthenia and its relations, as in the case of Dreiser and James, to Spencerian naturalism and cosmic philosophy:

> I read both day and night, grappling with Darwin, Spencer, Fiske, Helmholtz, Haeckel,—all the mighty masters of evolution. . . . Herbert Spencer remained my philosopher and master. With eager haste I sought to compass the "Synthetic Philosophy." The universe took on order and harmony. . . . It was thrilling, it was joyful to perceive that everything moved from the simple to the complex. . . . My brain young, sensitive to every touch, took hold of facts and theories like a phonographic cylinder, and while my body softened and my muscles wasted from disuse, I skittered from pole to pole of the intellectual

universe like an impatient bat. . . . Naturally I grew white and weak.
My Dakota tan and my corn-fed muscle melted away. . . . I had moments of being troubled and uneasy and at times experienced a
feeling that was almost despair.

Garland, like Dreiser, James, Beard, and Roosevelt, saw a link between brain-work, physical weakness, and despair, and like them he
looked for a solution in exercise and a "synthetic philosophy," a cure
of soundness in mind and body which required the development of
both muscle and what we might call a cosmic sociology.[2]
   Garland was originally a westerner; he began his career in the east
with corn-fed muscle and a Dakota tan and remained a spokesman
for the values of the Middle Border until his death in 1940. Unlike
Louis Rupert and Theodore Roosevelt, Garland did not look to the
West for a cure. What eventually cured him was integration into the
eastern intellectual establishment. His autobiography continues to
chart his decline, after the loss of his tan and muscle, as a starving
student unsure of himself and his place in society. Only when he is
appointed an instructor in English literature at a small college do his
health and spirits return. Garland had come East with a belief in his
own social trajectory. When that belief was threatened he noticed a
lack of vitality, but when his new position validated his sense of
success, he felt that all was again right with the cosmos and resumed
his mission as a spokesperson for literary values. Like Louis, Garland
wanted to go (back) west for "material" for his writing, but unlike
Louis, he returned as a healthy tourist. And he returned many times,
including once in 1903.[3]

Authorial Positions

   Crumbling Idols (1894) was Garland's literary manifesto, a battle
cry for realism and local color, two fictional modes that were already
prominent, in fact clearly dominant and critically defended in the
Atlantic, Harper's Monthly, and the *North American Review*. Garland
argued that western writers (like himself) rejected the aesthetic elitism of the East, and that the West was the new literary center of the
country, yet the book was published by two Harvard undergraduates,
in a style that appealed to eastern aestheticist taste—too aestheticist,
in fact, for the reviewer for the *Atlantic*, who ridiculed its "precious"
appearance.[4] In Chapter 4, "Literary Prophecy," Garland analyzes
realism in terms that parallel William James's understanding of religious life and Roosevelt's understanding of political life. The realist,

at the same time that he delineates the problems in society, Garland writes, is a prophet of the future life of peace. Unlike Roosevelt, who sought to deny his own "black care," Garland and James admit that the problems of life take their toll and need to be examined. The first step, for Garland in fiction and for James in religion, is the recognition of a problem, the second step the understanding or faith that there is a solution to that problem. But while both remain optimists, neither are what James called "healthy-minded." Garland continues:

> The realist or veritist is really an optimist, a dreamer. He sees life in terms of what it might be, as well as in terms of what it is. . . . He aims to be perfectly truthful in his delineation of his relation to life, but there is a tone . . . of sorrow that the good time moves so slowly in its approach. . . . He aims to hasten the age of beauty and peace by delineating the ugliness and warfare of the present; but ever the converse of his picture rises in the mind of the reader. He sighs for a lovelier life. He is tired of warfare and diseased sexualism, and Poverty, the mother of Envy. He is haggard with sympathetic hunger, and weary with the struggle to maintain his standing place on this planet, which he conceives was given to all as the abode of peace. (43–44)

As did the muckrakers and Christian reformers, Garland represented war, neurasthenic sexuality, hunger, and poverty as diseases that make people tired, haggard, and weary and that need to be fully recognized in order to be corrected.

Like James and such reformers as Jane Addams, Garland saw his own nervousness, at least in part, as a response to social conflict, something the healthy-minded Roosevelt and success-minded Dreiser denied in their own self-analyses. As in *The Varieties of Religious Experience*, the central image is one of disease lived and investigated and finally replaced by faith and peace. Because he "sees a more beautiful and peaceful literary life," the "haggard" and "weary" realist is "encouraged to deal truthfully and at close grapple with the facts of his immediate present. . . . Because he is sustained by love and faith in the future, he can be mercilessly true" (43). But this truth telling must be, for Garland, in the service of an optimistic reformism. While he praises Henrik Ibsen as the strongest influence on contemporary realism, he also criticizes his "morbid" characters. As Rashdall forgave James for his morbidity, so Garland forgives Ibsen, since the playwright "does not lose his grasp on surrounding facts, when studying these special cases" (91).

Edgar Saltus scoffed at such sentiments, writing poetry about "the aimlessness of all we undertake." Allied more to European decadence than to American literary movements, Saltus developed a version of the decadent aesthetic, an aesthetic beyond good and evil as it were, for American audiences. In "Morality in Fiction" Saltus called the ethical realism of Howells and Garland, hemmed in by propriety and purpose, the "sedative" element in fiction and argued for a pure aestheticism. "There is no criteria by which a story can be judged as moral or the reverse; there are but two classes of fiction—stories which are well-written and stories which are not." Saltus's friend and fellow aesthete Gelett Burgess, for instance, in his parodic doggerel version of James Russell Lowell's *Fable for Critics*, equated Norris's "naturalist" romance of 1903, *The Pit: A Story of Chicago*, with such best sellers as Alice Hegan Rice's *Mrs. Wiggs of the Cabbage Patch* (1901), making fun of both as ephemeral: "Each Morn a thousand Volumes brings, you say; / Yes, but who reads the Books of Yesterday? / And this first Autumn List that brings the New / Shall take The Pit and Mrs. Wiggs away. / Well, let it take them!" Mrs. Wiggs was explicitly of the optimistic school, despite living along the railroad tracks in a tenement, for as the narrator of Rice's novel says, "the substance of her philosophy lay in keeping the dust off her rose-colored spectacles." In Saltus's sardonic voice this could have passed as an apt insult to Garland's veritism. In closing, Mrs. Wiggs exclaims, "Looks like ever' thing in the world comes right, if we jes' wait long enough," a sentiment only slightly more Pollyannaish than Garland's ending to *Hesper*, or for that matter, Norris's ending to *The Pit*. Burgess also was perhaps referring to Garland a few years later when, in trying to define a "Bromide" (also known as Philistine, Conservative, Bore) he wrote that the Bromide "follows the main-traveled roads" and "goes with the crowd" and therefore never has an original thought or sentiment.[5]

Still, Saltus and Burgess represent just one of the possibilities for aestheticism in America, and Garland himself represented another. For contrast, a third is an academic version produced by one of the remaining practitioners of the genteel tradition. Edward Everett Hale's *New England History in Ballads* (1903), for instance, is a nice parlor book, or "gift book," which has good things to say about artistic book production, poetic tradition, nostalgia for oral culture, patriotic nostalgia, family values, and traditional intellectual heroes. The last poem is a ballad to the stars, which ends with these two stanzas:

> There are millions of loving thoughts and deeds
> All ripe for awakening,
> That never would start from the world's cold heart
> But for sorrow and suffering.

> Yes, the blackening night is sombre and cold,
> And the day was warm and fine;
> And yet if the day never faded away,
> The stars would never shine.

The idea that suffering is a moment in a progressive story, so convincingly argued by James, has become here a sentimental, polite background for silly rhymes, within an aesthetic of pure conventionality. Such sentiments, and such an aesthetic, too, are far from those of Saltus.

Although Saltus—in the mold of such European aesthetes as Oscar Wilde—positioned himself as a writer opposed to the realists, to gentility, and to the popular writers, he nevertheless created his own version of a progressive schema for literature. The novelist, Saltus wrote in "The Future of Fiction," has succeeded the troubador, whose duty was to please and amuse. But the novelist's "mission is no longer to entertain; it is to cure."[6] Written in 1890, this identification of the novelist as doctor was a "youthful" exuberance similar to that of Garland in *Crumbling Idols*, also published when the author was in his mid-thirties. And like those in *Crumbling Idols*, the literary directives in *Love and Lore* were very rarely, if ever, actually followed by the author. Like Garland, Saltus was a follower of fashions and dedicated to an aesthetic that changed as fast as fashion allowed.

While he was writing *Crumbling Idols*, Garland was under the influence of B. O. Flower, the editor of the *Arena*, and the group of contributors to that progressive Boston journal. This group was interested in a wide but interrelated range of concerns, most important evolutionary theory, literature, reform, and psychic research. Benjamin Orange Flower, like William James, was the son of a strongly religious but unorthodox father and had studied theology before turning to progressive publishing. Like James, he was a member of a society for psychic research. Flower and the *Arena* were at the forefront of nearly every reform movement of the 1890s, including labor rights, prison reform, federal control of liquor sales, women's dress reform, public works programs, unemployment relief, government ownership of natural monopolies, the eradication of child labor, slum clearance and urban muckraking, antitrust, single tax, higher education for women, suffrage, and so forth.[7]

Such a list would have provided a field day for the distantly amused scorn of a self-professed "idle dilettante" like Edgar Saltus. But the cluster of concerns also belies its own kind of dilettantism, grounded in a stridently bourgeois reformism, and thereby helps make sense of Garland's career as an antiestablishment establishment figure. Like Dreiser, Garland did not consider financial success and literary integrity to be compatible. And as was true for Dreiser and James, his social position and social trajectory remained a central concern: even as a young man, Garland was "weary with the struggle to maintain his standing," and the chapter immediately preceding the passage on realism in *Crumbling Idols* is titled "The Question of Success." Many critics have tried to explain Garland's "defeat" or his "decline" from his early years as a self-proclaimed literary radical to his years as a stodgy eminence remembering his own greatness. Larzer Ziff titled his chapter on Garland in *The American 1890's* "Crushed but Complacent," representing Garland as a youthful idealist who had been coopted. H. L. Mencken, who thought him a hopeless bore, created a fable in which Garland was "led astray when those Boston Brahmins of the last generation, enchanted by his sophomoric platitudes about Shakespeare, set him up as a critic of the arts, and then as an imaginative artist." But whatever story is told, it is clear that Garland's sense of literary professionalism, the "authorial ideology of professionalism" (to use June Howard's term) he shared with Norris, Dreiser, and others of his generation, is an adequate explanation of his attitudinal and generic decisions. He read his public and produced, at each point in his career, more of what sold best, whether that was reform-minded tracts, romantic love stories, or genteel memoirs.[8] He never declined; he remained a venerable, popular author into the 1940s.

Saltus, again like Wilde, was an author the public, more than the critics, loved to hate, the only "genuine exotic of the day" in America. What popularity he had grew through the 1880s, was maintained in the 1890s, and ebbed after 1900. It grew again in the 1920s, when the outrageous became once more a cachet rather than a mark of desperation, and a new uniform edition of his work was published. As Garland was in his own way, Saltus was a minor philosopher of desperation. All Garland's stories in *Main-Travelled Roads* (1891), his first and most important book, are about desperation, but his memoirs center on a denial of desperation. Garland recounted his life in volume after volume in a tone of wonder and nostalgia, since life was good, and life was to be lived and to be reflected upon. Saltus's first important work, *The Philosophy of Disenchantment*, argued for the validity of the "new pessimism" of writers like Arthur Schopenhauer and Edward Von Hartmann, and raised desperation to the level of a "first principle." "The world is a theatre of misery, in which, were the choice accorded it," Saltus writes, "it would be preferable not to be born at all." Life, according to Saltus, is an "affliction," and what people need from literature and philosophy is affliction represented, anatomized.[9]

The only way to make sense of Saltus's notion that representations of affliction would lead to cure is to rely on a homeopathic logic in which a small dose of a poison that causes symptoms similar to those of the disease is used as a specific. Homeopathy was itself an elite form of medical practice, and the fact that Garland's "cured" writings sold better than Saltus's "afflicted" books is another measure of the elitism of Saltus's texts. Saltus was the scion of a New York family, not an upstart from the Midwest. Like the characters he lightly ridicules, he was not beyond using claims to sickness as claims to privilege. His ironic tone—his friend and fellow writer James Gibbons Huneker claimed that Saltus should have been given an endowed chair in irony at some university, while Saltus himself suggested a chair in Love and Lucre—exposes the pretenses of his falsely afflicted characters and at the same time undercuts his philosophy of affliction. The rhetorical operation of this irony produces and requires a feeling of being one of the informed, of being at the same time a native in bohemia and a member of the highest society. And it was to an audience (necessarily somewhat small) that felt or wanted to feel in such a position that Saltus's work was directed.[10]

Saltus's ironically detached narrators present the social forms and personal experiences of nervousness in ways that invalidate neurasthenic symptoms and medicine at the same time that their prevalence in his stories underwrites the inevitability of the neurasthenic life style. In *The Pace that Kills* (1889), for instance (an early novel with a title that is itself an ironic warning against nervous wear and tear), we are presented with a reprobate who has been accused by his wife of sterility, which is, she says, the result of a "misspent youth."[11] He had married the woman to get his hands on her inheritance, which is in turn dependent on their producing a male child, and so he immediately looks for a solution to their barrenness: "With the idea of dulling the hurt and of ministering also to his own refreshment, he consulted a book which treated of certain conditions of the nervous system, and a work on medical jurisprudence as well. But literature of that kind is notoriously unsatisfactory. It may suggest, yet the questions which it prompts remain unanswered" (139). Here he seems to suggest that medicine has no answers and that theories of the nervous system have no application. But while the dismissive attitude of the protagonist negates medical authority, the ironic tone of the narrator in turn negates the dismissal of the protagonist. Saltus himself, in *The Philosophy of Disenchantment*, complicates his own rejection of neurasthenia when he locates his idea of disenchantment in the same cause as the one claimed by medical doctors. He likened philosophic disenchantment to the "symptoms of melancholy and disillusion" which were "patent to every observer" and which were "indubitably born of the insufficiencies of modern civilization" (161).

His treatment of neurasthenia in his novels and stories is similar to that of Henry James, to whom Saltus dedicated one of his novels in the 1890s. The possibility always exists that any character with neurasthenic symptoms is simply using the appearance of disease for other purposes. At times in Saltus's 1903 collection of stories, *Purple and Fine Women*, the false neurasthenic is exposed: "Trella, pretexting some one or other of those many malaises which women always have within beck and call, had disappeared for the night."[12] Two stories later, the same phrase (by 1903 Saltus had become quite sloppy) occurs: "If I asked, she answered at random, alleging fatigue, advancing any one of those myriad malaises which women when they wish have within beck and call" (104–5). Here neurasthenia is figured as a servant to be employed at whim. In addition, the narratives make fun of many of the common evaluative and medical assumptions of the neurasthenic world view. In "A Bouquet of Illusions," from this same 1903 collection, a widower tells the narrator a story in which he describes his obsession with the possibility that his wife is not dead, though he has had every indication that she is, since he arranged and attended her funeral. The widower reports asking a doctor in France, "I am mad, am I not?" The French doctor answers: "Pas plus qu'un autre. . . . Tout le monde est plus ou moins fou. You may have a delusion or two. What of it? Delusions are very delightful. What should we do without them?" (9–10). The French doctor, of course, represents the aesthetic of the Decadents and the bemused acceptance of affliction which Saltus championed. In another story in *Purple and Fine Women* the narrator delivers the epigram, "Love is a fever. Marriage is a febrifuge" (65), playing with the conventionally scandalous disease-metaphors of Saltus's bohemian set.

"The Princess of the Golden Isles," from the same collection, is set at Eichwald, a spa for neurasthenics, where the narrator has gone for the baths because of "a series of shocks, induced however by nothing more severe than baccarat." Making fun of the medical opinion that the speculative nature of gambling caused neurasthenia, Saltus then describes Eichwald as "the haunt of mattoids" (100). "Mattoid" was coined by the Italian criminal anthropologist Cesare Lombroso, whose theories were largely in line with those of the American doctors. Describing the "mattoid" in *Man of Genius* (1891), Lombroso wrote: "This variety forms the link between madmen of

genius, the sane, and the insane properly so called."[13] The link between the refined, civilized genius and the insane "properly so called"
articulated by Lombroso recapitulated Beard's neurasthenic theory
of refinement and insanity.

Saltus also made use of medical notions of insanity. "The Elixir of
Love," in *Purple and Fine Women,* is a story of dual personality cured
by love. "You know, however, that the mind is dual," the narrator
informs us. "Ordinarily the two hemispheres of the brain work together. Now and again there is discord. The result is insanity" (186).
And Saltus took the Jamesian view that the abnormal and the normal
were closely related. For instance, Saltus saw "dual personality" as
normal: "How often it happens that we do or say things that we have
no intention of doing or saying, things which afterward we are unable
to account for. In the course of every life there are such changes of
personality that, could each phase of our existence be incarnated into
distinct individuals and those individuals got together, so dissimilar
and antipathetic would they be, that it is only a question of time
when they would come to blows" (187). Again this is a somewhat
comic, yet fully assimilated notion of morbid psychology, a notion
that, as William James would say, there are always options for consciousness. The conclusion Saltus reached, again a variant of James's
notion of willed subjectivity, was that subjectivity was a pose. The
poseur, in Saltus's version of radical empiricism, became the model
for understanding human psychology, and an argument for a pragmatism of serial imposture.

Disorder and Disease

Garland's *Hesper* is pitched in a different key altogether. *Hesper* is
a reading of the reading public's desire for themes of power, money,
and heroism developed through an explicitly standard romantic formula. The same could be said of Frank Norris's *The Pit,* another
conventional sentimental novel by a self-professed literary radical.
Norris's naturalist manifesto in *Responsibilities of the Novelist* and
Garland's veritist manifesto in *Crumbling Idols* had less bearing on
the construction of these novels than did the plot structures of such
popular novelists as Winston Churchill and Mrs. Humphrey Ward. In
both *Hesper* and *The Pit,* the basis of the plot is the meeting of a
man and a younger woman; the woman finds something both crude
and attractive about the man; the man proves finally to be worthy;
love grows and prospers; and the backdrop to this main plot is a

large-scale economic confrontation. The plot of *The Pit*, as we will see, involves more, and draws on the naturalist themes of decay and resignation, economic and natural forces too large for human comprehension or melioration, and the relation of art to action. *Hesper*, on the other hand, draws the rest of its plot from a source as popular as Garland hoped his book would be: the dime western and its full-length elaborations.

Hesper was written while Owen Wister's *Virginian* topped the best-seller lists. Wister's book is both a nostalgic celebration of the frontier values of its hero and at the same time a celebration of the beneficial influence of eastern values, represented by the civilizing influences of the eastern schoolteacher the Virginian eventually marries. Like *The Virginian*, Garland's *Hesper* plays eastern and western values against each other to arrive at a compromise position at once rugged, masculine, sensitive, ordered, and civilized, a kind of neurasthenic utopia. In economic backdrop or subplot, however, the books that most closely resemble *Hesper* are a series of dime novels published by Beadle and Adams, particularly one first published in 1878, but still available in 1903, Edward L. Wheeler's *Deadwood Dick on Deck; or, Calamity Jane, the Heroine of the Whoop-Up.*[14] The upper-class health seekers in *Hesper* repeatedly refer to the degradation of the West in comparison to when, a generation earlier, Louis and Ann's father made a similar journey and found all in the West to be real and good. One of the marks of that degradation is the simmering class warfare between miners and mine owners, especially absentee owners from the East. While the old miners in *Hesper* echo the health seekers' indictment of the present, they blame the health seekers themselves. The miners feel that the best is gone, and they express their distaste for the overcivilized, intruding capitalists and for the colony of leisure-class invalids in terms that recall the political name-calling the prestrenuous Roosevelt was subjected to: "This is a collection of tenderfeet—a town of punkin-rollers," says one miner. "The real thing is gone forever."[15]

But *Deadwood Dick*, published in 1878, or roughly at the time of Rupert *pére's* visit, centers on economic problems remarkably similar to those in *Hesper*. In both *Hesper* and *Deadwood Dick*, a confrontation develops between western miners and eastern capitalists. In both books what is at stake are the egalitarian, humanistic values of the westerners, which are threatened by the economic exploitation of sophisticated and politely ruthless easterners. And in both books, the smooth-running, industrious, and exemplary community of miners is disrupted by the greed of eastern speculators. Wheeler's sympathy is entirely with the miners, and he makes the relation to eastern laborers explicit in this description of the hero: "Sandy was an enthusiast on the labor question, and if the country to-day had more of his make and resolute mind, there would, undoubtedly, be a change for the better, when every man would, in a greater or lesser degree, have an independence, and not be ground down under the heel of the master of money" (121). The eastern speculators are simply villains, and their "iron heel" does not belong in the West, where every man still has the ability to be his own master. Sandy's partner, who had originally owned the entire claim but had sold off small parts of it to independent miners, explains to the speculator why he had not sold the land to a corporation and received a much higher price:

> I'd ruther 'a' not got a cent out o' ther hull business, than to have sold et ter men who'd hev hed et all under three or four piratical pairs o' fists, an' w'ile hoarding up their pile ground ther workin' men down ter China-men's wages—'washee shirtee for five cents!' Mebbe ye cum frum out in Pennsylvania, whar they do thet kind o' playin', stranger, but et's most orful sure thet ye ken't play sech a trick out hyar among ther horny-fisted galoots o' this delectable Black Hills kentry—no sir-e-e-e! (109)

As Garland would twenty-five years later, Wheeler presents his miners as the middle term between effete wealth and the degrading Otherness of ethnic difference.

Other readings of the economics of the West were produced with the same settings in magazine fiction in 1903. In Rex E. Beach's "The Mule Driver and the Garrulous Mute," for instance, published in *McClure's* November issue, the medical metaphors are introduced immediately. " 'There's two diseases which the doctors ain't got any license to monkey with,' began Bill, chewing out blue smoke from his lungs with each word, 'and they're both fevers. After they butt into your system they stick crossways, like a swallered toothpick; there ain't any patent medicine that can bust their holt' " (93). Both of these "fevers" turn out in fact to be forms of speculation. " 'The first and most rabid,' he continued, 'is horse racing—t'other is the mining fever, which last heap is insidiouser in its action and more lingering in its effect' " (93–94). Bill is no eastern capitalist; Beach levels the classes and the economic analysis in his comic dialect rendering of the neurasthenic effects of speculative economics.

But the purely economic was only a portion of Garland's project, which was primarily cultural. Garland's nativism went far beyond his depiction of labor turmoil: an ethnically charged Americanism is one of the staples of Garland's authorial and cultural ideology. *Crumbling*

Idols is replete with nationalistic fervor in its condemnation of the use of European literary models and its repeated claims for a "broader Americanism." The theme runs throughout Garland's career and can be seen most clearly in a late article, "Limitations of Authorship in America" (1924), in which Garland argues that immigration is the major cause of what he perceived as a lowering of literary tastes and standards in magazines, drama, and the novel.[16]

Rather than use the Chinese as the laborer's Other as in the dime novel, however, Garland introduces a new division in *Hesper*, more in tune with the labor politics of 1903 in the East, between the true frontier Americans, who exist as laboring entrepreneurs, and the southern and eastern European immigrants who perform the worst jobs and are seen as having a position and set of concerns different from those of American miners. Nationally, American labor's anti-Asian activity had not at all abated since the time of Wheeler's story. In 1901 Samuel Gompers and Herman Gufstadt's *Some Reasons for Chinese Exclusion: Meat vs. Rice, American Manhood against Coolieism, Which Shall Survive?* was published by the American Federation of Labor, and in 1903 the AFL refused to grant a charter to the nation's first agricultural union, the Sugar Beet and Farm Laborer's Union of Oxnard, California, formed primarily by Mexican and Japanese workers, because it allowed Japanese membership. But in the East, the new wave of mass immigration from southern and eastern Europe—over 300,000 immigrants in 1900, over 600,000 in 1903—was the main fear of organized labor. In fact, the tripling of membership of the AFL between 1900 (548,000) and 1904 (1,676,000) represented fewer workers than the new communities of immigrants were adding to the workforce. In 1902 the AFL lobbied Congress for immigration literacy tests in an attempt to slow down the tide of immigration of what Garland has a character call "Dagoes and Rooshians," but this was to reduce competition among eastern workers, not among westerners.[17] The use of these minorities as refractions of economic exploitation and conflict marks the eastern perspective of this novel set in the West.

In *Hesper*, wealthy capitalists import immigrant labor to Colorado specifically to break a nascent union. The owners fear the union as anarchistic, but Garland represents it as harmless and "American." The owners are shown to be overreacting to the union; the few violent union men are aberrations rather than typical, and their violence is caused more by the owners's pigheadedness than anything else. But while the text condemns the capitalists' antiunionism and thereby seems to argue for open shops, it argues even more strongly for the entrepreneurialism (and the antiunionism) of American "free men."

Although on the surface this is a contradictory set of propositions, the primary distinction to be drawn is clarified by two embodiments of western values, Kelly and Raymond. Says Raymond:

> "The big owners in the Springs are sending East for their miners. They know that men like you and me will not do the deep work for them. He's right, too, in saying these cow-boys and farmhands from the States won't make miners. They don't intend to work underground."
>
> "Sure thing," said Kelly. "This gettin' under the crust o' the earth and livin' there is unholy business—not for free men like ourselves. It's all goin' to be done by the Rooshians and the Dagoes."
>
> "I didn't mean to say that a miner was a slave," replied Raymond. "I just meant that a man who is content to swing a pick in a mine all his life must be born and bred to it." (149)

This conversation takes place during an argument about whether or not the miners should unionize. Kelly and Raymond are the "free men" who are in fact small capitalists, and therefore do not need a union. Their workers are well treated (profit is shared) so they do not need a union either. But the wealthy eastern capitalists milk their labor unmercifully, and unions may be necessary for them, unless, of course, the workers are bred to misery like Russians and Italians.

The representation of the free, self-made entrepreneur as both the representative of western values and as a possible third term in an otherwise unresolvable conflict between capital and labor was, by 1903, somewhat anachronistic. The idea that each laborer, as Sandy in *Deadwood Dick* had put it, "would, in a greater or lesser degree, have an independence" was increasingly discredited. As Mineworkers' Union president John Mitchell declared in 1903, "The average wage earner has made up his mind that he must remain a wage earner. He has given up hope of a kingdom come, where he himself will be a capitalist, and asks that the reward for his work be given him as a workingman." Mitchell himself invoked aspects of neurasthenic discourse, as when he argued that if the union had been defeated in the 1902 strike, it "would have given the American Labor Movement a shock from which it would take years to rally and recover." At the same time he tried to argue against some of the commonplaces of the neurasthenic world view. Hard labor, he argued with overwhelming statistical evidence, destroys health and shortens life; manual labor is harder on the body than brain work.[18] Garland attempted, in his own way, to bring the West up to date and to replace earlier myths of western life, as when one rancher declaims: "The cattle business is on a new basis now, and what I want is not a wooly jack who shoots off his mouth and his pistol on the slightest provocation. I want steady, decent workmen" (85). His representation of the West as beset by the same labor problems as the East was considerably more accurate than the representation of the West in *The Virginian*, for instance, and its small-scale, entrepreneurial ranchers and rustlers living in a cultural vacuum. But Garland's notion of the western laborer on his way to becoming a small entrepreneur was nostalgic in its view both of the possibilities for labor and of the possible healthful effects of western values for the East.

Hesper was written against the background of a more specific event in the history of labor, the anthracite coal strike of 1902. The period from January 1902 to June 1904 was full of labor conflict, resulting, according to one contemporary observer, in 180 union laborers dead, 1,651 injured, and over 5,000 arrested. The coal strike, which virtually shut down coal production and caused a national crisis and "coal famine," was the most visible of these conflicts. Garland based his novel on research he had done into a strike a decade earlier in Cripple Creek, but the 1902 strike was on the front pages of all newspapers for as long as it lasted, which was roughly the period during which Garland was writing *Hesper*. In May 1902, fifty thousand members of the United Mine Workers in Pennsylvania struck for a 10- to 20-percent wage increase and an eight-hour day. After sending in the U.S. Army to keep order, Roosevelt appointed a commission to arbitrate the dispute; it came roughly half way between the demands of the Mine Workers and the position of the operators, who argued for no change at all. The *Report to the President on the Anthracite Coal Strike* invokes the nativism that remained one of the primary grounds of agreement among organized labor, management, and government. For instance, though immigrants live in shanties that are "not fit to be called habitations of men," the commissioners suggest, "it is impossible to say how much choice and volition have to do with their inferiority," and therefore no conclusions can be drawn.[19]

As soon as the commission was appointed the mine workers returned to work, and Roosevelt went on a bear hunt in Mississippi. There the president, to avoid negative comments in the press, refused to shoot a small bear brought into camp for him, even though he was happy to shoot the cub's mother. Roosevelt, conscious of his newfound image as the protector of the "little man" against the power of the big trusts and financiers, feared that the journalists traveling with his hunting party would draw connections between the little bear and the helpless workers and consumers he was pledged to protect. The incident led, after a series of political cartoons and satires on the subject, to the manufacture of the first teddy bear.[20] The commission's report was issued in May 1903, shortly before Garland submitted his proofs to his publisher.

Hesper is more in tune with the reform-minded muckraking journalists' comments on the coal strike than with the conservative press's condemnation of anarchistic elements in the unions. The main distinctions in the novel are not between kinds of laborers but between kinds of capitalists. At the height of a period of antitrust feeling, Garland used the fight between big capital and wage labor to celebrate the small entrepreneur. The enmity between the miners in his Skytown and the capitalists in the valley is represented as unresolvable:

> Sky-town had begun to hate the valley as the home of those who lived on the labor of others, and some of those in the valley, as Raymond well knew, expressed their contempt of those who dwelt in the Sky by calling them "red necks," in allusion to their tanned or drink-inflamed faces.
>
> These citizens of Sky-Town (who suffered little on account of sickness) retaliated by calling their neighbors of the Springs "dudes" and "one-lungers," in allusion to their having settled West for the sake of their broken health. Politically the two towns were as far apart as the poles. (145–6)

Munro, a union miner in *Hesper* whose personal craziness and sullenness discredit the claims of radical labor, puts the enmity most clearly when he says to Raymond, "I won't sit back and see the district done up by these capitalist thugs who never earned an honest dollar in their lives. And your friend Barnett—what good is he on earth? Just a blood-sucker on the bare back of labor" (207).

This polar opposition cannot be mitigated, for when the two armed groups finally confronted each other, when "at last the two forces of disorder—of passion and prejudice—were set face to face," writes the narrator, "Battle was . . . inevitable" (386). In this hopeless situation, we are supposed to see the justice of the small independent mine owners' remaining aloof from the conflict and the question of unionization. Unlike Norris's *Octopus*, which blames everyone involved for economic conflict, *Hesper* leaves Raymond and small entrepreneurship as viable and just models. Raymond is not greedy; in fact, his speculative endeavor, justified in part by his own labor, is further justified by his instrumental relation to whatever wealth might accrue. "Money is a measure of value," Raymond tells us, "and wealth I must have first; then leisure and the higher life" (150). In this and in Raymond's own relation to ill health, he is closer to the capitalists than he is to the laborers. "He looked the gentleman," Ann thought while she nursed him after a gunshot wound, "and his face was very handsome, very moving in its clear pallor; suffering had infinitely refined its lines" (109). One of Raymond's chief goals in life is to own a library as good as the Barnetts', but unlike theirs, his library is to be one in which the books are actually read.

As in Dreiser's work, agrarian values are played off against speculative values, and again Raymond provides a middle term closer to eastern capital than to western labor. The narrator describes the miners as men who have fled from farm and ranch life in search of a quick buck: "They had no gardens to grow thirsty for water, no vegetables to be nipped by the frost. Stocks and the daily output of this or that mine formed the staple of their interest, their chief anxiety. They could not endure the slow growth of grain, but they bore repeated failures of shafts or tunnels with smiling unconcern. Dreaming of sudden wealth and vast palaces of the future, they lived on bacon and beans" (129). The miners grew no flowers, either, and had no aesthetic sense. Again, although Raymond himself has left the ranch to mine gold, he is an exception, for his aesthetic sense is noted when we first meet him, reading Emerson. In 1903 perhaps more than ever before, during the much-celebrated Emerson centennial, reading Emerson functioned as a shorthand characterization, marking a character as someone at once aesthetically refined, learned, and worthy of the "higher things." Pure aesthetes and Emersonian nature lovers, like Louis or like the sculptor Parker in Garland's *Captain of the Gray-Horse Troop* (1902), are nervous and useless; Emerson and aesthetics are ethically necessary but not sufficient. And manly vigor is alike insufficient without the moral guidance of intellectual and literary culture.

Saltus attacked the Emersonian conflation of ethics and aesthetics from the other side. That wealth was a measure of one's ethical relation to nature, as Emerson had argued in a late essay, Saltus found ridiculous, but the idea that the "higher life" was approachable in a shack in eastern Colorado, even if one read enough Emerson, Saltus would have also found not only ludicrous but downright vulgar in its pretensions. The vulgarity of labor and laborers could only be compounded by the vulgarity of veritism, realism, or naturalism, from which, in Saltus's view, the vulgarity of Garland's romanticism was not far removed. Garland's transcription of the romanticized vulgate of his miners' language is perhaps an obvious example. Percival Pollard, another of the American aesthetes, lambasted Garland's romanticism in 1909 and took him to task for his lack of fidelity to the principles espoused in *Crumbling Idols*, introducing what was to become a critical truism, the idea that Garland had declined from his early radical days into a sloppy romantic.[21] Pollard, like Saltus, criticized romanticism not from the vantage of realism, but from the standpoint of the avowed aesthete. Pollard's own 1903 novel, *Lingo Dan*, makes fun of the realist as someone who relishes viewing others' misfortune. A consumptive playwright about to burn his rejected manuscript and die asks Lingo Dan: "Why don't you go?... Do you enjoy gloating? Are you realists? Is the suffering of others a delight to you?"[22]

In one of Jack London's books from 1903, *The Kempton-Wace Letters*, a similar dichotomy is set up between a young "realist" and an older "romantic" who argue in a series of letters about the nature of love. "Poetry is empty these days, empty and worthless and dead," the rationalist argues, and therefore the economist is more prophet than the poet, and workers "sing the song of today" with their hands.[23] The realist sees "beauty" and "use" as dichotomous and claims that the aesthete's production of beauty rests on the worker's useful productions. The romantic's preoccupation with topics such as love is a sign of illness, since "*Love is a disorder of mind and body*" (87). In an Emersonian, organicist comeback, the romantic argues that "love is not a disorder, but a growth" (95). Here Saltus, who saw love as a disorder, would appear to be on the side of London's old-fashioned romantic, and London's romantic also labels himself a decadent: "I, overcivilized, decadent dreamer that I am, rejoice that the past binds us, am proud of a history so old and so significant and a heritage so marvellous.... You are suffering from, what has been called, the sadness of science.... You discover that romance has a history, and lo! romance has vanished! You are a Werther of science, sad to the heart with a melancholy all your own and dropping inert tears on the shrine of your accumulated facts" (125). Suffering from the sadness of an empiricist's view of the world is part of the self-image of the realists, as we have seen.

"In this you are with your generation," the older romantic tells the young, fierce realist. "Just as every age has its prevailing disease of the body so has it its characteristic spiritual ailment.... As yet we do not know what to do with all we know, and we are afflicted with the pessimism of inertia and the pessimism of dyspepsia" (126). Here, London seems to attach pessimism to the realist and a kind of optimism to the romantic, which misses both Saltus, the jovial, pessimistic aesthete, and Garland, the despairing, optimistic realist who became a despairing, optimistic romantic. I have detoured through London's epistolary novel to show that the universe of aesthetics, pragmatism, literature, and disease was available for a variety of conflicting analyses. That Saltus and Garland so neatly oppose each other is more than coincidence, it is evidence for the practical identity of the cultural work they performed in redefining the structure of their culture. Their opposite constructions of the vulgar (for Garland, sexuality, excess, ethnic difference; for Saltus, false propriety, false Puritanism, class difference) mark both their margin of difference and the web of underlying agreements. Garland's neurasthenic tourists and healthy-minded entrepreneurs and Saltus's bohemian discontents together helped map out the shifting terrain of middle-class norms and values.

Boundless Emulation and Detachment

Garland's change of fictional locale from the Middle Border to the Rocky Mountains (the setting of *The Captain of the Grey-Horse Troop*, *Hesper*, and *The Tyranny of the Dark* [1905], among others) was related to his growing reputation as an expert on Indian affairs. Garland's attitude toward Native Americans is instructive. He argued, at times in Roosevelt's ear, that the Indian agents should be removed, that small settlements should be developed on watercourses, that missionary activity should be curtailed, and that free economic activity, especially that involving native arts, should be encouraged. This is one of the areas in which Garland's social thought maintained the general outlines of progressivism. His reasoning about the purpose of such policies was very much in tune with Roosevelt's. As he explained in a 1902 article, in terms echoing Roosevelt's, these policies were fitting for America as a nation: "Only when we give our best to these red brethern of ours," he wrote, "do we justify ourselves as the dominant race of the Western continent."[24] In *The Captain of the Grey-Horse Troop* he uses a Rooseveltian notion of evolution to expound his own version of the white man's burden: "We should apply to the Indian problem the law of inherited aptitudes. . . . Fifty thousand years of life proceeding in a certain way results in a certain arrangement of brain-cells which can't be changed in a day. . . . We must be patient while the redman makes the change from the hunter to the herdsman. It is like mulching a young crab-apple and expecting it to bear pippins."[25]

The Indians represented for Garland a field of action which appealed to his romantic sensibilities at a time when little appealed to his realist sensibilities. The Indian wars were over, and the generals who fought them were now in the Philippines, using the techniques of massacre and relocation practiced earlier in the West. The army enters the scene in the Indian novel as it does in the labor novel, as a force for order which never need fire a shot; its presence assures that the cooler heads prevail and that the love story, delayed by the threat of serious violence, can proceed apace.

Rather than veritist or realist texts, Garland was writing historical romances, the bugbear of veritists, realists, and naturalists. In "The Work of Frank Norris," published in the *Critic* in March 1903, Garland explained Norris's move away from realism and toward romance as a function of maturation: "Youth makes a savage realist, for youth has boundless hope and emulation in itself. When a man begins to doubt his ability to reform, to change by challenge, he softens, he allows himself to pity. Norris in 'The Pit' is more genial, that is to say, more mature, than in 'McTeague' and 'The Octopus.' He was thirty-two and successful. He was entering a less inexorable period. He was not written out" (216–18). Garland seems to be speaking from or to his own experience here, trying to convince himself that since he is no longer the savage realist he must no longer be at the mercy of "boundless emulation"; that to doubt his ability as a writer and reformer must have positive effects, since it gives him the ability to pity; and that since he is now forty-three and successful, he must not be written out.

Garland's diaries for 1903 show that he remained unconvinced. They show a man still at the mercy of emulation, unable to pity, and feeling that he had nothing left to write. After sixteen years away, Garland visited Iowa and worried that the people there seemed "uncouth" and "dirty," and rather than feeling pity he felt "cut off" from their experience:

> The old people of the town depress me. In an unexpected phase of western life the small town has become in a certain sense the hospital home into which farmers and their wives, old and gray, drift to wear out a few short years of decrepitude. (May 26, 1903)

> I have not trod these ways for sixteen years and it marks a period in my life. . . . All this commonplaceness, this definition, cuts me off from the past—or rather it separates me from these people and scenes. . . . My old-time world, the world that appealed to my imagination, is gone. This flat, stale and unprofitable world inhabited by melancholy ghosts of the past was a sad surprise. (June 1–5, 1903)

"I seem to have exhausted the fields in which I found *Main-Travelled Roads*," he had worried the year before, "In what direction I am now to turn I can not tell." Similar sentiments show up in entries from 1900 through 1903. Feeling blocked as a writer, cut off from the people with whom he used to sympathize, Garland continued trying to find models to emulate, including Howells and Roosevelt. Even his dreams show him emulating his notion of literary success: "My dreams are often literary. . . . I meet Howells or Roosevelt and talk important matters" (June 16, 1903). Perhaps even more significant is a dream expressing a love of boundless emulation, recorded on October 27, 1910: "I dreamed I had become a psychic. . . . I was for the time a medium and gave some remarkable exhibitions of my powers. I was a kind of wireless receiver, catching and restating fugitive words and phrases." Depending on one's outlook, catching and restating fugitive words and phrases may describe literary activity or may describe a literary decline.[26]

To dream of being a psychic, a medium, was not a chance occurrence, even though Garland insists that "this was only the second time in all my life I dreamed on this subject." Since his time with B. O. Flower and the *Arena*, Garland had had a keen interest in the occult and psychic research; two books, *The Tyranny of the Dark* and *The Shadow World* (1908) are based on his long involvement in psychic research. Garland's interest in psychic research, like that of Dreiser, William and Henry James, Wharton, Howells, and Freeman, was related to neurasthenia, as well as to his immersion in the Swedenborgian tradition in America and Spencerian positivism. "It is not a question of religion with me," he told a group in 1920 as he recorded in his diary. "It is a question of fact, biological fact" (93). Like neurasthenia, psychic research required a form of scientific piety, and like neurasthenia it was available as a way of affirming a life view that ultimately denied moral accountability, making human beings, especially sensitive human beings, mere transmitters of "fugitive words and phrases." Psychic research was also, at least symbolically, a comfortable replacement for Garland's earlier reformist tendencies. After going to a group to discuss psychic research in Pittsburgh in 1920 at a Dr. Arthur Hammerschlag's, Garland records in his diary a metonymic relation between muckraking and psychic research: "Pittsburgh was hot, dirty, dark, and hideously unkempt as I came into it at nine but at Dr. Hammerschlag's house all was harmonious." This harmoniousness could exist, Garland writes, with no "act of will" on anyone's part. Lincoln Steffens's articles on city corruption were written within the radical reform ideology that Garland maintained during his years with the *Arena*. Steffens, in his description of Pittsburgh in 1903, went beyond "hot, dirty, dark, and hideously unkempt" to a characterization of Pittsburgh as "Hell with the lid off." And Steffens maintained that partial responsibility for that hell was "conceived in one mind, built up by one will," that of the city's political boss, Chris Magee.[27] Garland's late psychicism, because of its neurasthenic rejection of the will in favor of a refinement of perception, is in direct contradiction to the philosophy of the reform movements he had earlier championed.

In *Hesper*, the neurasthenic bildungsroman of Louis Rupert's salvation through the example of Raymond's manly entrepreneurial capitalism, the "dagoes and Rooshians" represent a political unconscious, doing the work underground that no free white man would want to do. So too the laborers of Pittsburgh, in the Pittsburgh Survey of 1907, felt their own place as the national unconscious, as if they were all forced underground. As one worker told the survey, "We do not live in America. We live underneath America."[28] Garland's thesis in the novel reinforces the boot-strap ideology of entrepreneurial possibility that Mineworkers' president John Mitchell was ridiculing as a "utopian kingdom come." Garland argues that the right and ability of American-born white men to succeed as entrepreneurs is threatened primarily by the way they can get sucked up into the disputes between wealthy capitalists and immigrant laborers, disputes they should ignore, if possible. This is a thesis, but not a thesis about the labor question, which the novel relegates to the unconscious.

Likewise Hammerschlag, Garland reports with some pride, told him that he held his own at the psychical research meeting precisely because he had no thesis to uphold. Reviewers of his books on psychic phenomena found the same to be true, although they were often less congratulatory about the missing thesis. Perhaps the best reading of *Crumbling Idols, Main-Travelled Roads*, and other early works is that they, too, like his later works, are the work of a psychic receiver of fugitive words and phrases, the words and phrases on the run from the previous generation's literary world. Garland's move up the ladder of literary success, more than his movement through time, accounts for the changing nature of his reception. As a young man he was guilty of what he called in his review of Norris "boundless emulation"; he was a joiner of groups and of movements. As he grew older and more successful he became a chronicler of his own success. A chronicler but not an analyser: like Roosevelt, Garland had faith in the conventional pieties, and whether they were the pieties of his college friends, his early magazine associates, the psychic researchers, or the literary establishment rarely caused him any concern. As he recorded in his diary on his fortieth birthday in 1900, "Life will not bear close examination. It yields depressing results at best" (50). But

Garland's despairing complacency was not the way most people expressed their relations to labor or to the supernatural in 1903; for most, as the next section outlines, those relations were alternately a source of and an answer to nervousness.

Saltus, whose neurasthenia often functioned in the depressing last years of his life as a cover for alcoholism, was also, like Garland, interested in the supernatural. He wrote several ghost stories and his 1903 study of the world's religions produced a full-length survey titled *The Lords of Ghostland* (1907). According to Marie Saltus, "The writing of that volume marked his transition from materialism to the realization that there were higher realms of thought as yet unexplored by him."[29] His first forays into the field of the supernatural were sprinkled through a book significantly titled *The Anatomy of Negation*. Like Robert Burton's *Anatomy of Melancholy*, it is a cultural map rather than a physiological one and a celebration more than a therapeutic guide. Scandals, sicknesses, and divorces were the stuff of his fiction as well as the stuff of his life, and the social issues of labor, ethnicity, and economics raised by Garland's texts, in however nostalgic a form, never find a place in Saltus's. Saltus remained the ironist until the end. His work has been called a "comic supplement to Veblen's *Theory of the Leisure Class*," and we could say that in its ironic supplementarity to Veblen's ironic text, Saltus managed to produce the negation of a negation, an invalid notion of invalid leisure.[30] Or we could say that he sounds like an ironic, neurasthenically inverted Descartes when he declares, in *The Philosophy of Disenchantment*: "I am, therefore I suffer" (19). In that phrase, with all its self-pity and all its ironic undercutting of self-pity, neurasthenia had found one of its most succinct expressions.

PART II:
NEURASTHENIC SPIRITUALITY AND OTHER COMPROMISES

Supernatural Naturalism

In *Natural Supernaturalism* M. H. Abrams argued that the romantic writers of the early nineteenth century in England and Germany, at a time of profound cultural crisis, rewrote the Western tradition by secularizing inherited theological ways of thinking. My play on his title is meant to suggest both continuities and reversals in the thematics and motivations of cultural production in America from the time of romanticism to that of realism. Briefly, we can say that, for writers and intellectuals, continuities include (1) a revival of attempts at a secular expression of metaphysical culture, (2) a continued reliance on nature as central to that expression, (3) a continued belief in the social efficacy of metaphysical culture, (4) a continuation of romantic notions of art and the artist, and (5) a similar perception, by intellectuals, of cultural crisis. Reversals of romanticism include (1) a radical shift of ground from aesthetics, politics, and philosophy to economics and biology, or more broadly, from moral and natural philosophy to natural and social science, (2) a movement from naturalistic explanations of the supernatural toward supernatural explanations of the natural, (3) the use of supernatural imagery to express an understanding of nature rather than vice versa, and (4) the refitting of metaphors of prophecy, apocalypse, and revelation with images of material and social life. Harold Kaplan has written that the "apocalyptic themes in naturalist writing reflect the traditional need for metaphysical judgment." Or, we could say, the need for metaphysical judgment has been scientized in the discourse of neurasthenia; in any case, whatever one believed was the relation of neurasthenia to moral discourse and to actual neurology, the discourse still worked as a replacement for metaphysical judgment. As Kaplan says, "a whole structure of dependent values" can be built on either the apocalyptic or stoic revelation of naturalism, and both a notion of apocalypse or breakdown on the one hand and a notion of stoicism, or conservation of nerve force, on the other, were central to the elaboration of the medical response to neurasthenia.[1]

Scientists of various kinds appropriated the languages of romantic naturalism in their competition for cultural authority. A clear case is that of Simon Newcomb, a professor of mathematics and astronomy at Johns Hopkins, who published science-fiction stories in the monthly magazines. His "The End of the World," published in *McClure's* in May 1903, manages to make the extinction of the sun into a progressive parable of spiritual advance, suggesting that the end of the solar system would bring a "holy calm" and the reinstitution of life on a "superior" plane (14). Here he unwittingly recreates the neurasthenic plot, as did the scientific naturalists Roosevelt and Burroughs. Literary naturalism was a paradigm created by and responded to by writers, neurasthenia was a medical paradigm created by and then responded to by doctors, and these paradigms responded to each other as well, as Zola's essay "The Experimental Novel" demonstrates in its celebratory reliance on Claude Bernard's work on experimental medicine. Naturalism and neurasthenia share a belief in the practice of "a medical politics, a cruel science which heals."[2]

The antiromantic Friedrich Nietzsche was also interested in medicine, and spent the last years of his life reading medical treatises. The writings of the neurologists powerfully affected his own, and he saw quite clearly the religious nature of the battle for cultural authority. "There is from the first something *unhealthy* in such priestly aristocracies [here Nietzsche included all elites involved in cultural production] and in the habits ruling in them which turn them away from action and alternate brooding and emotional explosions, habits which seem to have as their almost invariable consequence that intestinal morbidity and neurasthenia which has afflicted priests at all times," he writes in *The Genealogy of Morals*. The neurologists' and other priestly aristocracies' cures, however—and again Nietzsche saw how closely their rhetoric followed that of other dominant cultural discourses—he characterizes as worse than the disease:

> As to that which they themselves devised as a remedy for this morbidity—must one not assert that it has ultimately proved itself a hundred times more dangerous in its effects than the sickness it

was supposed to cure? Mankind itself is still ill with the effects of this priestly naïveté in medicine! Think, for example, of certain forms of diet (abstinence from meat), of fasting, of sexual continence, of flight into the wilderness (the Weir Mitchell isolation cure—without, to be sure, the subsequent fattening and overfeeding which constitute the most effective remedy for the hysteria induced by the ascetic ideal): add to these the entire antisensualistic metaphysic of the priests that makes men indolent and overrefined, their autohypnosis . . . and finally the only too comprehensible satiety with all this, together with the radical cure for it, *nothingness* (or God—the desire for a *unio mystica* with God is the desire of the Buddhist for nothingness, Nirvana—and no more!)[3]

Nietzsche's brand of antiasceticism found expression in American culture only in greatly modified form. His critique of indolence and overrefinement and his glorification of action over reflection, however, were voiced by writers as diverse as Roosevelt, London, and his own sources, Mitchell and the other American neurologists. Nietzsche's medicalized antiromanticism is clear in his vituperation against morbid, dyspeptic introspection.

Literary naturalism both continues and contradicts the romantic idea of self-consciousness as a sickness, an illness that alienates the self from others. The idea lives on in the cultural fear of "morbid self-consciousness," one of the main causes and symptoms of neurasthenia, but appears reversed in cures that aggravate isolation by separating neurasthenics from their families and acquaintances, both in what Nietzsche calls the "flight into the wilderness" of the Mitchell rest cure and in the errand into the wilderness of the western exercise cure. Finally, "supernatural naturalism" is meant to suggest the incongruity of a body of purportedly scientifically informed, naturalistic texts that, in case after case, take positions in the important cultural debate between science and religion, idealism and naturalism, with a series of surprisingly supernatural and romantic compromises. Central to the understanding and representation of many formulations of this debate are the discourse of neurasthenia and the figure of the neurasthenic.

Even those farthest from acceptance of neurasthenic compromise, such as satirists of religion and "quack" medicine, relied on neurasthenic imagery. Thorstein Veblen inveighed against the devotional practices of his culture by linking them, in a characteristically double-barreled assault, to "predatory" sports and the glorification of athletic ability on the one hand and to wasteful, conspicuously unproductive leisure on the other. Oliver Wendell Holmes likened the practitioners of homeopathy to witch doctors and Catholics: "[Homeopathy] is image-worship, relic-wearing, holy-water sprinkling, transferred from the spiritual world to that of the body. Poets accept it; sensitive and spiritual women become sisters of charity in its service." Homeopathy's only effect was the relief of symptoms that were "trifling, ... merely troublesome," according to Holmes, and the homeopathist was "in the company of the quack, charlatan, and mountebank." Ambrose Bierce made the most specific references to neurasthenia in his symmetrical definitions of "devotion" and "indigestion" in *The Cynic's Word-Book*:

> Devotion, n. A mild form of aberration variously produced; in love, by a surplus of blood; in religion, by chronic dyspepsia.
>
> Indigestion, n. A disease which the patient and his friends frequently mistake for deep religious conviction and concern for the salvation of mankind.

Bierce's equation of romantic lovesickness with religious devotion and his relegation of reformist and religious seriousness to Nietzschean indigestibility make mockery of both the metaphors and the project of medicalized cultural politics.[4]

But this kind of curmudgeonism was a self-consciously idiosyncratic and marginal critique made possible by an effulgence of serious attempts at synthesis of the natural and the supernatural. And in the print epidemic of these syntheses the person of the doctor was often central. Sarah Orne Jewett, for one, celebrated the pastoral legacy of the general practitioner: "Nobody sees people as they are and finds the chance to help poor humanity as a doctor does.... Teachers of truth and givers of the laws of life, priests and ministers,—all these professions are joined in one with the gift of healing, and are each part of the charge that a good doctor holds in his keeping." A typical sentimental story in *McClure's*, "The White Glory," shows a wise old doctor providing wisdom, counsel, and support to a woman whose husband is dying. The fact that the doctor can do nothing about the illness is inconsequential, since he fulfills a more important, ministerial role. An article in the same magazine the month before on the Austrian orthopedic surgeon Adolf Lorenz, who was paid "fabulous sums of money" for his operations on the daughter of Philip Armour and on a few other wealthy clients but performed many operations for poor patients at little or no cost, was accompanied by a photograph of Lorenz, wearing an enormous beard and a surgical gown with a cowl, looking like a medicalized biblical patriarch.[5]

Popular ministers invoked images of sickness and health with a particularly neurasthenic cast. Charles Wagner's best-selling *The Simple Life* opened with the following sentence: "The sick man, wasted by fever, consumed with thirst, dreams in his sleep of a fresh stream wherein he bathes, or of a clear fountain from which he drinks in great draughts. So, amid the confused restlessness of modern life, our wearied minds dream of simplicity."[6] James's *Varieties of Religious Experience* provides a virtual catalog of writings by healing spiritualists of all stripes, and of movements—the Mind-curists, the Christian Scientists, the "Don't Worry Movement," Divine Healing, Mental Science, Menticulture, Theosophy, the Society for Psychic Research, Muscular Christianity—that each in its own way tried to redefine the classical Western, Christian split between the spiritual and the material in relation to the new scientific and cultural knowledges. Freud would later try to reverse these connections, as seen most clearly in a conversation with Carl Jung, as reported by Jung, about the sexual basis of neurosis. Freud asked Jung to promise never to abandon the sexual hypothesis, and when Jung asked why this hypothesis was so important, Freud replied that it was the only thing that saved them from sinking into the mud of occultism. Freud wanted to separate the study of abnormal psychology from the then-related study of occult, mystical, and other psychic phenomena; Jung in turn eventually revived the connection. By 1903 in America synthesis was almost the only game in town. In philosophy, not only James, as we have seen, but also such figures as Royce and Santayana were preoccupied by questions of knowledge and revelation, and Catholicism, German idealism, and Buddhism all had their vigorous proponents in intellectual communities. Even Peirce, despite his attempts to remain rigorously scientific and to maintain a common-sense, nonmystical view of religion, believed that transcendentalism, idealism, and the "monstrous mysticism of the East" were diseases that may have contaminated his thinking.[7]

Like William James, many intellectuals saw psychic research, for instance, not only as valid science but also as an enterprise central to the new scientific world view. Henry Adams, for instance, in the chapter "The Grammar of Science (1903)" in *The Education*, writes of the "revolutionary papers that foretold the overthrow of nineteenth-century dogma" and that according to Adams instituted the scientific "multiverse." The first of these papers "was the famous address of Sir William Cookes on psychical research, followed by a series of papers on Roentgen and Curie."[8] For Adams, not only was psychic research as important as the new physics, but prior to it. In some schools of psychology, as we have seen, psychic and spiritualistic

Advertisement for Dr. Thomas's diagnosis and bread, *Literary Digest*, 1903. Dr. Thomas's Christian iconography and clerical collar helped sell bread.

research, hypnotism, subliminal and unconscious mental life, mediums, thought transference, and the like were the subject of intense empirical investigation. Spencerian sociologists and social thinkers proclaimed new gospels of love and relaxation as ways to inner peace and higher knowledge. Popular and literary writers produced religious stories and ghost stories, and even the self-proclaimed naturalist and realist authors were consistently and unabashedly metaphysical.

The work of these last, the popular and literary writers of fiction, will be the subject of Part II, and in this fiction neurasthenia and the supernatural are central themes. The three novelists recognized as America's foremost naturalists, Theodore Dreiser, Frank Norris, and Jack London; America's most skillful proponents of realism, William Dean Howells, Edith Wharton, and Henry James; local colorists Mary Wilkins Freeman, Sarah Orne Jewett, Charles Chesnutt, Mark Twain, Margaret Deland, and Kate Chopin; the "veritist" Hamlin Garland; the aesthetes Gelett Burgess, Percival Pollard, and Edgar Saltus; popular writers Kate Douglas Wiggin, Francis Marion Crawford, O. Henry, Rex Beach, George Ade, Richard Harding Davis, and Stuart Edward White: all of these writers wrote about neurasthenic characters and the relation of nervousness to the supernatural. This relation, however, was represented in different ways: sometimes a neurasthenic personality is represented as a prerequisite to firsthand experience of the supernatural, sometimes experience of the supernatural is represented as a cause, or serves as a symbol of other causes, of neurasthenia, and sometimes the supernatural, or religious experience, is presented as a solution or cure.

William James invokes all three of these in *The Varieties of Religious Experience*. Neurasthenic personality—the sick soul—is a prerequisite to religious experience, James claimed, and the course of the religious life is therefore parallel to that of neurasthenia and its cure. In both cases, an "uneasiness" is felt and followed by willed activity (sometimes in the form of quiet contemplation) which results in peace, a solution to what is "wrong in us." In relating spiritual crisis to sickness, James draws on the neurasthenic discourse through which he understood his own relation to sickness and health. James saw the link between medical and religious discourses as very close; he himself obtained a Christian Science practitioner toward the end of his life to help him fight depression, as did Samuel Clemens (despite his tract, published serially in the *North American Review* in ,1903, blasting Christian Science), and Eugene Witla in Dreiser's autobiographical *The "Genius."* Radical empiricist, cynical cultural critic, and naturalist novelist met in their assumption of a link between sickness and the supernatural, and between the supernatural and science.

Christian Science was itself a response to the social, political, and cultural events and changes that formed the thinking of the psychologists, naturalists, and medical doctors at the end of the nineteenth century. Mary Baker Eddy began writing *Science and Health* in 1872, the year William James had the neurasthenic spiritual crisis described in *Varieties of Religious Experience*.[9] The Church of Christ, Scientist, was formed in 1879, the year Beard published *Nervous Exhaustion*. The transformation of the American economy, the challenge of science to traditional religion, the medicalization of complaint, the professionalization of intellectual and technical labor, spiritualism, and the changing status of women were among the important formative contexts of Christian Science, of James's philosophy, and of literary naturalism, as they were of neurasthenia. Again, each of these three formations had more in common with neurasthenia than with each other. Unlike neurasthenia, Christian Science elicited as much resistance and rejection as acceptance. Figures as different as Eugene Debs and Frank Lloyd Wright testified to the efficacy of Christian Science, while attacks came from medical doctors, psychologists, ministers, and culture critics. Wright wrote in a letter to a friend that he recognized Christian Science "as the flower of the highest and best of the religions of the ages . . . barring the Mrs. Eddy feature." While Mrs. Eddy was often attacked as a fraud (and sought conventional medical treatment herself at various times), even many of her worst enemies were themselves partial or intermittent believers, like Wright, James, and Samuel Clemens. In 1903, Clemens's attack on Christian Science focused on economic issues; he argued, among other things, that the dangerous difference between Christian Science and other forms of medical quackery was its organization as a trust, which gave practitioners economic as well as demagogic power. Clemens later procured Christian Science treatments for his daughter, his wife, and himself, and Eddy noticed the ambivalence even in Clemens's critique as it was being published serially in 1903. She wrote to one of her deputies that in the attack was "an undertone . . . which is very complimentary to Christian Science."[10]

But Christian Science was seen by some as economic exploitation or pure quackery, and other readers saw problems with the combination of sickness and religion in the *Varieties of Religious Experience*. Some worried that the view of the relation of religion to action might be pernicious, and felt that the spiritual sensitivity James seemed to be celebrating, however guardedly, might lead to transgressions of the work ethic and other social mores. In early 1903, H. Rashdall, the reviewer of *Varieties of Religious Experience* for *Mind*, the prestigious Anglo-American philosophical journal, brought up this fear and resolved it in James's favor, writing that "Professor James is quite alive to . . . the social uselessness and even perniciousness" of the "sick souls" he described. James was "alive" to the complicated social meanings of neurasthenic spirituality, but he argued specifically against the pernicious view, as we have seen. Neurasthenic characters in novels, the sick souls in fiction, were often represented as abnormal or at least problematic types (such as Louis in *Hesper*, Presley in *The Octopus*, Dreiser's protagonists, Lily Bart in *The House of Mirth*), and these characters, like neurasthenics in the actual culture, always remained open to the charges of "social uselessness and even perniciousness" that Rashdall saw in James's representation of ascetic religiosity.

In his review Rashdall is exercising a cultural disciplinary function, in other words, and the representations of neurasthenia in general, and neurasthenia in relation to the supernatural in particular, can be subdivided into different groups or kinds based on their relation to social discipline or to a cultural function much like Rashdall's. Rashdall, like Mitchell, Roosevelt, and others, represented neurasthenia and everything neurasthenic as aberrant and either anarchic or decadent, and figured cure as a reintegration into social life. Others—physicians like Beard, analysts like James, and writers ranging from Dreiser to Freeman, Chopin, Howells, and Norris—had a mixed attitude, desiring to validate the experience of the "socially useless" and at the same time offer the possibility of cure and reintegration. A third set of writers and commentators had an antidisciplinary message. Charlotte Perkins Gilman, Edith Wharton, and others represented the discipline involved in neurasthenic culture as strewing in its merciless path madness, destruction, and death. These last writers, even when they used neurasthenia in their representations of the supernatural, did so for very different reasons. Edith Wharton's ghost stories, for instance, use neurasthenia much as she did in *The House of Mirth*, as part of a criticism of the culture that had created the neurasthenic option. Gilman's "The Yellow Wallpaper" was originally read as a horror story in the neurasthenic tradition, but Gilman herself saw it as a very earthbound tale of misguided medicine and antiproductive patriarchy. It was the middle group—of whom Norris, Howells, and Freeman are representative—that in its ambivalence created the neurasthenia of religion and a religion of neurasthenia.

4 Frank Norris:
Nationalism, Naturalism,
and the Supernatural

God to start with is only nerve, not body, and akin therefore to the human soul. But unlike the human body, where nerves are present only in limited number, the nerves of God are infinite and eternal. They possess the same qualities of human nerves but in a degree surpassing all human understanding.

—Daniel Paul Schreber, *Memoirs of My Nervous Illness* (1903)

"Go out into the street and stand where the ways cross and hear the machinery of life work clashing in its grooves," wrote Frank Norris in "The Need of a Literary Conscience," in what sounds like a naturalist directive to novelists to portray the real, the mechanistic, natural life in the streets. Norris was one of the strongest voices in America at the turn of the century arguing for a "virile" literature, for a "heroic, drastic thrusting out" from "the life of the city and the comfortable stay-at-home, hour-to-hour humdrum, and a determined journeying out into the great wide world." Even more than Roosevelt, and invoking him, Norris explicitly related this virility and journeying out into the world to the new imperialism. American culture does not need writers who are scholars, Norris wrote, but writers who are the equivalent of men of action. A scholar's writing "is of as much use and benefit to his contemporaries as his deftness in manicuring his finger nails," he claimed, for "the United States in the year of grace of nineteen hundred and two does not want and does not need Scholars, but Men—Men made in the mould of the [hero of the Spanish-American War] Leonard Woods and Theodore Roosevelts."[1]

Norris's description of the hero and writer Condy in his novel *Blix* made the connection between militarism and male cultural production explicit. In the context of Norris's critical writings, the description has the ring of paranoid fantasy:

During the last week the story had run from him with a facility that had surprised and delighted him; words came to him without effort, ranging themselves into line with the promptitude of well-drilled soldiery; sentences and paragraphs marched down the clean-swept spaces of his paper, like companies and platoons defiling upon review; his chapters were brigades that he marshalled at will, falling them in one behind the other, each preceded by its chapter-head, like an officer in the space between two divisions. In the guise of a commander-in-chief sitting his horse upon an eminence that overlooked the field of operations, Condy at last took in the entire situation at a glance, and, with the force and precision of a machine, marched his forces straight to the goal he had set for himself so long a time before. (117)

Like Dreiser, Norris conflated sexuality and accomplishment; like Roosevelt, he reacted against the feminized man of the previous generation and produced a phallic rhetoric that, by privileging action over scholarship or reflection, calls into question his own activity as a writer. Norris was also arguing implicitly (and at times explicitly) for male writers as the true professionals in a market debased by the continued predominance of women authors.

After the opening exhibition of masculinist, hard-line pragmatism, however, and the comandeering of fledgling authors into the street, "The Need of a Literary Conscience" ends claiming that the best novelists are those who remain "unspoiled and unwearied and unjaded" so that they can find "a joy in the mere rising of the sun, a wholesome, sane delight in the sound of the wind at night, a pleasure in the sight of the hills at evening, and see God in a little child and a whole religion in a brooding bird" (216). "Wearied" and "jaded" are descriptions of two neurasthenic types; Norris's invocation of the unwearied and unjaded is antineurasthenic, and his advice to remain unspoiled may have sexual overtones or may serve as a standard American appeal to innocent experience, but in either case it is also again antineurasthenic. Norris is careful not to suggest a romantic, apocalyptic union with nature as an alternative to neurasthenic woe, which could encourage neurasthenic overexcitement. He offers instead a "wholesome, sane delight." This much is coherent. What, though, is the meaning of the romantic deistic sentiment at the end of the passage about seeing God in a child and "a whole religion in a brooding bird"? This invocation hardly fits the standard image of Norris as a Zolaesque materialist, a "chest-thumping" radical who railed against the gentility of literature and argued instead for a literature based on the "honest, rough-and-tumble, Anglo-Saxon give-and-take knockabouts that for us means life." How does the railing against gentility in literature fit with Norris's unerring, however unconventional, support for genteel beliefs about women, men, politics, and religion?[2]

An easy answer might be that Norris held many conflicting opinions without any sense of their contradictions. Or, as some have suggested, perhaps Norris remained committed to a world view developed in his fraternity at the University of California. Perhaps the contradictions are the result of high-jinks from a man who never grew up. Norris had his own theory of maturation, a theory of how and why a boy becomes a man. In such works as *Moran of the Lady Letty* (1898), *Blix* (1899), and *A Man's Woman* (1900) Norris represents male coming-of-age as catalyzed by male brutality and its concomitant, female dependency. Like Roosevelt's, Norris's gender politics, class biases, and international politics are based on a belief in evolutionary theory filtered by Victorian values, in particular a Victorian belief in the saving grace of women's influence on the male.[3] Donald Pizer has described this as "Norris's fundamental evolutionary ethical dualism, in which man must draw upon his animal past for strength but must be guided primarily by his higher and more distinctive attribute, the human spirit." As in Beard's work and Roosevelt's essays, the animal past is essentially masculine, and the higher spirit that man needs as a guide is essentially feminine. In *Moran, Blix,* and *A Man's Woman,* male characters are led to full masculinity only through a combination of the experience of their own animality and the civilizing influence of women.[4]

Pizer argues that these three novels are the second step in Norris's intellectual history, a movement from the determinism of *McTeague* and *Vandover and the Brute,* through the possibility of exercising human will in these "popular" novels, to an understanding, in the last novels, *The Octopus* and *The Pit,* of man's place in the "cosmic laws of nature." This sequence makes for a coherent intellectual history, in which Norris, after developing a shaky philosophy of determinism and then unwisely catering to the popular, antiphilosophic belief in the will, matured into a more subtle philosopher, espousing something more "cosmic" than determinism. But the distinction between Norris's "popular" and "literary" fiction makes no sense except in terms of the literary institutions of recent times. In fact, Norris's most popular books were, from the start, not *Moran, Blix,* and *A Man's Woman,* but *McTeague, The Octopus,* and *The Pit*: in Pizer's terms an early, deterministic novel, and two late, cosmic-philosophic novels. Norris's popularity throughout his career suggests that he was representing social relations in a form many people found compelling, and the greater popularity of the "literary" fictions suggests that his representations of such things as gender relations were found even more compelling in these books than in what Pizer calls the "popular" texts. There are contradictions in and among Norris's texts—between materialism and spiritualism and between traditional and modern literary and social ideas—but these contradictions have their own logic and force. His relative success at presenting apparent incommensurability in a form his audience found coherent and satisfactory gained him a wide readership. And the logic of these contradictions is the logic of neurasthenia.

The Inner Octopus

Norris died of appendicitis at the age of thirty-two in November of 1902, shortly after finishing *The Pit: A Story of Chicago*, the second book in his "Epic of the Wheat," following *The Octopus* (1901). Norris's martyrdom to his appendix—he refused to take his abdominal pains seriously until it was too late, acting the strenuous, healthy-minded male until the end—made him even more popular, and when *The Pit* was published in 1903, it outsold any previous book of his by almost three-to-one.[5] The novel seems a slight romance after the epic sweep of *The Octopus*, which for all its sophomoric melodrama remains an ambitious work, convincing in its attempts to represent the complexity and vastness of economic and natural forces at work in the agricultural and railroad businesses of the West. Neurasthenia is an important theme in both *The Octopus* and *The Pit*, but whereas the earlier novel has two neurasthenic characters in a large cast, nervousness provides the central drama and romantic complication to the plot of *The Pit*. The later novel, whether or not it was a conscious return on Norris's part to a more popular genre and theme than the muckraking naturalism of *The Octopus*, was easily recognizable to its original audience and to contemporary critics as a sentimental romance rather than a naturalistic epic. The foregrounding of nervousness in *The Pit* is a mark of a return from social reform to the problem of an individual's reformation, and thereby a return to a specific position in the popular literary landscape and the cultural politics of neurasthenic transformation.

The movement away from social reform, from the muckraking spirit that prompted Norris to write *The Octopus*, had begun before that book was finished. The protagonist of *The Octopus* is a young eastern writer, Presley, who has come west to write the great American epic, "The Song of the West." In Norris's notebook sketch for this character, the shorthand for the neurasthenic predominates:

PRESLEY.—... Searching for the *Epic*. Refinement gained at a loss of strength. Introspective. Morbid. ... Things without names, thoughts

for which no man had yet invented words, terrible formless shapes,
vague figures, colossal, monstrous, distorted, whirled at a gallop
through his imagination. Hates the ranch and the People at first.
Turns anarchist. . . . Excitable, easily impressed. Impressionable,
melancholic disposition, capable of extremes of exaltation. Almost
prophetic—seer—an unbalanced mind.[6]

Many of these phrases were incorporated into the introductory description of Presley in the first chapter. Presley is an eastern dude
who rides a bicycle instead of a horse, a brain-worker who writes
rather than works, and an amateur occultist with a morbid interest
in the cosmic musings of the mystic Vanamee. Presley has a neurasthenic relation to emotion (melancholic), to nerve force (refined, excitable, thus depleting), to psychology (morbid, unbalanced mind),
to politics (anarchist, the political equivalent of "excitable" and "unbalanced"), and to the supernatural (obsessive, almost prophetic).

The meaning of these relations is clear if this description, and its
combination of political and personal, profound and petty traits, is
compared to that of another Norris character, the girl Blix from the
novel of the same name:

She was young, but tall as most men, and solidly, almost heavily
built. Her shoulders were broad, her chest was deep, her neck round
and firm. She radiated health. . . . One felt that here was stamina,
good physical force, and fine animal vigor. Her arms were large, her
wrists were large, and her fingers did not taper. . . . She impressed
one as a very normal girl: nothing morbid about her, nothing nervous
or overwrought. You did not expect to find her introspective. You felt
sure that her mental life was not at all the result of thoughts and
reflections germinating from within, but rather of impressions and
sensations that came to her from without. . . . She never had her
vagaries, was not moody—depressed one day and exalted the next.
She was a good, sweet, natural, healthy-minded, healthy-bodied girl,
honest, strong, self-reliant, and good-tempered. (9)

The large, healthy girl is the prime mover of the plot of *Blix*, and manages in the course of the novel to make a somewhat irresolute young
man find a purpose in life. Moran, of *Moran of the Lady Letty*, is also
admirable because of her "fine animal strength of bone and muscle,
. . . indomitable courage and self-reliance, . . . her thick neck, her
large, round arms," and the fact that she is "vigorous, unrestrained,"
and makes the world conform to her needs. Presley, on the other

hand, makes very little happen in *The Octopus*. He is almost a by-stander in the main plot, uninterested for the first half of the novel in the "eternal, fierce bickerings between the farmers of the San Joa-quin and the Pacific and Southwestern Railroad," the economic warfare that flares up, smolders and finally erupts at the end of the novel.[7]

Presley came to California aspiring to produce in hexameter a "true and fearless setting forth of a passing phase of history," a song of "the West, that world's frontier of romance, where a new race, a new peo-ple—hardy, brave, and passionate—were building an empire" (13–14). Like Roosevelt and Frederick Jackson Turner, Norris saw west-ward expansion as empire building; like Roosevelt, he saw this as the inexorable march of the Anglo-Saxon and other hardy white races in their ascendency; like Turner and Roosevelt he saw the inevitability of expansion overseas once the frontier was "closed"; and like Roosevelt, he understood this movement in terms of virile energy. In "The Fron-tier Gone at Last," Norris writes that now that "there is no longer a wil-derness to conquer," overseas is an obvious place to spend the natural "overplus" of Anglo-Saxon energy which has pushed them in westward conquests since they lived in "the Friesland swamps." In the *Atlantic Monthly* in 1903, Turner made the same point in a retrospective arti-cle on events since he announced the closing of the frontier in 1893.[8] Presley's problem, at the outset, is that although he wanted to write truthfully, he had a desire "to see everything through a rose-colored mist" (15). The economic war that surrounds him does not fit either his eastern notion of the West or his effete view of poetry, and he fails to understand the violence involved in appropriation.

Lacking stamina and "easily impressed" by the cries of the ranch-ers, Presley finally abandons "The Song of the West" to write a short poem, "The Toilers," celebrating the virtues of the hard-working farmer beset by the octopus-like railroad trust and the pitiless eco-nomics of the modern world. "The Toilers" becomes a literary *cause célèbre*—an incident modeled on the reception of Edwin Markham's "The Man with the Hoe" (1899)—and makes Presley a nationally cel-ebrated "voice of the people." The reception of the poem effectively ends Presley's literary activity, as he decides to become "the champion of the people in their opposition to the trust. He would be an apostle, a prophet, a martyr of freedom" (278). But Presley's enthusiasm for this priestly role lasts only long enough for him to give a "red" speech to a crowd and then furtively throw a bomb into the empty house of the railroad agent (387–88). He then comes to see both of these acts as ineffective and unjustifiable and resigns himself to becoming sim-ply a spectator of events.

Presley remains ambivalent, in the end, unable to see a clear right or wrong side to the dispute. As a contemporary reviewer noted, this is "a novel without a hero; a romance without a heroine."[9] Presley's inability to function as a protagonist, like his inability to come to terms with or to evaluate the economic struggle he is witnessing, is the result of his inability to act in what Norris considers a responsible way. Presley has gone out and heard "the machinery of life clashing in its groove," and so he has fulfilled the first responsibility of the writer; but he hasn't performed the second responsibility, which is to see and tell the "truth." His inability to recognize the truth is a sign and symptom of both his irresponsibility and his nervousness: he is "irresolute" (15). In "The Responsibilities of the Novelist," Norris claims that an author needs to give "the People . . . an idea of life beyond their limits" (196), but Presley, until his initiation into the supernatural by Vanamee, can see only the limits themselves.

More important, Presley is unable to write about "real life" because of his neurasthenic sensitivity, because he is overcivilized. Even his physical features "argued education, not only of himself, but of the people before him" (12–13). As a result, "one expected to find him nervous, introspective, to discover that his mental life was not [in a simple reversal of the description of Blix] at all the result of impressions and sensations, that came to him from without, but rather of thoughts and reflections germinating from within" (13). These passages about germination do not represent male appropriation of the productive function in the face of anxiety over female generativity but an anxiety about feminization and overcivilization. Norris clearly opposes this feminine function in Presley; Presley's notion of art is both feminine and morbid because it germinates from within. Even Norris's heroines, like Blix, have the good sense to let their reflections germinate from without. Presley's feminity, his morbidity, and his sensitivity leave him necessarily indecisive. While his nervousness proves that he has enough "good taste" to avoid immorality, he doesn't have whatever it takes to obey the manly directive to "go out into the streets": "Though morbidly sensitive to changes in his physical surroundings, he would be slow to act upon such sensations, would not prove impulsive, not because he was sluggish, but because he was irresolute. It could be foreseen that morally he was of that sort who avoid evil through good taste, lack of decision, and want of opportunity. His temperament was that of the poet" (13). Like the scholar, the poet was effeminate, effete, and out of touch with the "real life of men," which was, for Norris, considerably more real than the life of women. Norris would agree with Marlowe that the "women are out of it—should be out of it," and the fact that Presley is "out of it" further feminizes him.

The flip side of Norris's feminization of the poet and scholar, however, was the masculinization of the novelist. In "Why Women Should Write the Best Novels," Norris explains why it is that women, who have the leisure, sensitivity, impressionability, and emotionality that should make them great novelists, fail to produce great novels as often as men. The reason, Norris writes, is that "it is inconceivably hard for the sensitive woman to force herself into the midst of the great grim complication of men's doings that we call life." Not only are women, because of their seclusion, not knowledgeable enough, but they lack the "physical strength" to get the job done anyway. "Is it not a fact that protracted labor of the mind tells upon a woman quicker than upon a man?" Norris asks, and then directly invokes the neurasthenic discourse: "A man may grind on steadily for an almost indefinite period, when a woman at the same task would begin, after a certain point, to feel her nerves, to chafe, to fret, to try to do too much, to polish too highly, to develop more perfectly. Then come fatigue, harassing doubts, more nerves, a touch of hysteria occasionally, exhaustion, and in the end complete discouragement and a final abandonment of the enterprise" (289). Presley, too, gets hysterical, both about his writing and about his politics. He chafes, frets, feels his nerves, is harassed by fatigue and doubts, is again troubled by his nerves, and finally abandons the project. Norris concludes that "woman" suffers mental fatigue because she "possesses the more highly specialized organ," and the indictment of Presley is the same: his "refinement" is "gained at a loss of strength." This effeminacy explains both his inability to write the Great American Epic and his bad politics, the latter linked already in Norris's notebook sketch: "Turns anarchist. . . . Excitable, easily impressed." The poet is linked to anarchism and femininity, while the naturalist strongman—Norris himself—writes the "Epic of the Wheat" that women and poets do not have the strength to write.[10]

Norris's own politics underwent an apparent shift during the composition of *The Octopus*. When he began the project, his publisher was Doubleday & McClure Company, and he was encouraged in his project by Sam McClure, the muckraking editor of *McClure's Magazine*, who suggested and then applauded Norris's antitrust themes. But before Norris finished the novel, McClure had sold his interest in the firm to Walter Page, who replaced McClure in what became Doubleday, Page, & Company, and the result was a new moral, political, and economic conservatism in editorial policy. Instead of the progressive McClure, Norris now worked for the publisher of *World's Work*, a magazine promoting "the twin ideals of the success ethic and beneficent capitalism." No longer having an editor encouraging a muckraking exposé, he faced instead a nervous conservative who abhorred the idea that Norris's novel might indict big business. Norris received a "nervous" letter from the editorial department asking him to look into the railroad's version of the battle, and shortly thereafter a meeting was arranged between Norris and Collis P. Huntington, president of the very trust he meant to expose, the Southern Pacific, the octopus incarnate.[11] Through Presley's change of heart after his meeting with a railroad magnate, Norris at least partially exonerated the railroad. Like Presley, readers are meant to see all parties to the dispute as equally responsible.

Although the change of editorial management and the meeting with Huntington were undoubtedly important to the way the novel was constructed, Norris's general attitude perhaps had been more like Page's than McClure's all along. Just as Norris's gender politics were similar to the Victorian conservatism of Roosevelt, his attitude toward success was similar to Dreiser's, and his attitude toward business similar to Page's. "Had Mr. Carnegie been alive at the time of the preachings of Peter the Hermit," Norris wrote, portraying the businessman as a holy warrior, "he would have been first on the ground in Jerusalem, . . . and would have hurled the first cask of Greek fire over the walls." And Norris, more than any other writer of his time, wrote about writing as one function in the larger world of the publishing business. His essays in *The Responsibilities of the Novelist* discuss retail booksellers, manuscript readers, reviewers, critics, royalties, education, the costs of setting oneself up in business in the various arts, and the number of short stories or copies of a novel that must be sold in order for a writer to make a living. Despite the fact that in "The True Reward of the Novelist" he disparages the writer who caters to his audience as a mere "business man," in "Novelists to Order—While You Wait" he insists that he doesn't mean to "claim that the artist is above the business man. Far from it."[12]

In his discussion of the various kinds of novelists and their relations to the publishing industry and to advertising, Norris was attempting to raise the status of the author, to professionalize his activity, and to shift the balance of prestige and power from reviewers, publishers, and "popular" writers (such as those actually employed by magazines) to the kind of writer—manly, professional, and "Anglo-Saxon"—he saw himself to be.[13] Norris also saw the relation between changes in the business of writing and the large-scale changes in America's economic position. In "The American Public and 'Popular' Fiction" he writes: "There must exist some mysterious fundamental connection between this recent sudden expansion of things American—geographic, commercial, and otherwise—and the demand for books. Imperialism, Trade Expansion, the New Prosperity, and the Half Million Circulation all came into existence at the same time."[14] The new economics of literary representation, like the new imperialism, trade, and prosperity, demanded a new set of responsibilities. When best sellers begin to sell over a hundred thousand copies, Norris writes in "The Need for a Literary Conscience," the author's responsibility is significantly increased. He points out that "it is a large audience, one hundred thousand, larger than any roofed building now standing could contain. Less than one-hundredth part of that number nominated Lincoln. Less than half of it won Waterloo" (213).

The political and military examples are significant, as they masculinize authorship and relate its importance to central forms of power and violence. In his essay "The Frontier Gone at Last," Norris discusses the martial metaphors in the language of business: "a commercial 'invasion,' a trade 'war,' a 'threatened attack' on the part of America; business is 'captured,' opportunities are 'seized,' certain industries are 'killed,' certain former monopolies are 'wrested away'" (224). This essay is one of the clearest statements of its time on the relation of the closing of the frontier to overseas expansion, and Norris makes clear the connection between violence, power, and economic growth when he equates the modern capitalist with the Anglo-Saxon warrior, the desire for conquest of Richard the Lionhearted and of the average American manufacturer: "We are now come into a changed time and the great word for our century is no longer War, but Trade. Or if you choose, it is only a different word for the same race characteristic" (223). Norris felt that his culture perceived his own activity as effeminate, since it was not clearly enough trade or conquest, and his response was to use martial metaphors for the act of writing, sometimes historico-dramatic ones such as Waterloo, sometimes more euphemistic ones such as rough-and-tumble Anglo-Saxonism. As with Roosevelt's perception of his rough-riding cure and Dreiser's of his symbolic boot camp at Muldoon's spa, Norris figured his own neurasthenic adaptation to his changing culture as a march of triumph.

"We are all Anglo-Saxons enough to enjoy the sight of a fight, would go a block or so out of our way to see one, or be a dollar or so out of pocket," Norris writes to explain the popularity of historical novels.[15] Norris also defended student violence at Berkeley in the same terms: "If the boys in our universities want to fight, let them fight, and consider it a thing to be thankful for. They are only true to the instincts of their race. We Anglo-Saxons are a fighting race; have fought our way from the swamps of Holland to the shores of the Pacific Coast at the expense of worse things than smashed faces and twisted knees.

One good fight will do more for a boy than a year of schooling."[16] Presley's decision to act violently, then, should be a positive step for him, a taking up of the cudgels for his race. But his one attempt to join the masculine, nationalistic fray is ineffective; his anarchist bomb-throwing is a kind of political violence which had few supporters among the dominant intelligentsia, the press, or the public. The McKinley assassination in 1901 destroyed much of what support anarchism had enjoyed in America, so that by 1903, Emma Goldman, long the most popular advocate for anarchism in America, was underground and was herself suffering from neurasthenia. A series of antianarchist bills was introduced in Congress, and the immigration law of 1903, in a measure that penalized immigrants for their political opinions for the first time in over a century, barred admission and allowed for the deportation of any foreigner believing in anarchism. The center of anarchist activity was among immigrant laborers, and anarchism was seen, however inaccurately, as a foreign, anti-American political philosophy.[17]

Presley's bomb, too, is represented as both futile and un-American. It is linked, in the novel, to "*unnecessary* violence" (360), the futile and hysterical attack by Hooven, an immigrant with a heavy German accent who fires the first wild shot causing the debacle at Los Muertes. Presley's decisions, like those of the easily excited Hooven, are based on his emotions rather than his rational understanding, and therefore on his feminine rather than masculine attributes. His action is itself neurasthenic, because it is not conquest, which would reinvest the energy expended, but harassment, the purpose of which is to waste energy, and also because it is a result of his natural overexcitability rather than a positive exercise of will.

Presley decides on his bombing mission after talking with the anarchist saloon keeper Caharrer, one in a series of many mentors. After Presley's anarchist period under Caharrer, he returns to Vanamee, the mystic. Vanamee is aloof from the political and economic battles ranging around them, much like the neurasthenic Presley in the first half of the novel. Some years before Norris's novel, Mitchell had written in *Doctor and Patient* that the neurasthenic "is in the grip of an octopus" and Presley is shown to have a private octopus that parallels the public one.[18] The neurasthenic despair created by the inability to "cure" the problem of the railroad trust pushes him toward mysticism as a treatment for his inner octopus. Most critics have been careful to point out that Norris does not fall for Vanamee's mysticism as much as Presley does. It would perhaps be more accurate to say that Norris does not fall for the mysticism of Vanamee as much as these critics do, for it is not Vanamee's mysticism per se that Norris and Presley admire, but his self-sufficiency and the relation to nature which his mysticism signifies.

Vanamee does not appear in Norris's notebook, which included sketches of all the other major characters, and this absence suggests that Norris created him to resolve problems that had arisen during the composition of the text. Still, Norris clearly sees Vanamee's as a valid position; Vanamee's experience is endorsed by the plot (he is one of the few characters that gets what he wants) and validated thematically (he is not motivated by the avarice the novel condemns). Vanamee's mysticism is simply one part of a larger perspective, one that represents an Emersonian relation to Nature, to literature, and to ethical living that the novel endorses. In an essay celebrating the Emerson centennial in 1903, George Santayana described Emerson's relation to nature and ethics. Although he was speaking of Emerson, the lines could be applied to Norris as well: "If he regarded any moral or political problem with sympathetic or steady attention, he immediately stated it in terms of some natural analogy and escaped its importunity and finality by imagining what nature, in such a conflict, would pass to next. What seems mysticism in his moral philosophy and baffles the reader who is looking for a moral solution, is nothing but this rooted habit of inattention to what is not natural law, natural progression, natural metamorphosis." Santayana's characteristically backhanded compliment holds for Norris's naturalist supernaturalism and for many other writers in 1903 as well. The habit of escaping importunity through a "rooted habit of inattention" to all but natural analogies was widespread, especially in the writings of such popular natural historians, nature writers, and nature novelists as John Burroughs, John Muir, Liberty Hyde Bailey, and Stuart Edward White. And what Santayana marked as the connection between rooted habits of inattention and mysticism Bailey makes explicit: "Nature-study is not science. It is not knowledge. It is not facts. It is spirit."[19]

Roosevelt, the natural historian and champion of strenuous physicality, was in the White House, and like Roosevelt, Norris was critical of the power of the trusts at the same time that he was pro-business, critical of "unnatural" political violence but convinced of the necessity for violence in the march of progress, and suspicious of all foreign influences despite the fact that he equated "Anglo-Saxonism" with "Americanism." For both men (again like Emerson) the supernatural was natural, and it naturally reaffirmed "law" and "progress," the hallmarks of American civilization. Norris and Roosevelt, the literary naturalist and the scientific naturalist, followed the same cultural program, came to the same nationalistic, naturalistic, and spiritual conclusions, and cured their own neurasthenia by activity they each helped constitute as professional.

Educated Men and Knowing Women

Three of Norris's books were published posthumously in 1903: *The Responsibilities of the Novelist*, *The Pit: A Story of Chicago*, and *A Deal in Wheat, and Other Stories of the New and Old West*. This last contains the title story, a look at the wheat trading in Chicago written when Norris was doing research for *The Pit*, a series of local-color stories from California, and two ghost stories. Three of the stories are based on material from an 1897 sojourn into the Sierras following his "collapse" in the spring of that year. Norris had felt "written out" and had alternated between "a listless indifference" and "fits of depression" according to his biographer. He felt that he was "exhausted, spiritually and physically." His depression, like Dreiser's, was related to the uncertainty of his status as novelist or journalist. His biographer claims "he was dangerously near to becoming a hack writer and remaining one," and as with Roosevelt, Remington, and Wister, the cure he decided on was a somewhat genteel errand into the wilderness. John Muir expressed this in terms of and for these men's class; on the first page of *Our National Parks* (1902) Muir connects nature and neurasthenia: "The tendency nowadays to wander in wildernesses is delightful to see. Thousands of tired, nerve-shaken, over-civilized people are beginning to find out that going to the mountains is going home." Norris left decadent San Francisco and stayed in a "wilderness" that was an active mining area, near Iowa Hill, California. His consciousness of class when watching the miners, prospectors, and vagabond cowboys of the mining camps left him feeling, as one of his narrators puts it, that he was "the one loafer of all that little world of workers." A combination of the invigoration of the "outdoor life" and some resolution of his attitude toward work helped Norris finish *McTeague* and reassert himself as a novelist.[20]

In *Blix*, the erstwhile writer is described as heroically laboring on the novel he is writing, "in the morning from nine till twelve, and in the afternoon until three" (117). This four- or five-hour schedule is apparently that which women do not have the stamina to take on. It also shows that whatever Norris's claims to a life of professional work rather than leisure, he never confused that with the work of laboring men. As with Dreiser, a short tour of the working class acted as a cure for his elite malady, and as with Garland, foreign-born miners are emblematic of the way problems of class and ethnicity had been pushed underground.

The stories from this period are saturated with nervousness and issues of class conflict. For instance, "The Wife of Chino," published in *A Deal in Wheat*, is the story of young Lockwood, a graduate of Columbia School of Mines who falls in love with Felice, the wife of Chino Zavalla, shift boss in one of the mines Lockwood superintends. Lockwood has become overcivilized through education: "Lockwood's student life had benumbed the elemental instinct, which in the miners, the 'men,' yet remained vigorous and unblunted. . . . For all Lockwood's culture, his own chuck-tenders, unlettered fellows, cumbersome, slow witted, 'knew women'—at least women of their own world, like Felice—better than he."[21] The answer, Norris hurries to assure us in the next paragraph, is not a return to slow-witted animal vigor. For Lockwood has a second problem, and that is that he has not been under the tutelage of women of his class. He has lost hold of his "deep-seated convictions, old established beliefs and ideals, even the two landmarks, right and wrong" (322), because he is alone. In class terms, he is in the woods: "Living thus apart from the world, Lockwood very easily allowed his judgement to get, as it were, out of perspective. Class distinctions lost their sharpness, and one woman—as for instance, Felice—was very like another—as, for instance, the girls his sisters knew 'back home' in New York" (324).

These two problems converge, then; the blurring of class distinction and the overcivilized lack of instinct leave Lockwood in a state he recognizes as "madness": "Yes, I know it—sheer madness; but, by the Lord! I *am* mad—and I don't care." He tries to control himself and stay away from Felice, but "the madness was upon him none the less, and it rode and roweled him like a hag from dawn to dark and from dark to dawn again, till in his complete loneliness, in the isolation of that simple, primitive life, where no congenial mind relieved the monotony by so much as a word, morbid, hounded, tortured, the man grew desperate—was ready for anything that would solve the situation" (325). In this neurasthenic state Lockwood is even easier prey to Felice's feline wiles, her "cat's green eyes" and "cat's purring, ingratiating insinuation" (322). Felice's animality is due, as in the analyses of Beard and Roosevelt, to her race, which reverses what would otherwise be the moral superiority of her gender. The Anglo-Saxon woman for all three men constituted, at best, the Victorian ideal of moral guiding force. David Graham Phillips, in *The Master Rogue* (1903), at most only half as seriously as Norris, praises a wife who is interested only in home and children. "That's the way a woman should talk and feel. When they get ideas that are only fit for men everything goes to pot."[22] But women of other ethnicities or classes were the opposite. "Felice being a woman, and part Spanish at that, was vastly more self-conscious, more disingenuous, than the man, the Anglo-Saxon" (322).

By the end of the story, after a somewhat rickety plot in which Lockwood shoots Felice's husband by accident and thereby brings on his own nervous collapse (" 'No; I—I've shot him' . . . Then the nerves, that had stood the strain already surprisingly long snapped and crisped back upon themselves like broken harp-strings" [332]), Lockwood sees Felice's true nature, for she mistakes the accidental shooting for an intentional act on his part, done so that she and Lockwood could be together, and she is happy. Although he had claimed that he would do anything to make her his and considers letting Chino die, he is horrified when he finds that she has had the same thoughts: "It was as though a curtain that for months had hung between him and the blessed light of clear understanding had suddenly been rent in twain by her words. The woman stood revealed. All the baseness of her tribe, all the degraded savagery of a degenerate race, all the capabilities for wrong, for sordid treachery, that lay dormant in her, leaped to life at this unguarded moment, and in that new light, that now at last she had herself let in, stood pitilessly revealed, a loathsome thing, hateful as malevolence itself" (333). The religious language of this passage, from the "blessed light" of revelation on, is not accidental; it marks the supernatural resolution of Lockwood's sexual neurasthenic crisis, much as William James's conversion experience cured his occupational neurasthenia. Norris makes clear that he is describing spiritual salvation in a reiterative passage that plays even closer with Pauline language: "It was a transformation, a thing as sudden as a miracle, as conclusive as a miracle, and with all a miracle's sense of uplift and power. In a second of time the scales seemed to fall from the man's eyes, fetters from his limbs; he saw, and he was free" (333).[23]

For Norris, and Norris's characters, pragmatic conversion is linked to an Emersonian view of nature, however, and this link marks a traditionalism more like Roosevelt's than James's. Franklin Walker, in his biography of Norris, inserts between his descriptions of Norris's nervous collapse and of his wedding later in 1897 a description of sexual "degeneration" in San Francisco in the 1890s and a discussion of Norris's puritanical attitudes toward sex. Walker's narrative implies that, like William James, and as Lockwood ought to have, Norris cured himself from sexual nervousness through marriage. The final words of "The Wife of Chino" are the protagonist's: " 'I *have* had a lucky escape,' shouted Lockwood. 'You don't know just how lucky it was' " (333).

The Nerve Center of the Industrial Body

The other stories in *A Deal in Wheat* also rely on neurasthenic themes, especially the supernatural tales and the comedies of failed ambition, "Two Hearts Beat as One," "The Ship That Saw a Ghost," "The Ghost in the Crosstrees," and "The Riding of Felipe." But even more than any of these stories, *The Pit*, Norris's most popular novel, is a neurasthenic tale.[24] The two main characters, Curtis and Laura Jadwin, grow more and more neurasthenic during the novel, each working, in gender-specific ways, toward a neurasthenic crisis and resolution at the novel's climax. The other characters are nervous as well: Landry Court is "astonishingly good-looking, small-made, wiry, alert, nervous, debonair" (17); the wheat traders in the pit at the Board of Trade are "nervous" (74); Miss Gretry is "excitable, nervous," which explains her nose-bleed during rehearsals for an amateur theatrical production (92); Cressler, like Jadwin, gets nervous when he speculates (208), and even the pigeons he feeds at the Board of Trade are "nervous" as they peck their grain (73).

Jadwin is a solid, stolid businessman, the owner of vast tracts of Chicago real estate, and a quiet and respected member of Chicago society. Laura is a typical Norris heroine: she is a bit too "masculine" until she finds and accepts her true role as dutiful, self-sacrificing wife; then she comes into her own as a moral guiding force. In the beginning of the novel Laura is courted by Landry Court, Sheldon Corthell, and Jadwin, and she gives mild encouragement to all three, though she claims to love no one. Her flirtation is the female version of the speculation that will eventually ruin her husband; like speculation, flirtation creates false value, confuses the real and the apparent, leads to excitement, nervousness and excess, and is inherently unstable. Laura's relation to Landry Court, just a boy who clearly does not interest her, functions to show that she is involved in real flirtation, that she is not just torn between the two very different and equally attractive suitors, Jadwin and Corthell.

These two, Jadwin and Corthell, are explicitly set up as types in opposition. Corthell, an effete artist who works in stained glass, is always impeccably dressed in the latest fashions and combs his mustache back in the French manner. He is, in Laura's mind, like a "beautiful artist-priest of the early Renaissance" (21). He has opinions about art, literature, and music, and in the novel's opening scene at the opera he is presented as far more interesting and far superior to Jadwin, who at first seems a slow-witted former hayseed. To Jadwin, the opera is "all very fine . . . but I would rather hear my old governor take his guitar and sing 'Father, oh father, come home with me now,' than all the fiddle-faddle, tweedle-deedle opera business in the whole world" (25). Corthell is cosmopolitan, informed, sensitive, aware, refined; Jadwin is provincial, thick as his huge body is thick, plodding, and ill at ease in Corthell's world. Jadwin refers back not to effeminate Renaissance spirituality but to the healthy-minded religion of his father.

Corthell is "a *woman's* man" (57), not a man's man, and as Mrs. Cressler tells Laura, "the kind of man that *men* like—not women— is the kind of man that makes the best husband" (58). The businessmen of the novel have "no use" for Corthell (116); in their eyes he is "pure affectation" (46). Laura, as was "inevitable," comes to compare Corthell to the businessmen:

> She remembered him, to whom the business district was an unexplored country, who kept himself far from the fighting, his hands unstained, his feet unsullied. He passed his life gently, in the calm, still atmosphere of art, in the cult of the beautiful, unperturbed, tranquil; painting, reading, or, piece by piece, developing his beautiful stained glass. Him women could know, with him they could sympathize. And he could enter fully into their lives and help and stimulate them. Of the two existences which did she prefer, that of the business man or that of the artist? (52)

Laura chooses, finally, the businessman, Jadwin: "After all, she was a daughter of the frontier, and the blood of those who had wrestled with a new world flowed in her body. Yes, Corthell's was a beautiful life. . . . But the men to whom the woman in her turned were not those of the studio" (52). This appears to contradict Mrs. Cressler's statement about the man women like, and the apparent contradiction marks Laura's difference from other women. The woman in her is manlike.

Laura's choice is one between the sterile, effeminate overcivilization of Corthell and the potent, masculine productivity of Jadwin. What amounts to a gender carnival is in full swing here, as the woman in her likes the woman in Corthell and the man in her likes the manly Jadwin, and while the women in general encourage her to be more manly, the men prod her to be more womanly. Jadwin finally conquers, however, because Norris believed in the value of "rough-and-tumble Anglo-Saxonism" and in business. The businessman, again, is represented as the modern reincarnation of the Anglo-Saxon warrior. Throughout the novel, business activity is represented in military terms: business is "The Battle of the Street" (51); Jadwin is "Napoleonic" (192), the "Napoleon of La Salle Street" (242); Bears and Bulls in the pit are in combat, and buying and selling are "aggression and resistance" (197). One passage, in what is less an extended metaphor than a habit of thought (this is, after all, the period which gave America its first overseas "possessions" and invented the advertising "campaign") contains "courier from the front," "in array," "manoeuvering for position," "captains," "the enemy," "grapple," and "the big conflict" (230). Toward the end of his attempt to corner the wheat market, Jadwin felt that "the time was come for the grand *coup*, the last huge strategical move, the concentration of every piece of heavy artillery. . . . Reserves, van and rear, battle line and skirmish outposts he summoned together to form one single vast column of attack" (270). This Napoleon, then, is Laura's choice for a husband, a true man's man, for as she indirectly muses:

> Terrible as the Battle of the Street was, it was yet battle. Only the strong and the brave might dare it, and the figure that held her imagination and her sympathy was not the artist, soft of hand and of speech, elaborating graces of sound and color and form, refined, sensitive, and temperamental; but the fighter, unknown and unknowable to women as he was; hard, rigorous, panoplied in the harness of the warrior, who strove among trumpets, and who, in the brunt of conflict, conspicuous, formidable, set the battle in a rage around him, and exulted like a champion in the shoutings of the captains. (52)

The choice between the two men is more explicitly related to neurasthenia as well. Corthell is not only a neurasthenic type, he is almost contagious. Whenever Laura is around him she gets overexcited, irrational, and nervous. Jadwin has the opposite effect: "Corthell again had asked her to marry him, and she, carried away by the excitement of the moment, had answered him encouragingly. On the heels of this she had had that little talk with the capitalist Jadwin, and somehow since then she had been steadied, calmed" (33–34). It is not just Corthell himself that overexcites Laura, but his art and music as well. When he played Beethoven and Liszt, or discussed painting or opera, "she felt all at once as though a whole new world were opened to her"; Corthell "evoked all the turbulent emotion, all the impetuosity and fire and exaltation that she felt was hers" (184). Corthell evokes neurasthenic sexuality.

Pulled in both directions, both before and after her marriage, Laura "wondered at herself." Her introspection takes a form that represents a movement from the health and sickness model of neurasthenia to the therapeutic model of the self that was to replace it; she explains herself to herself in terms of what both Henry James and W. E. B. Du Bois, in very different contexts in 1903, referred to as "double consciousness." Laura's double consciousness begins with the question of marriage, and with nervousness: "You don't know how nervous I am these days. One minute I am one kind of girl, and the next another kind. I'm so nervous and—oh, I don't know. Oh I guess it will be all right" (121). She is "changeable": "I know I'm cross, but sometimes these days I'm so excited and nervous I can't help it, and you must try to bear with me" (129). And despite the fact that "she was too nervous to so much as think" (129), she manages the following reverie:

> Surely, surely there were two Laura Jadwins. One calm and even and steady, loving the quiet life, loving her home, finding a pleasure in the duties of the housewife. This was the Laura who liked plain, homely, matter-of-fact Mrs. Cressler, who adored her husband, who delighted in Mr. Howells's novels, who abjured society and the formal conventions, who went to church every Sunday, and who was afraid of her own elevator.
>
> But at moments such as this she knew there was another Laura Jadwin—the Laura Jadwin who might have been a great actress, who had a "temperament," who was impulsive. This was the Laura of the "grand manner," who played the rôle of the great lady from room to room of her vast house, who read Meredith, who reveled in swift gallops through the park on a jet-black, long-tailed horses, who affected black velvet, black jet, and black lace in her gowns, who was conscious and proud of her pale, stately beauty—the Laura Jadwin, in fine, who delighted to recline in a long chair in the dim, beautiful picture gallery and listen with half-shut eyes to the great golden organ thrilling to the passion of Beethoven and Liszt. (184–85)

Each of the two faces of Laura combine a role option and a moral stance. In the first, a traditional role is coupled to traditional values, the only negatively tinged phrases having to do with either a lack of excitement ("plain, homely, matter-of-fact") or with a failure to cope with modernity ("afraid of her own elevator"). Both of these have sexual connotations as well, and it is the passion and excitement of the second option which is appealing. The role of the leisure-class wife is sexy as well as luxurious, and it is presented as opposed to the housewifely virtues of the traditional wife; the European, theatrical splendor of the sexualized option is, in Freud's term, *unheimlich*, literally "unhomelike."[25]

The moral cast of Laura Jadwin's options is complicated later in the novel when the life of luxury rather than the life of duty follows her marriage. Jadwin, through speculation, has become too rich, and his "absorption" in his business affairs leaves Laura home, alone and feeling neglected. Corthell reappears and, as his name suggests, Laura is clearly courting hell in her relations with him. Frustrated by the absence of her husband, and again excited by Corthell's presence, she alternately attracts and repulses him, and this struggle is represented in terms of both double consciousness and weakness of nerve: "This time she had prevailed once more against that other impetuous self of hers. Would she prevail the next time? And in these struggles, was she growing stronger as she overcame, or weaker? She did not know" (262).

Norris was not the only writer working this material, as the following excerpt from George Ade's *In Babel* (1903) shows. Just as *The Pit* is subtitled "A Story of Chicago," *In Babel* is subtitled "Stories of Chicago."[26] The story "Harry and Ethel" has its own Laura and a version of Corthell:

> "The idea! In this day and age of the world, and in Chicago, of all places, a man—a male man—letting his hair grow long, putting on nose-glasses and a white tie, and starting out to lecture before afternoon clubs on—what is it he lectures on, anyway?"
>
> "Oh, the True Somethingness of Beauty, I guess it is. Laura says he's terribly bright. She says there are very few people that appreciate him."
>
> "She's dead right about that. I know of twenty men that will pay him any price to come over to the club and put on the gloves. But the women seem to think he's all right."
>
> "Oh, some of them do, or they pretend to. Just at this minute he is a novelty, a fad."
>
> "Just at this minute and every other minute he is—a freak. Why do women get stuck on that kind of a fellow?"
>
> "They don't—except for a little while. They merely take him up, just to be doing."
>
> "Just to be done, you mean."
>
> "Do you know, just now Laura thinks he is the cutest thing!... She can't marry him, because she is already tied up to a commonplace, every-day broomstick of an old man, who works in the office fourteen hours a day so as to keep her supplied with luxuries."

"Such as lecturers."
"Yes—lectures, antique furniture, and Chihuahua dogs." (290–92)

Ade obviously finds less of the material of romance and melodrama here than Norris does.

Norris also uses double consciousness in a less dramatic vein when he makes clear that role confusion is not just the province of women. Landry Court, for instance, also has a double consciousness, and again the analysis is presented in terms of nerves:

> In a sense, Landry Court had a double personality. Away from the neighborhood and influence of La Salle Street, he was "rattle-brained," absent-minded, impractical, and easily excited, the last fellow in the world to be trusted with any business responsibility. But the thunder of the streets around the Board of Trade, and, above all, the movement and atmosphere of the floor itself awoke within him a very different Landry Court; a whole new set of nerves came into being with the tap of the nine-thirty gong, a whole new system of brain machinery began to move with the first figure called into the Pit. (71)

He not only has a double consciousness, he has two whole nervous systems. Court gets "rattle-brained," when he is not engaged in business, because he is then under the influence of women. As Cressler, an embodiment of traditional values until his own slide into speculation, puts it, "If you *women* would let that boy alone, he might amount to something" (116). For Cressler, the mark of Court's traditional masculinity is not just his strong business nerves, but his refusal to speculate: "I'd like to take that young boy in hand and shake some of the nonsense out of him that you women have filled him with. He's got a level head. On the floor [of the commodities exchange] every day, and never yet bought a hatful of wheat on his own account. Don't know the meaning of speculation and don't want to. There's a boy with some sense" (117). Court represents the possibility of a rational and nonneurasthenic commodities exchange. The pit is not necessarily a maelstrom, speculation makes it so. Speculation, according to Cressler, is "gambling": "I believe it's worse than liquor, worse than morphine" (98).

In 1896, Yale professor of economics Henry Crosby Emery described the stock and produce exchanges as "the nerve centers of the industrial body" and claimed that the economy needed them to function in a healthy fashion. Emery's analysis of speculation has other parallels with Beard's analysis of neurasthenia. According to Emery, there was more speculation in America at the end of the century than at any other time or in any other place; two of the causes for the increase were steam power and the telegraph. The American system of speculation had its basis in greater freedom (from governmental control) than the European; speculation as practiced in America was "a striking example of the confidence of the people of the Anglo-Saxon race." While futures trading had existed before, it became recognizable and epidemic only following the civil war. In the following passage, Emery seems to refer directly to Norris's novel, still seven years away:

> The only direct loser is the speculator.... A successful corner is of very rare occurrence. Most attempts in this direction have miserably failed.... It is a common saying in both the grain and cotton markets that the corner is a thing of the past. The difficulties of getting hold of the wheat supply or the cotton supply even in a single market, for a few days, are enormous.... If it be known a week or ten days before the end of the month that a corner is on in Chicago, the wheat of Minneapolis, and Duluth, and St. Louis can be poured into that market with astonishing rapidity.... Under these conditions it becomes a contest of capital and nerve.

Emery is interested in normalizing attitudes toward speculation and stilling fears. He tries to show that speculation is simply a part of any market economy and has no real or significant effect on consumer prices. He wants to counter widespread fears that speculation could lead to a weakening of these industrial nerve centers and eventually to a "panic."[27]

Norris is unconvinced, however, and speculation is the enemy in this novel, as it was for Dreiser. Norris represents the evils of speculation by tying it to neurasthenia. He clearly separates speculation from trade, which is an unmitigated good, in fact a curative force, as the narrator's hymn to the railroad suggests: "A train departed roaring. Before midnight it would be leagues away boring through the Great Northwest, carrying Trade—the life blood of nations—into communities of which Laura had never heard. Another train, reeking with fatigue, the air brakes screaming, arrived and halted, debouching a flood of passengers, business men, bringing Trade—a galvanizing elixir—from the very ends and corners of the continent" (49). But just as Corthell's weakness, his lack of business energy, represents the lethargic neurasthenia of the aesthete, speculation represents the overexcitement of the business impulse, the expenditure of nervous energy in a way that is doomed to final exhaustion because it operates outside the normal economic laws of production, supply and demand. The relation of the aesthetic sense and the desire to appropriate, the relation between (Corthell's) art and (Jadwin's) accumulation, is different from that represented in Dreiser's text. Corthell produces art and opinions that Norris feels should not be in demand, and part of the sickness of Jadwin's speculation is that he is accumulating a supply for which there can be no demand. But the two options are not equivalent: Norris clearly distinguishes between Jadwin's business activity and Corthell's art, as Jadwin is offered and refuses Corthell's way of life on moral grounds that the reader is supposed to sanction, and Jadwin's overexcited supply is rewarded by an orgasmic nervous breakdown while Corthell is simply, ignominiously sent packing.

Vandover, the spendthrift in *Vandover and the Brute*,[28] is also a neurasthenic, and many of the same phrases are used to describe both Jadwin and Vandover: Vandover feels a "strange numbness . . . in his head" (226), while Jadwin feels "a sort of numbness" in his (*The Pit*, 225). At the moment of crisis for Vandover, "all the objects in the range of his eyes seemed to move back and stand on the same plane" (*Vandover*, 226), while Jadwin wonders why "all the objects in his range of vision seemed to move slowly back and stand upon the same plane" (*The Pit*, 235). In both cases, an illness brought on by immoral economic activity has left the characters separated from the life around them, and therefore equidistant from all objects. Corthell, Jadwin, and Vandover all, then, misunderstand "the forces of demand and supply that ruled the world." Nervous energy, sexual energy, and money all need to be profitably reinvested if they are not to create panic or depletion. The spendthrift and miser both necessarily force themselves toward panic or depletion, and finally, as in neurasthenia, toward insanity and death. More important to Norris than issues of representation and aesthetic value are issues of the economics of civilized morality and the natural morality of economics.[29]

Jadwin is led into speculation by his otherwise praiseworthy inability to live the lethargic life of leisure: "What are we fellows, who have made our money, to do? I've got to be busy. I can't sit back and twiddle my thumbs. And I don't believe in lounging around clubs, or playing with race horses, or murdering game birds, or running some poor, helpless fox to death. Speculating seems to be about the only game, or the only business that's left open to me—and appears to be legitimate" (170). But despite his desire to appear legitimate, Jadwin is unable to withstand speculation's addictive and destructive pull. Speculation makes him more and more "nervous" (170), until "the tired brain flagged and drooped" (206). Laura, fearing for his "over-driven brain" (207), continually asks him what is wrong. Jadwin responds in physiological terms rather than moral: "It's hard to describe. A sort of numbness. Sometimes it's as though there was a heavy iron cap—a helmet on my head. And sometimes it—I don't know, it seems as if there were fog, or something or other, inside" (224). And when he promises to adapt to the life of leisure his wealth and wife are demanding, it is again in terms of the physiology of neurasthenia: "I'll take a good long rest this summer . . . by Jingo, I'll loaf" (225).

But he is unable to stop; the pit, often described as whirlpool, sucks him in and will not let go. The result is that his neurasthenia worsens: "I *am* touchy these days. There's so many things to think of, and all at the same time. I do get nervous. I never slept one little wink last night" (232). As with Corthell, Jadwin's neurasthenia seems to be contagious, for as he tightens his grip on the market, "the nervousness of the 'crowd' increased," and in the pit, "a feeling of nervousness began to prevail" (237). Eventually he has the first of a series of full neurasthenic "attacks":

He was weary to death; not a nerve in his body that did not droop and flag. His eyes closed slowly. Then, all at once, his whole body twitched sharply in a sudden spasm, a simultaneous recoil of every muscle. His heart began to beat rapidly, his breath failed him. . . . "Look here," he said to the opposite wall, "I guess I'm not a schoolgirl, to have nerves at this late date." . . . By degrees he lapsed into a sort of lethargy, a wretched counterfeit of sleep, his eyes half closed, his breath irregular. But such as it was, it was infinitely grateful. The little, over-driven cogs and wheels of the mind, at least, moved more slowly. (234–35)

But this reprieve is short lived, for as soon as the gong sounded in the pit, "instantly the jaded nerves braced taut again; instantly the tiny machinery of the brain spun again at its fullest limit" (236). His partner, Gretry, finds him "swinging nervously back and forth in the swivel chair" (244) and warns him that he is going over the edge, that he is already at the final stage of nervousness, insanity, and that at the same time his economic ability to continue his corner is at its limit. When Jadwin declares that he wants to continue his corner for another month, Gretry tells him he is "crazy," an assertion Jadwin proves by his crazed response, "going absolutely crimson" and declaring that Gretry is being "blasphemous" (252). Gretry immediately advises a rest cure: "Do you know, you ought to be in bed this very minute. You haven't got any nerves left at all. . . . If you should break down now—well I don't like to think of what would happen. You ought to see a doctor" (253).

Jadwin, completely absorbed in his speculative mania, will not listen, and we see him experience, slowly but steadily, the worst of his breakdowns, in what is the most detailed literary representation of a neurasthenic crisis:

> A new turn had been given to the screw . . . a slow, tense crisping of every tiniest nerve in his body . . . a gradual wave of torture that was not pain, yet infinitely worse. A dry prickling aura as of billions of minute electrical shocks crept upward over his flesh, till it reached his head, where it seemed to culminate in a white flash, which he felt rather than saw. . . . He put off consulting a doctor . . . [for] fear that the doctor might tell him what he guessed to be the truth. Were his wits leaving him? . . . How to grasp the morrow's business . . . with this unspeakable crumbling and disintegrating of his faculties going on? Jaded, feeble, he rose to meet another day . . . [with] hot, tired eyes, the trembling fingers and nervous gestures. . . . And then, under the stress and violence of the hour, something snapped in his brain. The murk behind his eyes had been suddenly pierced by a white flash. The strange qualms and tiny nervous paroxysms of the last few months all at once culminated in some indefinite, indefinable crisis, and the wheels and cogs of all activities save one lapsed away and ceased. (254–85)

In Norris's work the personality, the economy, sex, daily life, nature, the nervous system, and the trading pit, among other things, are described in terms of machines. Norris's use of machinery to describe organic life is an attempt to meliorate or find a middle ground in the cultural debate most succinctly represented by Henry Adams as that between the Virgin and the Dynamo. "The machinery of life work crashing in its groove," for instance, on the one hand a somewhat grating image of sexual intercourse, is on the other hand a complex resolution of Adams's dichotomy between the dynamo and what Norris termed "a whole religion in a brooding bird." The descriptions of neurasthenic crises invoke a mechanical, electrical notion of sexuality which is also continually linked to the possibility of religious conversion. The mind is a "complicated" machine, capable of "billions" of electrical impulses at once, which in its broken-down state looks most like inanimate machinery. The one "function of the complicated machine" which persisted after Jadwin's final breakdown is not named; we are simply told that "its rhythm beat out the old and

" BE SUNNY "

"Force-Thoughts"
By SUNNY JIM

DO you know that you get a new skin every month or six weeks—from four to twelve new skins for every gown or new suit of clothes you buy?

Do you know that your finger-nails are completely renewed every six months, and your toe-nails once a year, and that your eyelashes last about a hundred days?

¶ I grew up with the popular notion that one's body was completely renewed every seven years; in reality, the change takes place within about thirty months; and the only part that undergoes but little transformation is the enamel of your teeth.

No wonder, then, that the food you eat is the all-important thing. From it was made all you are to-day—and to-morrow's breakfast has a mighty big bearing on the way you'll decide an important matter two months from now!

¶ And you know it's not the amount of nutriment in the food but the amount that is available that counts. "FORCE" is a food containing the highest percentage of nutriment so far as materials are concerned, and the scientific cooking process renders all this nutriment ready for immediate transformation into brain and muscle.

It's because it is so easily digested that it helps us to

Be Sunny.

¶ Perhaps my book would help you—it's about "FORCE" and something else. I wrote it myself.

Yours truly,

Sunny Jim

Advertisement for "Force" cereal, 1903. Sunny Jim is a humorous character in part because he looks overcivilized.

terrible cadence: 'Wheat—wheat—wheat, wheat—wheat—wheat' "
(285). The monotonous—almost comic—repetition of the word is
meant to signify on the one hand the inexorability of the machinelike
"march of the wheat" as an "elemental force" that human action can
do little to control, and on the other hand Jadwin's monomaniacal
absorption in his attempt to control it.[30]

Absorption, in this novel, is a problem. "I hate speculation," Laura
tells Corthell. "It seems to absorb some men so; and I don't believe
it's right for a man to allow himself to become absorbed altogether
in business." Corthell, the dilettante, responds that there is no reason
to see absorption as simply a problem for business: "Is it right for
one to be absorbed 'altogether' in anything—even in art, even in religion?" (180) Laura's own problem is that she doesn't have anything
that even closely threatens to absorb her except flirtation, now curtailed by her married state; she is bored. She has everything, but
there is no "zest" in her possession. She redoes her wardrobe, buys
rare books, horses, carriages, but with "so much money at her command there was none of the spice of the hunt in the affair. . . . The
little personal relation between her and her belongings vanished
away."

In an attempt to reestablish a "personal relation" to her getting and
spending she breaks out of her nervous lassitude into nervous activity: "For a few days a veritable seizure of religious enthusiasm held
sway over her. She spoke of endowing a hospital, of doing church
work among the 'slums' of the city" (213). Within days, however, she
has dropped the whole thing and gone to the races, proving her reform
impulses to be nervous excess. She then has a stage built in the
ballroom and begins to rehearse the parts—Lady Macbeth, Juliet,
Portia, Ophelia—that she had always wanted to play on the stage.
Her highly sexualized impromptu performance for Jadwin makes him
quite nervous, and he gingerly denounces it as neurasthenic: "It's
sort of overwrought—a little—and unnatural. I like you best when
you are your old self, quiet, calm, and dignified. . . . I didn't know you
had this streak in you. You are that excitable to-night!" (228) As long
as Jadwin remains night and day at the exchange, however, Laura
continues to alternate between the poles of nervousness. Adjusting
her hair with "nervous fingers," she exclaims, "Oh, the ennui and
stupidity of this wretched life!" (257)

The flashing paroxysms of nervous breakdown or "brain-collapse,"
along with the flagging and drooping of neurasthenic exhaustion, signify complex fears of sexual spending and impotence. Jadwin's sudden spasms, nervous paroxyms, and pricklings of electrified nerves
are directly related to the "flag and droop" with which he meets his

wife at the end of the day. Such impotence explains why electric belts with genital attachments were advertised in the Sears catalogue and elsewhere, claiming to cure "flag and droop" by recharging the nervous system. In *The Pit*, the sexualized overspending of speculation leads to sexual impotence, and this impotence in turn creates the inevitability of both Laura's illicit temptations and her frustration and ennui. Laura and Jadwin are not necessarily stuck, however, looking for an option between absorption and theatricality, between an ungenteel overexcitement and the ennui of playing an inauthentic, genteel role. The place they both should look for the middle way, Norris makes clear from the beginning, is in their marriage. At first, Jadwin knew this better than Laura, as he told her during their courtship:

> Men need good women, Miss Dearborn. Men who are doing the work of the world. I believe in women as I believe in Christ. But I don't believe they were made—any more than Christ was—to cultivate— beyond a certain point—their own souls, and refine their own minds, and live in a sort of warmed-over, dilettante, stained-glass world of seclusion and *ex*clusion. No, sir, that don't do for the United States and the men who are making them the greatest nation in the world. The men have got all the get-up-and-go they want, but they need the women to point them straight, and to show them how to lead that other kind of life that isn't all grind. (94–95)

Before his long decline, then, Jadwin knows what he needs to relearn by the end of the novel, that a good wife is the answer to a man's need for moral guidance, guidance which would then necessarily bring about an economic use of the man's energy, including the "hot," "trembling . . . paroxysms" of sexual energy. And Jadwin, who early in the novel runs a Sunday school ("and I'll bet if D. L. Moody were here today he'd say, 'Jadwin, well done, thou good and faithful servant' "), equates the role of women with that of Christ, again adding a religious sanction to the acquisition of health.

Spiritual matters make their way into the text in a number of other ways as well. At one point the conservatives (Jadwin, Aunt Wess, and Cressler) "were deep in a discussion of mind-reading and spiritualism, . . . discussing psychic research and séances" (92–95). They then asked Laura whether she had ever had "presentiments," or " 'experiences'?" Laura answers "No, no, I am too material, I am afraid" (96). The question is asked of Jadwin, and he answers that he believes in "luck" and uses an example a coin toss related to his speculative activity (96–97). Both Laura and Jadwin are clearly placed in the wrong. Jadwin mistakes materialistic chance for supernatural activity, and Laura is as she admits "too material." Her lack of spiritual yearning mirrors her lack, at this early point in the novel, of any desire to marry. Jadwin's misrecognition of "gambling" as a spiritual experience is meant to be found by the reader, as it was by Cressler, "deplorable" and blasphemous. When Laura listens to Cressler's explanations of the folly of speculation and the workings of the exchange, "a whole new order of things was being disclosed, and for the first time in her life she looked into the workings of political economy" (98). The scales fall from her eyes, then, as a result of initiation into a moral explanation of economics.

Both Laura and Jadwin forget. Their neurasthenia is not due to moral laxity so much as it is to oversight. Laura has forgotten the traditional role she originally accepted, and the various attempts at staving off boredom—reform, racehorses, rare books—are emblematic of role options for the less traditional wife and are indicted as useless, frivolous, wasteful, and unsatisfying. Before the end of the book, however, Laura, at her lowest point, is inspired by her sister's rebuke to her for her selfishness. "If my husband had a battle to fight," her sister asks, "do you think I'd mope and pine because he left me at home; no I wouldn't. I'd help him buckle his sword on . . . and cry over his wounds" (291). Laura had instead been trying to compete with her husband's business interests and had started a war of her own; she would "panoply" herself, and glory in the strength of her beauty: "She felt the same pride in it as the warrior in a finely tempered weapon" (294) when she dressed to impress him. Their marriage has become not a haven but another battlefield. At the last minute, moments before her husband returns from the pit on the day of his defeat, she recognizes, besides the two Lauras, "a third— a third that rose above and forgot the other two, that in some beautiful, mysterious way was identity ignoring self" (295). She rejects the "cruel cult of self" (294) which had been directing her actions in favor of this higher identity, and she is thereby ready to perform her role as guide and helpmate when her husband returns hours later, broken down, financially and nervously bankrupt.

Jadwin several times during his downhill slide yearns for a return to the happy days when they were first married, and at one point announces: "Sometimes I think that we'd be happier—you and I— chumming along shoulder to shoulder, poor an' working hard, than making big money an' spending big money" (229). This plot is the right one: work hard, make and spend, husband and wife shoulder to shoulder rather than in any more exciting position. When their world finally falls apart, when Jadwin's corner collapses and all the mortgaged property is sold, his wish turns out to have been prophecy, and Laura and Jadwin leave with a few belongings to go west to start over, working together. The plot, then, follows the basic outlines of *A Man's Woman* and *Blix* in its representation of Norris's beliefs about gender and provides, in the end, a reassertion of traditional values with an emphasis on a return to traditional gender roles. Critics have used the double plot—and the question of how closely the "love" plot is related to the "wheat" plot—as evidence that *The Pit* is a "flawed" novel. Some have found the two plots unrelated; some have found that the love plot inexplicably takes "the upper hand" when it should, they think, remain secondary.[31] But Norris not only creates clear parallels between the two plots through the use of themes of flirtation and speculation (as Howard Horowitz has shown[32]) and their relation to neurasthenia, he further resolves the two plots at the end by referring them both to versions of supernatural naturalism. The love plot becomes an allegory about human types, expressed in the following conversation between Laura and Corthell:

> "Then, let's see, the individual may deteriorate, but the type always grows better. . . . Of course the type is more important than the individual. And that something that keeps it from going below a certain point is God."
> "Or nature."
> "So that God and nature," she cried again, "work together? No, no, they are one and the same thing."
> "There, don't you see," he remarked, smiling back at her, "how simple it is?"
> "Oh-h," exclaimed Laura, with a deep breath, "isn't it beautiful?"
> (181)

Jadwin, though he finally failed, managed the most spectacular corner in history. And though as an individual he may have suffered a setback, God and nature ensure that the type of the American businessman, the modern-day Napoleon and Crusader, continues to improve. Again the resolution is a combination of teleological naturalism, in its appeal to evolutionary theory, and supernaturalism, in its appeal to deity and a transcendental moral order. And the wheat plot is resolved in a similar way, with a reference to both natural law and blasphemy: "What had they to do with it? Why, the Wheat had grown itself; demand and supply, these were the two great laws the Wheat obeyed. Almost blasphemous in his effrontery, he had tampered with these laws" (272).

The reevaluation of the human will that Norris's naturalism produces is meant to be reassuring. In place of the Enlightenment belief that human will is the motor force of history, Norris offers a philosophy of the inefficacy of the human will, a common response, and for many a necessary response, to the impact of Charles Darwin and Charles Lyell. As William James would have it, the main use of the will is to will belief; what we need is not a new way of acting but a new way of thinking. Jadwin's "blasphemy" is his attempt to control what no human being can control. The wheat grows itself, it is an elemental force, as Jadwin realizes when he cries, "Corner wheat! It's the wheat that has cornered me. It's like holding a wolf by the ears, bad to hold on, but worse to let go." In Roosevelt's terms, it may be rough to ride so fast, but it is worse to slow down. Norris, James, and Roosevelt all offered meliorative philosophies—philosophies between the genteel and the anarchistic—for a world in which the traditional connections between will and morality were being transformed. These transformations are most clearly signaled by the way in which religious, metaphysical, and ethical questions and answers were represented in the language of economics. In the final passages of the novel, Laura's metaphysical struggle exhibits this transformation:

> For a moment, vague, dark perplexities assailed her, questionings as to the elemental forces, the forces of demand and supply that ruled the world. This huge resistless Nourisher of the Nations—why was it that it could not reach the People, could not fulfill its destiny, unmarred by all this suffering, unattended by all this misery?
> She did not know. But as she searched, troubled and disturbed, for an answer, she was aware of a certain familiarity in the neighborhood the carriage was traversing. (306)

The philosophical neighborhood she is transversing with these thoughts should not seem unfamiliar, because the novel offers, finally, the traditional consolations of philosophical distance and narrative closure. To look at the changing face of the world and consciousness, fearlessly and with sincerity, as Norris loudly demanded, requires, in the end, only that the human will be called in to reaffirm quotidian values. The physical neighborhood is also familiar because they are on La Salle Street, and the final image of the book is that of the Board of Trade building, "crouching on its foundations like a monstrous sphinx." It is the answer to the riddle of this sphinx, we are left to assume, that is the answer to Laura's questionings. Wheat follows the natural law of supply and demand, except when "man," the answer to every sphinx's riddle, tries to interfere. The vast land and its overwhelming natural productivity, and the enormous city, mark of the power and finality of the industrial order, have at their mysterious center the "nerve center" of the pit, of speculative finance and trade.

Supply and demand are natural laws, social laws, industrial laws, and domestic laws, and in another central theme of the book, parallel to the themes of business, wheat, and marriage, Norris shows that supply and demand are literary laws as well. He presents many opinions about literature in the book that advance his views on art and writing while they reinforce his other themes. Corthell, as an artist, is the most important representative of art in the novel, but it is a mistake to equate all of his views with Norris's. Larzer Ziff, for instance, argues that though Jadwin is a bull in the market, by the time he gets home his seed has been spilled; the primary tension in the book for Ziff is that between the image of masculinity presented by Jadwin, who is originally vital but eventually totally spent, and the image presented by Corthell, suspect in the culture at large as effeminate, but attractive, and sexually attractive, to Laura and Norris. Norris fails, Ziff writes, to "follow the implications of the Jadwin-Corthell tension to the very end."[33]

Ziff's reading makes some sense: the denial of businessmen's virility is perhaps a defense of Norris's own artistic activity as virile in an age that thought otherwise; the development in the novel of the "real" neurasthenic as Jadwin rather than Corthell, as we may have thought, supports this; and though Corthell is courting hell by his profession, Jadwin (Bad win? Bad wind? Can't win? Ruined? Jaded from winning?) is courting it even further because he has stopped being civilized by his woman. But this last point leads to the "implications" for Norris: marriage is not a corral for excess energy but a necessary part of spending. Money itself is not real spending, Norris seems to be saying; what Jadwin buys Laura doesn't count, for money is not the real issue. Norris is interested, finally, in keeping supply and demand in the moral realm rather than that of fiduciary accounting. Jadwin is overspending at the exchange, and that is a moral problem, and therefore only temporarily a problem with his virility, which we are to assume he has not lost, though he has been misdirecting it. We are told that he is heading west to start a new business; he has not lost his "get-up-and-go," he just needed his wife "to point [him] straight" (95). That Corthell is attractive to Laura only when Jadwin is unavailable implies that Corthell's aestheticism is only a substitute for real virility.

The text, then, seems negatively self-reflexive—the artist is inferior to the businessman, effeminate in his unproductivity, overly refined, overcivilized. Norris the artist, however, is not like Corthell the artist. Corthell's stained glass is medieval rather than modern like the novel. Norris had always claimed that the muse of American fiction would lead a writer "far from the studios and the aesthetes, the velvet jackets and the uncut hair, far from the sexless creatures who cultivate their little art of writing as a fancier cultivates his orchids." Norris is careful to portray Corthell in a more favorable light than that: he dresses carefully but conservatively, he keeps his hair cut, and he is far from sexless. Corthell expresses some opinions Norris agreed with and some he refuted. Corthell claims, for example, that the novel of the future will be a novel without a love story. Laura responds: "It will be long after I'm dead—that's one consolation" (46). Given the love plot of *The Pit* (and of *Moran, Blix,* and *A Man's Woman*) we might assume that Norris is also consoled. But, and here we can assume Norris agrees with him, Corthell admires not the "Bouguereau" (whose paintings, and name, became cultural symbols of decadent European sexuality [34]) on Laura's wall, but the landscape of a "Western artist": "And that little pool, still and black and sombre—why, the whole thing is the tragedy of a life full of dark, hidden secrets. And the little pool is a heart. No one can say how deep it is, or what dreadful thing one would find at the bottom, or what drowned hopes or what sunken ambitions. That little pool says one word as plain as if it were whispered in the ear—despair. Oh, yes, I prefer it to the nymphs" (182). Norris, the despairing naturalist, at times made similar pronouncements in his own critical writings, and in his fiction he often represented sexual morality as a choice between nymphs and despair, with the "still and black and sombre" mystery of neurasthenic despair the only morally righteous response to the neurasthenic overexcitement of specular or speculative sexual spending.

But in his own life he was far from despair and ruin. *The Octopus* had made him "suddenly successful," and as he writes of Jadwin, "he was full of triumph, full of the grim humor of the suddenly successful American" (187). He had taken to pronouncing, in the last year of his life, after the birth of his daughter, who, because it was "great fun," he called Billy, "*Maintenant je suis bon bourgeois, moi— père de famille!*" [35] He masculinized his own authorship as he masculinized his young daughter and the heroines of his fiction. Whatever preference he had for despair was, like Corthell's, based in the aesthetics of sentimentalism, that most conventional form of cultural criticism, the sentimentalism that informs the plot of *The Pit*, hinging as it does on the Christological significance of the long-suffering wife and the metaphysical meaning of everyday life. Norris, like

Hamlin Garland and William Dean Howells, was a literary radical nervously representing, with an aim of reinforcing, the economy of traditional values, including the most traditional of relations to the supernatural.

5 William Dean Howells:
Letters Home, Questionable Shapes, and the American *Unheimlich*

> The idea of duty in one's calling prowls about in our lives like the ghost of dead religious beliefs.
>
> —Max Weber, *The Protestant Ethic and the Spirit of Capitalism* (1904)

William Dean Howells celebrated his sixty-sixth birthday in 1903, and his letters that year return again and again to the question of his age, using two of the main strands of neurasthenic discourse—the depletion of nerve force and the problem of identity. Sometimes he invokes age as the cause of a lack of force or resolve, as when he wrote to Samuel Clemens, "Why is civilization such a carrion of falsehood?—That poor girl and her murdered baby," he went on, referring to a recent Clemens article, "it made me sick to read about her; but one is so limp and helpless in the presence of the injustice which underlies society, and I am getting so old." And sometimes age brought up questions of subjectivity and consciousness. "I should not mind being old, so much, if I always had the young, sure grip of myself," Howells wrote to Thomas Bailey Aldrich. "What I hate is this dreamy fumbling about my own identity, in which I detect myself at odd times. It seems sometimes as if it were somebody else, and I sometimes wish it were."[1]

Howells, whom the winner of the 1903 Nobel Prize for Literature, Björnstjerne Björnson, called "one of the greatest psychologists" of his age, perhaps overstated the firm grasp of self he attributed to his youth. Since the 1950s the biographical and critical literature on Howells has stressed his neuroticism, beginning with his self-proclaimed "very morbid boyhood." Howells suffered from nervousness all his life, with major breakdowns ("nervous prostration") at the ages of nineteen and forty-four. His letters, when not commenting on the neurasthenic illnesses of his wife and daughter, or the nervous illnesses of his correspondent or his correspondent's

William Dean Howells as pictured in a 1903 issue of *Century Magazine*.
Howells was nervous about the passing of time in 1903. (General Re-
search Division, The New York Public Library; Astor, Lenox, and Tilden
Foundations)

family, refer often to his own health and nerve strength. His wife, Elinor, suffered constantly from neurasthenia, beginning with the birth of their second child in 1868 until her death in 1910, with only minor recoveries, and she spent the majority of those forty-two years in bed. In 1880 his daughter Winifred contracted, supposedly from "psychic sources," a nervous illness that continued until 1889, when after six months under the care of S. Weir Mitchell in Philadelphia she died at the age of twenty-six.[2] John Crowley has argued, as Feinstein has of the Jameses, that there was an "economy of pain" in the Howells household, and that "Elinor, Winifred, and Will took turns, as it were, breaking down." Unlike Feinstein, who sees economic reasons for the timing of the Jameses' illnesses, Crowley sees the Howells family striving for "psychological balance" or equilibrium. In either case, Howells's life was suffused with nervousness, and nervousness was a constant backdrop to the issues of gender, class, and modernization which were, besides being the staples of the discourse of neurasthenia, the staples of Howells's fiction. As he once wrote—only half accurately given the concurrent epidemic of male neurasthenia—at times America seemed "little better than a hospital for invalid woman."[3]

Howells's neurasthenic breakdown at the age of forty-four occurred while he was writing *A Modern Instance* (1882), and this crisis has traditionally been attributed to the uneasiness its themes—sexuality, adultery, power and cruelty in marriage—produced in him. The unscrupulous journalist Bartley Hubbard commits crimes as a journalist and as a husband, and his wife sues him for divorce. What some critics have found to be the "unsatisfying" nature of the ending, in which the shady, philandering Hubbard emerges as a clear villain rather than the ambivalent character he had been earlier (and is suitably murdered by a man he has wronged), is usually attributed to Howells's reaction, once he had recovered from his nervous prostration, against the moral uncertainty of the text he had created.[4] Richard Brodhead, for instance, has analyzed the ending of *A Modern Instance* as "the means by which a lapsing social code rhetorically reconstitutes itself as a binding moral law, objectively sanctioned and universally enforceable." Because they reconstitute a social code no longer universally sanctioned or enforceable, we are suspicious of the conclusions or compromises that sympathetic characters come to and suspicious of the relation between those conclusions and the implied author. Brodhead, in fact, claims that Howells, too, "retains a certain suspicion of the fabrications" he constructed in the ethical realm, however necessary he felt such fabrications to be. Amy Kaplan, in her analysis of Howells's relation to the mass market, argues that the ending of *A Modern Instance* is not a failure or a retreat into conventionality but part of a coherent representation of (here Kaplan uses Warren Susman's terms) the "major social transition from the culture of character to the culture of personality." Howells resisted this transition, Kaplan argues, because of his commitment to the centrality of character.[5]

But even if Bartley Hubbard does represent mutable personality, and Ben Halleck, the good but indecisive man that has taken care of Hubbard's wife, represents stable character, both are shown to be unacceptable extremes through their relation to the supernatural and to neurasthenia. Hubbard is godless, and to him religious themes are simply raw material for journalistic exploitation: "Religion comes right after politics in the popular mind, and it interests the women like murder," he claims, and believes therefore that a newspaper should "give the minutest religious intelligence, and not only that, but the religious gossip, and the religious scandal."[6] And Halleck's belief in character is blasphemous in its own way, since for Halleck "character is superstition." Halleck's primary moral attribute is tainted by the archetypical invalid relation to the supernatural: superstition. As a result, Hubbard is dyspeptic and Halleck is sickly and "wasted."

Howells was, at times, both. He had a lifelong interest in psychic phenomena, psychic research, and the supernatural, seen in such novels as *The Undiscovered Country* (1880) and *The Shadow of a Dream* (1890), in the stories collected in *Questionable Shapes* (1903) and *Between the Dark and the Daylight* (1907), and in his editorial comments and letters. At times he took the connection between the supernatural and neurasthenia for granted, as when he refers in his letters to the psychic source of his daughter's illness, and when he represents Faulkner and his wife Hermia as both haunted and neurasthenic in *The Shadow of a Dream*. At other times the connection was both less explicit and more clearly in the service of conventional morality. In *My Literary Passions* (1895), Howells represents his feelings for classic American writers as "a passion surpassing the love of women" and his own writing as "communications" from "divinities" at whose "shrines" he worships, and he uses similar metaphors in his novelistic investigations of ethics and the will. *The Undiscovered Country* (1880), for instance, is a novel explicitly about mediums, spiritualism, psychic phenomena, and family romances: here Howells uses the image of mediumistic telepathy as a symbol of control, much as James would in *The Bostonians* a few years later.

Howells often represented intimate emotional relations as arenas of control and domination, and such representations, when worked out in fictional situations, tended to undermine conventional morality. *Their Wedding Journey* (1872), *A Hazard of New Fortunes* (1886), *The Minister's Charge* (1887), *The Shadow of a Dream* (1890), *An Imperative Duty* (1892), *The Son of Royal Langbrith* (1904), or *Fennel and Rue* (1908)—to mention an eclectic batch of the many possibilities—provide examples of the relation Howells represented between domination and intimacy and, in each of these cases, to nervousness and the supernatural as well. The use of metaphors of sexuality and spiritualism and a nervousness about the shifting bases of ethics, always central to his work, came into a new focus in his fiction in 1903. "We have indeed, in our best fiction, gone back to mysticism," Howells wrote in the "Editor's Easy Chair" for June of 1903, "if indeed we were not always there in our best fiction, and the riddle of the painful earth is again engaging us with the old fascination."[7]

Vulgar Dualism

Howells published two books in 1903—*Letters Home*, an epistolary novel, and *Questionable Shapes*, three stories of the occult—and wrote a third, *The Son of Royal Langbrith*, a novel. *Letters Home* introduces neurasthenic themes in the first epistle, written by Otis Binning, an older Boston bachelor suffering from nervous dyspepsia, to his neurasthenic sister-in-law, who is undergoing a rest cure. Like many of Howells's novels, *Letters Home* attempts to come to terms with issues of class, especially the emerging leisure class, and does so using another standard Howells theme—the difference between New York and Boston—to do so. As always, New York represents the new money and ways and Boston the old. The finicky nervous dyspeptic from Boston, who is visiting New York, writes home apologizing in his second sentence for using financial metaphors—"the local commercialism instantly penetrates one's vocabulary," he interpolates—and throughout he represents the Brahmin ways in Mammon, to mix, as that time did, religious metaphors.[8]

But Binning is also a critical thinker, as we see from his attitude toward neurasthenia in the first letter. Discussing his sister-in-law's "invalid leisure," he worries: "Your rest-cure may be good for you, or it may not." New York, despite all its vulgar and incessant activity, is a rest cure of sorts for him, he writes, because it is more relaxed than Boston, with its "moral tension" (3). Binning makes other, similarly sarcastic comments about his sister's neurasthenia in later letters: "I am glad to hear you are so much better, but having formed the habit of writing to you, I do not know that I can quite give it up, now, even in the presence of your convalescence" (145); "I am sorry to hear of your relapse, and I will gladly do what I can to comfort you with the woes of others, while you are renewing your care of yourself" (171); "But what I want you to own, Margaret, is that I could not have done more handsomely by the leisure into which you have relapsed" (177). "Invalid leisure," then, is the problem, since the phrase can be inflected to mean not only leisure enforced by sickness but also leisure for which there is no valid justification.

Thus the first letter has a structure of meaning built on the paired terms of rest and activity, rest and moral tension, leisure and sickness, leisure and health, money and morals, money and activity, new and old, male and female, vulgarity and commercialism. These terms are reworked throughout the book, along with oppositions between East and West, rich and poor, sophistication and naiveté, literature and journalism, work and leisure, spending and saving, and the rest of the cultural gumbo thrown in. The novel is self-consciously "minor." As Howells wrote to Henry Blake Fuller a few months after it was published, "My way is still the byway, not the highway; the minor, not the major means," and critics agreed: Thomas Wentworth Higginson and Henry Walcott Boynson claimed in 1903 that although Howells was "without equal" stylistically, he was not "expansive"; he was a "miniature" artist. The polite balance achieved for each opposition and the reliance on stock themes and situations—a young writer from the West agog at New York, nouveau riche midwesterners adrift in New York high society, the illnesses of poor people cured thanks to the selfless noblesse oblige of the leisure class, love triangles based on good-hearted misunderstandings—announce the book as pleasant and unimportant. It has received little critical attention and is rarely, if ever, taught. The book seems, in fact, to justify Mencken's criticism that Howells "really has nothing to say" in his "long row of uninspired and hollow books, with no more ideas in them than so many volumes of the *Ladies' Home Journal*, and no more deep and contagious feeling than so many reports of autopsies." The novel's somewhat insipid reinforcement of traditional values can reinforce Sinclair Lewis's comment that "Mr. Howells was one of the gentlest, sweetest, and most honest of men, but he had the code of a pious old maid whose greatest delight was to have tea at the vicarage."[9]

It is hard, then, to understand William James's effusive reception: "Dear Howells, You've done it this time and no mistake. I've just read *Letters Home*, which raised me from the dead almost, and which is the most absolutely flawless piece of richness as well as veracity that ever flowed out of human pen. I bar no one and no language. It is

nature itself, and the wit of it, and the humour of it and the goodness
of it! You may go—*that* will remain. Your ever thankful William
James."[10] One reason for James's enthusiasm may have been that
in the novel Howells is very free with his praises. In presenting the
New York-Boston opposition, Howells manages to praise both cultures, "the glittering new and the authoritatively old" (96). The "glittering new" in this case refers to "horseless vehicles" parked during
a large social gathering. The horseless carriage was still a very new
conveyance, and still finding new uses. In 1903 the first automobile
crossed the continent from New York to San Francisco, automobiles
were first used as police patrol cars (in Boston), and Henry Ford
organized the Ford Motor Company. But such glittering new realities
stay very much on the sidelines, and Binning the Brahmin has the
first and last word in a novel that shows at the same time the ob-
solescence, morality, and gentility of Binning's world view. As he
himself says of New York: "If you wish to lose yourself, this is the
shop; if you wish to find yourself, better go somewhere else. Our
quality, and the defect of our quality, in that obsolete Boston, was
from the wish to find ourselves, always" (65). Especially in the light
of Howells's own letter about distress at losing himself, this statement
works both ways; the narrative strategy of the entire text is that of
one hand taking away what the other gives. About the millionaire
midwesterner, Ralson, head of the Cheese and Churn Trust, who
Binning meets in New York, Binning says, "I must say, he looked the
part of an old barbaric aristocrat to perfection" (118). Still, the Ralsons "have a certain wilding charm," he admits, "and if they can
continue sylvanly themselves, they will be the *fine fleur* of the patriciate
in a few generations" (90). Elsewhere Binning says of Ralson: "He
early decided that I was intellectual, I think, and with the admirable
frankness of his class, he conceived of me—no doubt in a delicate
compliment to your sex,—as a kind of mental and moral woman, to
whom a real man, a business man, could have nothing to say after
the preliminary politenesses. I do not know why he should rank me
below Mr. Ardith, as I feel he does, unless it is because Mr. Ardith is
still young enough to be finally saved from intellectuality, and sub-
sequently dedicated to commerciality" (125). Here Binning himself is
managing the double entendres about gender, business, and intellectuality, but elsewhere Binning seems unable to control the spin of
his own play with gendered representation. When he claims that
Ralson began to patronize him "with condescensions suitable to a
woman of my years," the audience is encouraged to imagine Ralson's
condescension with a similar comic disregard. "He cannot make me
out," Binning continues, "I believe, but these money-getters, though

they are bewildered by the difference of some other man, are never abashed by it. I have no doubt but in his heart he despises the fineness of the pretty boy, and hopes to coarsen him to his own uses" (297). Some readers, including James, might agree that Binning is superior for bewildering Ralson, agree that to coarsen the pretty boy would be a shame, and agree that it is a fine quality of Ralson's not to be abashed, and may or may not realize that this series of agreements collapses the distinctions between the two characters' otherwise opposed positions.

Mrs. Ralson has her own newly found aristocratic manner, for like Binning's sister-in-law, she is a bed-ridden neurasthenic for whom a maid is hired, so that someone is always available to "talk her nerves down" (270). She thereby partakes of the "invalid leisure" that attempted to "cure" the contradictions Americans faced in adapting to a leisure-class ethic. Binning represents the aristocratic mannerisms and pretensions to which the Ralsons apparently aspire, and yet here Binning again manages to speak to both sides: "In the presence of the old American ideal [such pretension] might make one's flesh creep; but that . . . old American ideal was nowadays principally appreciable by its absence" (128–29), he writes, in as qualified a statement about the relation of aristocracy to democracy as might be made and still seem to uphold the values of both. Frances Dennam, the maid, and perhaps the most sympathetic character in the book, writes home to her mother, "You lose your bearings a good deal in New York, with the talk about classes, upper and lower and middle, and in some of the newspapers that try to be 'smart' you read things about common Americans that make your blood boil, if you haven't lost your bearings" (231–32). If you don't lose the bearings that you lose, in other words, you retain them. Ardith, the young author from Iowa, offers a similar collapse of contradiction in the relation of East to West. "We are queer, we Americans, and if any one takes up the study of us in that dark future when we shall have ceased to be Americans, he will find the New Yorkers, and not the frontiersmen, the queerest Americans of all," he writes to his editor back home. "In fact the New Yorkers *are* the frontiersmen, as I will explain to you, some day; but now the postulate would be too exhausting to handle" (191). Throughout the book, postulates too nervously exhausting to handle are resolved into double talk, paradox, and overdetermination through repeated qualification.

Nevertheless, James may have appreciated the dignity and nobility with which Binning's effeminacy and uselessness are robed, as well as the cosmopolitanism with which Howells characterizes the open-minded traditionalist. Or perhaps what James appreciated about the text was its very modern self-referentiality. More than any other text from 1903, *Letters Home* constantly refers to its own fictionality. In Binning's first letter, he remembers the eighteenth century, when everyone "willingly wrote such long letters as to give the epistolary novel a happy air of verisimilitude" (2). Ardith comments that he has a story he could tell but will not, for "as Miss Ralson says, . . . it would make a book, and I am not writing a book" (115). "I feel that I left you at the close of an exciting installment last night," he writes to his friend, "as if I were writing some wretched romance, instead of this wretched reality. . . . How strangely we are made, we who are born to scribble!" (188) "Did you suppose I was writing a story," he asks later, "and could make up a chapter whenever I chose?" (248) "I tried to collect my thoughts," he writes in telling his story, "as people used to do in the novels" (253). Earlier he had written, Essie "pulled herself up and kissed me, and then ran out of the room and left me to my thoughts, as they used to do in the novels" (140). And finally Binning tells his neurasthenic sister-in-law, in his last letter:

> I should be glad to know, some day after we meet, just how a Boston woman so completely of our old tradition as you, should have allowed herself to become so absorbed in the loves of my wild Westerners. I could understand, of course, if you had met them in the fine ether of one of James's stories—I wish he still wrote about Americans— you would have been bewitched with his delicate *précis* of that affair. . . . If they were not so intensely real to themselves, they might seem to me characters in a rather crude American story. In fact are not they just that? They are certainly American and certainly crude; and now that they are passing beyond my social contact, I feel as safe from them, and from the necessity of explaining them or justifying them, as if they were shut in a book I had just finished reading. (293, 298)

Howells then ends Binning's letter with a final self-referential flourish: "If I could find the author I should like to make him my compliment on having managed so skillfully that he left some passages to my conjecture" (299).

The self-referentiality of the text has the same effect as the over-qualified dualism: it signals playfulness, levity rather than gravity, inconsequentiality. The book, for all its evocation of cultural debates, ignores them in favor of the movement of its own prose and a fairly conventional love story. Howells, who along with Henry James had sworn to create a new novel that was not based on a love story, has Binning, again in the ironic mode of all Binning's statements, apologize for him: "It was so old, that love business, and though it had the conceit of an eternal novelty in its dim antiquity and did freshen itself up in the perpetually changing conditions, it really was the most decrepit of the human interests" (129). This last statement is not just humorous in its irony, but thought-provoking in its historicization of love and in the jarring intensity of the adjective "decrepit"; throughout the text little bits of psychology, cultural criticism, and cosmic philosophy are sprinkled amid the general playfulness. Like William James, Binning is a psychologist from Boston, albeit an amateur one, and his reflections on psychology, along with the youthful Ardith's responses to New York, provide the explicit philosophizing of the book. Ardith says that New York "completed the cure" for his lovesickness and, in a sentence that echoes the opening of Dreiser's *Amateur Laborer*, that in New York "you feel yourself not merely a witness of the great procession of life, but a part of it" (11). And later, in another passage that evokes Spencerian cosmology and neurasthenic discourse, he writes: "Life here is on such a prodigious scale, and it is going on in so many ways at once that the human atom loses the sense of its own little aches and pains, and merges its weakness in the strenuousness of the human mass" (61).

This kind of philosophizing could hardly have interested James, and it is possible that his letter was itself written with ironic playfulness, that its overstated praise mimics the text by glorifying the inconsequential and thereby constitutes flattery through imitation. The psychological issues that were of as much interest to James as to Howells are treated too lightly and glancingly to have excited James's positive or negative attention. The closest the novel comes to representing multiple consciousness, for instance, is that Ardith is in love with two women, one rich and one poor, at the same time. "I must be insane!" says Ardith, but the reader knows that his intentions are all of the best, that the situation is fairly benign, and that Ardith's sanity is not in question. "Just for the dramatic interest," Binning asks his sister, "wouldn't you like to imagine him playing some sort of double part, with that single selfishness which is the unique force of duplicity?" (240–41). But the novel eschews that much dramatic interest, and Binning, in his report on a conversation with Ardith, offers a reason why. "I expressed my surprise that the fact had never been adequately treated in literature, and he answered bitterly that life had never been adequately treated in literature, either because life was too bold, or because literature was too timid" (197).

This is one of Howells's favorite themes, the timidity of literature in the face of life; in this genteel novel the criticism seems like further self-reflexivity. Binning refers to the "fact" that literature has not addressed the multiplicity of affection in a monogamous culture, that "the affections . . . are of so many minds," but he concludes that to do anything but deny such multiplicity would make a man a "rascal" (196–97). Still, Ardith's "double part" is shown to be without duplicity, and everything works out in the end; Ardith marries the rich girl, the poor girl's honor remains intact, and the "fact" remains not "adequately treated"—either, we are to assume, because "literature was too timid" or because "life was too bold." Anything actually illicit, anything "unhomelike," is censored from the text, just as Howells claimed that his fiction was necessarily domesticated, since his own children acted as his censors.

When James praises the text for its "flawless . . . veracity," then, we might conclude that his praise is on the level of the letter he sent to his Radcliffe class after they sent him a potted azalea: "I will try to remain faithful to this one unique and beautiful azalea tree, the pride of my life and delight of my existence. Winter and summer will I tend and water it—even with my tears. Mrs. James shall never go near it or touch it. If it dies, I will die too; and if I die, it shall be planted on my grave."[11] This letter is flirtatious and directly plays on the relation of his affection for the young women in his class in relation to "Mrs. James." James warns his "Dear Ladies" not to "take all this too jocosely," since he really does appreciate the present, and we can assume that he also appreciated Howells's novel, however exaggerated his expression of that appreciation might have been. The ironic display of feeling makes even more sense given the dictum of Frances Dennam, the commonsensical maid in *Letters Home* who writes "real feeling is *always* vulgar" (251), and the fact that Howells and James so rarely were; better that young protagonists marry and live happily ever after and that older men make light of their affections.

Charles Eliot Norton, like James and Binning a neurasthenic Bostonian, also praised *Letters Home*. "You have never written anything more masterly in sympathetic dramatic characterization of widely contrasting types than these 'Letters,' " Norton wrote. "You do us others an immense service in exhibiting & interpreting to us America and Americans." In comparing this letter to another from Norton to Howells, we can construct a final possible explanation for James's praise. Not quite a year earlier, Norton had written about Edith Wyatt's *Every One His Own Way* (1901), which Howells had sent to him. Norton found the book "*almost* worthy of your praise. The temper, the spirit, the humor, the intent of the stories are quite exceptionally good, and the workmanship excellent,—but alas! the atmosphere, the milieu, the people are lacking in charm, in fact horribly true and ugly. Good people . . . people to celebrate as products of democracy in America, but not yet as pleasant to be familiar with or to read about as those who have risen a little further. We are, indeed, all of us on the make, and I like best those who are nearest made." When Norton praises the "widely contrasting types" in *Letters Home*, then, we can assume that he found all of them very nearly "made," that the offensive vulgarity of character and milieu evident in Wyatt's stories was absent from *Letters Home*, as in fact it was. One of the things both Norton and James appreciated about *Letters Home* is that it represented "America and Americans" in a way that crossed class and regional boundaries without ever crossing the line they felt separated them from the "vulgar."[12]

This avoidance of vulgarity could be accomplished only by representing the lower-class characters as middle-class people with no money. In effect, exactly what James praised is what many readers, such as Mencken and Lewis, for instance, find lacking: a real engagement with what Howells termed "unsmiling" aspects of American life. It is also what Cady finds central to Howells's "neuroticism," his uneasiness in the face of anything related to lower-class crime or immorality. Given the response of James and Norton, the "neuroticism" seems more cultural than personal. The gentility of *Letters Home* was perhaps already somewhat out of date in 1903, as Howells suggests in a letter to his sister Aurelia: "The name of 'Letters Home,' which I liked, is thought by the publishers to have hurt the sale of the novel. In this sophisticated age, people do not want letters nor homes, it seems." Some "sophisticates," like Charlotte Perkins Gilman, were, indeed, arguing that people need not want homes in the traditional sense (a proposal I examine in a later chapter). But Howells was less interested in declaiming against reformist ideas than he was in noting the traditionalism, and the anachronism, of his "culturally neurotic" desire to avoid contact with the vulgar. Howells's avoidance of vulgarity, on which he constructed both a psychology and a literary practice, also resulted in a constructed unconscious, the clues to which such readers as Mencken and Lewis miss even when they are as conspicuously planted as they are in *Questionable Shapes* and *The Son of Royal Langbrith*.[13]

Ghosts

Any praise by William James for *Questionable Shapes* would have been more readily understandable, since the three stories deal with one of James's special interests, psychic phenomena, and a psychologist (who quotes James) is featured in all three stories, in two as a central character. The first, "His Apparition," is a ghost story that discusses both the relation between the supernatural and everyday life and the relation between people's experience of the supernatural and the psychological study of it.[14] As a contemporary review put it: "Here is the modern 'scientific' or 'psychological' ghost-story, in which the interest attaches not what was seen, but to how it came to be seen."[15] The opening sentence of the story begins a discussion of the proper relation to the supernatural with a rejection of "professional spiritualism": "The incident was of a dignity which the supernatural has by no means always had, and which has been more than ever lacking in it since the manifestations of professional spiritualism began to vulgarize it" (5). Again, avoidance of the vulgar is a central concern of text; vulgarity defines the limits of metaphysical discussion and of communication in general.

The story is of one Hewson, who had retired from his law practice "and had contributed himself to the formation of a leisure class, which he conceived was regrettably lacking in our conditions" (60). Hewson saw his apparition while visiting at the country house of a friend, and as we will also see in relation to Mary Wilkins Freeman's fiction, Howells makes a link between property, propriety, and the supernatural: Hewson decides to tell no one about his experience so as to protect the market value of his friend's estate, since "the reputation of being haunted simply plays the devil with a piece of property" (14, 57). Hewson's adherence to the propriety of leisure-class social relations is represented as first and foremost a respect for property, property that needs to be protected, somehow, from a vulgar reaction to the supernatural.[16]

In fact, Hewson decides not only that professional spiritualists would vulgarize his experience and that it would be vulgar to compromise his host's property but also that to speak of his apparition at all would be to vulgarize it. The following winter he allows himself to tell his story several times, leaving out any mention of where it took place, but each time he feels less and less satisfied with his representations, and more and more vulgar for his misrepresentations, and disgusted at the "inadequate effect" on his listeners: "Some listened carelessly; some nervously; some incredulously, as if he were trying to put up a job on them; some compassionately, as if he were not quite right, and ought to be looked after. There was a consensus of opinion, among those who offered any sort of comment, that he ought to give it to the Psychical Research, and at the bottom of Hewson's heart, there was a dread that the spiritualists would somehow get hold of him" (25). Psychical Research, the society where professional psychologists like its former president William James discussed occult phenomena with other interested members, is equated with the professional spiritualists, the table-rappers and seance holders, and therefore we can assume that Hewson sees the researchers, too, as lacking in dignity. Only one woman adequately appreciates the meaning his apparition has for Hewson: the "spiritually slender," "nervous" Miss Hernshaw, a young woman he had met immediately after the event at his friend's estate.

One night at a dinner party Hewson meets Miss Hernshaw again, and they renew their agreement about the sacred quality of such experiences through a discussion of Henrik Ibsen's *Ghosts*, which was then playing in New York.[17] Howells also wrote *The Son of Royal Langbrith* during 1903, using the same basic situation as Ibsen's play, with important modifications, as well as an article on Ibsen printed in the *North American Review* after Ibsen's death in 1906. *Ghosts* is Ibsen at his darkest, a tragedy about inherited venereal disease, incest, adultery, corruption, and prostitution, and the play ends with the mother's piercing scream at finding the syphilitic body of her son after his suicide. Mention of Ibsen's play in "His Apparition" is one of the clear signposts Howells uses to cue readers to look for significance beyond that of the polite plot. For people who know Ibsen's play, the entire notion that Hewson's apparition is anything like a ghost becomes suspect, for in Ibsen's play there are no spectral ghosts, only the memory of evil and the effects of evil actions on future generations. Readers who do not know the play will unwittingly censor the illicit sexual connotations and move on to the next event as quickly as does the text, assuming that Hewson and Hernshaw were talking about a play about ghosts, about apparitions.

Their conversation is interrupted by Wanhope, a psychologist, who, himself apparently oblivious to the nature of the play and somewhat oblivious to the people around him, asserts that all the ghost stories he has ever heard are at third hand: he has heard of people who have known people who have seen ghosts, but he has never actually met a man who had seen a ghost. If he did, he said, he would be much more likely to believe in the possibility. Thus challenged, Hewson tries once more to tell his story, after which Wanhope "did not go back to his position that belief in ghosts should follow from seeing a man who had seen one; he seemed rather annoyed by the encounter" (45). Wanhope, who plays a more forceful role in the next two stories, plays the dupe here in being so obviously and easily ruffled, and the scene works to discount the possibility for a "professional" relation to the supernatural. Psychologists, like spiritualists and psychic researchers, prove inadequate.

Wanhope's name—"wan" suggests paleness due to illness or emotional distress, or a melancholy unhappiness, and is a convenient shorthand for neurasthenia—implies the pale hope of science in the face of such mysteries, and therefore the wan, one hope of all scientists. Hope is the only remaining recourse after the scientists and spiritualists are discounted. At the same time that Howells distances Hewson and Wanhope, he identifies them as well. At one point Hewson is described as falling "somewhat nervelessly back on Providence," or exactly as having a somewhat wan hope. This identification of Wanhope with Hewson is similar to the relation between Wanhope and Acton, the writer, in the second story, "The Angel of the Lord," and suggests a splitting of Howells, the writer, and Howells, one of the greatest psychologists of the age; it is also similar to that between Ardith, the young writer come east from the Midwest, and Binning, the voice of Boston and the "psychologist" in *Letters Home.* In the final story in *Questionable Shapes*, "Though One Rose from the Dead," Wanhope narrates in the first person, at least rhetorically resolving this split, but even here his narration is directed to Acton the writer.

Howells's view of the doubleness of consciousness is central to "His Apparition." A surface consciousness watches what is going on, but there is also a deeper consciousness, one which is less articulate, either for mysterious reasons or for reasons of propriety. When Hewson listens to his host's ironic story about his encounter, which leaves out any reference to the supernatural, the narrator tells us that "it was only [Hewson's] surface mind which was employed with what was going on; as before, his deeper thought was again absorbed with his great experience" (17). The surface mind is functioning socially, and the deeper mind is involved with the supernatural. At one point, Hewson is described as being "in a daze which was as strange a confusion of the two consciousnesses as he had ever experienced" (77). At this point in the story, his surface mind is attending to Miss Hernshaw's chaperone, and his "nether mind" to Miss Hernshaw herself. One effect of these two sentences is to separate the socially acceptable and the socially unacceptable into two different regions of the mind. As the formulation "nether mind" suggests, Howells creates a psychology based, fundamentally, on the idea of vulgarity.

The relation of this kind of psychological thinking to Freud's, especially given the sexual connotations of "nether" regions, should be obvious. It is possible that one of the difficulties for critics from the 1920s through the 1950s and later in seeing the importance of Howells's work is that his psychology, still new and exciting even for readers like William James and Björnson, had become such a common ground for various competing psychologies through the middle of this century that Howells seems not to take an interesting position at all. But to argue for two distinct consciousnesses at loggerheads with each other, one socially acceptable and one not, was a clear and still controversial position vis-à-vis the psychologies of his day, as we shall see in relation to Henry James and W. E. B. Du Bois. One could argue that Howells, in his notion of the two consciousnesses, was ahead of his time; I am more interested in arguing that Howells's psychology based on vulgarity is parallel to Freud's, constructed at the same time, with the same background of neurasthenic discourse and understanding and under similar cultural pressures, and that it might be used in a contextual study of the development of Freud's thought, as an aid in understanding the relation between the Freudian unconscious and Victorian consciousness. Both Freud and Howells relied on and argued against the theories of Beard and his followers.[18]

Another effect of this presentation of double consciousness in the story is to link Miss Hernshaw with Hewson's apparition once again. Miss Hernshaw is the only person Hewson tells about the exact circumstances of his "visitation." Miss Hernshaw retells the story, unwittingly in the presence of a correspondent to a newspaper, and the dreaded result follows: on publication of the story his host's house is depreciated to a tenth of its value. The shame Hewson feels is also represented in economic terms: "Hewson thought he had paid the principal of his debt in full through the hurt to his vanity in failing to gain any sort of consequence from his apparition, but the interest of his debt had accumulated, and the sorest pinch was in paying the interest" (50). Hewson does "the right thing" by his host and buys the estate at its former market value. Since she sees her own fault in the matter, Miss Hernshaw wants to buy the property herself, an intervention Hewson prevents. Hewson agrees with her when she says, "Of course I did not think—a girl wouldn't—of the effect it would have on the property" (84). Hewson and Hernshaw have come considerably closer, because of their relation to his apparition, and this closeness is represented as a similar relation to property, to the value of the host's estate.

The difference between them is one of gender, and it is this difference that decides Hewson's purchase; similarity in property combined with difference in gender results in chivalrous action. The chivalry does not free Miss Hernshaw from the web of property relations but leads instead directly to their marriage, which Hewson proposes by asking her to come with him to the estate he has just purchased. Miss Hernshaw is represented as a New Woman, one who is independent, says what she thinks, and is not answerable even to her own father: she is her own woman. Hewson has decided that she must be his, in the same way that the estate must become his and that the apparition is his. The title itself sets up a proprietary relation between the ghost and Hewson with the possessive pronoun. "His Apparition" remains his until the end, even after he marries and it in some sense becomes hers as well. "It had become so much her apparition that he had a fantastic reluctance from meddling with it" (104). If we read the apparition as related to Hewson's sexuality—it wakes him up in the middle of the night in the middle of his leisured bachelorhood and is resolved by marriage—then what he has done by the end is turn over control of his sexuality to her. Part of the fairy-tale character of the ending comes from the easy way in which the problems of shifting gender roles and those of the supernatural are resolved in marriage: the apparition is replaced by the "angel in the house," a figure linked both to the nether regions and to the supernatural.

At the beginning of the story, when Hewson first sees his apparition, he leaves the house to see if he can get a cup of coffee at the local inn, although it is still very early in the morning. There a "rude, sad girl," an "uncouth, melancholy waitress" serves him his coffee. He wonders if she has managed to wash her face and compares her "sloven dejection" to the "brisk neatness of the service at St. Johns-wort" (9, 10). Miss Hernshaw later takes up the waitress's defense when some of the guests make fun of her, and after this display of concern for girls "who have to work in that public sort of way," we hear no more about her. The "tragedy" of the girl's life, of girls who have to work in public, is particularly interesting in relation to Ibsen's play. In that play, the maid turns out to be the illegitimate daughter of the dissolute, and now dead, father of the household and a woman who worked "in a public sort of way." At the end of the play the daughter lays claim to part of the patrimony, which she had been unfairly denied, but she continues to angrily reject the hypocritical forms of the class above her. The maid's rejection is mirrored by Miss Hernshaw's rejection of her own class's hypocrisy, and Ibsen's maid and Howells's waitress add another dimension to our view of Miss Hernshaw's inheritance and Hewson's money, which he has acquired in his profession. "His acquisition" is of a different order from her patrimony, and even though disinheritance is not presented as a way of thinking about class, as it is in the Ibsen play, the somewhat uncanny appearance of the slovenly waitress adds a third term, a class unconscious, to what would otherwise be a standard representation of the relation of the new money to the old.

In addition, the phrase "His Apparition," given the subtext on the issue of an upper class in America, has echoes of such phrases as "His Excellency" or "His Lordship." Hewson's title to the property, given the way the American leisure class aped European nobility, was akin to having a title himself; perhaps, Howells seems to suggest, it should be the same as the title of the story. As in many of Howells's texts, the representational economy allows for two opposing readings simultaneously. In one sense, Hewson ends up the lord of a manor, the owner of an estate, and therefore fully equipped for his life in the class to which he aspired, he lives happily ever after. The story is a pleasant and innocuous one written for the kind of people it represents. At the same time, there is a sense in which the ironic portrayal of Hewson's dedication to the leisure class, which he later sees as vacuous and unfulfilling, undercuts this reading. The story charts the events in the lives of Hewson and Hernshaw over the course of more than a year, and so little happens that by the end of the story Hewson himself sees the life he had led before marrying as a waste of time and a series of empty forms. The only event of real interest in the vacuum of his life before marriage appears to have been the arrival of his apparition. "His Apparition" is never described, never fully cognized, and like the Emporer's new clothes, perhaps never existed. The story bristles with an irony that need not be read.[19]

The ending is a conversation between the newlyweds, again concerning the reason for the apparition's appearance. Hewson claims that it appeared in order to bring them together. His bride finds this blasphemous, finds it "out of proportion" for the occult to aid a "mere earthly love-affair." Hewson asks, "Is it merely for earth?" The new Mrs. Hewson replies, "Oh, husband, I hope you don't think so! I wanted you to say you didn't. And if you don't think so, yes, I'll believe it came for that!" (104–5) This could be read simply as an expression of belief in some kind of life after death, a further statement of belief in the occult. But since that belief has already been established, and since the phrase in contrast to the belief being expressed—"a mere earthly love-affair"—makes most sense in a Christian context (Howells, for instance, quotes Dante in the same book), we can assume that some kind of Christian afterlife is being invoked. The story finally, then, offers an appeal to conventional pieties. The supernatural enters human lives in order to marry confirmed bachelors (and therefore deliver them from temptation, including whatever temptation is represented by slovenly waitresses), and in order to provide an occasion for the profession of a mutual belief in Christian metaphysics. The bride's father had earlier suggested the same possibility in relation to the ghost: "If anything came to me that would help shore up my professed faith in what most of us want to believe in, I would take the common-law view of it. I would believe it was innocent till it proved itself guilty. I wouldn't try to make it out a fraud myself" (101–2).

This appeal to conventional piety is not one of simple conservatism, it is Howells's own "progressive" conclusion to the question of the relation of science and religion. Howells, who "vacillated between a despairing belief and a yearning hope," felt that to "meddle with things above" is to be "an arrogant ass," but "I *must* meddle with them, both in my own defective conduct and in the imagined lives of others." Howells's well-known championing of Tolstoy was based in part on Tolstoy's resolution of the question of belief into a notion of a social gospel. Like the pragmatists, Howells ended by believing that belief was not to be evaluated in terms of its relation to truth but instead in its relation to action. The meaning of the apparition, finally, has nothing to do with the true nature of the apparition but in its effects, in the way it can shore up belief and in the way such belief makes possible communal life, especially in its most elementary (for Howells) form, marriage.[20]

Thus though his characters appeal to a conventional piety, Howells's own religious conclusions are based in pragmatist and progressivist notions of social action rather than in a conservative retrenchment in faith. Of his main character, Howells writes: "Hewson might not have been in what he thought any stressful need of ghostly comfort or reassurance in matters of faith. He was not inordinately agnostic, or in the way of becoming so. He was simply an average skeptical American, who denied no more than he affirmed, and who really concerned himself so little about his soul, though he tried to keep his conscience decently clean, that he had not lately asked whether other people had such a thing or not" (29–30). This kind of healthy-mindedness in religious thinking was not exactly Howells's; as he has Frances Dennam say, "Some things are so sacred they make you sick." In his childhood the supernatural did quite literally make him sick with fear, and it was related in its "morbidity" to the hypochondria that led to his "nervous prostration" in 1856. Still, Howells at times saw himself as "an average skeptical American," and he, too, was not "inordinately agnostic." Hewson does not so much resemble Howells as he is represented in terms of an attitude Howells sometimes took to his own relation to the supernatural, a gentle and polite irony.[21]

In contrast to this irony, Howells also had had a well-documented fear of ghosts as a child and young man—he had had an "acute fear," a "special terror" of ghosts—and his autobiographical writings list episode after episode of terror of the supernatural, of his inability to walk past a tombstone-cutting shop, of having to be walked home instead of spending the night with a group of boys because he could not listen to their ghost stories, of being shaken "to the bottom of his soul" by a painting of Death. He writes of leading a "kind of double life" as a child, learning to hide his "riot of emotions behind the child's shy silence." The analysis of double consciousness in "His Apparition" does very little to suggest the horror and abhorrence Howells describes as his own relation to the supernatural: it suggests the ironic distance an adult has over childhood fears rather than the exciting cause of nervous prostration. And it does little to suggest the kind of concern Howells had throughout his life with religion.[22]

Howells wrote throughout his career about the relation of the supernatural to the kinds of professional inquiry he rejects in "His Apparition"; he had formulated the basic thesis of the story as early as 1875 in an article in the *Atlantic Monthly*: "In those fond dreams of a future life which some of us still furtively indulge, despite the hard skeptic air of our science-smitten age, nothing is more dismaying than the chaos which the conditions of eternal life seem to make of all our mortal relations." "His Apparition" shows how the supernatural can provide order rather than chaos in "mortal relations." The best way, the story seems to suggest, is not to meddle, not to question too thoroughly, to leave the question of doctrine, the question of the true nature of the supernatural, as vague as possible and reap whatever benefits one's relation to the supernatural might offer.[23] Metaphysical questions remain unanswered in favor of a pragmatic economics of belief.

Uncanny Coincidences

"The Angel of the Lord" begins where "His Apparition" leaves off, for just as the conclusion of that story denies that the apparition *is* anything except its effects, therefore denying doctrine in favor of action, "The Angel of the Lord" begins with a central problem in doctrinal thought, the personification of God. Wanhope, the psychologist, is holding forth at the club about what he calls the "primitive habit of personification." The story that follows is one example of what Wanhope sees as the continuance of this primitive thinking ("intensified in the more delicate temperaments" through time), a story of the clearly neurasthenic Ormond, who believed that the angel of death came to him in the form of an old tramp. It also continues the discourse on class, partly in the form of the tramp and partly in the form of Rulledge, one of Wanhope's auditors, who continually barks at Wanhope to "get down to business" and to get on with the story, since "we've no time to throw away!" "Being of no employment whatever," the narrator tells us in a sentence whose irony invokes neurasthenic discourse as well as the work ethic, "and spending his whole life at the club in an extraordinary idleness, Rulledge was always using the most strenuous expressions, and requiring everybody to be practical" (110). The story also continues the critique of professional inquiry in the fine distinctions Wanhope makes among psychologists, alienists, pathologists, and other doctors, distinctions that simply exasperate Rulledge and the others (117–18, 124). And it continues the investigation of the two consciousnesses, as when Wanhope states, for instance, that "though such a [personified] notion of death no longer survives in the consciousness, it does survive in the unconsciousness, and . . . any vivid accident or illusory suggestion would have the force to bring it to the surface" (115).

Just as Durkheim and Beard regarded neurasthenia as "elementary insanity," alienists would recognize Ormond's delusions, Wanhope asserts, "as one of the beginnings of insanity—*folie des grandeurs* as the French call the stage" (124). Howells clearly has a historicized notion of a disease like neurasthenia (and *folie des grandeurs*, for that matter), hence one of our clues to Wanhope's pomposity. Emotions themselves are historically conditioned, for as Wanhope says in an aside, the works of Laurence Sterne and Henry Mackenzie are "full of feeling, as people understood feeling a hundred years ago." At one point Wanhope meditates on a phrase of Mrs. Ormond's:

> Of course she thought he must be going to have a fit of sickness, as the people say in the country, or used to say. Those expressions often survive in the common parlance long after the peculiar mental and moral conditions in which they have originated have passed away. They must have once been more accurate than they are now. When one said "fit of sickness" one must have meant something specific; it would be interesting to know what. Women use those expressions longer than men; they seem to be inveterate in their nerves; and women apparently do their thinking in their nerves rather than their brains. (128)

Wanhope, though he adopts his own time's ahistorical view of the relation of gender to nerves ("Poor women!" he says. "They are always in double the danger that men are, and their nerves double that danger again" [138]), clearly has a historicized notion of nervous sickness in general.

Ormond's nervous sickness took a somewhat peculiar turn in that, after a long period of neurasthenic depression, he suddenly became quite happy. "I don't know why we shouldn't sometimes, in the absence of proofs to the contrary, give such a fact the chance to evince a spiritual import," says Wanhope. "Of course it had no other import to poor Mrs. Ormond, and of course I didn't dream of suggesting a scientific significance. . . . In view of what afterward happened, she regarded it as the effect of a mystical intimation from another world that was sacred, and could not be considered like an ordinary fact without sacrilege" (125). We are prompted to see the antineurasthenic development of Ormond's happiness as humorous by the response of a Holmesian doctor Mrs. Ormond consults, who "wrote back that if Ormond was so very happy they had better not do anything to cure him; that the disease was not infectious, and was seldom fatal" (131–32). Ormond's happiness is somewhat romantic, for he makes a religion out of nature: "His nature took hold upon what we call nature, and he clung fondly to the lowly and familiar aspects of it" (139). But his expression of his happiness is clearly fin de siècle: " 'I seem to have got to the end of my troubles. I haven't a care in the world, Jenny. . . . It sounds like nonsense, of course, it seems to me that I have found out the reason of things, though I don't know what it is. Maybe I've only found out that there *is* a reason of things. That would be enough, wouldn't it?' " (135). As in the case of "His Apparition," in which a purpose need not be defined to be a purpose and the ineffable quality of the supernatural is proof of its purposiveness, Ormond has come to a conclusion that both accepts and refuses to define the supernatural as purpose and fact. Ormond's belief—unlike, for instance, that of Norris's and Dreiser's mystical characters—is directly in opposition to naturalism. When Ormond reads the Old Testament, "there were some turns or phrases in it that peculiarly took his fancy and seemed to feed it with inexhaustible suggestion. 'The Angel of the Lord' was one of these. The idea of a divine messenger, embodied and commissioned to intimate the creative will to the creature: it was sublime, it was ineffable. He wondered that men had ever come to think in any other terms of the living law that we were under, and that could much less conceivably operate like an insensate mechanism than it could reveal itself as a constant purpose" (141).

Soon thereafter, however, Ormond starts to go wrong, for he decides that a tramp who shows up at their door in the country may be the very angel of the Lord that he has been reading about. This move from a figural and pragmatic interpretation to a literal and specific interpretation of scripture is the true mark, for Howells, of Ormond's *folie des grandeurs*, the standard theological mistake of a "sign-seeking generation." He has become "an arrogant ass," as Howells thought one must become when one strayed from the "earthly plane."[24] Ormond finally goes chasing after the tramp and, tripping and smashing his head on a rock just as he reaches him, dies at the tramp's feet. The violence of this ending to the anecdote, whether uncanny or slapstick, belies an anxiety stronger than we would expect Howells to evince about the interpretation of scripture. In Howells's Tolstoyan Christianity, poverty should be seen as a messenger from God, and therefore the tramp would necessarily be "commissioned to intimate the creative will to the creature" (143). But why must Ormond die if he is right?

Part of the answer lies in the incidents that occur between Ormond's meeting the tramp and his headlong rush to death at the tramp's feet. When the tramp first appears, Ormond tells his wife that "the fellow might be an angel of the Lord, and he asked her if she remembered Parnell's poem of 'The Hermit.' Of course she didn't, but he needn't get it, for she didn't want to hear it, and if he kept making her so nervous, she should be sick herself" (143). The incident immediately forces a contest, and the threat of sickness is Mrs. Ormond's counter both to his sickness and to his literary authority. This contest continues through the next five pages of text, with the Ormonds bickering in a way that Wanhope's auditors at the club recognize as the Ormonds' normal relations. Wanhope claims that Mrs. Ormond had admitted to him that they had "always quarreled a good deal. She seemed to think it was a token of their perfect unity. . . . I'm not sure that there wasn't something in the notion. . . . There is something curious in the bickerings of married people if they are in love. It's a way of having no concealments; it's perfect confidence of a kind—" (120). The "dark side" of marriage, which Howells's critics have recently written of in terms of a "terrifying uneasiness," of "sexual panic and frustration," and of the "bitterest anguish" concealed in even "the happiest marriage" is what intervenes between Ormond's joyous conversion and his running headfirst into a rock. Thomas Parnell's allegorical poem "The Hermit" was often reprinted in the nineteenth century as a pamphlet by tract societies. The story of a hermit's incomprehension of evil in the world is resolved by an angel, who explains that apparent evil is often God's will, whether to function as retributive justice or moral lesson, as when the angel murders the child of a doting parent to keep him from the evils of doting. Ormond jokes about the poem, claiming that maybe the angel-tramp might murder them to "save them from mischief." The text, through Wanhope's meliorative explanation, and through putting the criticisms of the Ormonds's bickerings in the mouths of the least sympathetic auditors, undercuts whatever criticism of the married state is implied, but the plot and the reference to Parnell inexorably indicts Mrs. Ormond's nagging for her husband's death.[25]

The events also call into question the very Tolstoyan Christianity with which Howells elsewhere is in such strong agreement. If Howells eschews the possibility of substantiating the insubstantial, as he clearly does in "His Apparition," for instance, then the idea of a heavenly messenger must also be eschewed. The tramp is not, in fact, the bearer of a message about Christian service but instead, as it turns out, functions as an unwitting and unconscious angel of death. The tramp's poverty and need—and the threat he represents to Mrs. Ormond—mark him as a symbol of class oppression. Tramps were, in fact, conventional symbols (as the homeless are today) of the severity and systemic intractability of the condition of the underclass. This was especially true for writers espousing the social gospel or socialism, as in Harold Bell Wright's *That Printer of Udell's* (1903) or several of Jack London's works. Howells imported a notion of class-based social responsibility from Europe, especially in the form of Tolstoy's novels and essays, but his version of it also had much in common with the social gospel preached by Washington Gladden and others and with American versions of socialism like London's. The tramp is a straight man in this black comedy, and the clubby talk of Wanhope and his dilettante friends simply heightens the grotesquerie of having a happily religious man career to his death running after a tramp he has mistaken for an angel, simply to ask the tramp about the whereabouts of his wife's hat. And finally any discourse on class, as it was in "His Apparition" (and in *A Hazard of New Fortunes*, among other works), is given second place to the discourse on marriage. In the first story marriage was represented as a purpose for the supernatural and a beginning of the safe life; here it is represented as a hindrance to supernatural experience and a danger to life itself. Given Howells's contention that in old age one is too tired to fight the ills of the world, and given his problems living for forty years with an invalid wife, "The Angel of the Lord" might have been a strong statement about the way in which religious energy, whether in the form of mysticism or social action in response to class injustice, is sapped by the "dark side" of marriage. This conclusion, however, is not demanded by the text by any means. At the end of the story, as in the end of "His Apparition," no specific resolution is offered to the questions raised, and narrative closure is effected by investing the ambiguity in the person of the professional. The last words are Wanhope's answer to a question about what his own conclusion to the story might be: he responds, simply, "Why, I haven't formulated it yet" (156).

Literary Guidance

In the third story, "Though One Rose from the Dead," which opens with a reference to William James's *Will to Believe*, Wanhope relates the story of Mr. and Mrs. Alderling's marriage to a writer, Acton, thus giving Howells an opportunity to comment on the difference between the literary and the psychological professions. The Alderlings, it seems, are able to exercise a kind of telepathy. As in *The Undiscovered Country* (1880), Howells uses telepathy as a metaphor for domination within sexual relations, since one person's suggestion controls another's response. But as in the case of the Ormonds' quarreling, a plea is also made for the normalcy of the Alderlings's relationship. Their telepathy—"the thought-transferences, and the unconscious hypnotic suggestions which they made to each other" (181)—is not strange, says Alderling, it is a part of the relationship of any married couple: "They pervade each other's minds, if they are really married, and they are so present with each other that the tacit wish should be the same as a call. Marion and I are only an intensified instance of what may be done by living together" (171).

But Wanhope notices that Mr. Alderling so controls Mrs. Alderling that she seems not to have any will of her own. One mark of this relinquishing of her own will is the fact that when they met they were both painters, but now only Alderling paints, and his wife sits for him. After some prodding from Wanhope, who suggests to Acton that Mrs. Alderling was in fact the better painter, Alderling himself admits his wife's abjection: "You know how some women, when they are married, absolutely give themselves up, try to lose themselves in the behoof of their husbands? I don't say it rightly; there are no words that will express the utterness of their abdication" (209). Wanhope tries again to construct a meliorative generalization to account for this abjection: "Such a woman's being is a cycle of self-sacrifice, so perfect, so essential, from birth to death, as to exclude the notion of volition. She is what she does." But he cannot approve, finally, of this unconscious pragmatism: "It appears pathetic when it is met with ingratitude or rejection, but when it has its way it is no more deserving our reverence than eating or sleeping. It astonishes men because they are as naturally incapable of it as women are capable of it" (209–10). Despite this attempt at contempt, Wanhope reproduces

Victorian notions of feminine passivity and feminine spirituality, since Wanhope's psychological analysis (itself a codification of the acceptable) is based, significantly, entirely on his conversation with Mr. Alderling. Wanhope "perceives" that it would be impossible to speak with Mrs. Alderling: "I perceived, in a manner, that her life was so largely subliminal that if she had tried she could not have met my question any more than if she had not the gift of speech at all" (177). At one point he even concludes that the problem with Mrs. Alderling is that she has been away from "society": "She could only have been entirely herself in society, where, in spite of everything that can be said against it, we can each, if we will, be more natural than out of it" (185).

As in the other two stories, the plot provides a counterpoint to the positions offered by the participants. The ability the Alderlings have to read each other—"I could always see them studying each other," says Wanhope, "he with an eye to her beauty, she with an eye to his power" (180)—becomes more and more oppressive for both parties. Mrs. Alderling, in compensation, overeats, and her overeating verges on the vulgar and therefore verges on the province of the psychologist. When she reads her husband's mind she sometimes follows "him into the recesses of his reveries, where it is best for a man to be alone, even if he is sometimes a beast there" (180); in other words, the supernatural again confronts a problem of vulgarity, here the natural beastliness of a man's inner life. In compensation Alderling paints his wife as the Madonna, the most clearly gendered religious symbol in the West.

One day when Mrs. Alderling goes out rowing and swimming on the cove, a fog rolls in, and Mr. Alderling, working in his studio, inexplicably jumps up, shouts "I'm coming" and runs down to the cove to save her. Wanhope is clearly impressed by Alderling's telepathic response, but hearing them call to each other in the fog, he can't help but wonder why their telepathy does not continue to work at this crucial time. They arrive back to shore safely, but within a short time she dies of typhoid fever. Alderling has a neurasthenic reaction and becomes morose and miserable. When Wanhope goes back to visit him, he finds him living in a melancholy and mechanical way, still brooding about his wife. He leaves the door open for her and the lights lit at night, and always sets a plate for her at table. He and Wanhope have long conversations about the question of life after death, which Alderling begins by affirming and ends by denying. Wanhope, too, would deny the possibility, except that, as he says, "men like James and Royce, among the psychologists, and Shaler, among the scientists, scarcely leave us at peace in our doubts, any more, much less our denials" (204). Alderling's neurasthenic depression is caused by the fact that he cannot believe and cannot deny.

Wanhope tells Acton, his literary amanuensis, that this, Alderling's neurasthenic lack of will to believe, should mark the end of the story, just as his reference to William James began it:

> Of course you know your own business, my dear Acton, but if you think of using the story of the Alderlings . . . it seems to me that here is your true climax. But I necessarily leave the matter to you, for I shall not touch it at any point where we could come into competition. In fact, I doubt if I ever touch it at all, for though all psychology is in a manner dealing with the occult, still I think I have done my duty by that side of it, as the occult is usually understood; and I am shy of its grosser instances, as things that are apt to bring one's scientific poise into question. (215)

Wanhope does not want to compete, he says, with his brother professional, the writer, and he does not want to bring his "scientific poise" into question by providing evidence for the occult. But, he continues, the story has another possible ending: as he and Alderling were involved in a discussion of the existence of an afterlife, Alderling, with no provocation that Wanhope can identify, again jumped up yelling "I'm coming!" and ran out into the cove where he promptly drowned. "I have a sort of shame for the aptness of the catastrophe," says Wanhope. "I shall respect you more if I hear that you agree with me as to the true climax of the tragedy, and have the heroism to reject the final event" (216).

There is a self-reflexive irony here as the writer (Acton, Howells) is held accountable for his lack of taste, or lack of "heroism," for he chooses the second ending. The idea that maintaining the indecisiveness of neurasthenia is itself a heroic stance, as opposed to a will to believe that is unjustified or "shamefully apt," had some currency in 1903—it is represented by the fin de siècle writers, Saltus and Pollard for instance, and by Thomas Eakins, who painted neurasthenic portraits and tried to show, in the suffering faces of his sitters, whom he often painted as older and more sick than they actually were, the "heroism of modern life."[26] On the other hand, the fact that the writer ignores Wanhope's suggestion and tells the end of the story implies a criticism of Wanhope, and thereby of psychology. Wanhope wants to leave the question poised in terms of the questionable shape of Alderling's psyche; the ending adds a tragic conclusion to the inability to decide and leaves a more serious doubt about the meaning of the entire story. The ending is not vulgar, it is simply melodramatic,

and Wanhope's distaste for it is therefore not justified. The melodramatic, as Howells knew it, was a necessary part of any adequate
psychology in 1903, and the melodrama of the Alderlings' lives, and
the relation of their lives to the occult, was not at all abnormal, as
far as he was concerned. Wanhope, in a cue early in the story, tells
us in effect not to read this as a ghost story, but as a story of the
"everyday life" of lovers and of readers:

> Of course I know that lovers are the life of fiction, and that a story
> of any kind can scarcely hold the reader without them. The love-
> interest, as they call it, is also supposed to be essential to the drama.
> ... Yet lovers in real life are, so far as I have observed them, bores.
> They are confessed to be disgusting before or after marriage when
> they let their fondness appear, but even when they try to hide it,
> they are tiresome. Character goes down before passion in them;
> nature is reduced to propensity. Then, how is it that the novelist
> manages to keep these, and give us nature and character while seem-
> ing to offer nothing but propensity and passion? Perhaps he does
> not give them. Perhaps what he does is to hypnotize us so that we
> each of us identify ourselves with the lovers, and add our own natures
> and characters to the single principle that animates them. The rea-
> son we like, that we endure, to read about them, may be that they
> are ourselves rendered objective in an instant of intense vitality,
> without the least trouble or risk to us. (161–62)

Melodrama invites identification without risk. "Ourselves rendered
objective," given a psychology with an unconscious vulgarity, is an
inherently dangerous proposition, but because of the banality of our
propensities and passions, the banality of lovers, and the banality of
a reader hypnotized by fiction, there is not "the least trouble or risk."
The encounter with fiction is here represented as therapeutic, since
like a psychologist the fictionist "hypnotizes" the client; thus though
Wanhope chooses not to compete with the writer, the writer necessarily competes with the psychologist.

The decision of Acton and Howells to use the melodramatic conclusion, in light of Wanhope's comments, can be better understood
in terms of Howells's major statement about the relation of the writer
to his market, "The Man of Letters as a Man of Business," published
in book form the year before.[27] The article starts with the sentence
"I think every man ought to work for his living" and goes on to discuss
how this applies to writers. Howells claims that he has never met a
publisher who was a rogue, but that he has heard of other people
who have, "just as I have heard of people seeing ghosts, and I have to

believe in both the rogues and the ghosts, without the witness of my own senses" (18). This statement may be pointedly disingenuous, since Howells aligns writers not with rogue capitalists like publishers but with workers. Writers and artists are laborers because they are producers, unlike businessmen, who manage and finance production but do not produce anything themselves and who eat from the "sweat of other men's brows." Howells wants artists and writers to recognize that "economically they are the same as mechanics, farmers, and day-laborers" and "to feel the tie that binds us to all the toilers of the shop and field, not as a galling chain, but as a mystic bond also uniting us to Him who works hitherto and evermore" (34). When Acton has no "shame" in the aptness of the ending, he is not, we can assume, just giving in to the romantic proclivities of his audience. He is announcing, for Howells, as the self-reflexivity of *Letters Home* announces, the fictionality of the account, the *produced* nature of the anecdote. The fact that self-reflexivity thematizes the productive professionalism of literary activity accounts for its rise at a time when that productivity was in question.

The self-reflexivity of Acton's lack of shame also suggests that the problem in the marriage of the Alderlings runs deep—given that her obsession with his power finally kills him—and that the "mystic bond" is as dangerous as marriage itself. The struggle for dominance is not over until they are both dead, and this, we are told by Wanhope, is the condition of all married couples. We both do and don't believe Wanhope, then, when he explains away the morbidity of the story of the Alderlings: "The thing was not quite what we call uncanny," he states. "The people were so honest, both of them, that the morbid character of like situations was wanting" (182). Wanhope in effect denies that the marriage of the Alderlings had its telepathic basis in a struggle for power and denies that the story is uncanny. The rest of the story makes clear that Wanhope is wrong—the issue is not one of James's notion of the will to believe, but one of Nietzsche's cor-responding notion of a will to power. The will to power of the Alder-lings, represented in the text in oblique relation to a traditional, gendered deference, is parallel to the will to power represented by Acton, the writer, in his deferential—we don't even hear Acton's voice—debate with his professional rival in the business of repre-senting the psychic economy. In equating beauty and power ("he with an eye to her beauty, she with an eye to his power"), the literary man and the psychologist are also equated, since psychology is based on nerve force just as literary art is based on beauty, and they therefore compete as equals for their market share of the economy of representation. And in so doing they take their different paths to the embrace and banishment of the uncanny.

Questionable Relations

In February 1903, Howells wrote that he was writing a novel "and feeling so much more interest in it than any reader will ever take that it is quite ridiculous. It is sort of a shame to be yarning away at my age," he continued, "but I might be doing worse things. I have got a good name for it from the old Tuscan proverb, '*Iddio non paga sabato*'; 'God does not pay Saturdays.' "[28] That title was rejected by the publisher in favor of *The Son of Royal Langbrith*. The stories in *Questionable Shapes* flirted with the uncanny as an unconscious struggle for domestic power, they and *Letters Home* talked around a class unconscious, but in *The Son of Royal Langbrith*, the novel Howells was writing in 1903, the uncanny and the unconscious come home to roost. In *Letters Home* the class issue centers on the relation of new money to old, and the lower classes are represented primarily as a way for noblesse oblige to manifest itself. In *Questionable Shapes*, the first story represents marriage as a cure for leisure, the second shows class domination forced into the unconscious by marriage, the third represents marriage as unconscious of its own relation to domination, and thus the stories of the occult display the gradual displacement of the lower classes in favor of the *unheimlich*. In Howells's work, class issues are regularly drummed into the background by the importunities of marriage and the proprieties of the family.

The Son of Royal Langbrith takes as its donnée the situation of Ibsen's *Ghosts*. In the novel, as in Ibsen's play, a son has been kept in the dark about his philandering father, and in both cases a weak-willed mother allows the son's ignorance to continue. In both pieces, a philanthropic project is inaugurated as a memorial to the deceased father, and in both pieces, the son finally learns the truth about his father. But here the similarities stop. In Ibsen's play, the son finds that he has inherited venereal disease from his father and that he is in love with the maid, who turns out to be his father's illegitimate child, his half-sister; the orphanage that was meant as the philanthropic memorial is burned to the ground with the aid of the director of the project, the local minister, who is working an insurance scam. The son's suicide provides the conclusion to a play of unremitting tragedy and evil. In Howells's novel, the duplicitous minister has been replaced by a wise medical doctor of unimpeachable integrity, the son has no disease and marries a "good girl," the memorial library, everyone in the novel agrees, is a fit and at any rate useful result of the father's life, and the fact of his illicit sexual spending and illegitimate children is kept a family secret. The *unheimlich*, in Howells's writing, remains a subtext, a wrinkle in the orderly recreation of the domestic sphere. It need not be brought to consciousness, because Howells's moral psychology is pragmatic: Royal Langbrith built a library, and that is good; he hurt people, but they are dead and so there are no longer observable results of his evil.

Howells's version takes a specific disease, syphilis, with a clear origin and translates it into a widely disseminated neurasthenia. It is unclear how often a diagnosis of neurasthenia in America was a cover for syphilis. Freud, in his case studies, is always careful to assert that all possibilities of an organic, especially syphilitic, cause of the symptoms had been investigated. But the question is rarely addressed in the American literature on neurasthenia. Beard, for example, in one paragraph on syphilis claims that the symptoms of the disease are becoming milder because its affects on a "nervous constitution" are less "furious and dangerous." Something called "nervous syphilis" is more common as well, he asserted, and is almost impossible to diagnose as other than neurasthenia without knowing "the history of the case." The section that immediately follows discusses the fact that nervousness can be inherited. But the huge literature on neurasthenia rarely refers more specifically to the problems these undoubtedly common alternative diagnoses posed for doctors and patients. Even though the fear of syphilitic contagion was not as central to the public discourse of sexuality in America as it was in England and elsewhere in Europe, some doctors in the late nineteenth century estimated that one out of every twenty people in the United States had the disease. Still, nerve specialists Beard, Mitchell, and others largely ignored it in their writings for lay audiences.[29] Howells's reversal of Ibsen's text parallels the denial of the prevalence of syphilis by that part of the medical profession which saw one its primary purposes as replacing the pulpit in providing moral advice for everyday living: propriety served as a replacement for other possible notions of responsibility in the same way that neurasthenia served as a denial of the will.

Just as doctors had replaced ministers in America, the doctor in *The Son of Royal Langbrith* replaces the minister of Ibsen's version. Doctor Anther is looked to in the community as a sage authority on topics ranging from love to ethics. S. Weir Mitchell, writer of "lay sermons," praised Howells's portrayal of the good doctor and espe-

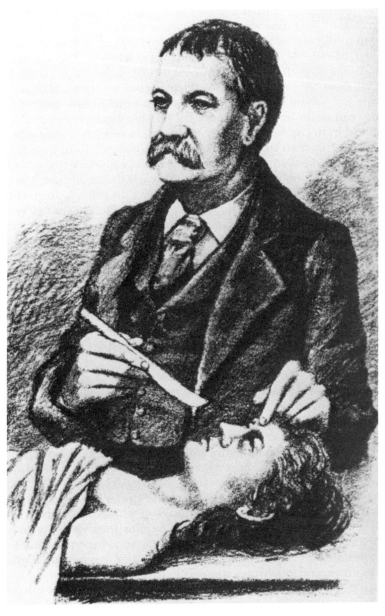

"William Dean Howells: Demonstrator of the American Girl," *Tid-Bits*, May 1, 1886. The novelist and medical doctor competed for cultural authority. (General Research Division, The New York Public Library; Astor, Lenox, and Tilden Foundations)

cially appreciated Anther's "noble sermons" and his name. Howells agreed that the name was a "fortunate invention."[30] An anther is the organ at the end of a flower's stamen that produces and discharges pollen, in other words, it is the male part of a flower. The sexual connotations of such a name seem more fitting for the philandering father than the chaste bachelor doctor, until we realize that Anther is the type of the vigorous, moral Victorian gentleman. Anther's potency can be assumed from the vigor and hardiness of the rest of his life and from the fact that after all his years as a bachelor he is still interested in marrying Royal Langbrith's widow. Royal Langbrith's vigor, we can assume, used itself up through his wasteful spending of seed and probably contributed to his early death. Anther, the doctor, then, is the truly potent man not only *in addition to* the fact that he is the truly moral man, but *because* of that fact. Nevertheless, the name is odd, since the anther's production of pollen is indiscriminate. The authors so fond of the name anther are also fond of broad dissemination, but the imagery points to the complex motivations of the late Victorian understanding of the relation of potency to sexual continence.

The doctor's moral strength is in direct contrast to the weakness of his patients, a point Mitchell makes continually in *Doctor and Patient*. Anther, for instance, "realized more and more that he had been having to do with weakness, and he realized this not in contempt of weakness, but in the compassion which was the constant lesson of his calling." Anther's quasi-religious calling leaves him with both a spiritual understanding of medicine and a medical understanding of the soul. Anther had "learned patience and mercy from his acquaintance with disease; and he had learned to distinguish between what was disease and what was an innate fault which no drugs, whether for the soul or body, could medicine" (300). Howells here makes the necessary connection between a psychology of vulgarity and a therapeutic view of character; in the person of Dr. Anther we can see the arrival of therapeutic culture in the bosom of Victorian values. A man can be the victim of forces of which he is unconscious, Anther and Howells tell us, as James Langbrith is victim of his unconsciousness of his father's past. But once he becomes conscious, in a formulation of the problem parallel to that of psychoanalysis, he is to an extent freed from its power. Howells and Anther go a step further, however, and state that while unconsciousness mitigates responsibility, consciousness implies total responsibility: "Up to a certain moment in every evil predicament men are victims of it, and after that, if they continue in it they are its agents, though as little its masters as before" (334).

Again, as in Howells's other stories, the working class is palpably present in the background, but the problems of class conflict are ignored in favor of attempts to work out the moral dilemmas of upper-class characters, moral dilemmas that center on issues of sexual propriety. Through the first half of the novel, when readers do not yet know what the crime of Royal Langbrith might have been, the possibility that his crime was purely economic is constantly suggested. He married his wife, whom he abused mercilessly, off the factory floor perhaps because she promised to be relatively inexpensive. He ruined his partner, Hawberk, and helped turn him into an opium addict, stealing Hawberk's half of the business and leaving his family impoverished. His former friends assume that his employees, especially the factory workers, might violently resent the building of a memorial to his honor. In the end, though, the workers agree that the memorial library is a great thing for the town, that the factory, however oppressive, brought whatever prosperity they had experienced, and that therefore they should perhaps be grateful to Royal Langbrith's memory. The evil of economic exploitation (and the text only implies such an indictment), is finally secondary to the evil of his sexual immorality, for which none of those few who know will forgive his memory. Nevertheless, his sexual crimes are kept secret so that the dedication and opening of the library can proceed, and this pious act of cultural dissemination manages the repression of class antagonisms and of sexual impropriety at the same time.

Langbrith's economic activity has so benefited everyone that it is necessary to hush up his illicit sexual activity for "the good of the town," and so Langbrith is forgiven in public but condemned privately by his family, intimates, and those in the know. The economy requires, somehow, the privatization of both rapacity and sexual morality. Whatever is *unheimlich* must necessarily remain in the home. The ghosts of Ibsen destroy homes and families, but while in Howells's work questionable shapes lurk in the background of marriages and families, they need not be destructive. Ibsen was recording the passing of a class in Europe, but Howells, despite his genuine horror at class oppression, was helping to create the cultural frame for the hegemonic power of the new dominant class in America. Like Hewson, he had dedicated his life to that class and its formation. "God does not pay Saturdays," went Howells's motto, at a time when those who worked on Saturday were of another class than those that rested on Saturdays, and in fact rested sometimes for years at a stretch. The motto, which Howells loved and which apparently no one else understood, sums up the complex consciousness Howells had of the relation of economic oppression to the leisure class, at the same time that it rests the problem itself, somehow, squarely on the shoulders of a God whose existence Howells was not willing to admit or refute.

6 Local Color,

Mary E. Wilkins Freeman,

and the Limits of Propriety

> You yourself have given the undoubted cause of the general nervous condition. I know of nothing that is worse for a girl than to have nothing to do. I would advise you to take up something as quickly as possible.
>
> —Dr. Emma Walker, M.D., "Hints about Good Health for Girls" (1903)

Local-color fiction, not surprisingly, is often the site of local critiques. Many local-color writers had local projects, and western writers such as Mary Austin and Andy Adams had a very different relation to neurasthenic discourse than eastern writers such as Sarah Orne Jewett and Mary Wilkins Freeman. In 1903 Jewett was suffering from what one critic claims were the "crippling effects, both physical and psychological," of a fall from a carriage, and though she continued to write letters, she never again wrote fiction.[1] In her work she often detailed New Englanders' neurasthenic attitudes toward health and medicine, and, as in the case of "The Passing of Sister Barsett" (1893), a tale of nervous hypochondria, she often ridiculed healthy-minded religion as an inadequate solution to the problems of a "nerve-shaken" world. When Edith Wharton wrote her New England local-color novel, *Ethan Frome* (1911), she returned to a neurasthenic mood and plot she had otherwise abandoned, and the neurasthenic protagonists in the local-color stories of Hamlin Garland in *Main-Travelled Roads*, although western in setting, bear the mark of his time in New England.

The western local colorists eschew both the ghost story and the neurasthenic indecision of the eastern writers in favor of healthy-minded religion and a common-sense naturalism closer to that of Emerson than that of Norris. Mary Austin came to writing "languid with convalescence" and experienced, during what was effectively a writing cure, a visitation: "As I wrote, two tall invisible presences came and stood on either side ... I suppose they were projections."[2] Nevertheless, Austin's *Land of Little Rain* (1903) combines a natu-

200

ralist's attention to flora and fauna with a conventional, if slightly mystical, piety.[3] It is "plain religion" that she respects in El Pueblo de Las Uvas, a town where people live in earth houses close to the natural processes of the earth. "Your earth-born is a poet and a symbolist. We breed in an environment of asphalt pavements a body of people whose creeds are chiefly restrictions against other people's way of life," Austin claims, and as an antidote to this overcivilized religion she offers to take her readers away to "the brown valleys and full-bosomed hills, to the even-breathing days, to the kindliness, earthiness, ease of El Pueblo de Las Uvas." (279–81). As with Roosevelt, naturalist classification and description—"the visible manifestation of the Spirit"—are at one with a healthy-minded religion; Austin reminds us that John Muir, who knows more of nature than most, "is a devout man" (247). And as Roosevelt and Muir both believed, immersion in nature and naturalist activity helped create the "ease" required by the overcivilized. Austin's project was to help protect the Southwest from predatory eastern business activity, and in this she was part of the conservationist movement, as were Muir and Roosevelt. To present the unspoiled Southwest as a cure for civilization denied its availability as an exploitable resource in other ways.

Andy Adams published *The Log of the Cowboy* in 1903, a book in the local-color tradition about cattle trail drivers in the 1880s, at the time that Roosevelt had his cattle ranch in the Dakota Territory.[4] Unlike Wister's *Virginian*, Adams's book is considered to be the most realistic account of cowboy life produced at the time. Adams went on to write cowboy novels, including *The Texas Matchmaker*, that followed a Wisterian formula, but *The Log of the Cowboy*, like Austin's *Land of Little Rain* (and Sarah Orne Jewett's *The Country of the Pointed Firs* [1896]), is hard to classify generically except as local-color prose. Like Roosevelt, Adams rejects "the blues" in favor of exercise and healthy-minded religion. Adams relates a story of cowhands sitting around a campfire telling "gloomy tales." The gloom depressed the men, and although one tried to make light of it—"At last Rod Wheat spoke up and said that in order to get the benefit of all the variations, the blues were not a bad thing to have"—the others fell under the spell and the "depression of [their] spirits was not so easily dismissed." Another cowhand began to tell a very long story about an itinerant cook who made mountains of doughnuts, but the story is interrupted when the herd begins to stampede. As the men jumped to their horses to try to control the dangerous and costly hysteria of the cattle, "All the fine sentiment and melancholy of the hour previous vanished in a moment, as the men threw themselves

into their saddles, riding deep, for it was uncertain footing to horses"
(275–86).

As Roosevelt had learned in a similar way, "black care," like Howells's "black heart's truth" can be banished by furious action or by intense work. The cowboys' work does not eliminate the uncertainty of the situation, for the horses still have treacherous footing; in fact, the gloomy stories had begun immediately after the men buried a hand that had fallen from his horse the same day. Still, the stampede itself occurred because the cattle had not been properly watered and bedded down. The cowboys had shirked work because they were blue; they told stories that made them gloomier; the gloom led to more gloom; and the missed work caused even more disaster. In the culture of Andy Adams's cowboys, "the blues" may be some benefit in giving one a sense of "all the variations," but they are otherwise unmanly and unwise. Adams's only excursion into religion is a description of another funeral service in which the minister's discussion of life, suffering, and the mystery of death leads to a healthy-minded notion of a correspondence between earthly life and the afterlife (303–6).

Theodore Dreiser, Hamlin Garland, Edith Wharton, Frank Norris, William Dean Howells, and Mary Wilkins Freeman all suffered neurasthenic symptoms and all published writings about the supernatural. The politically active neurasthenics, like Theodore Roosevelt, Emma Goldman, Jack London, Jane Addams, and Henry Adams, wrote little if anything about the supernatural, except Henry Adams, who, when his own involvement with politics was a thing of the past, wrote *about* spirituality as a thing of the past. The exercise of politics seemed to cure not just neurasthenia but the need for supernatural explanation. The exercise of cultural politics in the form of local-color fiction instead seems to have exacerbated both for eastern writers. And again, given a set of available discourses, individual writers adopted fictional and cultural stances of very different kinds, and in each case nervousness represented a mediation of the resulting conflicts. When those conflicts threatened to burst the bonds of even that most free-wheeling of turn-of-the-century discourses, neurasthenia, naturalism—whether Norris's philosophical naturalism, Howells's psychological naturalism, or Freeman's local-color naturalism—was pushed into the realm of the supernatural.

Humble Romances

When Horace Spencer Fiske of the University of Chicago, author of *The Ballad of Manila Bay and Other Verses* and *Chicago in Picture*

and Poetry, prepared his introduction to contemporary regional fiction for the Chatauqua Press in 1903, he did not use the term "local-
color." He referred instead to "sectional literature" and to "so-called
'realistic' fiction" and titled his volume *Provincial Types in American
Fiction*. Fiske discusses the fiction of Howells, Jewett, Page, Crad-
dock, Twain, Harris, Cable, Harte, Eggleston, Garland, Wister, and
others, and of all the authors he considers Mary Wilkins Freeman the
harshest.[5] "When the New England short story is mentioned the mind
naturally turns to Miss Wilkins (now Mary Wilkins Freeman)," Fiske
writes, whose "pictures" are of "the prevailing grimness and rigidity"
of New Englanders, "gaunt and 'set,' intensely and formally religious,
and lacking much in the spirit of mirth and the love of beauty. . . .
Conscience and will dominate these lives like passions" (43). Often
this results in what Fiske calls a story of "a lifelong tragedy of suffering
and misery" (43), in which Freeman's "provincial" characters are real-
istically, but hopelessly, bleak. Fiske elsewhere praises the "likable
darkies" of F. Hopkinson Smith (75) because they function, in effect,
as leading ideas: blacks should, Fiske feels, try to be likable. But
Freeman's writing he finds to be as devoid of social value as the
characters seem lost to the possibility of redemption.

Fiske's notion of reading is as naive and simplistic as his notions
of race relations, of course, for few of Freeman's readers could miss
entirely the nature of her leading ideas. Her fiction does often concentrate on religious and social morbidity, and in particular on the
connections in the culture of rural New England between the saving
of energy through the control of passion and the saving of the soul
through moral restraint. To overspend through passion leaves her
characters in nervous and moral bankruptcy, in need of being saved.
The poverty in which many of these characters live and the religious
culture that shapes them combine to make virtually impossible the
idea that cure or salvation might come from without. Their inability to buy salvation or to replenish their nerve capital, marks both
their provinciality and their backwardness. Her characters are old-
fashioned, and this can be seen in their futile attempts to save in a
world destined to drain their New England reserve.

Like Howells and Norris, Freeman is a neurasthenic writer with
neurasthenic themes who used the supernatural tale as a medium.
Born in 1852, she grew up in New England in a genteel family which
slipped further and further into poverty until the Panic of 1873 reduced them to boarding in a minister's house in exchange for work.
Freeman thus came of age witnessing the final loss of her genteel
patrimony. She tried working as a teacher but found it demeaning
and quit. Within ten years both her parents were dead and she had
turned to writing for magazines as a semigenteel form of employment.
She married for the first time when she was fifty years old, by which

time she was financially comfortable and famous for her short stories, but during the preceding decades she suffered the social stigma of spinsterhood and the psychological repercussions of downward mobility.[6] These were accompanied by a series of neurasthenic symptoms, the most pronounced of which was insomnia; eventually, like Hawberk in Howells's *Son of Royal Langbrith*, she became addicted to opiates in the form of sleeping sedatives.

Freeman published two books in 1903, *The Wind in the Rose-Bush, and Other Stories of the Supernatural* and *Six Trees*. The first, as the subtitle announces, is a collection of ghost stories. *Six Trees* is a collection of six naturalistic, local-color tales, in each of which a tree provides setting, symbol, formal frame, or all three. The different thematics of these two collections further clarify the use of the supernatural, particularly when linked to neurasthenia, as a normalizing device in the description of social relations.

Some of the stories in *Six Trees* are thematically consonant with those re-collected over the last decade, during a resurgence of critical interest in Freeman's work. While Freeman was never given the kind of sustained attention which the main canonized figures in American literary history received through the middle of this century, her work was not quite so neglected as her revivalists contend. She was considered among the top literary figures of her own day, was one of the first women elected to membership in the National Institute of Arts and Letters (in 1926), was championed by F. O. Matthiessen in the 1930s and Van Wyck Brooks in the 1940s. She was the subject of a full-length biography in 1956, and in the 1960s one critic points out, "Most anthologies of American literature . . . contain[ed] at least one selection from Mrs. Freeman's pen."[7] Still, with the revision of the American canon brought about by feminist criticism, Freeman's work has received more serious and useful attention, especially in terms of her thematicization of gender and class.[8] The critical reevaluation of Freeman's work centers primarily on stories reprinted in the recent collections edited by Marjorie Pryse, Barbara Solomon, and Michelle Clark, and the few stories regularly anthologized. In these stories Freeman represents New England village life, in particular the place of women and the poor, and she combines economic and emotional depression into a picture bleak save for the occasional active resistance of the protagonist. The editor of the first recent collection of Freeman's stories, Michelle Clark, for instance, claims that for her collection she chose stories that best represented Freeman's "recurrent themes: sexual repression associated sometimes with a lover who has gone off to seek his fortune, at other times with a tyrannical parent; the loss of a tiny livelihood or some cherished person followed by a rebellion against God or the village; piteous, envious, competitive gentility in poverty-stricken old ladies; do-gooders tyrannizing the elderly; maidens or young wives showing unexpected heroism; a girl pining for some young man, a second girl or sister retrieving the beau for her" (166). These are some of Freeman's recurrent themes, and described in this way they highlight the socioeconomic context Clark discusses: the economic and demographic devastation of New England accompanying western expansion and industrial urbanization. This context is important for an understanding of Freeman's themes, for Freeman's evocative realism relies on these developments, on the unavoidable facts of New England village life after the Civil War. These developments also describe Freeman's own situation, since they led to the loss of her inheritance and to such events as the disappearance of her "true love," a young man who, according to the standard biographies, left town like so many single men at the time to seek his fortune elsewhere and never returned.

But critics pass over many of Freeman's other stories (she published thirteen novels and over two hundred stories), at least in part because most are conventional magazine fiction in a sentimental mode, and there has not yet been a true revival of American late-Victorian sentimental fiction. Many critics speak of a decline in Freeman's later work, since by the turn of the century her stories were in great demand and her reliance on formula sentiment increased; therefore critical preference is usually given to the earlier stories, primarily those originally collected in the volumes *A Humble Romance* (1887) and *A New England Nun* (1891). All of the stories in the collections by Clark and Pryse, as well as eight of the fourteen in Solomon's collection, are from these two early books, which, as the titles suggest, concentrate on gender and class issues. Indeed, Freeman distanced herself from much of her early work: "The most of my work is not the kind I myself like. I want more symbolism, more mysticism. I left that out because it struck me that people did not want it, and I was forced to consider selling qualities."

The concentration on her early stories creates a somewhat warped vision of Freeman's work, one that can do little to account for many of her later fictions, such as her novel *The Portion of Labor* (1901), with its marriage-based resolution, its conventional piety symbolized as mysticism, and its heavy-handed legitimation of the economic status quo. Alice G. Brand, for instance, argues that Freeman's work became "angrier and bolder" as she grew older, a thesis clearly negated by *The Portion of Labor* and other works. Ann D. Wood finds the local colorists, Freeman included, to have abandoned the revolutionary potential of the sentimental writers by denying the possibility of the home as a haven and a source of women's power. Again, however, while this may be true of Freeman's early stories, it is less true of the late works, which return to some of the solutions of the sentimental novelists. Nan B. Maglin discusses *The Portion of Labor* but inexplicably finds it to be a realistic text devoid of sentimentalism and reads it as if it were similar in theme and intent to the short fiction of *A New England Nun* and *A Humble Romance.*[9] The disjunction, so often overlooked, between Freeman's "angry and bold," culturally resistant fiction and her merrily or serenely collusive texts raises a series of questions about her relations to genre, audience, criticism, and cultural process. And most centrally, it raises the question of the relation of what has been seen as Freeman's feminism to the reconstruction of class at the end of the Victorian era. As in the case of Garland, Norris, and Howells, conflicts about gender and sexuality relegate economic inequality to the political unconscious, and, as in the case of these men's work, this repression is accomplished in Freeman's work through appeals to the supernatural.

Natural Variation and Supernatural Justice

The formal frame of *Six Trees* seems, on the one hand, like a quaint, Victorian effect; on the other hand, it seems to be a protomodernist strategy, a formal device for the sake of a formal device, calling attention to the fiction's own artificiality. The trees that give title and form to each of the stories do not, for instance, necessarily signify the relation of the text to nature, and they stand in several different symbolic relations to the themes and subjects of the text. Compared to most local colorists, realists, and naturalists, Freeman makes use of nature very infrequently. Most of her spaces are interior to buildings and interior to human relationships. And the trees are not emblems of organic growth, natural cycles, development, or stasis. The trees perform as many functions thematically as there are stories. While the Lombardy poplar, for instance, represents the protagonist's determination, after years of conforming to other people's opinions, to define her own relation to the world and other people, the pine, in a number of ways, represents the limits of such individualism. And while the poplar represents the will to be different, the elm represents the protection afforded by traditional values. The very contradictory nature of the symbolic uses to which the trees are put signals a rejection of naturalistic interpretation. Here, as in Howells's fiction, self-reflexive technique thematizes, more than anything else, the work of the writer. It provides a way to call attention to the fiction's own production.

"The Lombardy Poplar" is the story of three elderly spinsters—Sarah Dunn, her twin sister Marah, and their cousin, Sarah Dunn—and centers on the problems of identity and individuation for such women, typecast into socially degrading roles. Freeman's use of proper names also creates a peculiarly modernist effect. The protagonists of the first two stories in *The Wind in the Rose-Bush* are both named Rebecca; there is otherwise no relation between the two. Not only are two protagonists of two different stories in *Six Trees* both named Sarah, but in "The Lombardy Poplar" Sarah Dunn's twin Marah dies and wills all her clothes to the cousin, also named Sarah Dunn, who then takes Marah's place as Sarah's housemate. These repetitions in "The Lombardy Poplar" are significant, for the story is about convention and individuation. But the repeated use of names in unrelated stories again seems to function as a flag of artifice.[10] Sarah Dunn is a "nervous" woman, unsure of her own thoughts and feelings, who follows the lead of first her sister and then her cousin. She comes into her own through an emotional movement from nervousness to "nervous indignation" (146), which allows her the strength to exercise her own will. In "The Balsam Fir," Martha Elder is made "nervous" and "fairly rebellious" by the smallest of domestic irregularities, such as curtains flapping in the wind. In the end, she, too, moves from nervousness to nervous indignation when a neighbor's hired hand nearly cuts down a Balsam fir she holds dear. Nervousness in these stories is a step toward rebellion; the nervousness is the outward sign of a perception of problems, and true to the structure of Christian reform thinking—although in somewhat sublimated form—the perception of the problem naturally leads to action.

This appropriation of nervousness in the form of nervous indignation runs through much of Freeman's fiction. The women in these stories who are not nervous are content with their roles. In James's terms they are "healthy-minded." The nervous women are sick souls, aware of their own degradation or insufficiency; they are "those persons who cannot so swiftly throw off the burden of the consciousness of evil," as James wrote in *The Varieties of Religious Experience*, "but are congenitally fated to suffer from its presence" (133–34). Sarah Dunn suffers from the consciousness of the evils of small-town censure, and Martha Elder from the consciousness of the pettiness of her own life and lost dreams. The religious response, according to James, "takes the form either of a lyrical enchantment or of an appeal to earnestness and heroism." Like the response to neurasthenia, in other words, the religious response can move either toward the rest afforded by lyrical enchantment or toward the exercise of earnestness and heroism. In *Six Trees*, four of the protagonists are male, two female; the men's response to their troubles takes the form of lyrical enchantment, and the women's response takes the form of earnestness and heroism. The women, Sarah Dunn and Martha Elder, end by heroically demanding their own rights and acting on them. The men in the other four stories end in reverie and acceptance of their lot. In "The Elm Tree," David, though he starts "in spirit a revolutionist and anarchist" (8), ends literally up a tree, from which we see his face peeking at the end of the story: "It was the face of a man in shelter from the woes and stress of life. He looked forth from the beautiful arms of the great tree as a child from the arms of its mother. He had fled for shelter to a heart of nature, and it had not failed him" (33). In reversing the gender specificity of the response to neurasthenia, Freeman is using neurasthenic discourse, transferred from the realm of the body to the realm of moral action, as a subtle challenge to the gender system.

The stories in *The Wind in the Rose-Bush* thematize neurasthenic issues as well, but with different results.[11] The title story, for instance, thematizes sexual neurasthenia, nervousness brought on by the effects of illicit sexuality. "The Wind in the Rose-Bush" is an evil-stepmother story, and, like the fairy tales, it rejects the mother who is not subservient to the demands of the mother's role. After the death of her sister and then, some time later, her brother-in-law, Rebecca travels from Michigan to Ford Village to take care of their child, her niece. Between the deaths of the sister and brother-in-law, the brother-in-law had remarried, and Rebecca arrives in Ford Village to find the stepmother with a well-warranted reputation for strange behavior, and the niece apparently inspiriting a rosebush. One of the townspeople worries out loud about the newly arrived Rebecca, saying "if it should be true, and she's a nervous woman, she might be scared enough to lose her wits" (8–9). The stepmother, it turns out, had neglected her stepdaughter, refusing to give her the medicine she required, whereupon the girl had died. Rebecca, on a traditional family errand (the father has died, she is a closer relative than the stepmother) is thwarted by the evil, sexualized stepmother ("What kind of woman is the second wife?" Rebecca asks. "I felt kind of hurt that John married again so quick" [7]). Rebecca doesn't lose her wits, as predicted, but she does end up neurasthenic: "The fatigue and nervous strain had been too much for her. She was not able to move from her bed. She had a species of low fever induced by anxiety and fatigue" (36). The stepmother in the process is exposed as the guilty party, which provides the resolution of the plot. Whatever Freeman's

challenge to the gender system, it did not include defending sexualized women. In fact, the stories of the supernatural all take a more
conservative position vis-à-vis the gender system and neurasthenic
morality than the stories in *Six Trees*.

In "Luella Miller," for instance, we get a representation of the type
of neurasthenic Mitchell called a "domestic tyrant." In *Doctor and
Patient*, Mitchell claimed that "for the most entire capacity to make
a household wretched there is no more complete human receipt than
a silly woman who is to a high degree nervous and feeble, and who
craves pity and likes power" (117). Luella Miller's story is an anecdote
of such a tyrant, told by an older woman who narrates in the New
England dialect Freeman is celebrated for transcribing. Luella Miller
is "nervous," so nervous, in fact, that when she marries, she is too
weak to do her housework. Her husband does all the household
chores, and when this load, on top of his own work and worries, saps
his nerve force, he slowly withers away and dies. Afterward, various
housekeepers and friendly neighbors come by to "help," since Luella
is essentially helpless, and they all, too, like her husband, defend her
helplessness. They all see her weakness as the effect of her refinement
and purity, but despite their greater strength they each, in turn,
slowly fade and die. Luella lives a life of "invalid leisure" while the
working-class people around her do her chores along with their own.
The invalid leisure of the neurasthenic tyrant here is used as a class
criticism of women who don't "do" for themselves and thereby sap
the lives of their servants. The economic criticism relies on a conservative notion of woman's place, for Luella's crime is that she does
not do her own laundry and cooking.

The relationship between neurasthenia and economics is central
in many of the other stories in *The Wind in the Rose-Bush* as well.
In "The Shadows on the Wall," three sisters and their brother live
together as adults in their dead parents' home. A younger brother
has died after a long nervous illness connected to the fact that he
squandered his inheritance and had never worked. The rest of the
siblings get progressively more nervous about the still-dwindling family fortune and about the brother's ghost, which appears as the titular
shadow on the wall. The financial insecurity of the remaining siblings
causes them to be nervous, and as they continue to spend without
producing, the ghost of their brother reminds them of their morally
untenable economic position. This nervousness is more explicitly tied
to civilized morality, since the nervousness of the three sisters is
exasperated by the tyrannical older brother, who insists that the
morbid topics of the dead brother, his perfidity, and his ghostly presence are all outside the pale of polite conversation. The tyrannical

Illustration from Mary E. Wilkins Freeman, *The Wind in the Rose-Bush* (1903). Old selves haunted the imagination of turn-of-the-century fiction.

brother is constantly demanding his sisters' silence, and the sisters collude by admonishing one another whenever they express strong emotions, which are continually brought on by the appearance, in shadowy form, of the dead brother. Freeman is the American turn-of-the-century writer whose work most resembles Freud's in its understanding of the relation of repression to symptom formation. As does Freud's late work, Freeman's clearly links symptom formation to social forms; the brother hopes that the repression of the nervousness caused by status deflation will prove a bulwark against further erosion of their social position. The nervous symptomatology of the sisters is in collusion with the enforcement of civilized morality spoken for by their brother, and it is this that allows a tyranny of false propriety to continue.

False propriety is one of Freeman's favorite themes, and it can take the form of a critique of gender roles as in "The Lombardy Poplar" and "The Revolt of Mother," a critique of emotional repression as in "The Shadow on the Wall," or a critique of class mannerisms as in her 1901 novel, *The Portion of Labor*. Intertwined with these is often a critique of property itself, as if the author were playing on the etymological relationship between propriety and property, and as in the case of Howells's fiction, neurasthenia provides a mediating discourse linking the two. The relation of Freeman's family's loss of their property and her own sense of propriety is a biographical context for the divided reaction—sometimes critical, sometimes approving—her texts display, just as her own neurasthenic symptoms are related to the ways in which she represented neurasthenia—sometimes as nervous collusion, sometimes as nervous indignation. The ghost stories, such as "The Shadow on the Wall" and "Luella Miller," play on the theme of contested ownership of property as a cause of a house's being haunted, as in the case of Howells's "His Apparition." This is most clear in "The Vacant Lot," from *The Wind in the Rose-Bush*, in which impropriety comes to haunt and devalue the property of future generations. What makes the family in "The Vacant Lot" nervous is a move to the city, where the crimes of their ancestors finally catch up with them. The father in the family, who is a Yankee trader and has bought, as his refrain goes, a "twenty-five thousand-dollar house for five thousand," fights against the mother, who is brought to a nervous collapse by the doings of various ghosts. The mother's sense of domestic safety finally wins out over the father's lust for a bargain and they move back to their small town. The mother's nervous collusion wins out over the father's nervous indignation, and rural, domestic, unbought serenity is allowed to prevail. In Freeman's shadow world, ownership is tainted if it is the result of a purchase, but not if it is the result of inheritance. Having is not the problem, getting is.

Nervous Politics

Impropriety in the getting of property is also a central theme in *The Portion of Labor*, Freeman's contribution to the genre of the labor novel, which features as its protagonist a nervous working-class girl who comes under the temporary protection of a nervous upper-class woman.[12] When Ellen, the girl, returns to her working-class home, she has a nervous sweetheart who is soon replaced in her heart by the nervous nephew of the factory owner. The factory owner, who has a nervous wife, is eventually shot by a nervous anarchist, and even the ministrations of a nervous doctor cannot save his life. Neurasthenia so pervades this economic novel that even the doctor's horses are nervous. In this book Freeman most thoroughly examines the interrelations between propriety and property, labor and capital, gender and class, social trajectory and the will, and through it all nervousness is the predominant motif.

The Portion of Labor also has, at the moment of its major crisis, a representation of a spiritual or mystical experience. As the novel moves toward its climax, Ellen, the neurasthenic protagonist who had never before been religious, walks out into a star-filled night, feeling "strangely nervous," and has a conversion experience. This experience leads her to a conclusion about the war between capital and labor: "There is something beyond everything, beyond the stars, and beyond all poor men, and beyond me, which is enough for all needs. We shall have our portion in the end" (411–12). Her nervous agitation not only leads to her religious conversion but is also a premonition of the crisis that follows immediately, when the anarchist shoots the factory owner, her sweetheart's father. As the psychologists who sympathized with psychic research, such as James and F. H. Myers, contended, her "subliminal self" contains both the key to her own religious self-discovery and occult powers of divination.

Ellen's realization is profoundly conservative and completely at odds with the critique of capitalism toward which the novel seemed to be headed. When the factory owner has been assassinated, the workers show up at the funeral with a floral wreath, and Ellen has to wonder whether "it were a sarcasm or a poetic truth beyond the scope of the givers, the pillow of laurel and roses, emblematic of eternal peace, presented by the hard hands of labor to dead capital" (431). We, too, have to wonder at the reversals of the text and the supernatural resolution, wonder whether there is some sarcasm or a real invocation of truth. The answer is given when Ellen's conversion experience is reinforced at the end of the novel with a quote from Ecclesiastes: "Live joyfully with the wife whom thou lovest all the days of the life of thy vanity, which He hath given thee under the sun, all the days of thy vanity, for that is thy portion in this life, and in thy labor which thou takest under the sun" (562–63). In the 1890s and the first decade of the twentieth century, Ecclesiastes was a prominent biblical text for literary writers, both in England and America. Thomas Hardy's *Far from the Madding Crowd*, Henry James's *Wings of the Dove*, and Edith Wharton's *House of Mirth*, to name just a few, like *The Portion of Labor* all take their titles from Ecclesiastes. The affinity felt for Ecclesiastes as an authoritative voice on the human condition can be seen as a sign of fin de siècle resignation and of the desire for a prophetic scriptural voice that speaks from outside the problems of revelation, history, mysticism, and belief. Not only is Freeman's appropriation of Ecclesiastes' celebration of personal resignation in the face of social problems politically reactionary, especially in the context of important and active socialist and anarchist movements, muckraking, and reform, but it also undercuts her criticisms of economic inequity.

The protagonist's father, who quotes the final passage from Ecclesiastes, is one of the laborers worst hit by the capitalists' inhumane practices, which are clearly represented by Freeman—such as unconscionably unsafe working conditions, cyclical layoffs for accounting convenience, and the constant manipulation of marginal wages, as in the repeated attempts to increase productivity through the slow lowering of the piece rate. Freeman represents anarchism as one form of neurasthenic crisis brought on by these conditions, and the stoical father feels the iron heel at one point acutely enough to consider anarchist action himself. Anarchism made people nervous: Alexander Berkman's 1892 attempted assassination of Henry Frick in Philadelphia, according to the journalist Ida Tarbell, caused a "general nervousness," as did the "anarchist" assassination of President William McKinley in 1901. When Congress legislated against the immigration of anarchists in 1903, it also prohibited the immigration of epileptics, insane persons, and beggars—that is, two forms of advanced nervousness and one form of degraded unproductivity.[13] The reformed anarchist "Harry Orchard" wrote in his "Confessions" that his anarchism was the result the "path of reckless living that so rapidly ends in ruin." He was reformed, he wrote, not through religious conversion per se: "No! it seems to me the order was first physical, second moral, and finally religious."[14] In *The Portion of Labor* the specific and contagious nervousness of the anarchist is also linked to spirituality. Ellen's premonition of anarchist violence is the result of her religious awakening, and the father's flirtation with anarchism leads him to a religious conclusion. One day, after the father has been turned down for job after job because at the age of fifty he is too old to keep up with the frantic pace of factory piecework, he ends up on a streetcar next to a rich man, and as the narrator tells us, the "spiritual bomb, which is in all our souls for our fellow-men, began to swell towards explosion" (393). By the end of the novel, though, the "spiritual bomb" has been defused by prosperity, when the father providentially makes a small killing with some mining stock he had speculated on years before.

The father's financial speculation had, in fact, brought on the worst of his neurasthenic symptoms, but these are erased when the speculation has been transmogrified into an investment. The father is a nervous wreck, convinced that he has squandered his family's small savings on an immoral desire to get rich quick, until he finds that the defunct silver mine he bought interest in contains vast quantities of another ore. The scam that fleeced him accidently ends up returning an enormous profit. Reflecting on this transubstantiation, the father waxes philosophical, through the indirect discourse of the narrator, and realizes "a new and further meaning" of the biblical verse: "He seemed to see that labor is not for itself, not for what it accomplishes of the tasks of the world, not for its equivalent in gold and silver, not even for the end of human happiness and love, but for the growth in character of the laborer" (563). All of the oppression and suffering detailed in the five hundred pages of the novel turn out to be character building; the cure for nervousness is resignation, work, sanctioned love, and wise reinvestment of any surplus wages. In other words, the cure for nervousness is adherence to a prescribed set of social roles, no matter how oppressive, for there one finds an individualized subjectivity that is not morbid but righteous. The novel had played with all of the current solutions to the labor question, including anarchism, labor unionism, worker-centered business decisions, a Frank Norris-like evocation of forces of production too large and esoteric for man to comprehend or meliorate, and liberal, individualized action. These are all rejected in turn, in favor of the resignation to fate which brings not joy but an end to vanity and nervousness.

Freeman's neurasthenic constructions tended to reject only one of the two contradictions she herself experienced. The gender construction she often reversed, but she eventually reinforced hegemonic understandings of class relations and social hierarchy, despite the wide sympathy for the poor evinced in the well-known story "A Church

Mouse," as well as in the stories of *Six Trees* and even in *The Portion of Labor*. In her own life, she found that while insomnia was not cured by marriage, and in fact was exacerbated by it, work could nonetheless create a solution to status erosion. While she never cured her own neurasthenic symptoms, she finally reversed her family's fortunes, becoming one of the highest-paid writers in America. Her endorsement of capitalism and status enhancement is clear in the advice she offered in an article for *Harper's* titled "For the Girl Who Wants to Write." It is not necessary, she writes, to have a noble purpose behind one's writing, for "in reality a man may write something that will live for the sake of something rather ignoble, and a woman may write something for money with which to buy a French hat."[15]

The naturalistic, local-color stories come the closest to making coherent critiques of the class and gender systems of her time, representing those systems as unfair but not uncanny. The supernatural stories fall closer to an endorsement of the dominant values and are shot through with neurasthenic characters and the uncanny. The labor novel, which also relies on supernatural evocations but which eschews any reference to the uncanny, and which is by far her work most riddled with the discourse of neurasthenia, is also her most conservative about both gender and class issues. Unlike the majority of her short fiction, the lovers in *The Portion of Labor* are allowed to marry, and the criticisms of property and all forms of nervousness are resolved by the deus ex machina of prosperity and by the closure provided by marriage.

Since Freeman is elswhere such a prescient and relevant critic of the abuse of power, economic wrongs, and gendered thinking, it is surprising to see her devote an entire novel to the supernatural legitimation of marriage and the hierarchies of the factory system. Freeman continued to write in both modes, both that of nervous indignation and that of supernatural legitimation, and thereby managed to speak to an audience for whom the transition to the modern was largely complete and to an audience for whom that transition was still in flux. Freeman's own early fears of spending and impropriety continued to exist uneasily alongside her acceptance of the accidents of prosperity and the pleasures of purchase. Her interest in new consumer products, like her statements about literature and writing and her fiction itself, were jealously followed by the various audiences looking for advice on consumption and life-styles. *The American Kitchen Magazine*, for instance, one of many magazines constructed around the new role of women as consumers of household and personal goods, ran an article in the October 1900 issue on the then newly popular art of cooking in chafing dishes, which included the proud claim that "Kate Douglas Wiggin and Mary E. Wilkins" were said to be "enthusiasts over chafing dish cookery." Just as Norris argued for the masculine professionalism of the role of the writer and thereby helped reinforce an ethic of masculine professionalism among male readers, so Freeman afforded women the idea that writing could be consonant with the role of woman as the consumer of personal and household items like French hats and chafing dishes, and thereby helped legitimize consumption for her readers.

Advertising was central to the neurasthenic world, in which the advertised services of doctors, potions, pills, electric belts, advice books, diets, and spas were offered for sale as antidotes to nervous overspending. The history of modern American advertising begins, in fact, with the advertisements for patent medicines just after the Civil War, providing a mirror history of neurasthenia itself.[16] Part of that history Henry James had encapsulated in his portrait of Selah Tarrant in *The Bostonians* (1886). Tarrant began his career as a seller of patent medicines before going on to the more lucrative and respectable (however marginally in his case) curative services involved in psychic media. ("Tarrant's Seltzer," from which James may have taken Tarrant's name, was a cure-all and specific remedy for nervous dyspepsia still widely advertised in the middle-class monthlies in 1903.) Central to this second career for Tarrant were his talents as an advertiser and self-promoter. At the same time that Freeman's name became regularly used in advertisements, the writing that originally seemed like a speculative gamble looked more and more like a wise investment, and the nervous indignation that infused her early fiction was accompanied by justifications for current social arrangements. As in the case of Howells's ghost stories, Freeman's use of the supernatural in her writing helped relegate the class issues that were one source of that indignation to a textual unconscious. As Garland had written about Norris, "youth had made a savage realist" of Freeman; but by 1903 realism was not her forte. And despite Fiske's castigations about her eschewal of leading ideas and her lack of "the spirit of mirth," her stories are full of what Norris called, referring to his less "savage" later self, "the grim humor of the suddenly successful American."

The morbidity of her early stories was by 1903 often replaced by paeans to a healthy-minded acceptance of one's allotted "portion." And both her early and late descriptions of moribund, provincial, small-town New England culture undoubtedly helped her urban, cosmopolitan readers accept their portion as well. Although the cultural center may delight in descriptions of the good life on the frontier or in the backwaters, careers like Garland's and Freeman's suggest that

Advertisements for Winchester's Specific Pill accompanied Mary E. Wilkins Freeman's stories in the monthly magazines.

it delights even more in descriptions of provincial poverty. Her indignant stories of gendered morbidity and the neurasthenic supernaturalism of her ghost stories and labor novel together helped justify the ways of the consuming secular city to itself. Her own place in the culture of advertisement—as pitchman, as product, as adviser—also helped inure women to their roles as consumers of cultural, personal, and household products.

Freeman's marriage to an alcoholic doctor in 1902 far from ended her personal involvement with neurasthenic issues, just as it did not end her reliance on the sleeping sedatives she bought in response to the advertisements for cure-alls carried by the magazines that bought her fiction. Dr. Hammond's Nerve and Brain Pills, for instance, advertised that they would:

cure you if you feel generally miserable or suffer with a thousand and one indescribable bad feelings, both mental and physical, among them low spirits, nervousness, weariness, lifelessness, weakness, dizziness, feeling of fullness like bloating after eating, or sense of emptiness of stomach in morning; flesh soft and lacking firmness, headache, blurring of eyesight, specks floating before the eyes, nervous irritability, poor memory, chilliness, alternating with hot flushes; lassitude, throbbing, gurgling, or rumbling sensations in bowels, with heat and nipping pains occasionally; palpitation of heart, short breath on exertion, slow circulation of blood, cold feet, pain in chest and back, pain around the loins, aching and weariness of the lower limbs, drowsiness after meals but nervous wakefulness at night, languour in the morning, and a constant feeling of dread, as if something awful was going to happen.

Freeman suffered from many of these complaints, especially the last several, and she described almost all of them at one time or another in her fiction. Dr. Hammond's was one of the many products advertised to cure all of these problems, and like the advice columns, Freeman's fiction analyzed such problems in practical and moral terms. "BEWARE OF QUACK DOCTORS" the ads for these Nerve and Brain Pills recommend, for Dr. Hammond can show you "HOW TO CURE YOURSELF." As a consumerist ethic gained ground, legislation would be aimed at misrepresentations in advertising and attempts made to separate fiction and advertising. Some of the earliest legislation regulating advertising practices followed the publication of muckraking journalist Samuel Hopkins Adams's *The Great American Fraud* (1906), which effectively and dramatically exposed patent medicines and their manufacturers. In Freeman's world and in her fiction, local custom, propriety, religious experience, advertising's incitement to desire, and advertising's promised products all functioned as cause and cure of nervous conditions. Like the quack doctors and the real doctors, Freeman and her fellow fiction writers advertised solutions and resolutions that none of them could or perhaps would want to deliver, as they attempted to reconstruct the rights of women and the portion of workers.

PART III:

NEURASTHENIC REPRESENTATION AND THE ECONOMY OF CULTURAL CHANGE

Reconstructing Subjectivity

As a cultural complex, neurasthenia was in constant flux. Although a generalized description of the disease of the 1910s would look much like that of the 1880s, in that thirty years there had been significant changes in its relation to systems of prestige, to the professional ideology of physicians, and to basic cultural constructions of gender, economics, intellectual production, and the supernatural. These last pages suggest some of the ways those changes took place through a look at the appropriation of neurasthenic discourse by Charlotte Perkins Gilman, Edith Wharton, Henry James, and William E. Burghardt Du Bois. Despite their resistance to some of the underlying assumptions governing neurasthenic logic, each had a stake in holding on to many of the other foundational assumptions of the discourse. What we might call their resistant readings of the disease helped to redefine the discourse in ways that necessarily undermined it. The wide interpretability of neurasthenia, which made it so important as a cultural space for individual adaptation to a great variety of social and cultural changes, was also, in turn, that which made for its demise.

James and Du Bois are installed in very different canons. My decision to link them here is based largely on the relation of their texts to the argument I have just outlined, but the strangeness of the link points to the fact that in constructing alternative canons and alternative traditions, literary scholars can sometimes reinstitute the very categorical differences to which they are theoretically opposed. A related impulse led me to link Wharton and Gilman. Critical concentration on issues relating to the traditional and the expanded canon has led to certain forms of comment on these writers which have obscured both some striking similarities and some serious and thoroughgoing differences in the two women's approaches to literature, culture, gender, and economics. A quick look at the work and lives of Charlotte Perkins Gilman—whose short story "The Yellow Wallpaper" has perhaps more than any other single text helped to maintain literary historians' interest in the disease—and of Edith Wharton—who in some ways expanded Gilman's critique of the disease—will demonstrate the identity and difference in the widely divergent appropriations of the disease, and, as in the section on Du Bois and James, show some of the ways in which these appropriations can be seen as empowering new discourses and practices that would eventually replace neurasthenia as a cultural force.

Each of the figures studied so far had a different kind of neurasthenia, each understood the disease somewhat differently, and each used it for different literary, personal, and polemical purposes. These last sections focus on the effects of individual rewritings of the discourse on the discourse's own history and show, among other things, that although discursive formations have wide-ranging effects on the ways in which people experience and shape their lives, human agency shapes and continually reshapes the discursive universe in and through which people move. Thus Part I, largely about action and subjectivity, and Part II, largely about the nature of reality and subjectivity, are followed by this third, about a series of neurasthenic constructions of the nature of individual consciousness, and how these constructions and constructors were important to the disappearance of neurasthenia in America, and to reconstructions of the issues of gender and economics with which we began.

7 Women and Economics in the Writings of Charlotte Perkins Gilman and Edith Wharton

The denial to woman of an equal share in man's intellectual and physical career is not, as the near-sighted advocates of feminine enfranchisement would have us believe, a useless relic of barbarism and savagery.... It flows from an ancient and profound realization of and respect for an inexorable law of nature—a law that never fails to deprive intellectually developed woman of her fecundity.

—Margaret Bisland, "The Curse of Eve," *North American Review* (1903)

Neurasthenic women worked at the forefront of many fields in 1903. Edith Wharton and Charlotte Perkins Gilman both wrote literary fiction and essays about (among other things) women's work, economic life, and the management of the home. Both started their careers in the midst of neurasthenic illness and appropriated the main strands of neurasthenic discourse in their writing. Other women did the same. Fannie Farmer was not (and still is not) taken as seriously as a brain-worker as was Edith Wharton or Charlotte Perkins Gilman, but in her time she was taken more seriously than either of them as a guide to everyday life and household management. As the author of the *Boston Cooking-School Cookbook*, countless articles on cooking for the middle-class journals, and several other books including *Food and Cookery for the Sick and Convalescent* (1904), Farmer was undoubtedly more widely known than either Wharton or Gilman. Like the more elite writers, Farmer had spent many years as an invalid before beginning her career, and her courses on cooking for the sick and invalid were known as specialties of Miss Farmer's School of Cookery, opened in 1902. Farmer brought to culinary ideas a new emphasis on presentation, on dishes with visual appeal. Rather than stress the medicinal properties of foods, as in the tradition of John Harvey Kellogg and Sylvester Graham, whose ideas about nervousness and health were used to advertise myriad food products, Farmer emphasized the stimulation of appetite through creating food that was its own best advertisement. And for nervous patients, this presentation included appealing to the patient's sense of self, as she lectured to the staff of the Adams Nervine Asylum: "Never serve a patient custard scooped out from a large pudding dish. He wants to feel that he is being particularly looked out for, and the individual custard suits him."[1] Farmer helped revolutionize culinary thinking away from the needs of productive laborers toward the desires and the inciting of desires of food consumers.

Mabel Dodge Luhan was in Europe trying to cure her neurasthenia in 1903, having suffered a nervous breakdown after the first of her four husbands died in a hunting accident in 1902. Luhan recovered, to become a spokesperson for the first sexual revolution, seeking a "spiritual communion" in sex and yet, according to one commentator, treating "her husbands and lovers like possessions of the same order as the beautiful objects with which she filled her houses."[2] Jane Addams had spent from 1881 until 1888 in a neurasthenic depression, "sickened," according to her own account, by her "advantages" and "leisure." She had gone on to found and direct Hull House, which she was running in 1903. The year before she had written of the "unlovely result" whenever "the entire moral energy of an individual goes into the cultivation of personal integrity," which might seem a fit epitaph for Luhan or for Wharton's Lily Bart.[3] Luhan and Addams emerged from neurasthenic despair with their sense of self reconstructed. Luhan became an avatar of desire, Addams of renunciation, both in the name of spiritual communion, the self, and the end of despair.

Margaret Deland, in "The Grasshopper and the Ant," a story in *Dr. Lavender's People*, told a modern fable of self and appropriation for 1903. Lydia, who is so poor that the town takes up a collection to help her repair her chimney, claims that she is not in fact poor, because of her wealth of "interest."[4] The text plays off the double meaning of interest—interest in other people (and therefore connection, community), and financial interest. "No one who has an interest is poor," Lydia says (132), and Deland suggests that Lydia's sunny nature is the result of her poverty, the result of having no wants. She describes three classes of people, the destitute, who are "without the spiritual muscle to manufacture an interest," although they sometimes learn how through financial setbacks; the manufacturing class, who through philanthropy, art, or intellectual pursuits get up an interest; and the aristocracy, rolling in wealth because of "a zest for living" (133). All of these categories play with the standard financial metaphors for moral relations. "I am always contented and I'll tell you why," Lydia exclaims: "*I don't want things.*" At the same time, she insists that she does not lack desire. "I don't want to lose my appetite for life by getting too much of it," she says; instead she wants to be like her friend the minister, Dr. Lavender, who "wants to get up from the banquet of life *still hungry*" (148). By creating the doctor as a minister rather than a medical man, Deland marks her text as a quaint return, a provincial fable rather than a realistic text. But Lydia's championing of an ascetic form of eternal desire is directed at cosmopolitan culture.

Lydia's opposite number is Willy, the spendthrift of the town, who never has as much as he desires and is always ready to receive more, no matter the moral cost. He is sickly, as a result, with a series of undefined complaints. While Luhan and Addams retained a set of tangential relations to the cultural reconstruction of desire and the market, Deland is much more involved in exploring the consequences of both. Deland, in this story and others, describes the revamped attitude necessary to maintain desire and energy in a changing world: think of all your relations as "interests," deny the desire for "things," remain "hungry," and, through "spiritual muscle," maintain a "zest for living." Deland's formula manages to remain metaphorically applicable along much of the continuum from asceticism to conspicuous consumption.

Ruth St. Denis, often called the "mother of American art-dance," was born into the center of the neurasthenic tradition of American womanhood. Her mother, Ruth Emma Hull, practiced medicine for a year after graduating from the University of Michigan Medical School in 1872 and then succumbed to "nervous prostration" and took a water cure.[5] A superstitiously religious woman, Hull found in "Delsarte movements"—cultish spiritual and physical exercises introduced from France to America by Steele Mackaye—a form of aesthetic gymnastics which melded her spiritual desires and her scientific training in physical hygiene. Delsarte movements had specific spiritual meanings (sometimes accompanied by inspirational texts) and promised both relaxation and energizing, cutting a wide swath through the neurasthenic market for cure. Ruth St. Denis learned the Delsarte movements from her mother and they influenced her career as a dancer. She began as a skirt dancer in vaudeville in the 1890s and then moved on to musical comedy. By 1903 she was dancing for David Belasco, bringing art-dance movements to the American stage, as Isadora Duncan and Maud Allen were first performing such dance in Europe.

Born Ruth Dennis, the "Saint" in her stage name was a mark of the continued influence of her early religious exposure. Sometime around 1903 St. Denis introduced her mother to Christian Science, and the "spirituality" of her dance always had the tinge of both the spiritual claims of the physical culture movement and the medicalized mysticism of Mary Baker Eddy. At the same time, the sexuality of her vaudeville skirt dances and of her later art-dance helped to continue the relaxation of religiously based notions of sexual propriety. Other originators of modern dance also had connections to the neurasthenic: Isadora Duncan began with the health-conscious mysticism of Delsarte as well, and Loie Fuller supposedly discovered her style of dancing while rehearsing for a musical comedy entitled *Quack, M.D.* American art-dance was constructed from neurasthenic ideas of the relation of body to self to soul and like neurasthenia was surrounded by the aura of sexuality. A self-consciously aesthetic alternative to vaudeville and musical comedy, art-dance rejected the vulgarity of the market while creating its own market as did Wharton and the other practitioners of what Henry James insisted was "the art of fiction." The self-conscious modernism of women as diverse as St. Denis and Farmer, and as different as Wharton and Gilman, was also, like neurasthenia, both a rejection and an incorporation of Victorian ideals of gender, selfhood, and desire.

Changing Home Economics

"In those days a new disease had dawned on the medical horizon," Gilman wrote in her autobiography. "It was called 'nervous prostration.' No one knew much about it, and there were many who openly scoffed, saying it was only a new name for laziness. To be recognizably ill one must be confined to one's bed, preferably in pain. That a heretofore markedly vigorous young woman, with every comfort about her, should collapse in this lamentable manner was inexplicable. 'You should use your will,' said earnest friends. I had used it, hard and long, perhaps too hard and too long; at any rate it wouldn't work now."[6] The story of lamentable collapse told in Gilman's autobiography is similar in many details to that of the narrator of her 1892 story, "The Yellow Wallpaper." In "Why I Wrote the Yellow Wallpaper" (1913), Gilman explained that she wrote the story to expose the abusive and detrimental nature of the rest cure, a regimen she had herself suffered through.[7] The narrator of the story—who might today be diagnosed as suffering from postpartum depression—is ordered to bed by her husband, a doctor, and is forbidden any activity, even reading or writing, and is allowed no visitors. The cure's enforced inactivity and isolation is shown to be worse than the illness, which at least allows a modicum of activity, and the narrator slowly goes mad. The story is told within some gothic conventions, including the setting in an ancestral mansion, the removal of the madwoman to an attic, and a powerful character—the husband—who seems beneficent when he is present but who emerges as the absent source of evil when he leaves the scene. The story is as much a critique of the patriarchal family and society as it is of medical practice; the two are, in the person of the husband/doctor, shown as two sides of the same coin. Gilman's desire to expose the rest cure is related to her main economic arguments, as presented in *Women and Economics* (1899) and *The Home: Its Work and Influence* (1903): women should be allowed to be as productive as men and a gender system that disallows women's productivity is harmful not only to women but to society as a whole.[8]

"The Yellow Wallpaper" draws on Gilman's own experience of neurasthenic illness. In her description of that illness in her autobiography, we can see several significant differences between Gilman's story and her narrator's story. First is the representation of the husband. *The Living of Charlotte Perkins Gilman: An Autobiography* was written some forty years after the event, and to tell the story of her life Gilman relied on journal entries she made at the time of her illness. (In the following excerpt the journal entries are within quotation marks.)

A lover more tender, a husband more devoted, woman could not ask. He helped in the housework more and more as my strength began to fail, for something was going wrong from the first. The steady cheerfulness, the strong, tireless spirit sank away. A sort of gray fog drifted across my mind, a cloud that grew and darkened.

"Feel sick and remain so all day." "Walter stays home and does everything for me." "Walter gets breakfast." October 10th: "I have coffee in bed mornings while Walter briskly makes fires and gets breakfast." "O dear! That I should come to this!" By October 13th the diary stops altogether, until January 1, 1885. "My journal has been long neglected by reason of ill-health. This day has not been a successful one as I was sicker than for some weeks. Walter also was not very well, and stayed at home, principally on my account. He has worked for me and for us both, waited on me in every tenderest way, played to me, read to me, done all for me as he always does. God be thanked for my husband."

February 16th: "A well-nigh sleepless night. Hot, cold, hot, restless, nervous, hysterical. Walter is love and patience, personified, gets up over and over, gets me warm wintergreen, bromide, hot foot-bath, more bromide—all to no purpose." (87–88)

I quote the autobiography at length to show what a consistent and insistent picture is painted of a devoted husband as servant rather than master. The husband/doctor of "The Yellow Wallpaper" is an evil, unfeeling tyrant, whereas the husband of the autobiography and journal is kind, compassionate, and supportive. Although keeping a diary is forbidden the narrator in "The Yellow Wallpaper," in the autobiography it has been not forbidden but "neglected." In the story, the woman is confined to her room, allowed no company that might overstimulate, and offered no succor; in the autobiography the husband brings her coffee, warm wintergreen, and hot footbath.

Immediately after the passage above comes this description of the birth and postpartum experience, again relying on Gilman's earlier diary:

Then, with impressive inscription: "March 23rd, 1885. This day, at about five minutes to nine in the morning, was born my child, Katharine."

> Brief ecstasy. Long pain.
> Then years of joy again.

Motherhood means giving. . . . [ellipsis in original]

We had attributed all my increasing weakness and depression to pregnancy, and looked forward to prompt recovery now. All was normal and ordinary enough, but I was already plunged into an extreme of nervous exhaustion which no one observed or understood in the least. Of all the angelic babies that darling was the best, a heavenly baby. My nurse, Maria Pease of Boston, was a joy while she lasted, and remained a lifelong friend. But after her month was up and I was left alone with the child I broke so fast that we sent for my mother, who had been visiting Thomas in Utah, and that baby-worshipping grandmother came to take care of the darling, I being incapable of doing that—or anything else, a mental wreck.

Presently we moved to a better house, on Humboldt Avenue near by, and a German servant girl of unparalleled virtues was installed. Here was a charming home; a loving and devoted husband; an exquisite baby, healthy, intelligent and good; a highly competent mother to run things; a wholly satisfactory servant—and I lay all day on the lounge and cried. (88–89)

After this passage comes the description of neurasthenia as a new disease with which I began this section. The force of these combined passages is not to indict patriarchy and medical practice but to express helplessness and a lack of understanding, expressed almost as apology. When a friend offers advice (" 'Force some happiness into your life,' said one sympathizer. 'Take an agreeable book to bed with you, occupy your mind with pleasant things'"), Gilman does not plead oppression but inability: "She did not realize that I was unable to read, and that my mind was exclusively occupied with unpleasant things" (91). Whereas the narrator of the story is forced into inactivity by her husband and doctor, Gilman reports herself forced into inactivity by the disease. "'If you would get up and do something you would feel better,' said my mother. I rose drearily, and essayed to brush up the floor a little, with a dustpan and a small whiskbroom, but soon dropped those implements exhausted, and wept again in helpless shame" (91).

Gilman by 1903 was well known as an economist. Her *Women and Economics* received wide attention, and despite its controversial thesis it was often used as a college textbook into the 1930s. This book had as its guiding principle the idea that women, like men, needed to be productive citizens and that for that to happen some basic restructuring of social practice was necessary. She suggests that the home as we know it should be abolished, that all services should be centralized—the providing of food, laundry services, education, child care—and that separate quarters should be provided only for sleeping. In 1903 she published *The Home: Its Work and Influence*, in which she both expanded and tried to make more palatable to a wide audience the ideas in *Women and Economics*.

Gilman's main argument in *The Home* is that the current system of family life is incredibly wasteful. Domestic economy "is the most wasteful department of life," Gilman writes. "The most effort and the least result are found where each individual does all things for himself. The least effort and the most result are found in the largest specialisation and exchange" (52). Women are relegated to an area of production that is not only "primitive" in that it has not kept up with industrial progress but also one which, if organized on industrial principles, could be done with a small fraction of the current amount of labor. The book combines criticism of gender relations with criticism of inefficient social organization, and it is the latter that she emphasizes. "A method of living that wastes half the time and strength of the world is not economical," Gilman writes, and this waste is the great crime that results from our woeful lack of progress (53).

At the same time, home life has secondary effects on women's lives and health. Because men's lives have advanced so far beyond the primitive, women feel their own backwardness, and this realization makes women feel cramped and useless, a state of affairs "positively injurious" to the health of women (10). "Confined to the home, [she] begins to fill and overfill it with the effort at individual expression," and the overfilling of a house, like the overspending of energy, is unhealthy (35). The text argues that the overfilling and overspending are based on a desire for individual expression and on a related desire to perform useful work, both of which are normal and necessary processes thwarted by women's place in the home. These normal processes thereby become pathological. "The physiologist knows that where normal processes are arrested abnormal processes develop," Gilman writes, again agreeing with the neurologists. "Social life has this possibility of morbid growth as has the physical body" (196–97). These normal processes turned abnormal are the cause of women's "morbid modesty," "unfounded pride," and "domineering selfish-ness" (174, 178) and of homes that are "hotbed[s] of self-indulgence" (181). Gilman then explicitly addresses neurasthenia: "The wide-spread nervous disorders among our leisure-class women are mainly traceable to this unchanging mould, which presses ever more cruelly upon the growing life. Health and happiness depend on smooth ful-fillment of function, and the functional ability of a modern woman can by no means be exercised in this ancient coop" (225–26). Tra-ditional home life simply cannot keep up with the modern world and its pace: "Among the splendid activities of our age it lingers on, inert and blind, like a clam in a horse-race" (315). The role of housewife creates the disjuncture between the pace of the subject and the pace of the world which necessarily results in neurasthenia. And yet leisure-class consumption is not the answer, since that is itself a form of overspending and of morbid self-absorption.

Gilman also provides a psychological reading of women's home life which has parallels with the notions of multiple consciousness rep-resented by Howells and, as we shall see, by James and Du Bois. The primitive and wasteful nature of housework, the lack of organized, specialized approaches to the work that needs to be done to fulfill basic human needs, means that each woman does thousands of tasks each day, all different, all inefficient, and all replicating similar efforts in every other household. The psychological effect is that the woman has to "adjust, disadjust, and readjust her mental focus a thousand times a day; not only to things, but to actions; not only to actions, but to persons; and so, to live at all, she must develop a kind of mind that does *not object to discord*" (151). The multiplicity of chores cre-ates a multiplicity of consciousness which is dissipative. "The cur-rents of home-life are so many, so diverse, so contradictory, that they are only maintained by using woman as a sort of universal solvent; and this position of holding many diverse elements in solution is not compatible with the orderly crystallisation of any of them, or with much peace of mind to the unhappy solvent" (152). Self-contradictory consciousness is represented as so impossibly complex that resolution is possible only if the entire position of women is changed, since what men have always seen as the disabilities of women are instead simply "the disability of the house-bound" (226). And it is the fact of this enforced disability which proves that the frenetic level of psychological discord is not to be confused with adequate mental exercise. Women, like men, need physical exercise, "else would their muscles weaken and shrink, and beauty and health disappear. For the health and beauty of the body it must have full exercise. For the health and beauty of the mind it must have full exercise," Gilman writes, and then refers again to neurasthenia. "No normal human mind can find full exercise in dusting the parlor and arranging the flowers; no, nor in twelve hours of nerve-exhaustion in the kitchen. Exhaustion is not exercise" (261).

In *Herland*, Gilman's feminist utopian novel, published serially in *The Forerunner* in 1915, the male explorers who accidently find an all-female utopia are amazed at the lack of neurasthenia: "We looked for nervousness," says the narrator, "there was none."[9] The women these explorers find are physically fit and mentally able and alert, which the narrator finds confusing: "College professors, teachers, writers—many women [at home] showed similar intelligence but often wore a strained nervous look, while these were as calm as cows, for all their evident intellect" (22). References to neurasthenia and nerve force abound in her other works as well, as in, for instance, "Just to Be Out of Doors," a poem published in the May 1905 *Cosmopolitan*, which recapitulates Muir's and Burroughs's endorsement of the restful, curative powers of nature.

These examples of polemical deployment might suggest that Gilman knew the discourse of neurasthenia well and knew how to manipulate it rhetorically, and that she also maintained a fully skeptical attitude toward its standard deployment. But it is also clear that Gilman still accepted many of the basic tenets of the neurasthenic understanding of the world. In 1903 Orison Swett Marden's *Success Magazine* asked a group of successful women what they would do differently if they had their lives to live over, and the results of these interviews were published in a series of articles titled "If I Were a Girl Again." Gilman, by then famous for her economic writings, replied: "The only line of conduct pursued in girlhood which I now consider injudicious lay in a too lavish expenditure of nerve force, and on that point I may give useful warning." She then relates this view to her own philosophy of work: "Nerve force is capital. Use the interest carefully, saving some to increase the principal for your heirs; [and here she even seems to accept the notion of the necessity of women to conserve their energy for the purposes of childbearing] but never break into the principal unless some issue of life and death compels. The world needs helping and we all want to help it; but the best service is in a lifetime's strong and steady work, rather than a few years of feverish struggles."[10]

And so Gilman, like Henry James and Edith Wharton a writer with an ability to see the discourse inside and out and to deconstruct it forcefully in her fiction, turns out to believe quite firmly in the disease after all. In "Why I Wrote the Yellow Wallpaper" Gilman claims that she wrote the story in the hopes that other women would not be driven "to the borderline of mental ruin" by doctors' advice, especially by advice not to work, which as we have seen was part of the process and purpose of the rest cure. What Gilman wanted to argue was that women's work as it existed, since it was wasteful, led to neurasthenia, but when women's work would become the same as men's work, it would be a reinvestment of nervous energy and lead away from nervousness. Completely involved in the medical discourse and its moral and economic correlatives, Gilman used it to make her political points, and what seems to be a criticism of the disease is actually a criticism of aspects of its deployment made from a ground constructed of the same materials. The argument's lack of cogency, given the high incidence of neurasthenia among men in the professions, also points to its polemic rather than mimetic function.

There is other evidence of Gilman's belief in the allied medical theories of her time. For one, patterned wallpaper (and Gilman claims this motif in "The Yellow Wallpaper" has no strictly autobiographical basis), had its medical detractors, and the critique of domesticity many readers find implied in this central metaphor turns out itself to have had a medical history. Citing medical opinion in 1883, Robert W. Edis wrote, "The endless multiplication and monotony of strongly-marked patterns . . . [is] a source of infinite torture and annoyance in times of sickness and sleeplessness." Not only did patterned wallpapers fail all aesthetic tests, but they "could materially add to our discomfort and nervous irritability, and after a time have a ghastly and nightmarish effect upon the brain."[11] And at the same time, John Harvey Kellogg, who also treated neurasthenics, warned readers of his *Household Manual of Domestic Hygiene, Food, and Diet* (1882) to stay away from certain kinds of wallpaper because of the use of poisonous dyes, many containing arsenic. The two worst culprits, Kellogg wrote, were red and yellow wallpapers. Children had died scratching at pieces of wallpaper and ingesting fatal amounts of arsenic. Not only is the narrator's abnormal response to the wallpaper a normal process according to medical opinion, but she is poisoning herself in her attempt to tear the wallpaper from the walls: this strongest image of the woman's attempts to break free from the constraints of domesticity is also an image of self-poisoning.

Gilman claimed that S. Weir Mitchell changed the regimen of his cure after reading "The Yellow Wallpaper." Whether he did or not, the cure and the disease changed radically, eventually changing right out of existence. And it is clear that although Gilman had no interest in changing the neurasthenic understanding of sickness and health, this well-known and controversial story had an effect. Gilman's appropriation bought more than she had bargained for, as her use of the disease to make her own points helped undermine the position of neurasthenia and the neurasthenic. Patricia Meyer Spacks claims that Gilman's adoption of sickness as an alternative to the roles of wife and mother "exemplifies the remarkably devious relationship possible between a woman and her work," in which she "achieves greatly as a mysterious corollary to self-deprecation."[12] In outlining the relationship between women, work, and ill health, Gilman validated her own decision to write, validated women's intellectual labor in general, and helped, finally, to invalidate neurasthenia as a role option. She represented neurasthenia as poisonous, as a mark of leisured affluence and what was poisonously wrong with such affluence.

Edith Wharton's Backward Glance

Edith Wharton also knew something of wall coverings and something of the leisure class. In *The Decoration of Houses* (1902), she declared that "it was well for the future of house-decoration when medical science declared itself against the use of wallpapers." While wallpaper was sometimes convenient and inexpensive, she went on, "a papered room can never, decoratively or otherwise, be as satisfactory as one in which the walls are treated in some other manner."[13] Aside from this mention of medical opinion, Wharton's interest in interior decoration had little in common with Gilman's. In her autobiography, *A Backward Glance* (1934), she wrote a long description of the interior of her parents' house and of her mother's cooking and concluded: "I have lingered over these details because they formed a part—a most important and honourable part—of that ancient curriculum of house-keeping which, at least in Anglo-Saxon countries, was so soon to be swept aside by the 'monstrous regiment' of the emancipated: young women taught by their elders to despise the kitchen and the linen room, and to substitute the acquiring of University degrees for the more complex art of civilized living. The movement began when I was young, and now that I am old . . . I mourn more than ever the extinction of the household arts."[14] Again we have a woman writing in her autobiography in ways that do not sit well with current evaluations of her writings, evaluations that argue, among other things, that those writings presciently deconstruct the combination of gender and class constraints which faced women at the turn of the century.

Wharton's 1903 novel, *Sanctuary*, is a genteel novel of manners, but one in which she already, as the narrator says of one of the characters, "had begun to perceive that the fair surface of life was honeycombed by a vast system of moral sewage."[15] And the novel that Wharton began writing in 1903, *The House of Mirth*, has been lauded as paving the way for "a new hope—the New Woman" and as marking the "death of the lady novelist."[16] But Wharton was never a New Woman, and she remained a "lady" until the end of her life. She was never, as she said of a character in *Sanctuary*, "patently of the 'new school': a young woman of feverish attitudes and broadcast judgements" (84). She held to her ideas about civilized living until her death, and these included finding the "complex art" of household management and the management of servants more important than the "substitute" of "acquiring University degrees"—hardly the attitude of the New Woman or of a woman no longer concerned with being a lady. Her stance has always been a problem for feminist critics. The most recent attempt to deal with it is in Gilbert and Gubar's "The Angel of Devastation," in which they argue that Wharton was adept at portraying the "arts of the enslaved" and that this project explains her celebration of interior decoration and household management at the same time that she devastatingly deconstructs the traffic in and containment of women.[17] I do not mean to make Wharton out to be simply an "angel of decoration" but to examine this ideological conundrum one more time through an examination of Wharton's various appropriations of neurasthenia and its imagery.

Edith Wharton suffered from neurasthenia from 1891 until 1894 or 1895 and had a serious neurasthenic breakdown in 1898. She had a textbook diathesis: a woman of leisure who did brain work. Like many of the neurasthenic writers examined here she wrote realistic novels, romances, and ghost stories and was very concerned with her professional existence as a writer, despite the fact that she did not need the money. After her 1898 breakdown she traveled to Philadelphia for a rest cure under S. Weir Mitchell's direction. For many years there was a rumor in literary circles that Wharton began writing fiction in response to Mitchell's encouragement.

Mitchell, at the time a fiction writer of some repute, was supposed to have suggested fiction writing as a way of fending off morbid self-consciousness and as an aid to recovery, and if this is so, "The Yellow Wallpaper" had indeed had a significant impact on him. R. W. B. Lewis, in his biography of Wharton, declares that the rumor is pure myth, claiming that Wharton first met Mitchell in 1898, after she had already published several volumes. It is not at all improbable that Mitchell started the rumor himself, having no great respect for the truth when it came to self-aggrandizement.[18]

We have examined some of the relations between neurasthenia and the supernatural, and Mitchell, himself a writer of ghost stories, in a late autobiographical writing made the connection between religion, ghosts, and neurasthenia in discussing his own childhood:

> I began very early in my life to be disturbed by religious matters. I remember asking my mother what the Holy Ghost was, and as she knew no better than I, I remained with the conviction that it was some form of dreadful apparition which would appear to me at some time in the night; and many a time I lay awake, frightened lest I should see the Holy Ghost. . . . It was too sober a life for an imaginative child, and of it and its many repressions I carry away chiefly a memory of hated Sunday School and incomprehensible church; of passionate love for my mother and a sort of veneration for my father, and, over and above all, of wearisome ennui.

Mitchell's confusion of religion and superstition, as in the case of Howells and others, fed immediately into the kind of hyperreverence for traditional Victorian values which fascinated Freud, here represented as passionate love of the mother and veneration for the father. Wharton, who when she was young was haunted by ghosts and read religious tracts, also, like Mitchell, wrote ghost stories and evinced a certain ennui (however forced) toward the family romance. In the manuscript for *A Backward Glance* she wrote that until the age of twenty-eight she was unable to sleep in a house in which there were ghost stories in the library. That would date her ability to handle ghosts as a theme to the time her neurasthenic illness commenced. She then wrote her first ghost story, "The Lady's Maid's Bell," shortly after being treated by Mitchell in 1898.[19]

In this compelling and dense story with overtones of adultery and incest, neurasthenic illness in one or another of its forms plagues most of the characters.[20] The mistress of the house, who seems to be having an affair with the neighbor, is an invalid, the master is a profligate and inebriate, and the new maid is nervous and recuperating from an illness. The ghost in the story, who was the former maid, is a free-floating double, the conscience of all the characters at the same time. The new maid feels she is being watched from the moment she arrives, and the ghost is apparently watching the other characters as well. When the new maid tries to ignore what appears to be the adulterous relationship, the ghost tries to make her see and prompts her into becoming a watcher as well. When Wharton was first in Philadelphia under Mitchell's care, she was disturbed by the constant surveillance required for her cure, annoyed that the doctor and nurse popped in continually to check on her. Mitchell and others insisted that this surveillance was essential (and Freud singled out this feature of the rest cure for favorable comment in his short review of *Fat and Blood*). Wharton and her friend, Walter Berry, fresh from reading Henry James's latest story, *The Turn of the Screw*, nicknamed the doctor and nurse Peter Quint and Miss Jessel. For Wharton, it would seem, ghosts are representations of the policing of custom in neurasthenic society.[21]

Wharton returned to the theme of surveillance in *The House of Mirth*, which she began writing in 1903, while her husband was suffering from nervous illness and Wharton herself sought treatment for asthma.[22] Like some of Dreiser's neurasthenic characters, Lily Bart, after losing what tenuous status she had and her ability to raise her status through marriage, slowly wastes away and dies. The rest of the complex surrounding neurasthenia, sexuality, and success comes into play as well. Lily is an object of speculation, and speculation, linked early in the novel to gambling, makes everyone involved nervous. Lily, herself speculating in the marriage market, makes other people nervous, in part because of the status anxiety aroused and in part because of the power of female sexuality implied by and increased by the pecuniary value of Lily's beauty. What Lily continually finds most soothing to her nerves is male appreciation of her beauty, the main sign of her economic viability. Gerty Farrish suggests that marriage might cure Laurence Selden's nervousness. George Dorset is a nervous dyspeptic in part because his wife Bertha is spending too much money and in part because she is spending her sexual energy equally freely. Gus Trenor's speculation in stocks for Lily's benefit, in return for what he assumes should be sexual favors, makes Lily nervous. Simon Rosedale's knowledge of Lily's indiscretions make her "evidently nervous," and Rosedale "was not above taking advantage of her nervousness" (185).

It is Lily's uselessness, an idea introduced by Selden in the opening pages, that makes her status questionable. In one of the most telling phrases in the introductory chapter, Lily leans back "in a luxury of discontent" (9). But it is in the discontent that comes without the trappings of luxury that Lily finally dies. Her leisure was invalid in part because she did not have the money such leisure required and in part because she was presenting herself dishonestly to the society that was watching her—she was not in fact on the laissez-faire market (she was not for sale to the highest bidder; she refuses the wealthy aristocrat Percy Gryce, the nouveau riche Rosedale, and the married Trenor) and yet her actions, her flirtations, suggested she was. Her final discontent comes when she is without prospects, and then she is without surveillance as well. While she is in society, all eyes are on her; she is constantly being watched, as is everyone else, by one another and by such outsiders as the society gossip columnist. In the novel society's system of surveillance is trained most acutely on those, like Simon Rosedale, who attempt to enter its ranks on the strength of their new wealth, and it ignores those with neither position or wealth. When Lily is forced out of society, she is also freed from the system of surveillance which governs it.

The novel produces interesting divergences from standard neurasthenic understandings. Lily is susceptible to the disease because she is "fine," but her fineness is seen as a lack rather than a positive attribute; it is because she is fine that she has no ideas, because she is fine that she has no skills, and because she is fine that she has little compassion and little ability to act on what compassion she does have. At the same time, the fact that she is highly refined and civilized matters much less than the fact that she has no money. Rosedale has money, so his lack of refinement does not matter. Lily is related to old money, but old money that is either gone or denied her, and she rejects the new money because she is banking on coming up with some of the old. Wharton may criticize Old New York, but never as savagely as she criticizes the New, and it is in part Lily's attempt to ride some middle line which dooms her. The class issues Selden introduces when he muses that Lily "must have cost a great deal to make" and that "a great many dull and ugly people must in some mysterious way, have been sacrificed to produce her" (7), recur in the person of the charwoman who brings Lily the damning letters Bertha Dorset wrote to Selden, in Gerty Farish's ministrations to working-class families, and in the ending's representation of total impoverishment. Selden is himself finally not to be trusted, we find, as a guide to class relations for Lily or for the reader, and his untrustworthiness is immediately signaled by his attribution of mystery to economic processes.

Selden's idea of success as personal freedom, which he presents as an alternative to monetary success, turns out to require a level of

worldly success Lily is unable to muster. And the other representations of class-conscious people, such as Gerty Farish, who has dedicated herself to charity work, are not flattering. The enervation of the
upper classes may rest on the suffering shoulders of the underclass,
but the "work" of Farish and Selden (his very part-time lawyering) is
not presented as an answer. Rosedale has managed to rise, and he
neither works in the old sense of the word nor suffers, nervously, for
his speculative gains. The new money of Rosedale and the other upwardly mobile characters is exactly what destroys Old New York: the
new money is outside the old moral economy, and it not only invalidates but displays the moral bankruptcy of that economy. At the
same time, Wharton shows, in the new people's mawkish aping of
the old society, that the only thing morally more tainted than the old
money is the new money.

Wharton's representations of "new" sexual moralities, like her representations of new money, work in both directions at once. Her
representations of female desire, for instance, run the gamut: she
implies criticism of Bertha Dorset's greedy and inhumane pursuit of
sexual gratification, but also, at the other extreme, she damns Ethan
Frome's wife, Zeena, whose renunciation of sexuality (and accompanying dyspeptic invalidism) is shown to be as stupid as it is tragic
in *Ethan Frome* (1911). Mattie Silver's flirtation with Ethan Frome
ends when they ride their sled with total abandon into a large elm
tree. Their sexualized activity results in a punishment to Mattie's
nervous system which leaves her paralyzed, while Bertha Dorset's
adulterous affairs do not even make her neurasthenic (although her
husband is forced to take the cure at Engadine [43]). *Summer* (1917)
traces the sexual awakenings of Charity Royall, who experiences
strong emotions, from ecstasy to despair, but who never becomes
nervous or neurasthenic and whose renunciation of her own desires
is neither heroic nor ennoblingly tragic. In *Ethan Frome*, Wharton
plays off the difference between what Zeena calls nervous "troubles,"
which are common, and "complications," which can be fatal. Wharton
ridicules the respect given those with "complications" and Zeena's
awe of them, and at the same time she shows that what really complicates health are the human desires that crash headfirst into the
elm trees of social custom. The explicit, illicit eroticism of Wharton's
unpublished fragment "Beatrice Palmato," which represents ongoing
father-daughter incest, is Wharton's clearest statement that sexual
spending incurs only social costs. The author of "Beatrice Palmato"
has left the neurasthenic economy of sexuality far behind.

Still, Wharton came to accept many of the social mores she criticized
in *The House of Mirth*, so that by the time she wrote *The Age of*

Innocence (1920), set at the turn of the century, the ways of Old New York are represented as worthy of respect. The "broadcast judgements" against the New Woman, against the "new people," and against the new economy appear throughout Wharton's works. But *The House of Mirth* has an added animus against the pieties of her Old New York set which is contained in the various twists and turns given neurasthenic discourse. The sexual spending of the upper classes has no negative or neurasthenic effects on the spenders, and so the moral neurasthenia of Lily, who dies for a principle related to chastity, becomes detached from the system of values Wharton was criticizing. Lily's death, like the injuries of Ethan Frome and Mattie Silver, is a result of severe self-discipline, and like the accident in which they were crippled, however tragic, it was finally unnecessary.

This, then, is the antidisciplinary message of Wharton's representation of neurasthenia, and one way to answer the perennial question of the nature of her critique. In *Sanctuary* the idea that "the social health must be preserved" through the "hygienic" ignorance of evil is mouthed by the old-fashioned Mrs. Peyton, who had for years "remained enthroned in a semi-invalidism which prohibited effort while it did not preclude diversion" (61,45). This attitude is ridiculed by the text, as is the falsity of maintaining a neurasthenic mask for egotism. By locating moral responsibility in the manners and actions of individuals rather than in social structure, and by representing those actions within a realist aesthetic (in which criticizing manners is a convention of social critique), Wharton manages to seem both radical and reactionary at the same time. She represents neurasthenia as the result of immoral individual actions rather than oppressive socioeconomic structures; what is wrong with Lily and the Dorsets, for instance, is that they are spending their energy unwisely. Money is not the problem. Rosedale knows how to spend his time and energy and money in ways that get him what he wants; while at first he seems to be nervously trying to buy what has been suggested is useless—the society life—it turns out that he has been a shrewd investor all along and that it is Lily, on the contrary, who does not know how to spend within her means. That spendthrift mentality is as foolish from Wharton's perspective as it was from Beard's. The youthful idealism that led Lily to reject Gryce and Rosedale as suitors was very expensive, as it destroyed her chances to take part in the society that would have allowed her to continue to spend without self-deterioration. That Wharton's own youthful idealism and animus helped, in some little way, destroy the world she came to treasure is one of the ironies of literary and intellectual history. Like Henry James, Wharton lived to rue the passing of a society they had both shown at its worst. Wharton's backward glance, in her late novels and autobiography, may reinvent a turn-of-the-century sense of propriety, but in these late writings nostalgia has replaced nervous complaint, and the function of saving has been reversed from a need for the future to an attitude toward the past. At that juncture, the revaluation of Wharton's critical values is complete.

Consumption

Despite their involvement with economic issues, neither Wharton nor Gilman were ready to make any fundamental changes in their thinking to account for the rise of consumer society. The tension between production and consumption in "The Yellow Wallpaper" and *The House of Mirth* is a tension central to the discourse of neurasthenia: if women are not allowed to produce, they have no interest to spend (and perhaps no interest in spending), and since the main productive forum for women is domestic work, when that possibility is denied, through illness or choice, they spend principal, to their own detriment. Production implies the creation of a surplus that can then be spent; without production all one can spend is capital. If one starts spending one's nerve capital, one spends (wastes) oneself. The rest cure is necessarily a failure not because its premises about gender and economics are flawed, but because *not* consuming is impossible: there is no rest, even for the weary. Only the stodgy and wealthy Mrs. Peniston in *The House of Mirth* believes that lying down is a "panacea for all physical and moral disorders," and being wealthy and ascetic she can afford to think so.

The problem for the narrator of "The Yellow Wallpaper" is that she has, like the young Gilman and like Lily Bart, started going at too fast a pace, as an older Gilman herself argued, and that her investments of energy were not wise. Lily Bart creates a commodity-self that is consumed by the society for which she produced it, and her illness is both the sign and the effect of the fact that she has been discontinued. She demurred from women's work, whether it was the contractual obligations of marriage, the sexual return on investment expected by Gus Trenor, or the various forms of social work represented by Carry Fisher, Gerty Farish, and Grace Stepney. When Lily first begins to feel her insignificance, she realizes "that a woman's dignity may cost more to keep up than her carriage; and that the maintenance of a moral attitude [is] dependent on dollars and cents" (273). The self she performs requires a moral attitude she cannot afford, and therefore she finds she has spent herself. The narrator of

"The Yellow Wallpaper" also writes herself not into a self but into the destruction of the self, and as her doctor has warned, her writing depletes her nerve force; the circle she runs at the end of the story reinforces our sense of her waste of energy. Lily Bart does not write, she is written about and written around, and although her self-production is represented as performative rather than textual, the plot remains largely the same.

The understanding of the self which informs Gilman's writing is, then, moral, physiological, economic, medicalized, and sociological: it is infused, in other words, with the logic of a deployed discourse on neurasthenia. Gilman was not a philosopher and not interested in epistemology, she was a political economist interested in what she thought of as material forces. Nevertheless "The Yellow Wallpaper" is neither an endorsement of consumer capitalism nor a critique of it. Gilman seems unaware of consumer capitalism as a problem for two reasons: she was interested not in changing the structure of capitalism but in changing the relation of women to economic life, and she was more interested in correcting women's relation to production than in directing patterns of consumption. About the order of her society she says in *The Home*: "Change this order. Set the woman on her own feet, as a free, intelligent, able human being, quite capable of putting into the world more than she takes out, of being a producer as well as a consumer" (321). Her orientation toward production is similar to that of the *New York Times* editorial with which I began this study. Consumption is a given, and only a problem if it is wasteful, and waste, of course, like other moral-economic categories, is in the eye of the beholder. In *The Home* Gilman uses the signs of increased consumption—complex systems of newly acquired household products and the bric-a-brac markers of hours of shopping—as an indictment of wasted effort. Unlike Gilman, most modern economists would find the fact that every home has its own pots and pans and dishes and appliances and furniture and luxury goods as a sign of a healthy economy, but Gilman's production-oriented economic understanding required her to see this as a sign of inefficiency and thus of a sick economy. Gilman's neurasthenic agenda in her economic writings and her fiction (as Wharton's agenda in *The House of Mirth*) made the issues of capital, production, and spending central, but it never explicitly addressed the value of consumer society as a form of practice. Gilman was, as Dolores Hayden has argued, a "romantic advocate of benevolent capitalism," but neither a direct supporter nor detractor of consumerism.[23]

While Gilman took little notice of the consumer revolution, much of its advertising was in line with her ideas. Advertisements for household products often touted the productive, efficient sentiments of

Gilman's economic writings. "ECONOMICAL HOUSEKEEPERS use Walter Baker's Cocoa and Chocolate, Because they yield the MOST and BEST FOR THE MONEY," one ad reads. The Postum Cereal Company offered cash prizes and "diplomas" to winners of their contest to stimulate improvements in the "culinary department" which will put "humanity farther along the road to civilization, health, comfort and happiness." The Natural Food Company's "Shredded Wheat Biscuit is made in the most hygenic Food Laboratory in the World" and Libby's Food Products are made in large hygienic kitchens; these claims suggest that the best kitchens are those most similar to industrial facilities. Jello and Horlick's Malted Milk advertised that their simple preparation required fewer steps. Pearline detergent and Bissell sweepers are advertised as saving time and effort by making fewer jobs for housewives. Pearline ran a series of ads in many of the major monthlies which suggested that a housewife or servant could eliminate fatigue and drudgery by using the detergent. "Is your exercise healthy or deadly?" one ad in this campaign asked, illustrated with parallel photographs of a disgusted and disgruntled washerwoman in a work bonnet and a very modern younger woman in a ribbed turtleneck sweater hoisting a medicine ball. "Pearline takes the deadly exercise out of Washing and Cleaning. Intelligent Women save health and find safe, time, labor and Clothes Saving Washing by following the directions found on each package of PEARLINE The Modern Soap." (The syntax here helps explain the prevalence of advertisements for advertising copywriters, several of which could be found in the major journals each month.) The dissipation of energy in housework can be alleviated, these ads suggest, by products that do some of the work before they are purchased. Gilman's analysis of the neurasthenia induced by housework—by too many steps, too many chores, too much exercise that it not healthy, too little return on the investment of energy, too preindustrial a model of work, too unhygienic an environment—is assumed by the copywriters, whose promises Gilman would have recognized as freeing women for more productive labor.

In "The Women Do Not Want It" (1898), a suffrage poem, Gilman writes:

> We were told of disabilities,—a long array of these,
> Till one would think that womanhood was merely a disease;
> And 'the maternal sacrifice' was added to the plan
> Of the various sacrifices we have always made—to man.
>
> Religionists and scientists, in amity and bliss,
> However else they disagreed, could all agree to this,

Advertisement for Pearline soap, 1903. The medicine ball was not only more healthy than washing, it could cure illness caused by housework.

> And the gist of all their discourse, when you got down to it,
> Was—we could not have the ballot because we were not fit!

Gilman goes on to say that "whatever ails those arguments—we do not hear them now!" for the argument replacing those about women's lack of fitness is that women themselves do not want the vote. The rest of the poem describes all of the things (customs, roles, oppressions) women have been given without asking for. These are primarily, as in the case of the question, "Did we seek to be forbidden from all the trades that pay?" about women's desire to produce, not to consume. The poem concludes that "what women want has never been a strongly acting cause."[24]

Gilman also argued, however, in *The Home*, in accordance with her belief that the home should be reorganized along industrial lines, that whenever modern industry or institutions had replaced women's domestic labor, the result had been good. Kindergartens, she claimed, were an obvious improvement over education at home. Bread had "risen greatly in excellence as we make less and less at home." Store-bought clothes were superior to those made at home. Everything that one could buy was better than what one could do by oneself. Just as men no longer go off and kill what their families eat and wear, so the modern woman should no longer perform the myriad tasks of the women of previous centuries. She should, instead, sell her labor and buy the domestic products she and her family need. Gilman's emphasis on the productive desire of women led her into a backdoor defense of consumption. It led her to defend, in fact, the consumption of manufactured products, exactly those products advertised in the magazines that provided Gilman with her largest audiences.

Edith Wharton, although her tastes ran to other than the mass-produced goods advertised in the women's magazines, also provided, in her picture of Lily Bart's finally tragic inability to market herself, the ineluctable conclusion that the only thing worse than vulgar buying and selling is having no sale at all. Even if marketing oneself leads to self-degradation, it is nonetheless inescapable. To remove oneself from circulation is to die, and therefore the rest cure is counterproductive. To be denied productivity is, like the narrator gone mad at the end of "The Yellow Wallpaper," to enact some kind of horrible mimicry of real circulation or, like Lily Bart, to enact a gothic parody of the prescription for rest and isolation. Like Freeman, who used neurasthenic discourse to maintain a measured distance from cosmopolitan consumer culture, Wharton and Gilman never embraced the "new basis of civilization." Wharton actually argued that civilization was losing its basis rather than getting a new one. Freeman's representations of the provincial morbidity of New England helped deny the rural rejection of cosmopolitan spending. Wharton's omnidirectional jeremiad against accumulated money helped usher out a capital-based notion of the personal economy, and Gilman's desire to allow women productive work helped reshape women as consumers. When the smoke cleared, neurasthenia had disappeared.

8 The Blues and the Double Consciousness of Henry James and W. E. B. Du Bois

There's always enough of one's old self left to suffer with.
—Edith Wharton, "Quicksand" (1904)

Henry James and W. E. B. Du Bois are rarely seen as writers within a single tradition and are rarely discussed together, despite a series of striking similarities in background and activity. Both men were from the Northeast and had, in fact, many acquaintances in common, not least of whom was William James, Henry's brother and Du Bois's teacher at Harvard. Both also had grandfathers who were very successful businessmen and fathers less successful as businessmen, and both published novels and essays. Most important for our purposes, both published what many have considered to be their chefs d'oeuvre in 1903—James's *Ambassadors* and Du Bois's *Souls of Black Folk*. Each of these texts constructs a notion of psychology which existed then on the periphery, but was soon to be seen as at the forefront, of psychological understanding: both speak of a double consciousness.[1]

Surface and depth models of consciousness like Freud's, and models of multiplicity based on a real and an apparent self—such as those represented by döpplegangers, Jekylls and Hydes, and the like—were more widespread than the model both James and Du Bois employed. Mary Austin, for instance, in *The Land of Little Rain* (1903), uses a surface-depth model when she writes about yucca cacti, related in her text to the lives of the Shoshone and other tribes of the desert: "The real struggle for existence, the real brain of the plant, is underground." In popular fiction, images of danger in depths abound, from the snakes underfoot in Claude H. Wetmore's adventure story *In a Brazilian Jungle* (1903) to James Lane Allen's *Mettle of the Pasture* (1903), where the heroine "rises above" her evil suitor's perfidity but only as "deep changes were wrought out in her," changes deep within her psyche. "All the deep displacement and destruction . . . within," the narrator tells us, is partially cured by rest, for "while we have slept we have still been subject to that onmoving energy of the world that incessantly renews us yet transmutes us—double mystery of our permanence and our change." The climactic chapter of Booth Tarkington's *Cherry* (1903) is titled "The Double Villain" and is replete with images of being covered by snow and stuck under heavy weights to compliment the theme of duplicity. F. Marion Crawford's *Man Overboard* (1903) is a ghost story in which the döppleganger, the unconscious twin, is a presence represented as worse than the plague and which the plot consigns to rest under the sea. In Alfred Henry Lewis's *Peggy O'Neal* (1903), a romantic comedy that explores issues of class, gender, and ethnicity, the unsympathetic character, a retired general, concludes that the difference between men and women is that women are weak while men are "deeper": "For she [woman] is a child, and nowise deep nor fortified of any rooted strength. Your man, on the other hand . . . is cold like an iceberg, and like an iceberg he rides steadily throughout every gale with nine-tenths of him beneath the sea." For the general, depth is safety, since "your tempest can go no deeper than the surface; it cannot search the ocean's depths, and so the man swims safely." But the protagonist is quick to remind us that such thinking is wrongheaded, and the black servant concludes that "D'Marse General is a pow'ful fine soger an' all that, but he shore don't know enough 'bout women folks to wad a gun."[2]

In the 1903 issues of *Records of the Past*, a monthly journal devoted to archaeological exploration, in which surface-depth language might seem appropriate, very little of such rhetoric is applied to the work of archaeologists, but in the advertising pages it is used to describe books dealing with religion, especially those attempting to reconcile religion and science. The advertising copy and the excerpts from reprinted criticism cited in the ads refer to the "deep things of God," the "real substance at the bottom" of doctrine, "very deep" subjects, and the like. The kind of doubleness represented by the advertisements is in direct opposition to the more scientific view, in which such supernatural doubleness is denied or at least elided, and hence the absence of such language in the text of articles in the journal itself. Sherwin Cody's *Art of Writing and Speaking the English Language* (1903), despite the use of the word "art" in the title, claims that grammar is science, a purely logical set of relationships, and that, for instance, "there are not two ways to punctuate the same passage and still convey exactly the same meaning."[3] James and Du

Bois reject both the scientific denial of doubleness and the popular hierarchal doubleness of moral surfaces and depths. In a more than coincidental adoption of a new psychology, both recast doubleness as a necessary psychological fact related to changing social relations.

Diplomatic Resolution: James's *Ambassadors*

There is a doubleness in James's style, as in all irony, and in James's case the doubleness has a certain intensity, for despite all the self-assurance of the prose and the self-proclaimed mastery of his style, it is a nervous irony that James produces. We can see in James, as he writes of the "double-consciousness" that Strether feels in *The Ambassadors*, a certain "detachment in his zeal and curiosity in his indifference" (18). Detachment, zeal, and indifference are words it would be fairly easy to link to neurasthenia. Curiosity is somewhat out of the ken, except insofar as it is related to the nervous fascination with psychic phenomena and the supernatural. Strether's curiosity, however, is of a decidedly worldly sort. Neurasthenia, as I have said, had a history, and James, through Strether's double consciousness, can illustrate for us the movement of that history. In particular, neurasthenia changed over time, as some other historians have noted, from a fashionable disease to a popular one before it disappeared altogether. F. G. Gosling, for instance, has discussed the democratization of nervous disease, but his conclusion—"The recognition of nervous disorders as diseases that transcended both class and gender boundaries was an important step in the transition from Beardianism to Freudianism"—places the change in a narrative of the rise of psychoanalysis.[4] Freudianism could instead be considered one aspect of a democratization of (or a widening of the market for) the professional management of emotional life, which is itself related to widespread changes in economic life and economic thinking. James's recognition of diseases that cross class boundaries may represent part of a transition from Beardianism, but not simply one within the intellectual history of Freudianism. As *The Ambassadors* makes clear, it is not the history of the therapeutic, or what we might call the marketing of advice, that intervenes to marginalize neurasthenia, it is advertising, or marketing advice, that finally replaces the economy of nerve force.

Although Henry James was neurasthenic when the disease was fashionable, by the time it had started to become popular he had stopped referring to himself in the terms of neurasthenia. It had become the "American disease" and, for James, a symptom of American provincialism. In *The Ambassadors*, and in the stories in *The Better Sort* (1903), we see neurasthenia as either no longer a mark of distinction or at best a false marker. Characters maintain their nervousness only inasmuch as they maintain their provinciality, or they are shown to be somewhat déclassé to begin with. In "The Birthplace," for instance, the Gedges, who take over the management, including tours, of the birthplace of some unnamed literary figure (often taken in the critical literature to be Shakespeare), were "nervous, anxious, sensitive persons" whose "exhaustion" had "overtaken" them some time before.[5] But the Gedges had, we are told, "a pride . . . above their position," and although Mr. Gedges's view of cultural history may have been decidedly superior to that of either the visitors or the Board of Directors, he also had some very rough edges, and without this fairly humiliating job as caretaker he and his wife would be penniless and out on the street, as he himself fears, "beg[ging] for bread" or "taking in washing" (292). As the always discriminating Charles Eliot Norton wrote to Howells: "I am fond of Harry James & recognize his admirable and exceptional gifts, but I cannot read his late books without repulsion & wonder. If these people are his 'Better Sort' what can the Worst Sort be? How can he spend his days & himself on such an unredeemed lot, whom he, no less than you or I, would shrink from, at least would not wish to associate intimately with in real life.'"[6] One can also imagine Norton shrinking from intimacy with the "unredeemed lot" of upstart neurasthenics such as Theodore Dreiser and Emma Goldman.

Still, James was not ready to throw over the entire neurasthenic world view. Strether is committed to get nothing for himself, and James, too, represents himself as not ready to embrace the consumption economy or the ideas and values that were replacing the ideal of capital reinvestment on which the discourse of neurasthenia was based: in *The American Scene*, which he began on his return to America in 1904, James would rail against commercialism, advertising, and the rest of the complex that announced loudly, however little it was heard, the arrival of a reconstructed economic order. Max Weber (also a teacher of Du Bois's), after his 1904 visit to America wrote his foreboding conclusion to *The Protestant Ethic*, bewailing a modern ethic he did not fully understand and yet forcefully analyzed. In a similar way, James's visit in 1904 caused him to reject much of the development that was in important ways the mirror of his own artistic development. Despite the fact that his prose is itself marked by a neurasthenic style—a highly refined and "civilized" style in which force is diffused, in which indecision is syntactically figured, and which is at the same time both enervated and hyperactive—his psychology and ethics had stepped into the modern as surely as the New York City skyline had changed during his twenty-year exile. This combination of a postneurasthenic moral psychology and a neurasthenic style is abundantly clear in *The Ambassadors*.

James had a very complex series of relationships to neurasthenic discourse. Although he eventually came to reject it as provincial and outdated, he used the diagnosis, perhaps quite consciously, to his own profit when young. And even though in his later rejection he came to see the relation of neurasthenia to systems of discipline and to personal readjustment more clearly than any of his contemporaries, like Edith Wharton he held conspicuously to some of the values— particularly values of style—of the society that had created the disease, and he held onto them longer than almost anyone in what we might call his cohort. After reading James's *Notes of a Son and Brother* in 1914, for instance, Henry Adams wrote a letter—which James in his often-quoted reply called a "melancholy outpouring"— claiming that they had both outlived their time. Adams also wrote to Elizabeth Cameron about James's autobiography: "Poor Henry James thinks it all real, I believe, and actually still lives in that dreamy, stuffy Newport and Cambridge, with papa James and Charles Norton—and me! Yet, why! It is a terrible dream."[7]

Invalidism, as Ruth Bernard Yeazell has put it, "always seems to have had its strange attractions for the Jameses," and although it should be clear that the attractions were not strange in the sense of being abnormal or exceptional given the epidemic of invalidism in which they found themselves, the particular forms invalidism took for each of the Jameses were highly idiosyncratic. William James's work—in his theory of the will, for instance, as well as in *The Varieties of Religious Experience*—maintained, for all its modernity, a neurasthenic logic, while Alice James both insisted on and resisted the medical interpretation of her position; both William and Alice remained committed to neurasthenic problematics until the ends of their lives, though they explicitly rejected some of the social underpinnings of the disease. Their brother Henry, though he argued for the maintenance of those same underpinnings even while he bemoaned their passing, was eventually able to see neurasthenia as a passing aspect of culture and, in fact, one already on the way out in 1903.[8]

Henry James believed that historical perspective itself worked as a kind of cure—a modern replacement and reversal of neurasthenic views of progress—but such a perspective came fairly late. James's early life, according to his own autobiography, was suffused with sickness. The earliest neurasthenic episode in the autobiography recapitulates (it was written after) the description of Strether in *The Ambassadors*. In *A Small Boy and Others* James describes one moment in his childhood as "crucial, as supremely determinant." In 1855 the James family was in Europe, and twelve-year-old Henry was suffering from intermittent fever associated with a malarial condition. He describes his time in bed as "short sweet times when I could be left alone," in which "I first tasted the very greatest pleasure I was ever to know," the pleasure of the "fine art" of "taking in" (158–59). Like Strether, the young James is pleased most of all with the view of Paris from a little balcony.

What James says his young self took in, in this "supremely determinant" instant, was the "ecstatic vision" of " 'Europe,' sublime synthesis," in the form of a ruined castle and a peasant woman. Although this was but "the momentary measure of a small sick boy," James writes of this feudal vision, "it made a bridge over to more things than I knew." The joy he experienced was "doubtless partly the sense of fantastic ease" of the sickbed and partly the "invidious luxuries" he was awarded for being sick, and all of this together he describes as "the whole perfect Parisianism I seemed myself always to have possessed mentally—even if I had just turned twelve!" To complete the neurasthenic passage, James gives us the economistic version as well: "We seize our property by an avid instinct wherever we find it, and I must have kept seizing mine at the absurdest little rate, and all by this deeply dissimulative process of taking in, through the whole succession of summer days." "Dissimulation" is used in a letter from Henry James, Sr., to Henry, Jr. (reprinted in *Notes of a Son and Brother*), in which the father worries about William's dissimulation and speaks of his hope that William will overcome being " 'hypochondriachal.' " Henry, Sr., comments that William "used that word, though perhaps less in substance than in form," and of course with both hypochondria and neurasthenia substance and form are impossible to distinguish even in cases where dissimulation is not an issue. In the autobiographies of Henry, Jr., sickness is more than just dissimulation. *A Small Boy and Others* returns, in its last paragraph, and last sentence, to an evocation of the "strong sick whirl" of these early moments. Sickness functions as both climax and conclusion of the first volume of James's autobiography.[9]

At exactly the time of the invention of neurasthenia, that is at the time of the Civil War, Henry James suffered from his now famous "obscure hurt," which has been speculated to be anything from back strain to castration, but which at any rate left James unfit, by his own reckoning, to enter the service. The doctor he saw about his malady, again by James's own account, treated him with "a comparative pooh-pooh," despite the fact that he was suffering from a "huge comprehensive ache." His self-administered cure was "agitated scraps of rest." One possibility, which again he suggests himself, is that the pain was trumped up, though he admits that "to have trumped up a lameness at such a juncture could be made to pass in no light as graceful" (411–16). Howard Feinstein has shown very convincingly that James quite consciously used trumped-up illnesses to get money for European travel from his parents in the later 1860s.[10] Whoever was "sickest" in the James family (unless it was Alice) got to go to Europe, and Feinstein details the correspondence with which James elongated his stays in Europe through reports of near-cures and relapses. The "manipulative politics of invalidism" abounded in the family, and Henry, particularly when presenting himself as needing European travel as a cure, was the most adept at maintaining the appearance of illness and the promise of improvement.

Feinstein's argument suggests, in short, that Henry James quite consciously manipulated neurasthenia for his own ends. James had what according to the doctors was a textbook diathesis, a background, occupation, sensitivity, education, and environment that would all contribute to a nervous constitution, yet he was the least ill of his siblings and seemed to use the disease as simply one more part of the social machinery he worked with such ease. During 1903, for instance, there is no sign of personal nervousness, none of the usual symptoms. Edith Wharton would speak of the "morbidly delicate sensibility" of James at this time, but nothing in his letters, notebooks, or elsewhere indicates any such self-perception. In his letters, James sometimes ironically inflates his distress at not fulfilling some ideal notion of his social obligations (sometimes described as being "sick" about his own shortcomings), but he certainly feels the distress even less than he wants his correspondent to think he feels it.[11] His manipulation of the language of illness betrays a consciousness of its multiple uses and of the inadequacy of medical explanations.

More in the late novels than elsewhere, perhaps because of what Adams called James's terrible dream of tradition, and perhaps because his style represents the culmination of a lifetime of refining neurasthenic explanation, James's celebrated and refined prose has a neurasthenic quality. Ian Watt has argued that, in *The Ambassadors*, "the main grammatical subjects are very often nouns for mental ideas . . . and the verbs . . . tend to express states of being rather than particular finite actions." Watt also talks of James's "slowness and deliberation" and sees a "bewilderment" written into the text. William Veeder has shown how James's style was developed from the materials of popular fiction, which I in turn have shown are suffused with neurasthenic themes and language. John H. Raleigh writes that James's characters have certain traits in common which necessitate his prose style—"their sensitivity, their acquisitiveness, their individualism, the ambiguous quality of their motivations, which are always concerned with ethical choice, but never have reference to an explicit moral code, their supreme esthetic sense." Although Raleigh argues that the source of the complex is Lockean empiricism, the sociology of neurasthenia was closer to home for the writer and his readers.[12] The reliance on abstract nouns and intransitive verbs, the passive constructions, the repeatedly qualifying phrases which divorce the subject from what few active verbs are used, the minutely detailed refractions of consciousness and moral conundrums, all combine to create a prose that is at the same time enervated and enervating, measured and intense, a prose as high-strung and finely organized as an ideal neurasthenic patient.

James believed, according to his Preface to *The Ambassadors*, that whatever "headlong energy" was used in presenting a story, it should "pale before the energy" of the story itself. The result, he claimed for *The Ambassadors*, was a "splendid particular economy." James goes on in the Preface to compare his work as a novelist to that of a "chief accountant" who must "keep his head at any price." But for the characters and for the reader, the economy of the telling, as many critics have pointed out, is linked to indecisiveness. Critics have been tempted to take the text's indecisiveness as an invitation to decide for or against the characters and their actions, to tilt the scales of the text's carefully constructed neurasthenic balance. Such temptation led E. M. Forster to claim in *Aspects of the Novel*, for instance, that "maimed creatures alone can breathe in Henry James's pages—maimed yet specialized." While such a reading ignores half the balance, Forster is right that James's prose necessarily recreates a neurasthenic world. As William C. Brownell wrote, responding to the manuscript of *The Sacred Fount* for Scribner's: "It is surely the n + 1st power of Jamesiness. . . . It gets decidedly on one's nerves. It is like trying to make out page after page of illegible writing. The sense of effort becomes truly exasperating. Your spine curls up, your hair-roots prickle & you want to get up and walk around the block."[13] The curling spine was one of Norris's favorite descriptions of neurasthenia, the prickling hair-roots one of Dreiser's, the exercised response Roosevelt's.

James is far from accepting the medical theorists of neurasthenia at face value, however, and in *The Ambassadors* none of the sufferers suffers in ways or for causes in line with the medical theory. *The*

Ambassadors was published in monthly installments in the *North American Review* from January to December 1903, and through most of the year the lead article in the *Review* was Mark Twain's *Christian Science*. Each month on the title page Twain's series of articles and the chapters of James's novel were displayed in larger, bolder type than the rest of the contents, Twain's at the top, James's at the bottom. These very different texts on the medicalization of complaint and its relation to changing economic conditions framed the rest of the reading in this important elite intellectual forum through most of 1903. The opening of the novel, with its repeated references to nervous prostration and nervous remedies, seems like a late-Victorian version of *Marat-Sade*, in which various "sick" people, each with a different notion of reality, attempt to take care of one another. Strether's friend and compatriot Waymarsh, we are told, is coming to meet him from Malvern, an English town famous for its water cure. Waymarsh, in coming to Europe, had "barely escaped, by flight in time, a general nervous collapse," the collapse that functioned as the "very proof of the full life, as the full life was understood at Milrose," his home town. Already James has signaled his distance from the social understanding of neurasthenia, since *The Ambassadors* continually shows the full life as it is understood in Milrose to be anything but full.

Strether, too, has trouble squaring his own notion of Waymarsh's "success," both personal and financial, and the "rigour with which, on the edge of his bed, [Waymarsh] hugged his posture of prolonged impermanence. It suggested to [Strether] something that always, when kept up, worried him—a person established in a railway coach with a forward inclination" (30). This worrying, forward inclination is an attitude that Strether more strenuously abjures as the novel progresses, but in our first exposure to it there is something comic. Waymarsh is at first a caricature of intense nervousness, and in his posture is ridiculously old-fashioned; he is a rail traveler from the middle of the previous century, uncomfortable and nervous. James has Waymarsh himself mouth one of the ironic critiques of medical opinion when he claims that despite his cures he is still "dog-tired," saying "it's this wild hunt for rest that takes all the life out of me" (32).[14]

Right after we learn of "the sufferer" Waymarsh's "overwork" and "prostration," we learn from Waymarsh that Strether, himself, has supposedly come to Europe because of his own case of "prostration." And Waymarsh in his turn throws doubt on that. "You don't appear sick to speak of," he tells Strether, and Strether admits that although he was, in fact, "dog-tired" when he left, he was already feeling better:

"I guess I don't *feel* sick now that I've started. But I had pretty well run down before I did start." The emphasis on feeling sick—as opposed to being sick—signals the direction James will take the discourse. In a novel that illustrates both the complexity and the relativity of moral values and social reality, notions of sickness, especially those so closely tied to morality as neurasthenia, are shown to be created intersubjectively, and thereby to be intersubjectively modifiable. Sickness not only will vary according to who is performing the diagnosis, but a valid diagnosis also needs to take into consideration the possibilities that one can be sick, feel sick, act sick, feign sickness, or feign health. The testimony of the patient at least potentially becomes more important than the theories of the doctor. But the testimony of the doctor remains important for purposes of dissimulation, a fallback when the patient's own testimony is ill-advised. When Waymarsh asks Strether what is "back of" his prostration, hinting that Strether is feigning, however, Strether's smile dims and he answers, in what may or may not be a feint to the doctors, simply that "back of" his prostration, "There are all the causes of it!" (32).

But whatever the causes of either man's neurasthenia, the European cure does not seem to be working on the prostrate Waymarsh, whom Strether has elaborately tucked in like "a patient in a hospital," while Strether himself seems instantly cured. With a feeling like "that of a nurse who had earned personal rest by having made everything straight" (32–33), Strether has made, on his first day in Europe, a complete *volte face* from his own position as a nervous patient. Waymarsh on the other hand comically retains the idea of his own imminent collapse, despite the fact that he seems quite energetic and untroubled during the rest of the novel, except for the regularity with which the dark clouds of his disapproval of Strether tend to gather.

The third principal American character, if that is the right word for a woman never directly represented in the text, is also a neurasthenic. According to James's preliminary "Project" as sketched for his publisher Mrs. Newsome, whose son Strether has come to Europe to rescue from unnamed infamy, is "high, strenuous, nervous, 'intense' (oh, a type!)... invalidical, exalted, depressed, at once shrill and muffled, at once extremely abounding and extremely narrow."[15] This description—"oh, a type!"—again highlights the ironic distance James held, by the turn of the century, regarding the sufferings of the "invalidical." James also deconstructs the distinction between the neurasthenic and the strenuous life in offering "strenuous" and "nervous" as metonyms or at least aspects of a syndrome. Mrs. Newsome is the one person in the text who does not come to Europe and is the one person whose rigid moral code does not undergo any change: she remains both strenuous and nervous throughout. As a type, she functions all the more clearly as one of the moral poles in the book. All the other Americans—including the further ambassadors sent to rescue the obviously failing Strether—are affected by Europe to the point where they no longer clearly represent any moral code at all.

The great oddity about her son, Chad, from the point of view of neurasthenic morality, is that he is not sick; by rights, since he is not properly reinvesting his energy, and seems to be wasting his energy sexually, he should be the one who is prostrate. Strether's great surprise is that Chad is not prostrate from all his dissipation; in fact he seems all the more energetic and healthy for it. Instead of being nervously bankrupt, as expected, Chad is found to be quite literally flush. When Strether first meets Chad's friend Little Bilham, he is amazed at Bilham's "serenity" and further amazed when he realizes that this is related to the fact that Bilham "hadn't a prejudice." Strether had thought that moral prejudice, moral rigor, was necessary in order to avoid nervousness and to attain serenity, and therefore he unsuccessfully tries, at first, to see Bilham's serenity (his "general exemption from alarm, anxiety or remorse" about his lack of occupation, for instance) as the "trail of the serpent, the corruption, as he might conveniently have said, of Europe." But instead Strether finds that he agrees with Maria Gostrey that Bilham is "far and away . . . the best of them" (83–86).

Chad presents the same dilemma: he has become more "refined"—a "refinement that had been a good deal wanted"—through the activity that was supposed to be his undoing. To express what had been "a good deal wanted," the narrator suggests people might have wanted him to look more like his mother, the morally rigorous parent, rather than his rapacious father. Instead Strether finds him improved very much despite the fact that "no resemblance whatever to the mother had supervened. It would have been hard for a young man's face and air to disconnect themselves more completely than Chad's at this juncture from any discerned, from any imaginable aspect of a New England female parent" (92). Though he has lost any relation to the "New England conscience" as well as the New England female parent, Chad's manner had nonetheless become, from the neurasthenic point of view, admirably efficient. "He had formerly, with a great deal of action, expressed very little; and he now expressed whatever was necessary with almost none at all" (97): he had learned to speak softly. All the signs of Chad's distinction, ease, refinement, and "improvement" distress Strether precisely because they work against his neurasthenic notions of ethical cause and effect. At one point Strether does manage to see some sign that Chad is "really nervous" despite appearances, and this, the narrator tells us, he took "as what he would have called a wholesome sign" (97). But Strether later decides that he has misinterpreted as nervousness a shyness that is simply another example of the "good manners" Chad has assimilated.

Chad, Strether decides after his first meeting, is a "Pagan." "Christian" is, of course, one of the most common overarching terms for describing the general tenor of Woollett and of New England in general, and in particular that class of New Englanders represented by the Americans in the novel. This is "Christian" in the sense that Theodore Roosevelt and robber barons like Robert Baer used the term, to describe the self-perception of cultural elites in such a way as might still garner hegemonic consent. The "Christian gentleman," however, was apparently becoming a bit of an anachronism. Strether would like to think that "Pagan" and "gentleman" are descriptions at odds with each other but finds that they are not. Waymarsh, whose brooding possessiveness Strether early on describes as the "sacred rage," is a typical Christian gentleman of the neurasthenic type, and his "success" in Paris is due to his being so easily identifiable as such, an American type with some physical resemblance to, and going the way of, the buffalo. The combination of Waymarsh's brooding propriety and his frenetic shopping is what makes him a comic character, a moral dodo bird in the cosmopolitan world of the Parisian fashion system, and subject to that system all the more for his relation to tradition.[16]

The desire for Chad to come home is based on the plans of his deceased father, who, in his infinite business wisdom, had foreseen the economic wave of the future and had laid out plans for vast expansion. This expansion was to be based on the latest marketing techniques, which were not yet applicable when he was alive, but which he predicted would be by the time his son was ready to take the helm. Therefore, Strether muses, though as readers we don't yet know why, "a Pagan was perhaps, at the pass they had come to, the thing most wanted at Woollett" (99–100). The lack of "Christian" morality implied in Chad's inoculation against nervousness and in his sensuality make him more fit for pulling the strings of the market than perhaps any other qualification. Some ten years after Baer declaimed about the "Christian gentlemen to whom God in His infinite wisdom has entrusted" the future of America and while Roosevelt continued to orate on the Christian duty to export peace to the heathen, James argued that it is instead godless men who are most fit to be entrusted with the business of America. In the face of this new order, Strether, though he never makes reference to Christian values himself, feels he has nevertheless become an anachronism in a number of ways.

At the beginning of the novel, woven through all the talk of sickness, prostration, and hospitals, is the theme of success. Waymarsh is a financial success; Strether so far is not. Strether wants to be successful in his ambassadorial role, which will insure his marriage to Mrs. Newsome. Gostrey assures him, even before she knows of his mission, that he is going to be a huge success, as will Waymarsh, although of a different sort. Chad's father was most obviously a success, and Chad has been a success of sorts. All of this reaches a tentative conclusion at the end of Book I when Gostrey says to Strether: "Thank goodness you're a failure—it's why I so distinguish you! Anything else to-day is too hideous. Look about you—look at the successes. Would you *be* one, on your honor? Look, moreover . . . at me." When Strether agrees that she, too, is "out of it," she replies that "the superiority you discern in me . . . announces my futility." Superiority and distinction are associated with futility—Gostrey, Strether, Little Bilham—and success with hideousness, paganism, toilets (or whatever the article is that is manufactured by the Newsome concern), and modern advertising programs.

On the one hand this schematization of values is similar to that of the various neurasthenic gospels of relaxation, the appeal of which lay in their ability to calm fears of the future and relax the standards of the past at the same time. In other words, James's arrangement of values remains very close to the arrangement he is apparently criticizing. He retained an aristocratic distaste for business success— it was Henry James who claimed that his family had not been "guilty" of any business activity for two generations—and for anything smacking of the primitive or vulgar, and at the same time sought success in the literary market at every juncture. Even to worry about business at this level is naive, and compared to the economic thinking of Thorstein Veblen, Eugene Debs, Emma Goldman, other socialists and anarchists, or the new demand-side economists Simon Nelson Patten and Richard T. Ely, James's is a fairly naive and reactionary response to economic developments. It is hard to read James's reactions to economic and social change in *The American Scene*, for instance, without continually receiving the impression that he is "out of it." Norris and Garland wrote of economic realities in large degree already part of the past and remained tied to a capital-based, moralistic, and somewhat ascetic view of economic activity, as did such economists as Charlotte Perkins Gilman and Edward Atkinson, whose *The Industrial Progress of the Nation: Consumption Limited, Production Unlimited* sums up in its title the preconsumerist view of the economy still held by many economists. James, on the other hand, is able to point to the pertinent variables and innovations and to show the importance to cultural perceptions which those changes imply.[17]

Most central of these is the way that economic theory was being shorn of any moral or ethical meaning. Neurasthenia was constructed of both a moralistic economics and an economistic morality dressed up with a medical lexicon and thereby provided seemingly scientific evaluative criteria for moral judgments about success and failure. But if Strether is a success in Europe, he is a failure in America. What looked like his moral (and financial) responsibility in America are reversed when he gets to Europe, so that what he comes to see as his moral responsibility and his financial security are absolutely at odds. James is charting the moral effects of cultural relativism and quite accurately predicts that those who can move easily in different moral universes stand the best chance to benefit financially from the changing economic world. Cultural relativism is itself produced by money—Americans go to Europe when they have enough money, museums fund field research for anthropologists when they have enough money, immigrants come to America to make money—and Strether's mission is to bring back a man who because of his relativism can make even more money for the firm. Chad, since he moves most easily in all worlds, is the man most fit for financial leadership. The world of moral force and nerve force is being replaced, and we are told quite explicitly with what: "Advertising scientifically worked, presented itself thus as the great new force" (339).

Nervous Renunciation

Henry Adams, writing from Paris in November 1903, told James he had written the story of the life of all Bostonians of their generation, of the "type bourgeois bostonien," and, more particularly, Adams specified "your own and mine—pure autobiography, the more keen for what is beneath, implied." And Adams recognized as essential to the typical and autobiographical portrait what he called a "nervous self-consciousness" in which "self-distrust became introspection." Adams was talking about another of James's works published in 1903, *William Wetmore Story and His Friends: From Letters, Diaries and Recollections*, which was, in fact, a biography of a bourgeois bostonien.[18] But it might be applied no less to the story of Waymarsh and Strether. James saw the essential theme of the novel as widely applicable, if not universal, and in fact in his 1903 article on Zola he described the French naturalist novelist as "a man with arrears of personal history to make up," who like Strether was possessed of "a spirit for which life, or for which at any rate freedom, had been too much postponed," a spirit that was "treating itself at last to a luxury of experience."[19] Strether's position is not simply that of the Bostonian; his life in Massachusetts determined only the forms his postponements took. His relation to freedom and experience, according to James, is in general terms the same as that of the French novelist.

The forms that Henry James's postponements took were in some ways more like those of Chad Newsome than Strether's, since James, like Newsome, came to Europe as a young man and ignored the familial desire for his return to America. During the crisis of the novel Chad removes himself from the fray and goes to England to study the latest developments in the art of advertising, much as James removed himself from family pressures to pursue his art and career in England. But James also clearly identified with Strether, as when writing to his young and recent enamorado Jocelyn Persse in late-Stretherian tones in 1903—"may you suffer yourself to be pelted with as many of the flowers of experience as you can"—or more directly when he gave Persse *The Ambassadors* and asked that he "try to like the poor hero, in whom you will find a vague resemblance (though not facial!) to yours always Henry James."[20] The doubleness of representation here is emphasized by Strether's apparent imitation of Chad. When Strether arrives in Europe, he finds Chad to have been marvelously remade, remarkable and refined, and Strether begins to become, in many ways, more and more like him. The ambassador, in his double consciousness, has become a double agent.

The novel is a bit of a mimetic carnival, in fact: Strether wants at first to be more like Waymarsh and then more like Chad, and when the imitative Strether finally comes down in judgment on Chad he becomes immediately worried about Chad's judgment of him. More important, since this is a novel about perception, Strether imitates the perceptions of everyone around him, and he is happiest when he can get Maria Gostrey to imitate his perceptions. Veblen's *Theory of the Leisure Class* argued that emulation was at the center of the construction of class and class consciousness, and James is representing emulation in an even more comic light than Veblen does. Strether has moved from a country where people imitate each other's sicknesses to one where they imitate each other's pleasures, and it is this apparently unavoidable process of imitation that is constantly surprising him. Finally he finds that he has imitated Chad's love for Mme de Vionnet, the woman from whose snares Strether is supposed to rescue Chad.

Thus his double consciousness persists. Although he has, through imitating the Parisians and expatriates, adopted a new way of life and a new set of social relations, he has not been able to slough off the old Strether, the old values. As James wrote in a lecture given during his American tour in 1904, a people's social relations are constructed by their speech, and Strether has had no way of speaking of his new relations to his old relations except in the old language of relation. He cannot find a way to advertise his new improved self, and when he tried to advertise Chad as new and improved, not only did Strether find that perhaps he had exaggerated the improvement, as a good advertiser must, but he also found that no one that he was trying to convince bought the story anyway. Strether may be a much less questionable salesperson than Selah Tarrant of *The Bostonians*, but Strether has less of Tarrant's ability as well. Strether knows literature, but he does not know advertising.

Strether therefore does not try to speak his way free of the original half of his double consciousness, but returns to America. Freedom is something he has tasted, but not something that one can "have." He is left feeling, as he says, that his "only logic" is the logic of neurasthenic asceticism that he began with, the logic of renunciation and social norms. Julie Rivkin has argued that the prevailing logic in *The Ambassadors* is one of delegation, of Derridean supplementarity. I quote from her article at length because it makes many of my points, however divergent our conclusions. In *The Ambassadors*:

> An economic theory of representation as the preservation of the original is replaced with a theory of representation as a potentially infinite dispersal of delegates without a guiding origin or authority. And a New England economy of experience as holding in reserve or saving is replaced with a Parisian economy of experience as necessitating an expenditure without reserve, loss without a guaranteed gain. . . . By displacing the economy of representation that governed Strether's initial conception of experience, Mme de Vionnet also displaces the economy of commercial transaction that governed his initial conception of his mission.[21]

My only argument with this is that James's Parisian economy, within which Chad the nascent advertiser is quite obviously at home, is itself a representation of the new New England economy, the economy whose essence is advertising and dissimulation; that Strether's initial conception of his mission in relation to the economy of commercial transaction turns out to be as anachronistic as his conception of moral and bodily economy; and that therefore Strether has not renounced commercialism in favor of a Parisian economy of loss and dispersal, as Rivkin would have it, but has renounced the new commercialism represented (for the American ambassadors) by Paris and the new Chad, in favor of an older, neurasthenic notion of economics. His renunciation is one governed by the New England economy of saving rather than the Parisian ethic of spending, an ethic Chad is being brought home to encourage in Woollett and environs. Chad's consumerist denial of neurasthenic economy was foreseen by the farsighted businessman-father, who projected the need for incitements to spending and left as his legacy a son with the moral aptitude and a business with the capital accumulation which would make transition to the new economy possible and profitable.

But all this is somewhat dissimulative itself. James, who renounced his country and perhaps his sexuality, was no stranger to renunciation as a cure for double consciousness, especially double consciousness that is directly related to personal freedom and social expectation. Like Strether and Waymarsh, James managed to have his time in Europe, a time marked by the relaxation of some of those expectations, and like Strether's and Waymarsh's, James's time in Europe was originally what he had "bought" with his neurasthenia. Invalidism could be the price of leisure or, in the James family, the price of a trip to Europe. And though events, both cultural and personal, may have led to the conclusion that the neurasthenic world had passed and that the age of advertising had arrived, advertising retained the immoral aura of speculation. James's last major attempt at advertising his own work, the massive New York edition of 1908, ended in failure in the marketplace and was surrounded by stretches of nervous invalidism.[22]

If there is a romanticization of self in the representation of Strether it is the idea that he has "not, out of the whole affair, to have got anything for [him]self," which is clearly a denial both of dissimulation and of exchange. Although in the end Strether is "out of it" in a different way than he was at the beginning of the novel, he still claims being "out of it" as a kind of moral victory. After all its detours into modern consciousness, the novel returns to modernism's incommensurate double, neurasthenic retirement. The forced recuperation of Strether comes too late, however, for even in the guise of wisdom, renunciation is powerless in an age in which advertising is the great force. As with Howells's psychology, renunciation has become the province of the lower classes, and Strether, whatever fate awaits him after he renounces his chance to marry Mrs. Newsome, will not, we assume, become a factory worker. *The Ambassadors*, like the other classic texts of American realism, ends by rejecting its own analysis, trying—more or less ineffectively depending on the particular reader—to subvert its own subversion, yet another example of the doubleness inherent in the adaptive strategies of the neurasthenic. *The Ambassadors* is thus a nervous advertisement for the questionable promise of the postneurasthenic world.

The Blues as Social Psychology:
Du Bois's *Souls of Black Folk*

Du Bois was never neurasthenic. But these same issues of freedom and social expectation are expressed in his own concept of double consciousness, one of the several major contributions to African-American cultural thought advanced in *The Souls of Black Folk* and one of the clearest statements of the new psychology in America at the turn of the century. What follows does little justice to Du Bois's life work or even to the text under examination. In some sense it does an injustice to Du Bois's work to insist on its similarities to that of James, since Du Bois himself insisted on difference. Insisting on difference, however, was itself common to the neurasthenic world view. When Du Bois claims that he had "a flood of Negro blood, a strain of French, a bit of Dutch, but thank God! no 'Anglo-Saxon,'" he is playing off, however ironically, the discourses of differential inheritance which formed an important strand of neurasthenic explanation.[23] Du Bois's concept of double consciousness (briefly, that black Americans have a conflicted, double consciousness as free, equal Americans and as unfree, unequal blacks) is in important ways similar to James's concept of double consciousness, and Du Bois's use of this particular conceptual and rhetorical strategy, like James's, is related to neurasthenia on the one hand and to notions of social life which, however common now, were new to the cultural horizon of the time. Just as Howells could be considered the premier psychologist of his generation because of his examination of multiple consciousnesses within individuals, and just as Freud was seen as discovering the unconscious, Du Bois and James can both be seen as examining the relation of the psychology of individuals and groups to social norms and practices in new and surprisingly similar ways. Although both men started in the same place, however, Du Bois's conclusions amount, in this analysis, to a criticism of James's notions of freedom and responsibility.

Both Henry James's and Du Bois's ideas were related, at some distance, to William James's and Charles Peirce's notions of habit and pragmatism. In the Preface Du Bois wrote for the Jubilee Edition of

The Souls of Black Folk in 1953, he claims that he had been a student of James, Royce, and Santayana and "was therefore not unprepared for the revolution in psychology which the Twentieth Century has brought." Nevertheless, he continues, the book "does not adequately allow for unconscious thought and the cake of custom in the growth and influence of race prejudice." This is a somewhat strange caveat, since Du Bois in 1903 used what now looks like a Freudian notion of repression, claiming, for instance, that if people are silenced, they either internalize their discontent, which leads to "paralysis," or "burst into speech so passionately and intemperately as to lose listeners" (45). Frantz Fanon, just a few years after Du Bois's retrospective apology, would use Freudian explanations for the same phenomena. But Du Bois's self-criticism makes sense if, when he claims that he had not adequately allowed for "the cake of custom," he means that he had taken too seriously the optimistic voluntarism of pragmatist notions of habit. Du Bois's invitation to his reader to take a ride with him in the Jim Crow car invokes the rhetoric of reform journalism and pragmatism, in a belief that he might, through exposé, persuade his audience to change basic habits of thought. *The Souls of Black Folk* in this sense shares the optimism and idealism of the reform movements that strongly influenced, and were most clearly codified by, William James's philosophical psychology.[24]

The other main revolution in early twentieth-century psychology, behaviorism, was also available to Du Bois. Edward L. Thorndike, professor of genetic psychology at Columbia, was a pioneer in the use of statistics in educational psychology and an important proponent of a behaviorist approach. By maintaining an evolutionary idea of mental functioning, however, he remained as optimistic as the reformers, without, at the same time, having any agenda for change. Thorndike wrote in *Educational Psychology* (1903) that "the universe of mental forms" is created by interaction with the natural and cultural environment, and that the resulting "new species of thought" are then in conflict with the old: "Species of thoughts like species of animals prey upon one another in a struggle in which survival is the victor's reward."[25] What Du Bois and Henry James show are species of thought not so much locked in a struggle to the death as mutually, however antagonistically, coexisting. Strether develops new species of thought without letting them kill off the old, even though they are in conflict, and Du Bois says American blacks necessarily carry with them the conflicting consciousnesses of their equal and unequal status.

In 1903 another pioneer of behaviorism, Ivan Pavlov, was performing and reporting on his first experiments in conditioned response, experiments that would suggest that Strether, for instance, simply could not learn the lessons of Europe as quickly as he does, since he learns new responses and abandons some of his old ones without the requisite conditioning. And Du Bois's theory would also simply not make sense in Pavlovian terms: conditioned more by their status as blacks than by their status as Americans, internal contradictions should be so clearly weighted toward the black and away from the American that no effective problem of response would develop. This is not to suggest that Du Bois was behind the times in his differences with behaviorism. On the contrary, his complex notions of the relation of ideology, practice, position, tradition, and socialization in the conditioning of response are more postbehaviorist than prebehaviorist. And his criticism of the use of statistics in sociology as a way to dehumanize subjects and mask the facts of political and cultural power is similar to criticisms of behaviorism and sociology which have been surfacing recently after the long hegemony of that approach in the social sciences.[26]

For both James and Du Bois, the doubleness of consciousness is a problem. For Du Bois, one half of black consciousness is an agent of debilitation, and double consciousness thereby a fact that incapacitates blacks. Similar to Veblen's notion of "trained incapacity," in which businessmen develop ways of thinking which inhibit their ability to respond to new phenomena, Du Bois's double consciousness is clearly a less optimistic concept than James's. Strether's exceptionality can be described as his capacity for innovation and improvisation, which allows him to act in new ways despite his training. Strether's peculiar problem is created by his training, but he somehow manages to act in a way that rebels against that training and jibes with it at the same time, and thereby is able to maintain both his dignity and his integrity. When Du Bois discusses American blacks and "the peculiar problems of their inner life" in *The Souls of Black Folk*, he sees two sets of possibilities:

> All this must mean a time of intense ethical ferment, of religious heart-searching and intellectual unrest. From the double life every American Negro must live, as a Negro and as an American, as swept on by the current of the nineteenth while yet struggling in the eddies of the fifteenth century,—from this must arise a painful self-consciousness, an almost morbid sense of personality and a moral hesitancy which is fatal to self-confidence. The worlds within and without the Veil of Color are changing, and changing rapidly, but not at the same rate, not in the same way; and this must produce a peculiar wrenching of the soul, a peculiar sense of doubt and be-

wilderment. Such a double life, with double thoughts, double duties, and double social classes, must give rise to double words and double ideals, and tempt the mind to pretence or revolt, to hypocrisy or radicalism. (148–49)

Strether, too, displays "an almost morbid sense of personality and a moral hesitancy which is fatal to self-confidence." But pretense or revolt, hypocrisy or radicalism, are not, we are shown, Strether's only choices. The romance of James's text lies in Strether's heroic ability to come up with a middle alternative. In this James remains more closely tied to the ethical idealism of both pragmatism and realism than does Du Bois, whose pragmatic optimism is rarely close to the surface.

The language Du Bois uses in this passage invokes neurasthenic discourse several times: "painful self-consciousness," "morbid sense of personality," "moral hesitancy," are both cause and effect of "intense . . . ferment" and "unrest," of "a peculiar wrenching of the soul, a peculiar sense of doubt and bewilderment," the result of which "is fatal to self-confidence." In the neurasthenic understanding of Beard these are not negative markers, of course, but signs of sensitivity, refinement, and civility. Earlier in the book Du Bois also uses neurasthenic description when talking about Josie, his student in Tennessee: she was "a little nervous . . . she had about her a certain fineness, the shadow of an unconscious moral heroism": Josie, despite Beard's pronouncements, is a neurasthenic type (56). And thus Josie, and all blacks, since all blacks suffer double consciousness, Du Bois argued, are as sensitive, refined, and morally heroic as that cream of white society that suffers, inwardly, because they have these same qualities. Du Bois is culturally enfranchising blacks by claiming that they are all, in effect, neurasthenic. Only the civilized and refined can suffer as Du Bois argued that blacks suffer.

But Du Bois does not stop there. "All in all, we black men seem the sole oasis of simple faith and reverence in a dusty desert of dollars and smartness. Will America be poorer if she replace her brutal dyspeptic blundering with light-hearted but determined Negro humility?" (22) As James did with Strether, whose determined humility is one of the marks of his integrity and who demonstrates simple values in a "desert of dollars and smartness," Du Bois uses the neurasthenic idiom—"dyspeptic blundering," which conjures up "dyspeptic plundering" as well—to indict commercialism. Part of Du Bois's criticism of Booker T. Washington is that the latter thoroughly accepted the values of "triumphant commercialism, and the ideals of material prosperity" (393). When Du Bois allows Washington a backhanded compliment, it is again in the language of neurasthenia: "And yet this very singleness of vision and thorough oneness with his age," Du Bois goes on, "is a mark of the successful man. It is as though Nature must needs make men narrow in order to give them force" (393). Du Bois, like James, uses both sides of the neurasthenic argument: force equals success equals narrowness equals neurasthenic lack of force.

And like William James, Du Bois centered part of his discussion on religion. Not only does he discuss Afro-American religion in detail, but his language itself is often biblical, as Arnold Rampersad has pointed out.[27] The title already suggests as much; his use of the plural "Souls" gives his discussion of double consciousness a spiritual resonance, and shows the kinship of his thought with that of William James in *The Varieties of Religious Experience*. James's "sick souls" and Du Bois's "Souls" are rhetorically aligned. As James writes, the essence of the sick soul's religious experience is the recognition of a fundamental problem; likewise, in "Of Our Spiritual Strivings," the first chapter of *Souls*, Du Bois rhetorically asks, "How does it feel to be a problem?" It is in his main chapter on religion, "On the Faith of the Fathers," that he introduces the idea of double consciousness. The paragraph from which the long quote above was taken begins: "It is difficult to explain clearly the present critical stage of Negro religion" (148). In both *Varieties* and *Souls*, religious experience is a sign of personal worth, and in both books the recognition of problem and cure completes the analysis of the meaning of religious experience. In both books religious striving represents that combination of the highest cultural aspirations and severe social sanctions which are at the heart of neurasthenia as a cultural phenomenon. The great difference, of course, is that Du Bois insists that the only "cure" possible is social change.

Du Bois was not alone among turn-of-the-century black writers in using neurasthenic discourse. The heroine of Pauline Hopkins's *Contending Forces* (1900) is a refined, nervous woman named after the Greek poet who first introduced the concept of double consciousness, Sappho. Hopkins's 1903 novel *Of One Blood* opens with a neurasthenic young man, an authority in "brain diseases" and a psychic researcher, who is despondent and considering suicide.[28] Charles Chesnutt opened *The Marrow of Tradition* (1901) with a portrait of a white woman who is a neurasthenic invalid, who has had a "nervous shock" brought on by seeing, from her bedroom window, her half-black half-sister in the street. Her unhealth highlights her half-sister's stoicism and moral conviction.[29] Chesnutt also edited a collection of essays in 1903, *The Negro Problem*, with essays by himself, Booker T. Washington, Du Bois, Monroe Trotter, and others.

Chesnutt's essay talks of racism as a disease and rejects the idea that time alone—a rest cure of sorts—will cure it. H. T. Kealing in the same collection constructs a catalogue of the "inborn," or racial, and "inbred," or socially conditioned, "characteristics of the Negro." The inborn characteristics, according to Kealing, include, on the one hand, blacks' spirituality, imaginativeness, eloquence, sensitivity— all parts of the nervous diathesis—and, on the other hand, cheerfulness, physical ability, and endurance, which are most decidedly not neurasthenic qualities. Inbred characteristics, those necessarily learned because of the position of blacks in American society, include improvidence, extravagance, indolence, and lack of initiative, neurasthenic symptoms all. Washington's essay begins with a similar premise, that "all forms of labor are honorable, and all forms of idleness are disgraceful." Although the baldness of Washington's statement seems to be a clear directive (Washington wants blacks to accept a place below whites for the present), he at the same time completely invalidates leisure, whether it be the indolence of blacks or the disgraceful idleness of the white leisure class.

Du Bois, who by 1903 had become one of Washington's most influential and unrelenting critics, contributed "The Talented Tenth" to Chesnutt's collection, and here again the claim for black equality is framed in terms related to neurasthenic understandings. In particular, Du Bois adopts the notion that a refined and educated few are the repositories of progress and civilization. Like Roosevelt in his arguments about race suicide, Du Bois argued that "the unrisen" will "pull the risen down" if the risen are not "strengthened."[30] Again Du Bois plays both sides by proving that educated blacks are not "spendthrifts" (he provides figures for the assessed value of real estate owned by college-educated blacks) but bewailing at the same time the fact that "the fortune of the millionaire [is] the only stamp of true and successful living" (56). Still his basic message is clear: the Talented Tenth are "missionaries of culture among their people" and "The Negro race, like all other races, is going to be saved by its exceptional men" (75).

Du Bois tends to be described as "complex," a writer and thinker full of paradox and contradiction. This label, of course, fits his own analysis: as a black and an educated American, he must have an interior life marked by contradiction and therefore complexity. But more to the point, the discourses out of which his own are woven, be they from sociology, religious study, or medicine, were themselves fraught with contradiction. August Meier described him as representing "the epitome of the paradoxes in American Negro thought," and we can add that this was at least in part because he was more thoroughly versed in the paradox-laden discourses of American high culture than most of his peers. Some of his contemporaries argued precisely this point in the language of neurasthenia.[31] Washington Gladden, for instance, after meeting Du Bois in 1903 and reading *The Souls of Black Folk*, found him to be "the most cultivated man among American Negroes; his is a highly organized, sensitive, practical nature." Although it was "easy to charge hypersensitiveness and morbidity" upon the man as an author, Gladden argued (specifically in relation to the section on double consciousness), the book is not "altogether morbid"; it is, in fact, the best book on the race problem yet written.[32]

One of the paradoxes Du Bois addresses and transcribes in *The Souls of Black Folk* is the place of music in black American culture. After quoting from a German song he learned while a doctoral student in Germany, he devotes his last chapter to black American music. What is the double consciousness of black music in America? Du Bois's argument here is perhaps the most confused and internally contradictory of his volume. He argues that these songs are (1) the only beauty America has bequeathed to the world, that they are (2) the only truly American music, that they have (3) influenced American music, but that they are (4) found only in "debased" form in American music. The songs are "primitive," they are the "siftings of centuries." They are an expression of hope, an expression of despair. It seems that Du Bois hoped to provide a typological review, but then despaired and tried a story of historical development instead. Some music, he decides, is "African," later it became "Afro-American," and then came "a blending of Negro music with the music heard in the foster land." But then he seems to despair of a historical explanation and gives it up in favor of a catalogue of impressions filled with denials of his own authority to comment.[33]

The music Du Bois describes, and at the head of each chapter as well as elsewhere musically transcribes, are spirituals, and this decision is in itself pointedly anachronistic. As early as 1874, the introduction to a collection of spirituals published by Hampton Institute announced the need for preservation: "One reason for publishing this slave music is that it is rapidly passing away. The freedmen have an unfortunate inclination to despise it as a vestige of slavery; those who learned it in the old time, when it was a natural out-pouring of their sorrows and longings, are dying off." And spirituals were markedly anachronistic since Du Bois was arguing for their validity and centrality to African-American culture during what was the peak of popular interest in ragtime and coon songs (then two of the most popular musical forms in the country) and while the blues, which would completely transform American popular music, was first emerging.[34]

These musical forms are the degraded African-American music against which Du Bois made his claims for the meaning and artistic value of spirituals. Du Bois was not alone in his dim view of this music. In 1902 one commentator noted both the popularity of ragtime and what he felt was the "debasement" of that form since the early 1890s: "A hopper is fitted into the press and into it are poured jerky note groups by the million, 'coon poetry' by the ream, colored inks by the ton, and out of the other end of the press comes a flood of 'ragtime' abominations, that sweeps over the country." Others felt that ragtime was more debasing than debased, at least in part because of its origin in bordellos, still one of the main public performance spaces for rags in 1903 and one of the places where ragtime music was disseminated to untrained musicians. Eubie Blake, for instance, claimed that he found out that he was playing ragtime (which he had overheard coming out of the brothel in his Baltimore neighborhood as a child) when his religious mother, who thought it the "devil's music," yelled at him: "Take that ragtime out of my house!" Blake worked at what he called a "hookshop" from the time he was fifteen, in 1898, until 1901, when he did a brief stint with a medicine show. That the two main performance spaces for ragtime were urban houses of prostitution and middle-class parlors expresses the doubleness of Victorian sexual nervousness, and that the third space was the medicine show makes the tie to neurasthenia complete. And ragtime was accused of causing other forms of nervousness as well. Ragtime is a musical form that encourages a lack of moderation, one critic argued as late as 1918, it "overstimulates; it irritates." And this overstimulation can lead in the two descending spirals of neurasthenia: mental and physical illness. Ragtime is "syncopation gone mad," pianist Edward Perry claimed, and its "victims," like dogs with rabies, went mad themselves. The *Negro Music Journal* in its inaugural issue in 1903 claimed that ragtime "is an evil music that has crept into the homes and hearts of our American people regardless of race, and must be wiped out as other bad and dangerous epidemics have been exterminated." Other writers brought the medico-moral discourse even closer to that of the neurological version of neurasthenia and claimed that ragtime "disrupts normal heart rhythms and interferes with the motor centers of the brain and nervous system."[35]

Unlike the editorialist of the *Negro Music Journal* or Du Bois, many black writers embraced ragtime. Paul Laurence Dunbar published the lyrics to "The Colored Band" (1901, music by J. Rosamond Johnson, who along with James Weldon Johnson published the pioneering

American Negro Spirituals collections in the 1920s) in his 1903 collection of poetry *Lyrics of Love and Laughter*. This collection of poetry, for which Howells wrote an introduction and which he promoted as the first "true poetry" of the "African race," established Dunbar's national reputation. In *Letters Home* Howells describes, with some distance but some approval, a vaudeville show in which "coon songs" were performed as encores. Du Bois considered all of these ragtime songs and "coon songs" debased, appropriated music, or Afro-American music, or blended music—the boundaries of these overlapping categories remain somewhat unclear. But the "coon songs" outstripped simple questions of musical genre by relying on explicitly and virulently racist lyrics, and it is these lyrics that Du Bois undoubtedly found debased and debasing.

"Coon songs" reveled in negative stereotypes that were produced in part through the spin given neurasthenic maxims. The resulting reinvigoration of racist clichés, according to some analyses, helped provide rationales for the continued subordination of blacks and, by extension, the native peoples of the new American possessions. The song "A Hot Time in the Old Town Tonight" was the unofficial theme song of Roosevelt's Rough Riders in Cuba and was sung so often by soldiers occupying the Philippines that it was thought by some Filipinos to be the American national anthem. "Coon songs" used the same syncopations as ragtime songs (and thus the two names were sometimes used interchangeably), and the two forms came in for some of the same criticisms, although the less virulent ragtime received more bad press than the songs doing the cultural work of racism.[36]

One of the recurrent themes in racist popular song was what Sam Dennison has called the "money fantasy," in which "the protagonist is shown as a caricature of the white moneyed class." The otherness of blacks is represented as their imperviousness to the nervous debilitation that should be caused, according to neurasthenic theory, by immoral activity, especially activity that involved immoral relations to money. In 1903 songs of this kind included "The Coontown Billionaire" and "When a Coon Opens a Department Store," both of which rely on comic images of impossible excess. This and related song genres represented black men as lazy dreamers or as rich through the iconic forms of speculation: card playing and wagering on horses. The cover art for the sheet music of "I'm a Lucky Coon," for instance, shows a black man winking at the viewer as he is being driven (by a white chauffeur) away from the racetrack with a fistful of cash. The cover of "The Luckiest Coon in Town" shows a healthy and happy "Zip Coon"-type figure fondling his ill-gotten winnings.

The lucky Edith Wharton and Henry James go for a drive in 1904. (Lilly Library, Indiana University, Bloomington, Indiana)

The art for "The Coons' Paradise" shows a sleeping black man dreaming scenes of himself energetically playing cards, stepping out in conspicuously fancy clothes, and stealing chickens from a coop—all stereotypical forms of immoral getting and spending. These images are of course exactly those that Du Bois was countering in *Souls* with images of black industry, spirituality, and nervous debility.[37] Du Bois's rejection of debased music follows (as does his corresponding representation of blacks as physically and mentally debilitated by their economic standing) the same cultural imperatives, and involves

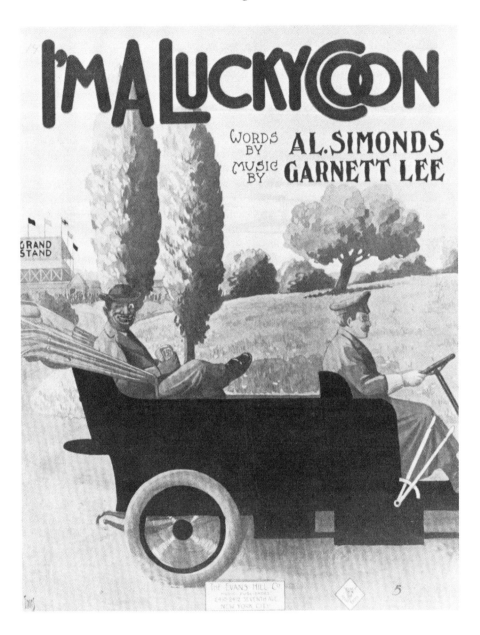

The mode of transportation, the source of income, and the reversal of racial hierarchy all mark the black gambler as a primitive unable to become nervous. (Sheet music cover courtesy Garland Publishing, Inc.)

similar moral commitments, as James's condemnation of Chad's callousness.

The other major development in African-American music at the turn of the century was the emergence of the blues, which Du Bois also necessarily rejected as debased. W. C. Handy, the man often credited with bringing the blues to a wide audience in the late teens, claims that he first discovered the blues in Mississippi in 1903. Gertrude "Ma" Rainey claims she first heard the blues sung in Georgia in 1902, two years before her first tour with a minstrel show. Both blues and ragtime have roots in spirituals, and so, like neurasthenia, they form an important cultural expression of secularization, and again as with neurasthenia, the complete secularization and popularization of these forms of musical experience made them ripe for interpretation in either denigration or defense. Both spirituals and blues songs can have moments of what might be seen as spiritual crisis and nervous prostration. Like neurasthenia, which combines high sensitivity and low spirits, the blues as a musical idiom maintains a doubleness, both lyrically and musically, of joy and sorrow, of raucous celebration and base despondency, or at times of base celebration and raucous despondency.[38]

The blues has other ties to neurasthenia. Like neurasthenia, the blues did not offer a monolithic reorientation toward spiritual despair or the more modern appropriations of depression. The emergence of the blues is related to the migration of blacks to northern cities at the end of the nineteenth century, a migration accompanied by what Ben Sidran calls the "fall of black Christian authority" and a secularization of many aspects of black life, including the secularization of musical expression and the contemporaneous emergence of music as a profession for blacks.[39] Because many early blues and ragtime players made a living playing in houses of prostitution, the blues is tied culturally to one of the dominant paradigms of illicit, nonregenerative spending. The blues is also tied to drinking and drugs, other neurasthenia-inducing forms of spending: "barrelhouse" piano, for instance, originated in bars that served directly from barrels, that is, inexpensive, no-frills honky-tonks. Perhaps most significant, many early blues players also earned a living by traveling with the patent medicine salesmen that sold nerve tonics and neurasthenic cure-alls. (Other popular musicians got their start in medicine shows as well, including Dreiser's brother, Paul Dresser, the best-selling songwriter of the first years of the century.)[40] Thus in terms of cultural presence, neurasthenia, advertising, secularization, song forms based in black musical idioms presented to white audiences, and an increased expression of the joys of spending all follow a similar historical trajectory from the Civil War through the turn of the century.

"The blues," in fact, was used as a name for neurasthenia before it was used as a name for the musical form, and by the turn of the century it was widely used in its medical sense, as in *The Blues: Causes and Cure* (1904), a popular book on neurasthenia and mind cure by Albert Abrams, M.D. In 1903, *Ladies' Home Journal* writer Martin Petrey went so far as to suggest that music is a better cure for nervous morbidity than mind cure: "Music as a medicine in the home [is] better than any system of mental therapeutics . . . so much the fad today. . . . In all nervous illnesses music is very potent as a sedative, and, strange to say, in cases of despondency and melancholia the minor chords are the most effective and act as a tonic [no musical pun intended, apparently]." As Albert Murray has argued much more recently, blue notes and blue chords do not intensify low spirits but can, as Petrey puts it, "dispel any gloomy winter's scene . . . and will cast out any fit of the 'blues.' " The relation between double consciousness, the blues, and what might be called cure, in fact, has been seen by some critics as central to the entire history of African-American culture.[41]

Du Bois's own double consciousness led him to write about spirituals as African music from the vantage point of his own American form of historical sociological meditation. But this doubleness in his work has very little in common with the "blended" form of ragtime, which by 1903 had a largely white audience and which had adopted the racist lyrics of the "coon song." Du Bois ends *The Souls of Black Folk* with a song and an afterthought. The song repeats the line, "Let us cheer the weary traveler," and the afterthought hopes that out of the book will spring "vigor of thought and thoughtful deed." From weariness to vigor, these last two strategies reiterate the neurasthenic logic of the text. Du Bois himself remained vigorous enough in his ninetieth year to combine parts of his voluminous writings into the latest volume of his autobiography, and for all his invocation of the neurasthenic, he remained free himself of the symptoms. His later writings rely less and less on the imagery of neurasthenia, as might be expected. By 1958, when Du Bois was ninety years old, the word "nervous" had lost most of its earlier connotations, and only the "nervous breakdown" remained a popular form of sickly distinction.

Henry James, "The Master," on the other hand, for all his ability to critique the neurasthenic world view, had a relapse in 1909, after a thirteen-year hiatus, of the "black devils of nervousness"—a "nervous breakdown," according to his brother William, at least partially

Immoral forms of getting and spending exact no nervous cost from this leisured dreamer because of his inheritance. (Sheet music cover courtesy Garland Publishing, Inc.)

the result of a temporary setback in finances and a feeling of failure due to the small sales of the New York edition of his complete works. He began to feel better after he received several thousand-dollar advances. James, who ridiculed the use of the disease and the dissimulation it involved, continued to suffer from its symptoms and experienced recurrent periods of depression; Du Bois, who simulated the disease in his prose and claimed the disease as a badge of honor for all blacks, was untouched. The work of the two men had one effect in common, however—it helped convince people that neurasthenia transcended class bounds. When this idea was generally accepted, neurasthenia disappeared. The blues became a musical form more and more central to American culture as it disappeared as a medical form, and while James's neurasthenic novelistic style gave way to modernism, colloquialism, and plain styles, his aesthetics remained an authoritative source for arguments and positions on art and distinction long after the neurasthenic correlatives of his language were forgotten. And Du Bois's social psychology, less dependent on moralistic physiology than James's, has remained an important part of cultural understanding and of political activism in the postneurasthenic world.

9 Concluding Anecdotes: "The Death of the Strenuous Self"

A few last anecdotal reports serve as my somewhat open-ended conclusion. The impulse to narrativize historical reports is encoded in my subtitle and in its invocation of conclusion figured as a death, and the impulse toward generalizing the experience of historical actors is represented by the use of the definite article in front of the word "self." The radical conjuncture of the turn of the century has, obviously enough, passed, and in the course of its passing both individuals and cultural complexes can be said to have died. But as soon as one says, even in quotation marks, "the death of the strenuous self," it sounds melodramatic, overly dramatic. The hegemonic recreation of privilege, the putting aside of formerly useful ideological strictures, the revamping of spirituality, the refurbishing of the medical and political lexicons—these seem hardly to constitute a death. But they do demand a number of disappearances.

Billy James, son of William and Alice Howe James and favorite nephew of Henry, graduated from Harvard in 1903. In a letter to his class secretary twenty-five years later he wrote:

> When I was in College I supposed that life was achievement and that the price of achievement was strenuous and disagreeable exertion.
> . . . And I recall doing, in the same spirit, a piece of "original research work" in the Medical School on *Enemata*, and reading about the blame things in three languages at the Boston Public Library. I supposed life was like that. Strenuous, muscular, overcoming kind of stuff. But I now think it does not matter so much what we

accomplish as what we *are* in our daily human relations, and that unless what we call knowledge helps us in these, it's not of much account.[1]

Many things had changed between 1903 and 1928 for men like the younger William James. His father's pragmatism had evolved more clearly into an instrumentalism concerned with the way "knowledge helps." The ideas of accomplishment, achievement, and mutability central to the notion of a self-made man had been replaced with the fragmented but essential self that is constructed by one's relations. And in the case of James, at least, the turn away from the medical was accompanied by a relaxation of the work ethic and related "strenuous, muscular overcoming stuff." Here and there, among the neurasthenic cultural producers in 1903, such changes were already in the works, although they were rarely expressed with James's sincere and condescending nonchalance.

Jack London ran for mayor of Oakland in 1903 as a socialist. In *The Kempton-Wace Letters*,[2] his older correspondent mouths the rejection of muscular overcoming in the language of a teleological, sensual naturalism: "The day of asceticism is gone, or shall we say the night? We are not afraid of sense delights. We are intent upon living on all sides of our natures, roundly and naturally," the old romantic Kempton tells his young rationalist, socialist nephew Wace. "You have a fine gospel of work and I congratulate you upon it, but you make no mention of the purpose of it all" (194). Kempton goes on, like a mellow Henry Adams scolding his alter ego:

> I, overcivilized, decadent dreamer that I am, rejoice that the past binds us, am proud of a history so old and so significant and of a heritage so marvellous. . . . You are suffering from, what has been called, the sadness of science. . . . You discover that romance has a history, and lo! romance has vanished! You are a Werther of science, sad to the heart with a melancholy all your own and dropping inert tears on the shrine of your accumulated facts. . . . In this you are with your generation. Just as every age has its prevailing disease of the body so has it its characteristic spiritual ailment. . . . As yet we do not know what to do with all which we know, and we are afflicted with the pessimism of inertia and the pessimism of dyspepsia. (125–26)

The young scientific socialist Wace rejects all sentimentality, romantic love, and pleasure for a scientific view of human relations and economic life, and his uncle, attempting to stand outside the fray, claims that modern dyspepsia is caused by knowing too much. He insists that he knows less than his nephew and therefore he "has" more. London's book comes down nowhere in particular on the issues it supposedly addresses, issues of labor, socialism, emotion, "reality," and gender. Kempton claims (unlike Wharton, James, and Thomas Hardy, but like Freeman, as we saw) that Ecclesiastes can be read "with a triumphant lilt in the voice. After all, it is the modulation that carries the message of the text" (131). Modulation would have to carry London's text, since the competing voices coexist without being ideologically organized, without being very skillfully orchestrated, as Mikhail Bakhtin would say. The only message that comes through is a rejection of the strenuous life, since the young Wace is never so much a fool as when he is being strenuously dyspeptic.

Gertrude Stein, like the younger William James having left the strenuous world of medicine behind, and having left William James's philosophy department behind as well, wrote her first novel in 1903, *Q.E.D.*[3] Here she echoes Kempton's position about the sadness of too much knowledge, however less earnestly: "A little knowledge is not a dangerous thing," the narrator intrudes, "on the contrary it gives the most cheerful sense of completeness and content" (3). In *The Making of Americans*, which Stein began in 1903, her representation of the "self-made" merchant Henry Dehning talking to his children also has some echoes of Kempton's nostalgia for a moral past, but in a slapstick version of first-generation immigrant vernacular:

> Yes, I say to you, I don't see with all these modern improvements to always spoil you, you ever will be good to work hard like your father. ... Yes, what, well, tell me, you all like to be always explaining to me, tell me exactly what you are going to get from all these your expensive modern kinds of ways of doing. Well I say, just tell me some kind of way so that I can understand you. You know I like to get good value for my money, I always had a name for being pretty good at trading, I say, you know I like to know just what I am getting for my money and you children do certainly cost a great deal of my money, now I say, tell me, I am glad to listen to you, I say you tell me just what you are going to do, to make it good all this money. Well what, what are all these kinds of improvements going to do for you. (9)

Unlike Strether, Dehning wants to know what he will get out of it for himself. But his quaint distress at "the expensive" and his old-fashioned notion that economic activity is "trading" mark him as an anachronism. " 'Yes,' he would often say to his children, 'Yes I say to you children you have an easy time of it nowadays doing nothing. Well! What! yes, you think you always have to have everything you can ever think of wanting' " (8). His children want to consume rather than produce, and so no "good" will come of them. The children laugh and tell him that they will probably be good for something someday, but he answers " 'No you children never will be good for something if I have any right kind of a way to know it' " (9). Dehning doesn't, of course, have a right way of knowing. The narrator tells us that the homes of self-made merchants are like the cities in which their fortunes are made and that in London such a house would be rich and gloomy, in Paris cheery and "filled with pleasant toys," while in America it would be "neither gloomy nor yet joyous." The Dehning house, we are told, was "of this sort. A nervous restlessness of luxury was through it all" (28).

Stein left for Paris in 1903, not as an ambassador like Strether but as an emigré. She had none of Strether's economic confusion, none of Dehning's nervousness about luxury, and few illusions about neurasthenic self-presentation. *Q.E.D.* begins with three young American women, Adele, Helen, and Sophie, sailing to Europe. "The last month of Adele's life," we are told, "has been such a succession of wearing experiences that she rather regretted that she was not to have the steamer all to herself. . . . Heigho it's an awful grind; new countries, new people and new experiences all to see, to know and to understand." In such declarations early in the novel Stein ridicules the false and weary ennui of Adele (often taken to be a self-portrait) and Adele's defense of middle-class ideals. But in the process of working through the complications of a love triangle with Helen and Sophie, and confronting the intricacies of mimetic desire, social prohibition, love and domination, Adele comes to reject the false advertising of neurasthenic self-presentation. Quarreling with Helen, her lover, Adele shouts: "You have no right to constantly use your pain as a weapon!" (60), rejecting, in that one line, all of the self-serving moralism of the neurasthenic life-style. As Lisa Ruddick and others have noted, Stein's writing style itself constitutes a rejection of the theory of the will of her teacher William James. If James's notion of the will to believe, by making the control of mental activity rather than the control of behavior the essence of moral action, was a step toward recognizing the unconscious will to power of the neurasthenic, then Stein's rejection is simply another step in the same direction—one person's monism may be another's pluralism.[4]

Richard Harding Davis's *About Paris* (1903), much less ambiguously, retains the moral pluralism of *The Ambassadors*, claiming that "Americans who go to Paris might be divided . . . into two classes— those who use Paris for their own improvement or pleasure, and those who find her too strong for them, and who go down before her and worship her, and whom she either fashions after her own liking, or rides under foot and neglects until they lose heart and disappear forever."[5] The instrumentalist "use or be used" logic of neurasthenic appropriation informs Davis's satiric portraits of the young expatriate artists in Paris, whom he presents as ridiculous fadists, and of the "American colony" in general. Still, the artist remains interesting, he writes, because of a naive integrity: "It is only when he ceases to develop, and sinks into the easy lethargy of a life of pleasure there, that he becomes uninteresting" (213). Davis tells the story of a young artist who had a picture in the Salon his first year but no success the following year; therefore he walked around Paris, "flushed and nervous and tired looking" (217), in a neurasthenic fog. The best, the kind who "made the Columbian Fair what it was," are those artists who study in Paris and come back to work in America: "They are the best examples we have of the Americans who made use of Paris, instead of permitting Paris to make use of them" (219), Davis writes. "The wise man and the sensible man takes the button or the medal or the place on a jury that Paris gives him, and is glad to get it, and proud of the recognition and of the source from which it comes, and then continues on his way unobserved, working for the work's sake. He knows that Paris has taught him much," and here Davis might be talking directly about Strether, "but that she has given him all she can, and that he must now work out his own salvation for himself" (181–82).

Davis could as well be referring to Thomas Eakins. Eakins had spent his years in Paris, received his training and accolades, and came back with a clear sense that he needed to do something like "work out his own salvation." Eakins also spent his time in the West, having been sent by his friend Dr. Horatio Wood, to cure his "exhaustion." Wood, whose portrait Eakins painted in 1890, believed that modern life "tends to produce nervous exhaustion," as did Beard and Mitchell, the latter another of Eakins's friends. Eakins himself, according to Elizabeth Johns, came to believe that whatever heroism was available consisted of stoically resisting exhaustion, of enduring with grace the wear and tear of modern life. Eakins's early paintings of action—surgery, sculling, hunting, baseball—were succeeded almost entirely by portraits in his later years. In those portraits he often made his sitters look older than they actually were, feeling that the added wear and tear gave dignity and "character" to the portraits, made them look more "heroic," and thus helped transform a representation of the real into a work of art. Three of Eakins's paintings from 1903—*Miss Alice Kurtz, Portrait of Archbishop William Henry Elder*, and *An Actress (Portrait of Suzanne Santje)*—represent their subjects as sturdy but resigned, looking as if they had all just decided not to cry. Santje and Elder grip the arms of their chairs as their bodies lean in a slight slump. All three look away from the beholder in various stages of a melancholy self-absorption, but an absorption interrupted by an imperative to look, with a certain sadness, at the world as it is.[6]

Eakins's own "exhaustion" came after he was dismissed from his position at the Pennsylvania Academy of the Fine Arts, a forced retirement due at least in part to his insistence on the use of naked models in coed life drawing classes. Eakins was facing a career crisis, as were Frederic Remington, Owen Wister, and Theodore Roosevelt when they were sent west. When he returned, Eakins still sold very few paintings and continued to live in his father's house most of his life. His neurasthenic resolution remained central to his theory of portraiture, but this theory was idiosyncratic enough that some sitters, aghast at the neurasthenic heroism of their portraits, paid for them but never bothered to take them home.

S. Weir Mitchell was at the height of his career in 1903, one mark of which was having his portrait painted by John Singer Sargent. He published *A Comedy of Conscience* in 1903, a novel in which professional anxieties are woven into the love story from the first page, when Serena Vernon's spinsterhood is announced as her "profession" by her cousin and suitor, John. John's "profession" is leisure, primarily in the form of hunting in various parts of the world, interspersed with periods of idleness. The classic professional competitors of the neurologist are disposed of in the form of a minister with lax morals and an old-fashioned medical man with more bedside manner than medical training. The older doctor has the complete faith of his female patients, we are told, "and if men liked or trusted him less completely it was of small moment in general practice, where it is the verdict of women which decides the fortunes of a doctor."[7] Professional journalists are presented as rude and grasping fools. Even the neurologist himself takes a poke in this frenzy of professional neurasthenia.

The story begins as Serena's purse is snatched in a New York train. In the process, the thief manages to drop his own diamond ring in another bag Serena is carrying. The comedy of conscience is that Serena cannot decide what she should rightfully do about the ring. The priest and the doctor each advise her to donate it to his favorite cause. John suggests she tour Europe. She has much too firm a conscience to make use of someone else's property, and she advertises for the owner. In the process, a reporter gets hold of the story and she becomes a minor celebrity in the daily press, a freak of unselfish

Thomas Eakins. *An Actress* (1903). Eakins's portraits emphasized the effects of modern wear and tear on his sitters. (Philadelphia Museum of Art: Given by Mrs. Thomas Eakins and Miss Mary Adeline Williams)

Thomas Eakins. Self-portrait (1902). Eakins turns a morbid eye upon himself and exaggerates his own debility. (National Academy of Design, New York City)

honesty. Reporters come for interviews, which she refuses, but the story of her selfless deed is copied from paper to paper across the nation, getting farther and farther from the facts as it travels. One story, after piling up exaggerations, distortions, and sensational additions, announces that Serena's "nerves [had] given way, and she is about to consult the distinguished neurologist, Dr. von Neuron" (100). Finally, the thief shows up to claim his ring, manages to make clear that the ring itself was stolen from someone else, and is sent packing by cousin John, whereupon John makes great progress in his suit for Serena's hand.

Serena is remarkably self-possessed, and is the "least nervous woman" John has ever known. Only in the heat of the last scene, with drawn guns and police wires, does she become nervous. She then straightaway becomes ready to answer John's suit, which at that point had been pending for some seven years. Although bachelorhood (and by extension spinsterhood) is called "a curable malady" early in the book, Serena has shown only one symptom—an overactive conscience—up until her final nervousness, and it is that nervousness which makes marriage possible. Her nerves are impervious to some of the common mechanisms of wear and tear, such as rail travel, urban mayhem, and her passing the age of marriageability. What turns the tide is the unbidden celebrity. The attention of the press is an "outrage" she is forced to "suffer." In her diary she confides what amounts to an outline of the relations of privacy and publicity, propriety and sexuality: "poor, innocent me, who have lived in what Helen calls a cocoon of privacy. Alas! I think I might once have married, but the unpleasant publicity of it all seemed so shocking, and now I am *affichéed* like an opera-dancer. It does seem too atrocious" (81).

The doctor who invented the rest cure here represents neurasthenia as an adjustment to the public nature of the modern self. The modern self was *affichéed*, posted, advertised, announced, publicized. Modern selves were represented in fiction in all their internal complexity, mirrored by and flanked in the magazines by columns of products announcing their qualities and availability and by columns of advice by journalistic specialists in etiquette and home economics. These selves were studied by anthropologists and sociologists and psychologists and novelists, some of whom worked under cover, like Wyckoff, Pettingill, Dreiser, and London, as the system of surveillance multiplied to match the new multiplicity of selfhood. At the same time, as Alfred Thayer Mahan wrote in the *Atlantic Monthly*: "To communicate with others that which one's self has acquired, be it much or little, be it money or any other form of human possession, is not only a power, but a *duty*. . . . If it be in any measure a reproach to a man to die rich, as has been somewhat emphatically affirmed, it is still more a reproach to depart with accumulations of knowledge or experience, willingly locked up in one's own breast."⁸ One's self "acquires" experience, and it is one's duty to publicize those experiences, to advertise and circulate them, not to keep them locked up as possessions. As William James, Jr., wrote, "what we *are* in our daily human relations" was of central importance, and the private character, in the nineteenth-century sense of character, had been correspondingly devalued. Thorstein Veblen had, already in the late 1890s, noted the relation between consumption and display, the public meaning and role of spending, but his was a resistant reading. Publicity was, as Wharton argued through Lily Bart, necessary to the very survival of the new self, and the recognition of the self by others the key to that self's ability to fulfill its desires, represented as acquisitive desires. The modern self is not required to be strenuous; it is required to be simply, in Wharton's terms, presentable, to be in circulation.

Hegemonic Recreation

The theory that spoke to such a self, finally, was not the transitional medicalizations of Mitchell, Wood, and Beard, but psychoanalysis, with its ability to account for a self constructed through imaginative appropriation of others, its ability to interpret the self in terms of its specific and general desires, and its ability to create the publicity necessary to keep such a self alive, since psychoanalysis requires that the subject reconstruct a self, and that self's desires, under medical scrutiny. Freud in 1895 made a distinction between "psycho-neuroses" (which were psychogenic) and "actual neuroses" (which were organic), and he placed neurasthenia in the second category and thereby outside the ken of psychoanalysis. But before he appropriated them as distinct syndromes, the majority of symptoms of what he termed psychoneuroses had been considered symptoms of neurasthenia, not specific disease entities. Nevertheless Freud continued to maintain the importance of neurasthenia as a general term and argued for the value, for instance, of Mitchell's rest cure. And in his middle writings neurasthenia, anxiety neurosis, and other "actual neuroses" were analyzed as psychogenic as well.

In his writings up until 1913, Freud's radical depoliticization, depathologization, and desocialization of the neurasthenic theories of Beard and Nietzsche accomplished three things that mark the success of the psychoanalytic and the downfall of the neurasthenic economy: (1) In its insistence on the intrapsychic nature of conflict, Freud's theory placed responsibility, even more than did the isolation cures of Mitchell, on the individual, since now even the problems caused by relations were interpreted as facts about the individual psyche. Therefore adaptation, compromise, integration, and sublimation became the measure of the growth and happiness of the individual subject. When this idea is elaborated, in Freud's later writings, into a theory of culture and society (which development, too, could be analyzed in terms of Freud's specific debts to Beard and Nietzsche), adaptation, compromise, integration, and sublimation are again keys to order and progress, and the radical individualism of the earlier theory is justified and itself compromised, adapted, integrated, and sublimated into a vision of society which is at once somberly Victorian and characteristically modern. (2) When a person experiences alienation, the solution is not a cure, but an adjustment, accomplished through an office visit for psychoanalysis. Although office visits to alienists were available before Freud, it was Freud who successfully medicalized the moral authority of the physician *independent of the physician's ability to heal the body*. While this turning away from the body was his most important elaboration of the practices of Beard, Mitchell, and other doctors who had slipped their "lay sermons" in between their ostensible doctorings, Freud's medical practice nevertheless clearly relied on the model begun by the neurologists. (3) When the office visit replaced the isolation cure, therapy became available to a much wider group; it was no longer necessary to have the time and resources to go to a sanitarium, a dude ranch, Nauheim or Marienbad, or to have a separate room and a private nurse, to enter the heroic ranks of the therapized. Freud's theories made possible the neurasthenicization of the petite bourgeoisie (who had previously relied on nostrums and patent medicines) and thereby the integration of this group, growing in size and importance, into therapeutic culture.[9]

Psychoanalysis also helped to theorize the relation between the publicity of the self and scandal, a relation the neurologists had helped to repress. In 1903 Daniel Paul Schreber published, in Germany, his *Memoirs of My Nervous Illness*, and Schreber quickly became what his translators called the "most frequently quoted patient in psychiatry."[10] The *Memoirs*, like many American accounts of neurasthenia, represented nervous debility in relation to the concept of the soul and the supernatural; for Schreber, in fact, the "human soul is contained in the nerves of the body" and "God . . . is only nerve" (45–46). Schreber's illness was the "most gruesome" time of his life, but also "the *holy* time of my life when my soul was immensely inspired by supernatural things, which came over me in ever increasing number amidst the rough treatment which I suffered from outside; when I was filled with the most sublime ideas about God and the Order of the World" (79–80). Schreber's father, who also suffered from nervous illness, was a physician and author of books about the healthful and moral effects of exercise for the individual and for the nation. Schreber himself, as a lawyer and chief judge at a superior court of appeals, would have been considered by American doctors as a brain-worker at risk through both inheritance and station. When Freud analyzed Schreber's case in 1911, he was not interested in Schreber's "sick soul" or the possibility of a diseased body. He isolated instead the scandal of Schreber's homoerotic desire.

Schreber's case went well beyond the experience of the neurasthenics I have discussed—none of them spent years screaming in a padded room, hallucinating little men in their feet and the scalpel of God at their anus. Still, scandal led Edna Pontelier and Lily Bart to suicide, and Dreiser's Carrie (and Dreiser himself) to fame and alienation. Suicide and alienation are represented by these novelists as caused by a society with too strenuous a reaction to scandal and too disciplinary a reaction to scandalous desires. In *The House of Mirth*, Bertha Dorset's actual adulteries are condoned because they are not made public; the rumored indiscretions of Lily are deadly because of the ensuing publicity, especially as institutionalized by the representative of the culture of print, the society columnist. Wharton's progressive polemic, in condemning Lily's condemnation and exposing the falsity of neurasthenic morality, argues that the work of publicity in policing and constructing subjectivity should be freed from neurasthenic morality.

In 1905, Simon Nelson Patten would argue that "the economic revolution [the new economy of surplus] is here, but the intellectual revolution that will rouse men to its stupendous meaning has not done its work." In the neurasthenic economy, the repression of desire was like money in the bank, and consuming always potentially a scandal. "We try to suppress vices when we should release virtues," Patten lectured; we "voluntarily surround ourselves with obsolete discomforts for the cure of our souls." Such discomfort and suppression made sense only in an economy of scarcity, Patten claimed, which was now past. "The new morality does not consist in saving, but in expanding consumption," and this new morality, as Patten became famous for announcing, required "a new type of man." Patten also answered neurasthenic fears (like those of the editors of the *New York Times*) that the working class would become consumers: "the surplus energy of the well-paid laborers points out to him new objects of desire, and if they seem attainable, enthusiasm is generated within the man to carry him thither. Enthusiasm is born of energy and varied desires." Following one's desires creates more energy, not less. Desire, if it is not like money in the bank, nevertheless creates a kind of credit economy of energy, allowing the consumer to pay as he or she goes. This theory of expenditure necessarily confuses the moral economy, since illicit desires could no longer be identified by the wear and tear of such an enthusiastic subject. Therefore Patten also offers a new theory of sin: "Vice is energy aborted by the lack of variety, the imprisonment of desires." As has been often noted, in Patten consumer capitalism found its ideal economic theorist, and the "triumph of the therapeutic" reconstructed by Richard Wightman Fox, Jackson Lears, Christopher Lasch, Philip Rieff, and other historians found its perfect spokesman. Patten's revamping of the notion of moral energy is one of many indications that his work represents not so much a reversal as a renovation and grand reopening of a therapeutic discourse created some thirty years earlier.[11]

By 1911 Patten's argument was repeated in the presidential campaign, as the strenuous Roosevelt lost to the priestly Woodrow Wilson, a man whose most famous campaign speech was "The Liberation of a People's Vital Energies." Wilson's call for the "emancipation of the generous energies" of Americans recapitulates Patten's arguments and is perfectly antithetical to Roosevelt's progressive conservationism. By 1913 Chopin, Norris, Remington, Clemens, and William James were dead, and Roosevelt, Eakins, Henry James, Howells, Freeman, and Garland seemed to many to be hopelessly old-fashioned. Already in 1903, while John Singer Sargent was painting the portraits of Theodore Roosevelt and S. Weir Mitchell, Henry Adams claimed that "the generation of Harry James and John Sargent is already as fossil as the buffalo."[12] The neurasthenic approach did not die out completely, as sporadic manuals such as Paul von Boeckmann's *Nerve Force* (c. 1920) and Richard Blackstone's *New Nerves for Old* (1931) attest. Bernarr MacFadden, editor of *Physical Culture* magazine, continued to argue the strenuous line, publishing his *More Power to Your Nerves* as late as 1939. Although many candidates for liminal or resistant utilitarian medical discourses exist now (chronic fatigue syndrome, Epstein-Barr virus, bulimia, stress), neurasthenia itself, as a discursive space of transformation, is extinct in America, as extinct as asceticism construed as capital formation, as extinct as the electricity cure for syphilis, and as extinct as the strenuous virtues of wifely duty and the fear of poisoned wallpapers. Neurasthenia is still, however, an important diagnostic category in Asian countries, countries that are reconfiguring the moral culture of spending.[13]

Henry Adams, just back from France in January of 1903, continued to "nurse [his] blooming nerves" and wrote to his brother Brooks: "It is no joke to run and catch onto a train moving like these U. States. A few days of effort exhausts me till I want to lie down and cry." To Elizabeth Cameron: "There is no longer any idea of order, relation or sequence; only police or force, and not much of that." To his brother Charles: "We have had no dividends and no profit from our investment. Reform proved a total loss, and abstract morality went into bankruptcy with the Church. All our ideals turned out to be relative." Racist, classist, antisemitic, elitist, and constitutionally bitchy, Adams as a "nervous old man" saw that his dissatisfaction existed despite the fact that he had been able to take in "all the cream of society, and lap it up, like a cat, with a contemptuous curl of whiskers." His *Education*, which attempts to provide a philosophical basis for the eternalization of desire freed from sexual objects, in inventing the third person autobiography also provides a model for the introjected, alienated self. Adams, the perfect neurasthenic, saw through the discourse at every level ("I loathe the strenuous life!" he could write, and "I know that behind [the Bostonians'] apparent dogmatism and self-esteem, there is really the same self-distrust and absolute depreciation of self that has marked the whole puritan stock, . . . acute egoism") and helped exhaust the very discourse that has made him a spokesperson for the intellectual culture of his time.[14]

Henry and William James, W. E. B. Du Bois, Edith Wharton, Charlotte Perkins Gilman, William Dean Howells, Frank Norris, Mary Wilkins Freeman, Theodore Roosevelt, Hamlin Garland, Edgar Saltus, Theodore Dreiser, and the numerous lesser neurasthenic lights I have mentioned responded to, and in so doing helped recreate, the discourse of neurasthenia, a process central to the economy of representation, to both the creation of discursive value and the forms of discursive exchange, at the turn of the century. To continue this study, to examine the neurasthenic aspects of the work of Willa Cather, Sarah Orne Jewett, Josiah Royce, George Santayana, Samuel Clemens, John Fox, Jr., Lincoln Steffens, Mary Baker Eddy, John Burroughs, Helen Keller—just to mention a few of the dozens of other influential writers, artists, and activists who were themselves neurasthenic and/or who strategically used the discourse rhetorically or otherwise—to look at these figures would broaden and further complicate the picture I have constructed. To add these figures to the mosaic, to emphasize the experience and work of yet another set of exemplary figures, or to orchestrate the voices differently would also alter the tenor of some of the arguments. But neurasthenia, whether used as a mark of distinction or shabiness, as an individual moratorium, as evasive banality, as a forerunner of the therapeutic, as hypochondriacal escapism, as a critique of patriarchy, as a refusal (or embrace) of the market, or as a new role option, clearly helped people negotiate the transformations in social structure and economic activity which reshaped cultural life in America between the Civil War and World War I.

The diverse appropriations of the disease do not describe historical movement as much as they describe cultural heterogeneity, as the concentration on the year 1903 has shown. And it is precisely pluralism and its emergence as a cultural fact which created the role neurasthenia played in 1903. The "management" of diversity afforded by neurasthenic discourse helped ensure the recreation, along somewhat new cultural lines, of the hegemony of a group that came to identify itself with "the middle class." The double inflection of invalid leisure is not resolved by recasting it as hegemonic recreation, any more than the nervousness aroused by pluralist consumerism was quieted by advertising and the role of the shopper. The double consciousness of consumer morality has often been recast since 1903, but a certain amount of nervousness seems endemic. While "stress" is an engineering term more suited to an economy with a crumbling infrastructure, its links to the medical complaints of 1903 are many, and its availability for plural appropriation rivals that of neurasthenia. But that is many other stories.

Notes

An Introduction to Nervousness

1. Freeman Champney, *Art and Glory: The Story of Elbert Hubbard* (New York, 1968), 101.

2. Kate Douglas Wiggin, *Rebecca of Sunnybrook Farm* ([1903] New York, 1986), 124.

3. William James, *The Varieties of Religious Experience* (Boston, 1902). These are terms commonly used by James throughout this work. Frank Lloyd Wright, "The Art and Craft of the Machine" (1901), in *Writings and Buildings*, ed. Edgar Kaufmann and Ben Raeburn (New York, 1960), and *An Autobiography* (New York, 1943), 50, 151.

4. George M. Beard, M.D., *American Nervousness: Its Causes and Consequences* (New York, 1881), 176, 96. See also Beard, *Nervous Exhaustion* (New York, 1879), *Sexual Neurasthenia* (New York, 1884, 1902), and "Neurasthenia, or Nervous Exhaustion," *Boston Medical and Surgical Journal* 3 (1869): 217. For other medical literature see F. G. Gosling, *Before Freud: Neurasthenia and the American Medical Community, 1870–1910* (Urbana, Ill., 1987), which cites over a hundred contemporary medical articles; Susan E. Cayleff, "'Prisoners of Their Own Feebleness': Women, Nerves, and Western Medicine—A Historical Overview," *Social Science and Medicine* 26 (1988) 12: 1199–1208; and John S. Haller, Jr., and Robin M. Haller, *The Physician and Sexuality in Victorian America* (Urbana, Ill., 1974). Although I am concentrating on neurasthenia in America, neurasthenia was an international concern; the *Index Medicus* for 1903 lists articles on neurasthenia published in Paris, London, Vienna, Berlin, St. Petersburg, Madrid, Leipzig, Milan, Kiev, Tokyo, and elsewhere; see also the special issue of *Culture, Medicine, and Psychiatry* 13 (1989): 105–241, on neurasthenia in Asian cultures.

For other recent scholarship on neurasthenia see Anita Clair Fellman and Michael Fellman, *Making Sense of Self: Medical Advice Literature in Late Nineteenth-Century America* (Philadelphia, 1981); George F. Drinka, M.D., *The Birth of Neurosis* (New York, 1984); Suzanne Poirier, "The Weir Mitchell Rest Cure: Doctors and Patients," *Women's Studies* 10 (1983): 15–40; Mark Olfson, M.D., "The Weir Mitchell Rest Cure," *Pharos* 51 (1989): 30–32; Barbara Sicherman,

"The Uses of Diagnosis: Doctors, Patients, and Neurasthenia," *Journal of the History of Medicine and Allied Sciences* 32 (1977): 36, and "The Paradox of Prudence: Mental Health in the Gilded Age," *Journal of American History* 62 (1976): 890–912; John S. Haller, Jr., "Neurasthenia: The Medical Profession and the 'New Woman' of the Late Nineteenth Century," *New York State Journal of Medicine* 71 (1971): 478; Philip P. Weiner, "G. M. Beard and Freud on 'American Nervousness,'" *Journal of the History of Ideas* 17 (1956): 269–74; Charles E. Rosenberg, "The Place of George M. Beard in Nineteenth-Century Psychiatry," *Bulletin of the History of Medicine* 36 (1962): 245–59, and Introduction to Beard, *American Nervousness* (New York, 1972); T. J. Jackson Lears, *No Place of Grace: Antimodernism and the Transformation of American Culture, 1880–1920* (New York, 1981), esp. 47–58.

5. Beard, *American Nervousness*, 96; Henry Adams, *The Education of Henry Adams* ([1907] Boston, 1973), 379–90.

6. "Elementary insanity" is Emile Durkheim's chaacterization of neurasthenia in *Suicide: A Study in Sociology* ([1897] New Yor, 1951), 68.

7. Beard, *American Nervousness*, vii–viii. See S. Weir Mitchell, *Fat and Blood and How to Make Them* (Philadelphia, 1878), *Lectures on Diseases of the Nervous System, Especially in Women* (Philadelphia, 1881), *Wear and Tear, or Hints for the Overworked* (Philadelphia, 1897), *Doctor and Patient* ([1887] Philadelphia, 1904), and "The Evolution of the Rest Cure," *Journal of Nervous and Mental Diseases* 31 (1904): 368–73. Mitchell was also a poet and novelist. For gender relations see *Dr. North and His Friends* (New York, 1903) and *A Comedy of Conscience* (New York, 1903); for medicine see *The Autobiography of a Quack and the Case of George Dedlow* (New York, 1900). For a taste of the poetry see "Books and the Man," in *Proceedings of the Charaka Club*, vol. 2 (New York, 1906), 1–4. For a tribute from a patient see Owen Wister, "S. Weir Mitchell, Man of Letters," in *S. Weir Mitchell, M.D., LL.D., F.R.S., 1829–1914. Memorial Addresses and Resolutions* (Philadelphia, 1914). The standard biography is Ernst Earnest, *Silas Weir Mitchell, Novelist and Physician* (Philadelphia, 1950).

8. Beard, *American Nervousness*, 186, 16. Marrs is quoted in Haller and Haller, *Physician and Sexuality*, 8. Baer is quoted in Anthracite Coal Commission, *Report to the President on the Anthracite Coal Strike of May–October, 1902* (Washington, D.C., 1903), 35.

9. Anonymous, "What the Year Will Bring Forth," *New York Times*, January 1, 1903, 8; Ray Stannard Baker, "The Right to Work," *McClure's* 20 (January 1903): 323–36.

10. For discussions of changes in economic thinking in the late nineteenth century, see Laurence Birken, *Consuming Desire: Sexual Science and the Emergence of a Culture of Abundance, 1871–1914* (Ithaca, 1988), 22–39; Daniel Boorstin, *The Americans: The Democratic Experience* (New York, 1973), 89–164; Robert Higgs, *The Transformation of the American Economy, 1865–1914: An Essay in Interpretation* (New York, 1971); Stuart Chase, *The Economy of Abundance* (Port Washington, N.Y., 1971).

11. See John Pierce, "The Telephone and Society in the Past 100 Years," in *The Social Impact of the Telephone*, ed. Ithiel de Sola Pool (Cambridge, Mass., 1977), 161; Boorstin, *The Americans*, 330; U.S. Department of Commerce, *Historical Statistics of the United States* (Washington, D.C., 1949); James D. Hart, *The Popular Book: A History of Literary Taste in America* (Berkeley, Calif., 1950); Mark Sullivan, *Our Times: The United States, 1900–1925*, vol. 1 (New York, 1931); Alan Trachtenberg, *The Incorporation of America: Culture and Society in the Gilded Age* (New York, 1982); Robert H. Wiebe, *The Search for Order* (New York, 1967).

12. Roosevelt, "Expansion and Peace," *Independent*, December 21, 1899: 3405; "Race Decadence," *Outlook*, April 8, 1911: 763–69. See also David Axeen,

" 'Heroes of the Engine Room': 'American Civilization' and the War with Spain," *American Quarterly* 36 (Fall 1984): 481–502.

13. Thorstein Veblen, *Theory of the Leisure Class* ([1899] New York, 1953), 134, 141. Daniel Horowitz, *The Morality of Spending: Attitudes toward the Consumer Society in America, 1875–1940* (Baltimore, 1985), 39, sees Veblen as criticizing "moral accounting," but Veblen does so entirely in its own terms. See also Joseph Dorfman, *Thorstein Veblen and His America* (New York, 1934), 14–197.

14. Frederick W. Taylor, "Shop Management," *American Society of Mechanical Engineers Transactions* 24 (1903): 1337–1480. On Taylor, see Daniel Nelson, *Frederick W. Taylor and the Rise of Scientific Management* (Madison, Wis., 1980); Frank B. Copley, *Frederick Taylor: Father of Scientific Management* (New York, 1923); and Sudhir Kakar's Freudian interpretation, *Frederick Taylor: A Study in Personality and Innovation* (Cambridge, Mass., 1970).

15. Simon N. Patten, *Heredity and Social Progress* (New York, 1903). Patten argued that the energy-storing female and the energy-dissipating male together made social evolution possible. A review by R. R. Marett (*Economic Review* 13 [1903]: 498–501) voices skepticism for Patten's project in the nervous language of a fear of dissipation. A. C. Pigon rejects Patten's views for similar reasons in "Some Remarks on Utility," *Economic Journal* 13 (1903): 58–68. Richard T. Ely's *Studies in the Evolution of Industrial Society* (New York, 1903) argued that "never before has there been such a high average of strength and vigor" and that this was leading to increased spending and, finally, to "social progress and race improvement." C. F. Bickerdie's review claimed that "that does not prove that there is no fear of ultimate deterioration" and that increased comfort and convenience was bound to lead to "mental and moral decay" (*Economic Journal* 13 [1903]: 598–602).

16. Marshall Sahlins, *Historical Metaphors and Mythical Realities: Structure in the Early History of the Sandwich Islands Kingdom* (Ann Arbor, Mich., 1981), 68, and *Islands of History* (Chicago, 1985), xiv, 125, 152–53.

17. Jackson Lears and Richard Wightman Fox also note the relation between neurasthenia and economic issues, from consumer spending to imperialist expansion, in their Introduction to *Culture of Consumption: Critical Essays in American History, 1800–1980*, ed. Richard Wightman Fox and T. J. Jackson Lears (New York, 1983). See also Gillian Brown, "The Empire of Agoraphobia," *Representations* 20 (1987): 134–57.

18. Alice Brown, *The Mannerings* (Boston, 1903), 102.

19. James, *A Pluralistic Universe* (New York, 1909), 254.

20. Pierre Bourdieu, *Distinction: A Social Critique of the Judgement of Taste* (Cambridge, Mass., 1984), 97–115. According to Bourdieu, the "objectively classifiable conditions of existence" and the individual's social position condition the "habitus." The habitus, which Bourdieu describes as "a structured and structuring structure," receives its structure from the conditions and position of the subject, and it in turn structures the subject's systems of practical and perceptual schemes. These schemes then condition an individual's practices and works, which are recognized by the subject (and often by others) as a "Life-Style": "a system of classified and classifying practices, i.e., distinctive signs ('tastes')." One of Bourdieu's arguments is that the "differential experiences" people have of a cultural product is "a function of the dispositions they derive from their position in economic space." I will be making a similar argument about the "differential experiences" of neurasthenia.

21. Arnold Van Gennep, *The Rites of Passage* ([1908] London, 1960). See also Émile Durkheim and Marcel Mauss, "De quelques formes primitives de classification: Contribution à l'étude des représentations collectives," *L'Année sociologique* 6 [1903]: 1–72. Victor Turner's quote is from *The Ritual Process: Structure and Anti-Structure* (Chicago, 1969); see also Turner's *Dramas, Fields, and Meta-*

phors (Ithaca, 1974), Preface, chap. 1, and passim, and "Social Dramas and Stories about Them," in *On Narrative*, ed. W. J. T. Mitchell (Chicago, 1981), 137–64; James A. Boon, *Other Tribes, Other Scribes* (Ithaca, 1982).

22. Smith-Rosenberg, *Disorderly Conduct*, 11–52, 151, 161. See also Karen Halttunen, *Confidence Men and Painted Women: A Study of Middle-Class Culture in America, 1830–1870* (New Haven, Conn., 1982). Halttunen sees the liminal nature of the figures she studies as related to reorganizations of status and to the hypocritical nature of bourgeois propriety, of a false front obscuring more authentic desires. I will instead argue that turn-of-the-century bourgeois propriety, more hypochondriacal than hypocritical, was a formation based in authentic desires and was at times adopted to further those desires.

23. Roland Barthes, "Semiology and Medicine," in *The Semiotic Challenge*, trans. Richard Howard (New York, 1988), 210; American Psychiatric Association Task Force on Nomenclature and Statistics, *The Diagnostic and Statistical Manual of Mental Disorders*, 3d ed. (Washington, D.C., 1980), known as DSM–3. Neurasthenia was left out of the first edition of the APA's manual (DSM–1, 1952) but was added to the second edition (DSM–2, 1968) in response to a wave of internationalism, since neurasthenia was then an active diagnostic category in certain Asian countries. This attempt at internationalism was reversed in DSM–3, despite the fact that interest in neurasthenia (and its occurrence) in Asia is increasing. On current views of neurasthenia, see recent articles in the *Boston Medical Journal* 66 (1989): 1199–200, and *Canadian Medical Association Journal* 139 (1988): 198–99.

24. In *The Republic* Plato discusses the evolution of society as a progressive disease; in *Ion* he discusses artistic production in relation to disease. See Jeffrey Meyers, *Disease and the Novel: 1880–1960* (London, 1985), 2–11; Sander L. Gilman, *Disease and Representation: Images of Illness from Madness to AIDS* (Ithaca, 1988), especially 1–17, 50–80; Michel Foucault, *The Birth of the Clinic: An Archaeology of Medical Perception*, trans. A. M. Sheridan Smith (New York, 1973), 34, 38, and *Madness and Civilization*, trans. Richard Howard (New York, 1965), x, 158, 224–36.

25. Roger Chartier, *Cultural History: Between Practices and Representations*, trans. Lydia G. Cochrane (Ithaca, 1988), 13; Robert Weimann, "Text, Author-Function, and Appropriation in Modern Narrative: Toward a Sociology of Representation," in *Literature and Social Practice*, ed. Philippe Desan, Priscilla Parkhurst Ferguson, and Wendy Griswold (Chicago, 1989), 30, 31.

26. See V. N. Voloshinov, *Marxism and the Philosophy of Language* (New York, 1973), 23, 45–63; Jacques Lacan, *Écrits: A Selection*, trans. Alan Sheridan (New York, 1977), 146–78, 281–91.

27. See Anthony Giddens, "Action, Subjectivity, and the Constitution of Meaning," in *The Aims of Representation: Subject/Text/History*, ed. Murray Krieger (New York, 1987), 159–74, *The Constitution of Society* (Cambridge, 1984), chap. 2, and *Central Problems in Social Theory: Action, Structure, and Contradiction in Social Analysis* (Berkeley, Calif., 1979), esp. 9–95, 230–33, 253–57.

28. Grant McCracken outlines what he calls "three decisive episodes in the history of consumption," the first in sixteenth-century England, the second in the eighteenth century, and the third with the emergence of the department store in the mid-nineteenth century. For McCracken the world of goods and the social world had become, by the end of the eighteenth century, mutually transformative. My argument here is that the turn of the century was another "decisive moment," one in which "brain-workers" first attempted a systematic overhaul of ethical and sociological thinking to account for the primacy of economic "demand." It is no accident that McCracken relies from time to time on Thorstein Veblen's 1899 analysis of consumption. See Grant McCracken, *Culture and Consumption: New Approaches to the Symbolic Character of Consumer Goods and Activities* (Bloom-

ington, Ind., 1988), 10–30. See also Neil McKendrick, John Brewer, and J. H. Plumb, *The Birth of a Consumer Society: The Commercialization of Eighteenth-Century England* (Bloomington, Ind., 1982); Rachel Bowlby, *Just Looking: Consumer Culture in Dreiser, Gissing, and Zola* (New York, 1985); and Birken, *Consuming Desire*, 22–39.

29. Jane Addams, *Twenty Years at Hull House* (New York, 1910); Christopher Lasch, *The New Radicalism in America, 1889–1963: The Intellectual as a Social Type* (New York, 1965), 3–37.

30. See Josiah Strong, *Expansion* (New York, 1900), 80; Daniel T. Rodgers, *The Work Ethic in Industrial America, 1850–1920* (Chicago, 1978), 27; Ray Ginger, *The Age of Excess: The United States from 1877 to 1914* (New York, 1965), 53–55.

31. F. Marion Crawford, *The Novel: What Is It* (New York, 1893), 23. See also James D. Hart, *The Popular Book: A History of America's Literary Taste* (Berkeley, Calif., 1950), 185. Hart finds the increased circulation due to a mass audience "hesitant of its own taste."

32. Susan Sontag, *Illness as Metaphor* (New York, 1978), 3; W. V. O. Quine, "A Postscript on Metaphor," in *On Metaphor*, ed. Sheldon Sacks (Chicago, 1979).

Neurasthenic Economies

1. Carroll Smith-Rosenberg has thus described hysteria, according to Beard a fairly severe form of neurasthenia (*Disorderly Conduct: Visions of Gender in Victorian America* [New York, 1985]). See also Ann Douglas, " 'The Fashionable Diseases': Women's Complaints and Their Treatment in Nineteenth-Century America," *Journal of Interdisciplinary History* 4 (Summer 1973): 25–52, esp. 35–37; David M. Kennedy, "The Family, Feminism, and Sex at the Turn of the Century," in *The Private Side of American History*, ed. Thomas R. Frazier (New York, 1979), 124–33; S. Weir Mitchell, *Doctor and Patient* ([1887] Philadelphia, 1904), 13, 84, 89, 122.

2. William Dean Howells, *Suburban Sketches* (New York, 1871), 96; Mitchell, *Doctor and Patient*, 10.

3. S. Weir Mitchell, *Fat and Blood and How to Make Them* (Philadelphia, 1878), 48.

4. Mitchell, *Doctor and Patient*, 13.

5. Mitchell, *Doctor and Patient*, 142–43.

6. Thorstein Veblen, *The Theory of the Leisure Class* (New York, 1899); *The Autobiography of a Neurasthene: As Told by One of Them and Recorded by Margaret A. Cleaves, M.D.* (Boston, 1910), 5, 17; R. W. B. Lewis, *Edith Wharton: A Biography* (New York, 1975), 82–84; Cynthia Griffin Woolf, *A Feast of Words: The Triumph of Edith Wharton*, 85–91; Martha Solomon, *Emma Goldman* (Boston, 1987); Alice Wexler, *Emma Goldman: An Intimate Life* (New York, 1984).

7. Edith Wharton, *The Age of Innocence* ([1920] New York, 1970), 19.

1. Making It Big: Theodore Dreiser, Sex, and Success

1. Dreiser, *An Amateur Laborer*, ed. Richard R. Dowell, James L. West, III, and Neda Westlake (Philadelphia, 1983), 3; Dreiser left *An Amateur Laborer* unfinished, and it was first published in its current form in 1983. Biographical information is drawn from W. A. Swanberg, *Dreiser* (New York, 1965); Ellen Moers, *The Two Dreisers* (New York, 1969); Thomas P. Riggio, Introduction, *Theodore Dreiser: The American Diaries, 1902–1926*, ed. Riggio (Philadelphia, 1982); Richard Lingeman, *Theodore Dreiser: At the Gates of the City, 1871–1907* (New York,

1986); Richard P. Dowell, Introduction to Dreiser, *An Amateur Laborer*; F. O. Matthiessen, *Theodore Dreiser* (New York, 1951); Helen Dreiser, *My Life with Dreiser* (Cleveland, Ohio, 1951); Vera Dreiser, *My Uncle Theodore* (New York, 1976); Robert H. Elias, *Theodore Dreiser: Apostle of Nature* (New York, 1949); Donald Pizer, *The Novels of Theodore Dreiser* (Minneapolis, Minn., 1976); Richard Lehan, *Theodore Dreiser: His World and His Novels* (Carbondale, Ill., 1969); Laurence Hussman, *Dreiser and His Fiction* (Philadelphia, 1983); *Letters of Theodore Dreiser*, ed. Robert H. Elias (Philadelphia, 1959); Dreiser, *Dawn* (New York, 1931), *A History of Myself: Newspaper Days* ([1922] New York, 1931), *The "Genius"* (New York, 1915). Indirectly autobiographical novels include, I will argue, *The Financier* (New York, 1912) and *An American Tragedy* (New York, 1925).

2. During 1903 such articles were still quite popular. Most middle-class monthlies regularly ran articles such as the *Saturday Evening Post* series titled "Money Kings of the World" and the *Cosmopolitan* series on wealthy and famous businessmen. The muckraking classics, including Ida Tarbell's *History of the Standard Oil Company* with its detailed portrait of John D. Rockefeller, are less celebratory works in the genre.

3. Dreiser, *A History of Myself*, 33. See Arun Mukherjee, *The Gospel of Wealth in the American Novel: The Rhetoric of Dreiser and Some of His Contemporaries* (London, 1987).

4. David Graham Phillips, *The Master Rogue* (New York, 1903), 19.

5. Phillips, *Master Rogue*, 19.

6. Brooks Adams, *The Law of Civilization and Decay* ([1896] New York, 1955), 4–5, 285–308; "The Criterion is Success" is from *The New Empire* ([1902] Cleveland, Ohio, 1967), xxxii; Elias, *Dreiser*, 94.

7. The later version is in Dreiser, "The Toil of the Laborer," in *Hey Rub-a-Dub-Dub: A Book of the Mystery and Terror and Wonder of Life* (New York, 1919), 98; the manuscript fragment is published in *An Amateur Laborer*, 177.

8. Muldoon was one of the four most famous sports heroes of the 1890s along with Eugene Sandow, bodybuilder, John L. Sullivan, boxer, George Hackenschmidt, wrestler. See Harvey Green, *Fit for America: Health, Fitness, Sport, and American Society* (New York, 1986), 213. On the activities at the spa, see Dreiser, "Culhane, The Solid Man," in *Twelve Men* (New York, 1919), 134–86; Dowell, Introduction, xxi–xxii; Dreiser, *An Amateur Laborer*, 64–97; Elbert Hubbard, *Health and Wealth* (East Aurora, N.Y., 1908), 51–72; Edward Van Every, *Muldoon: The Solid Man of Sport* (New York, 1929).

9. Amy Kaplan claims that Dreiser insists he was an amateur laborer as a way of claiming the status of a professional writer. But Dreiser was already a professional journalist and by 1903 was interested instead in the "amateur" status of the aristocratic man of letters. See Kaplan, *The Social Construction of American Realism* (Chicago, 1988), 132–33.

10. See Alphonso D. Rockwell and George M. Beard, *A Practical Treatise on the Medical and Surgical Uses of Electricity Including Localized and General Electrization* ([1871] New York, 1903); the advertising pamphlet for "Professor Chrystal's Electric Belts and Appliances" (Marshall, Mich., c. 1900) is quoted in Green, *Fit for America*, 265; Sears, Roebuck Catalogue ([1902] Chicago, 1975).

11. Dreiser, *Diaries*, December 4, 1902, p. 70; December 29, 1902, p. 77. For a review of this literature see Graham Barker-Benfield, *The Horrors of the Half-Known Life: Male Attitudes toward Women and Sexuality in Nineteenth-Century America* (New York, 1976). Also see Charles E. Rosenberg, "Sexuality, Class, and Role in Nineteenth-Century America," *American Quarterly* 25 (1973): 131–53, Nathan Hale, *Freud and the Americans: The Beginnings of Psychoanalysis in the United States, 1876–1917* (New York, 1971), 33–34; and Anita Clair Fellman and Michael Fellman, *Making Sense of Self: Medical Advice Literature in Late Nineteenth-Century America* (Philadelphia, 1981).

12. Thorstein Veblen, *Theory of the Leisure Class* ([1899] New York, 1953), and "The Barbarian Status of Women" (1898) and "The Economic Theory of Women's Dress" (1894), in *Essays in Our Changing Order* (New York, 1934). See Theodor Adorno, "Veblen's Attack on Culture," *Studies in Philosophy and Social Science* 9 (1941): 396; John Patrick Diggins, *The Bard of Savagery: Thorstein Veblen and Modern Social Theory* (New York, 1978), vii.

13. See Laurence Birken, *Consuming Desire: Sexual Science and the Emergence of a Culture of Abundance, 1871–1914* (Ithaca, 1988), 22–56.

14. Quoted in F. O. Matthiessen, *Theodore Dreiser*, 27.

15. Walter Benn Michaels, *The Gold Standard and the Logic of Naturalism: American Literature at the Turn of the Century* (Berkeley, Calif., 1987), 279–81.

16. Jürgen Habermas, *Theory of Communicative Action*, trans. Thomas McCarthy (Boston, 1979), 225, 236.

17. Dreiser, "Neurotic America and the Sex Impulse," in *Hey Rub-a-Dub-Dub*, 126–41.

18. Adams, *The New Empire*, xviii.

19. Alice Brown, *The Mannerings* (Boston, 1903), 128.

20. Kate Chopin, *"The Awakening" and Selected Stories*, ed. Barbara H. Solomon (New York, 1976), 123–24. One of the last thoughts Edna is represented as having is "Perhaps Doctor Mandelet would have understood . . . " (124).

21. Per Seyersted, *Kate Chopin: A Critical Biography* (Baton Rouge, La., 1969), 68.

22. *Independent* 15 (1903). The *Independent* ran eighty of these stories or "lifelets" between 1902 and 1908; seventeen of them have been reprinted in *Plain Folk: The Life Stories of Undistinguished Americans*, ed. David M. Katzman and William M. Tuttle (Urbana, Ill., 1981). See also Julian Ralph, *The Making of a Journalist* (New York, 1903); Joseph R. Buchanan, *The Story of a Labor Agitator* (New York, 1903). See also Robert H. Bremner, *From the Depths: The Discovery of Poverty in the United States* (New York, 1967), 145–49.

23. Dowell, Introduction to *An Amateur Laborer*, xxx.

24. For a comparison to Durkheim, see Irving Howe, "[*An American Tragedy*]," in Pizer, ed., *Critical Essays* (Boston, 1981), 294; Émile Durkheim, *Suicide*, trans. John A. Spaulding and George Simpson (New York, 1951), 68.

25. Jack London, "How I Became a Socialist," *Comrade* 2 (March 1903): 122–23; Lester Ward, *Pure Sociology* (New York, 1903), 381–89, 401–3; Albion W. Small, *General Sociology* (Chicago, 1905), 38. See also George E. Mowry, *The Era of Theodore Roosevelt, 1900–1912* (New York, 1958), 16–37.

26. Dreiser, *Twelve Men*, 134. See Moers, *The Two Dreisers*, 138–41; Laurence Hussman, *Dreiser and His Fiction* (Philadelphia, 1983) (Fred See, in *Desire and the Sign: Nineteenth-Century American Fiction* [Baton Rouge, La., 1987], however, goes so far as to claim that there is no metaphysics in Dreiser's writing).

27. Dreiser, "Reflections," *Ev'ry Month*, February 1897, 3; Dreiser, *Twelve Men*, 142; Herbert Spencer, "Imperialism and Slavery," "Rebarbarization," "Regimentation," *Notes and Comments* (London, 1902), 112–41.

2. The Big Stick and the Cash Value of Ideas: Theodore Roosevelt and William James

1. *Letters of Theodore Roosevelt*, ed. Elting E. Morison (Cambridge, Mass., 1951–54) (hereafter *LTR*).

2. Roosevelt is quoted by David Axeen, "'Heroes of the Engine Room': 'American Civilization' and the War with Spain," *American Quarterly* 36 (Fall 1984): 482. William James, *Memories and Studies* (New York, 1911).

3. John S. Haller, Jr., and Robin Haller, *The Physician and Sexuality in Victorian America* (Urbana, Ill., 1974), ix–xi: "Like the priest's confessional, the minister's study, or the lawyer's office, the doctor's consultation and examination rooms became a sacred setting in which confidential conversation might take place" (x). Competitors for the preistly role abounded. For priestly journalism, see Ida Tarbell, *History of the Standard Oil Company* (New York, 1904), and Lincoln Steffens, *Shame of the Cities* (New York, 1904). Among the priestly economists were Richard T. Ely (see "The Control of Natural Monopolies," *World Today* 5 [December 1903]: 1633–34, "If You Can't Go to College," *Success Magazine* 6 [February 1903]: 85, 102, and "The Economic Aspects of Mormonism," *Harper's Monthly* 106 [April 1903]: 667–78) and Simon Nelson Patten (*Heredity and Social Progress* [New York, 1903] and *The New Basis of Civilization* [New York, 1909]). See also sociologist Albion W. Small, "Immoral Morality," *Independent* 55, March 26, 1903, 710–13. Most important of the natural scientists were Nathaniel S. Shaler (see "Faith in Nature," *International Quarterly* 6 [March 1903]: 281–304), John Muir, John Burroughs, and Roosevelt. See also Nathan Hale, *Freud and the Americans* (New York, 1971), 50; Bruce Kuklick, *The Rise of American Philosophy: Cambridge, Massachusetts, 1860–1930* (New Haven, Conn., 1977), 131–38; Warner Berthoff, "Culture and Consciousness," *Columbia Literary History of the United States*, ed. Emory Elliott et al. (New York, 1988), 488–90; Burton J. Bledstein, *The Culture of Professionalism: The Middle Class and the Development of Higher Education in America* (New York, 1976); Thomas L. Haskell, *The Emergence of Professional Social Science: The American Social Science Association and the Nineteenth-Century Crisis of Authority* (Urbana, Ill., 1977).

4. James, "Address on the Philippine Question," Report of the Fifth Annual Meeting, New England Imperialist League, 1903 (in *William James: The Essential Writings*, ed. Bruce D. Wilshire [New York, 1971]). "Can Lynching Be Stopped?" *Literary Digest*, August 8, 1903; "Epidemic of Lynching," *Boston Journal*, July 29, 1903; "The PhD Octopus," *Harvard Monthly* 36 (1903); "The True Harvard," *Harvard Graduates' Magazine* 12 (1903); *Address at the Centenary of Ralph Waldo Emerson* (Concord, Mass., 1903); "Herbert Spencer Dead," *New York Evening Post*, December 8, 1903.

5. Roosevelt was, of course, a generation younger than James, and in fact had taken James's course on Herbert Spencer in 1876. Basic biographical material on Roosevelt is from Owen Wister, *Roosevelt: The Story of a Friendship* (New York, 1930), David McCullough, *Mornings on Horseback* (New York, 1981), Howard K. Beale, *Theodore Roosevelt and the Rise of America to World Power* (New York, 1962), Edmund Morris, *The Rise of Theodore Roosevelt* (New York, 1979), and John Morton Blum, *The Republican Roosevelt* (Cambridge, Mass, 1977). Biographical material on James is from Ralph Barton Perry, *The Thought and Character of William James* (Cambridge, Mass., 1935), 2 vols. (hereafter *TCWJ*), Howard Feinstein, *Becoming William James* (Ithaca, 1984), Gay Wilson Allen, *William James: A Biography* (New York, 1967), and Gerald Myers, *William James* (New Haven, 1986).

6. James, *The Varieties of Religious Experience* ([1902] New York, 1982), 83.

7. Allen, *William James*, 222; Feinstein, *Becoming William James*, 183; James, *Letters of William James*, ed. Henry James (Boston, 1920), 1:79; Perry, *TCWJ*, 2:323.

8. Allen, *William James*, 228, 437, 317–32; Perry, *TCWJ*, 2:670–98.

9. See Havelock Ellis, *Study in the Psychology of Sex: The Evolution of Modesty, the Phenomena of Sexual Periodicity, Auto-Eroticism* (Philadelphia, 1900), *Man and Woman: A Study of Human Secondary Sexual Characters* 4th ed. (London, 1904), *The Criminal* (London, 1890); Richard von Krafft-Ebing, *Psychopathia Sexualis* (London, 1890); Cesare Lombroso, *Crime: Its Causes and Remedies*, trans. Henry P. Horton (Boston, 1911), *The Man of Genius* (New York,

1891); Enrico Ferri, *Criminal Sociology* (London, 1897); Max Nordau, *Degeneration* (London, 1897). See Kelly Hurley, "The Novel of the Gothic Body: Deviance and Abjection in Late Victorian Gothic Fiction" (diss., Stanford University, 1988).

10. James, *The Varieties of Religious Experience*, 22; Allen, *William James*, 383.

11. Kuklick, *Rise of American Philosophy*, 131–38.

12. Kuklick, *Rise of American Philosophy*, 461; Mark Twain, "A Dog's Tale," *Harper's Monthly* 108 (1903): 11–19; James, *The Principles of Psychology*, 2 vols. (New York, 1890), 1:vi, 137, 401, and 2:669–70.

13. Kuklick, *Rise of American Philosophy*, 583.

14. James, *Principles of Psychology*, 2:46; James, "Frederic Myers's Services to Psychology," *Popular Science Monthly* 59 (1901), 380–89; James, *Presidential Addresses of the Society for Psychical Research, 1882–1911* (Glasgow, 1912), 75–85; James, "Frederic Myers's Services," 389.

15. See the letters from William James to his wife and father in Perry, *TCWJ*, 2:323, 706–16. For an interpretation of the relation between father and son see Feinstein, *Becoming William James*, bk. 2.

16. James, *Varieties*, xxxvii, 163, 483, 508.

17. The consensus on the autobiographical base of the passage is represented by Allen, *William James*, 165–67, and Feinstein, *Becoming William James*, 241–42. Allen assumes the original experience to have happened in 1870, Feinstein in 1872. Sander L. Gilman has also, in passing, commented on "the question of career choice and the economic definition of the self," in "Masturbation and Anxiety: Henry Mackenzie, Heinrich Von Kleist, William James," in *Disease and Representation* (Ithaca, 1988), 63–80.

18. *Letters of William James*, 1:79; letter to Holmes, quoted in Max Fisch, "Was There a Metaphysical Club in Cambridge?" in *Studies in the Philosophy of Charles Sanders Peirce*, 2d ser., ed. Edward C. Moore and Richard S. Robin (Amherst, Mass., 1964), 4; Kuklick, *Rise of American Philosophy*, 48.

19. James diary and notebook entries, February 1, 1870, and April 30, 1870, in Perry, *TCWJ*, 1:622–23.

20. Henry James, Jr., *A Small Boy and Others* (New York, 1913), 190.

21. George F. Drinka, *The Birth of Neurosis* (New York, 1984), 283.

22. James, "The Energies of Men," in *On Vital Reserves* (New York, 1916), 3–39.

23. Simon Nelson Patten, *The New Basis of Civilization* (New York, 1909). See also Jackson Lears, *No Place of Grace* (New York, 1981), 54, 123, and Warren I. Susman, " 'Personality' and the Making of Twentieth-Century Culture," in *Culture as History: The Transformation of American Society in the Twentieth Century* (New York, 1984), 271–85.

24. James, "The Gospel of Relaxation," in *Talks to Teachers on Psychology; and to Students on Some of Life's Ideals* ([1899] New York, 1958), 132–48.

25. H. Rashdall, review of *The Varieties of Religious Experience*, *Mind*, n.s. 46 (April 1903): 246.

26. James E. Amos, *Theodore Roosevelt: Hero to His Valet* (New York, 1927), 118; Roosevelt, *Ranch Life and the Hunting Trail* in *The Works of Theodore Roosevelt*, ed. Hermann Hagedorn, 20 vols. (New York, 1926), 1:329 (hereafter *Works*); TR to Anna Roosevelt, *Letters of Theodore Roosevelt*, ed. Elting E. Morison (Cambridge, Mass., 1951–54), 1:56 (hereafter *LTR*); Howells to H. B. Fuller, March 14, 1909, *Life in Letters of William Dean Howells*, ed. Mildred Howells (Garden City, N.Y., 1928), 2:264. See Morris, *The Rise of Theodore Roosevelt*, 131–32, and McCullough, *Mornings on Horseback*, 221–58.

27. John Burroughs, *Camping and Tramping with President Roosevelt* (Boston, 1907), 3.

28. Mark Sullivan, *Our Times, 1900–1925*, 4 vols. (New York, 1946), 2:215–18; the one reporter is John Walsh (*Kansas City Star*, February 12, 1922); Morris, *Rise*, 161–62.

29. David Graham Phillips, "Owen Wister," *Saturday Evening Post*, January 3, 1903, 13. See Darwin Payne, *Owen Wister: Chronicler of the West, Gentleman of the East* (Dallas, Tex., 1985), 70–76; Wister, *Roosevelt*, 28; Payne, *Owen Wister*, 75–76, 209; Donald E. Houghton, "Two Heros in One: Reflections on the Popularity of *The Virginian*," *Journal of Popular Culture* 4 (1970): 497–506; Lee Clark Mitchell, " 'When You Call Me That . . . ': Tall Talk and Male Hegemony in *The Virginian*," *PMLA* 102 (1987): 66–77. G. Edward White, in an analysis parallel to this one, claims that Wister, Remington, and Roosevelt were "participants in a reorganization of status, with particular overtones for families of established wealth but with ramifications for all of eastern America" (*The Eastern Establishment and the Western Experience: The West of Frederic Remington, Theodore Roosevelt, and Owen Wister* [New Haven, Conn., 1968], 58–59, 73).

30. For the relation of ranchmen, plantation owners, and imperialists, see McCullough, *Mornings on Horseback*, 317, and TR to Paul Dana, April 18, 1898, *LTR* 2:817.

31. Roosevelt, *Oliver Cromwell*, in *Works*, 13:358–59.

32. TR to Henry Cabot Lodge, May 18, 1895, *LTR* 1:508; TR to George Otto Trevelyan, November 30, 1903, *LTR* 3:662–63; TR to Anna Roosevelt Cowles, December 17, 1899, *LTR* 2:1112–13.

33. TR to Hugo Münsterberg, June 3, 1901, *LTR* 3:86; cf. the opposite views in his senior thesis at Harvard, "The Practicability of Equalizing Men and Women before the Law," in which he advocated suffrage and property rights for women. Roosevelt's address is quoted in Henry F. Pringle, *Theodore Roosevelt: A Biography* (New York, 1931), 472. For programmatic statements by Roosevelt see "Twisted Eugenics" (1913) and "Race Decadence" (1911), in *Works*, 14:151–78.

34. See Thomas G. Dyer, *Theodore Roosevelt and the Idea of Race* (Baton Rouge, La., 1980), 14–15. "Mr. Dooley" is quoted in William M. Gibson, *Theodore Roosevelt among the Humorists: W. D. Howells, Mark Twain, and Mr. Dooley* (Knoxville, Tenn., 1980), 55, 59.

35. These were not published in Peirce's lifetime; see *Collected Papers of Charles Sanders Peirce*, 6 vols., ed. Charles Hartshorne and Paul Weiss (Cambridge, Mass., 1931–35), vol. 5, and sections scattered in the editions of Justus Buchler (*Philosophical Writings of Peirce* [New York, 1955]) and Philip P. Wiener (*Charles S. Peirce: Selected Writings* [New York, 1966]).

36. Charles S. Peirce, "What Pragmatism Is," *Monist* 15 (1905): 165–66; Perry, *TCWJ*, 2:409. See J. David Lewis and Richard L. Smith, *American Sociology and Pragmatism: Mead, Chicago Sociology, and Symbolic Interaction* (Chicago, 1980), 27–58.

37. James, *Pragmatism* ([1907] New York, 1955), 133, 125. See also William H. Gass, "The High Brutality of Good Intentions," *Accent* 18 (Winter 1958): 62–71.

38. James, *Essays in Radical Empiricism* ([1912] Cambridge, Mass., 1976), 25, 22. I derive the description of modernity from Jürgen Habermas's in *Theory of Communicative Action* (Boston, 1984), 35n; for others, Peirce's emphasis on semiology places him in the vanguard of modernity.

39. See Wister, *Roosevelt*, 126–27.

40. See Perry, *TCWJ*, 2:10; Allen, *William James*, 171–210.

41. Perry, *TCWJ*, 2:410–11.

42. As Peirce wrote to James (June 13, 1907): "Truth is public." See Roosevelt, "The Duties of American Citizenship," Address to the Liberal Club, Buffalo, N.Y., January 26, 1893, in William H. Harbaugh, ed., *The Writings of Theodore Roosevelt* (Indianapolis, Ind., 1967), 3–16.

43. See Allen, *William James*, 391. For Roosevelt, see memoirs by a friend, a servant, an acquaintance, and a detractor, respectively: Wister, *Roosevelt*; James Amos, *Theodore Roosevelt*; John Burroughs, *Camping and Tramping with President Roosevelt*; Annie Riley Hale, *Bull Moose Trails (Supplement to "Rooseveltian Fact and Fable")* (New York, 1912). On stable characters and developing personalities, see Warren I. Susman, *Culture as History*, 271–85.

44. James to Schiller, April 8, 1903, in Perry, *TCWJ*, 2:375; James to Charles William Eliot, March 3, 1895, in Perry, *TCWJ*, 2:416–17; Peirce to James, March 16, 1903, in Perry, *TCWJ*, 2:427.

45. James to Peirce, December 22, 1897, and Peirce to James, December 26, 1897, in Perry, *TCWJ*, 2:418–20.

46. But see also John Milton Cooper, *The Warrior and the Priest* (Cambridge, Mass., 1983), in which Roosevelt is figured as the warrior and Woodrow Wilson as the priest.

47. Peirce, "The Concept of God" (c. 1906), in *Philosophical Writings of Peirce*, 267, 376–77; *Collected Papers* 5:197.

48. Burroughs, *Camping*, viii.

49. John Muir, *Our National Parks* (Boston, 1902), 3. John Higham, *Strangers in the Land: Patterns of American Nativism, 1860–1925*, 2d ed. (New York, 1963), 110–23; "Mr. Roosevelt's Tour and Speeches," *Independent* 55, April 16, 1903, 879–80.

50. Anthracite Coal Commission, *Report to the President on the Anthracite Coal Strike of May–October, 1902* (Washington, D.C., 1903), 42–43; TR to W. H. Taft, 1906, quoted in Richard Hofstadter, *The Age of Reform* (New York, 1955), 239.

51. Roosevelt, speech, May 30, 1903, quoted in Dwyer, *Roosevelt and the Idea of Race*, 97; TR to Rudyard Kipling, November 1, 1904, *LTR* 4:1007–8.

52. Arthur M. Schlesinger, Jr., *The Crisis of the Old Order*, vol. 1 of *The Age of Roosevelt* (Boston, 1957), 17.

53. James to Carl Schurz, March 16, 1900, in *Selected Letters of William James*, ed. Elizabeth Hardwick (New York, 1961); Adams, *Education*, 265; Ida Tarbell, *All in the Day's Work: An Autobiography* (New York, 1939), 189–90; James to C. F. Adams, December 29, 1898, *The Letters of William James*, ed. Henry James (Boston, 1920); James to F. C. S. Schiller, August 6, 1902, quoted in Richard E. Welch, Jr., *Response to Imperialism: The United States and the Philippine-American War, 1899–1902* (Chapel Hill, N.C., 1979).

54. James, "The Moral Equivalent of War," in *William James*, ed. Wilshire, 349–61.

55. Roosevelt, quoted in Axeen, "Heroes of the Engine Room," 482.

56. Friedrich Nietzsche, *Beyond Good and Evil*, trans. Walter Kaufmann and J. R. Hollingdale (New York, 1969), §32; Percival Pollard, *Lingo Dan: A Novel* (Washington, D.C., 1903), 36; Henry Adams to Brooks Adams, 1898, *Letters of Henry Adams*, ed. Worthington Chauncey Ford (Boston, 1938), 2:178.

57. James, "Address at the Emerson centenary in Concord," in *William James*, ed. Wilshire, 290–91; Ralph Waldo Emerson, "Fate," *Conduct of Life*, centenary ed. 6 (Cambridge, Mass., 1904), 13.

3. Hamlin Garland's Despair and Edgar Saltus's Disenchantment

1. See also Billy M. Jones, *Health-Seekers in the Southwest, 1817–1900* (Norman, Okla., 1967), who claims that the heyday of health seeking was over by 1900.

Jones writes primarily about consumptives, however, and very little about neurasthenics.

2. Garland, *A Son of the Middle Border* (New York, 1917), 322, 323, 326; Garland's early relation to Spencer has been discussed by, among others, Donald Pizer, in "Herbert Spencer and the Genesis of Hamlin Garland's Critical System," *Tulane Studies in English* 7 (1957): 153–68.

3. Garland, *Son*, 332.

4. Hamlin Garland, *Crumbling Idols: Twelve Essays on Art Dealing Chiefly with Literature, Painting, and the Drama* ([1894] Cambridge, Mass., 1960); "New Figures in Literature and Art," *Atlantic Monthly* 76 (December 1895): 842. See Jane Johnson, Introduction to Garland, *Crumbling Idols*, x.

5. Saltus, "Akosmism," in *Love and Lore* ([1890] New York, 1970), 20; Saltus, "Morality in Fiction," in *Love and Lore*; Gelett Burgess, *The Rubaiyat of Omar Cayenne* (New York, 1904), 7; Burgess, *Are You a Bromide? or, The Sulphitic Theory* (New York, 1907), 17.

6. In *Love and Lore*, 36.

7. See Lars Åhnebrink, *The Beginnings of Naturalism in American Fiction: A Study of the Works of Hamlin Garland, Stephen Crane, and Frank Norris with Special Reference to Some European Influences, 1891–1903* (New York, 1961), 75–77; Johnson, Introduction, xi; Robert Mane, *Hamlin Garland: L'homme et l'oeuvre* (Paris: Didier, 1968).

8. See Johnson, Introduction, xi; Larzer Ziff, *The American 1890s: Life and Times of a Lost Generation* (Lincoln, Neb., 1966), 119; H. L. Mencken, *Prejudices: First Series* (New York, 1919), 136; June Howard, *Form and History in American Literary Naturalism* (Chapel Hill, N.C., 1985), 179. For an earlier evaluation, which although more judgmental than this one comes to very similar conclusions, see Bernard I. Duffey, "Hamlin Garland's 'Decline' from Realism," *American Literature* 25 (1953): 69–74.

9. Alfred Kazin called Saltus an exotic in *On Native Grounds: An Interpretation of Modern American Prose Literature* (New York, 1942), 66. On Saltus and the "new pessimism" see Claire Sprague, *Edgar Saltus* (New York, 1968), 14; Saltus, *The Philosophy of Disenchantment* (New York, 1885), 34.

10. Homeopathy was a form of medical practice that in the 1880s was procured almost entirely by upper-class patients. See Michael Sartisky, Afterword to Elizabeth Stuart Phelps, *Doctor Zay* ([1882] New York, 1987), 259–321; Paul Starr, *The Social Transformation of American Medicine* (New York, 1982), 96–99; and the Introduction to Part II, herein.

11. Saltus, *The Pace That Kills: A Chronicle* (Chicago, 1889), 128.

12. Saltus, *Purple and Fine Women* ([1903] New York, 1968), 81.

13. Cesare Lombroso, *Man of Genius* (London and New York, 1891), 3 vols., 3:209.

14. Philip Durham, ed., *"Seth Jones" by Edward S. Ellis and "Deadwood Dick on Deck" by Edward L. Wheeler* (New York, 1966). Calamity Jane was a real person as well as a fictional character; she died in 1903.

15. Garland, *Hesper* (New York, 1903), 128.

16. In *Bookman* 59 (May 1924): 257–62.

17. See Philip S. Foner, *First Facts of American Labor* (New York, 1984), 5, 12; John Higham, *Strangers in the Land: Patterns of American Nativism, 1860–1925* (New York, 1981), 112.

18. Quoted in Thomas R. Brooks, *Toil and Trouble: A History of American Labor*, 2d ed. (New York, 1971), 114. Mitchell was often criticized for hobnobbing too energetically with the likes of Roosevelt, and indeed Mitchell often imitated Roosevelt's rhetoric, as when he suggested that mine workers should be "moderate in speech" but insistent about their rights. He also was one of the most prescient observers of the economic scene, as when he argued that workers should organize

not just as producers but as consumers. See *Minutes of the 15th Annual Convention of the United Mine Workers of America* (Indianapolis, Ind., 1903), 22, 35, and *Minutes of the 14th Annual Convention of the United Mine Workers of America* (Indianapolis, Ind., 1903), 24–26.

19. Anthracite Coal Commission, *Report to the President on the Anthracite Coal Strike of May–October, 1902* (Washington, D.C., 1903), 42–43. On other strikes see Slason Thompson, "Violence in Labor Conflicts," *The Outlook* 78 (1904): 969.

20. See Mark Sullivan, *Our Times: The United States, 1900–1925*, 4 vols. (New York, 1931), 2:445–46.

21. Percival Pollard, *Their Days in Court* (New York, 1909), 230–36. This view was reiterated by H. L. Mencken, Carl Van Doren, in their own ways by Fred Pattee and Vernon Parrington, and by Granville Hicks, Larzer Ziff, and others. See *The Critical Reception of Hamlin Garland, 1891–1978*, ed. Charles L. P. Silet, Robert E. Welch, and Richard Boudreau (Troy, N.Y., 1985).

22. Percival Pollard, *Lingo Dan: A Novel* (Washington, D.C., 1903), 152.

23. Jack London, *The Kempton-Wace Letters* (New York, 1903), 19–20.

24. Jean Holloway, *Hamlin Garland: A Biography* (Austin, Tex., 1960), 177–78; Garland, "The Redman's Present Needs," *North American Review* 174 (April 1902): 488. To quote this one line out of context may be slightly unfair. Jack L. Davis, for instance, although he does not mention this part of Garland's argument, finds the article to contain "penetrating and persuasive" proposals for reform of the government's handling of Indian affairs. See "Hamlin Garland's Indians and the Quality of Civilized Life," in Silet, Welch, and Boudreau, eds., *The Critical Reception*, 426–39.

25. Garland, *The Captain of the Grey-Horse Troop* (New York, 1902), 56.

26. *Hamlin Garland's Diaries*, ed. Donald Pizer (San Marino, Calif., 1968), 268, 3, 51, 98, 93.

27. Lincoln Steffens, "Pittsburgh: A City Ashamed," *McClure's* (May 1903); reprinted in *The Shame of the Cities* (New York, 1957), 101, 104.

28. *The Pittsburgh Survey*, 6 vols., ed. Paul Underwood Kellogg (New York, 1909).

29. Marie Saltus, *Edgar Saltus, the Man* (Chicago, 1925), 112.

30. Harry T. Levin, "The Discovery of Bohemia," in Robert Spiller et al., *Literary History of the United States*, 2 vols. (New York, 1948), 2:1074. Saltus's devotion to style has led Claire Sprague to see a connection to Veblen's "instinct of workmanship" (*Edgar Saltus*, 67).

Neurasthenic Spirituality and Other Compromises

1. Harold Kaplan, *Power and Order: Henry Adams and the Naturalist Tradition in American Fiction* (Chicago, 1981), 130, 9. Kaplan, without direct reference to neurasthenia, goes so far as to define naturalism as "the effort to value things for the energy they embody" (2).

2. Émile Zola, *The Experimental Novel and Other Essays*, trans. B. M. Sherman (New York, 1893), 45.

3. Friedrich Nietzsche, *The Genealogy of Morals*, trans. Walter Kaufmann and R. J. Hollingdale (New York, 1969), 32.

4. Thorstein Veblen, *Theory of the Leisure Class* ([1899] New York, 1953), chap. 12; Oliver Wendell Holmes, review of *Homeopathic Domestic Physician*, "Literary Notices," *Atlantic Monthly*, December 1857, 252; Holmes, *Medical Essays: 1842–1882* (Boston, 1911), 74, 69; Ambrose Bierce, *The Devil's Dictionary* ([1911] New York, 1958), 65. On Holmes and Veblen see Perry Miller, *American Thought: Civil War to World War I* (New York, 1954), intro.

5. Sarah Orne Jewett, *The Country Doctor* (New York, 1886), 253; Keene Abbott, "The White Glory," *McClure's* 20 (February 1903): 470–75; John Swain, "Dr. Lorenz, Straightener of Children," *McClure's* 20 (January 1903): 314–22.

6. Charles Wagner, *The Simple Life* ([1901] New York, 1904), iii. Wagner's example of the complicated life is a wedding requiring dressmakers, milliners, upholsterers, jewelers, decoraters, and caterers, betrothal dinners, dinners of presentation, the settlement dinner, receptions, balls—the audience is upper middle class, in other words; the complexities are the complexities of wealth. See also George C. Lorimer, *The Modern Crisis in Religion* (New York, 1904), which argues that the solution to the "decadence" of modern religion is to further modernize it (41). These arguments had been rehearsed since Herbert Spencer's "Gospel of Relaxation" and Henry Ward Beecher's sermons of the Civil War era.

7. Carl Jung, *Memories, Dreams, Reflections*, trans. Richard and Clara Winston (New York, 1965), 150; Charles Sanders Peirce, *Philosophical Writings*, ed. Justus Buchler (New York, 1955), 339.

8. Adams, *The Education of Henry Adams* ([1907] Boston, 1973), 450. "Phrases and motifs from *The Education of Henry Adams* begin appearing at random" in Adam's letters in 1903, according to J. C. Levenson, Ernest Samuels, Charles Vandersee, and Viola Hopkins Winner, editors of *The Letters of Henry Adams* (Cambridge, Mass., 1988), 5:433.

9. See Howard M. Feinstein, *Becoming William James* (Ithaca, 1984), 241–42, although Gay Wilson Allen (*William James*, 165–67) dates James's crisis in 1870.

10. Frank Lloyd Wright, letter to D. D. Martin, December 10, 1903, *Letters to Clients*, ed. Bruce Pfeiffer (Fresno, Calif., 1986); Robert Peel, *Mary Baker Eddy: The Years of Discovery* (New York, 1966), esp. 243–46; Peel, *The Years of Authority* (New York, 1977), 201, 422. For examples of ambivalence in Twain's *Christian Science* (in *What Is Man? and Other Philosophical Writings*, ed. Paul Baender [Berkeley, Calif., 1973]), see pp. 266, 268, 284; his ambivalence was also noted in reviews in *Harper's Weekly*, *Philadelphia Medical Journal*, and *The Nation*. See also Edward Wagenknecht, *Mark Twain: The Man and His Work* (Norman, Okla., 1961), 184ff; Washington Gladden, "Truths and Untruths of Christian Science," *Independent* 55, April 2, 1903, 776–79.

4. Frank Norris: Nationalism, Naturalism, and the Supernatural

1. Norris, "The Need of a Literary Conscience," *Responsibilities of the Novelist* (New York, 1903), 214. The machinery of life also clashes in its grooves in Norris's novel *Blix* ([1899] New York, 1903), 130. See also "Salt and Sincerity," *Responsibilities of the Novelist*, 305. And see Ronald Takaki, *Iron Cages: Race and Culture in Nineteenth-Century America* (Seattle, Wash., 1982), 253–79, for what he calls the "masculine thrust toward Asia" of the late 1890s.

2. Larzer Ziff calls Norris a chest-thumper and quotes the line about Anglo-Saxon knockabouts in *The American 1890s: Life and Times of a Lost Generation* (New York, 1966), 252–53. See also June Howard, *Form and History in American Literary Naturalism* (Chapel Hill, N.C., 1985), and Donald Pizer, "The Masculine-Feminine Ethic in Frank Norris's Popular Novels," *Texas Studies in Literature and Language* 6 (Spring 1964): 84–91.

3. Until two months before his death Norris was a big fan of the "Anglo-Saxon fighting spirit" of the football team at Berkeley, his alma mater (Franklin Walker, *Frank Norris: A Biography* [Garden City, N.J., 1932], 300 and passim); and see Joseph R. McElrath, Jr., "Frank Norris: A Biographical Essay," in *Critical Essays on Frank Norris*, ed. Don Graham (Boston, 1980), xxxiv–xxxv.

4. Donald Pizer, "The Masculine-Feminine Ethic in Frank Norris's Popular

Novels," 84–91. See also Pizer, "Evolutionary Ethical Dualism in Frank Norris's *Vandover and the Brute* and *McTeague*," *PMLA* 76 (1961): 552–60. Victorian ethics are already central to Darwin's theory in *The Origin of Species*, but the responsibilities and abilities for a civilizing morality were not, in Darwin's text, given primarily to the female of the species. Mark Seltzer has written that naturalism is "an emphatically 'male' genre" because of its "abstract conceptions of force" which countered "female generativity" ("The Naturalist Machine," in *Sex, Politics, and Science in the Nineteenth-Century Novel: Selected Papers from the English Institute*, ed. Ruth Bernard Yeazell [Baltimore, 1986], 121). This approach makes what was a scientific, material concept for Norris into an abstract concept and creates a series of contradictions out of what were coherent concepts for him. Where Seltzer sees "thermodynamic" logic creating a system of "crisis management" and a new "biomechanics of power," I see neurasthenic logic and its own notions of crisis management: neurasthenia was a "technology of regulation" which preceded the naturalist novel, and neurasthenic logic already provided the link between economics and sexuality Seltzer claims motivates the recourse to thermodynamics.

5. Sales for the original editions of Norris's novels were: *McTeague*, 3,974; *The Octopus*, 33,420; *The Pit*, 94,914. By 1932, the figures had reached the following levels, with *The Pit* still in front three to one: *McTeague*, 67,272; *The Octopus*, 59,985; *The Pit*, 189,751 (Walker, *Frank Norris*, 286n). The first lines of the following reviews in January 1903 indicate the effect of Norris's death on the reception of *The Pit*: (1) "The death of Frank Norris was a serious loss to American literature" (Issac F. Marcosson, "Frank Norris' Last Book: Lamented Novelist at his Best in *The Pit*—The Wheat Motive Again," *Louisville Times*, January 3, 1903, 7); (2) "It is with mingled feelings of regret and admiration that many readers will approach the last novel of Frank Norris" (Anon., "The Epic of the Wheat—The Pit," *Indianapolis News*, January 10, 1903, 8); (3) "After a careful reading of 'The Pit'—the last work by the late Frank Norris—one feels more keenly the loss to American letters by his death, just when he was coming into the full sense of his mastery of the story-teller's art" (George Hamlin Fitch, "Good Reading," *San Francisco Chronicle*, January 11, 1903, 18); (4) "By the death of Frank Norris, at the age of thirty-two, American literature lost its greatest known potentiality" (G. H. S., "Book of the Day: *The Pit*: Frank Norris's Last Novel," *Boston Evening Transcript*, January 21, 1903, 16); (5) "Had Frank Norris lived he might have achieved who knows how much?" (Anon., "Books That Are Being Read at This Time," *St. Paul Globe*, January 26, 1903, 8). Even the mixed reviews began on the same tack: "Just how much American literature lost by the death of Frank Norris is a difficult question, to which there will be many answers, none conclusive" (Anon., "A Dispassionate Examination of Frank Norris's Posthumous Novel," *New York Times*, January 31, 1903, "Saturday Review of Books and Art," 66). All quoted from Joseph R. McElrath, Jr., and Katherine Knight, *Frank Norris: The Critical Reception* (New York, 1981), 186, 194, 198, 213–14, 230, 235; an even greater number of examples can be found in the reviews of February and March (238, 240, 246, 253, 255, 259, 263, 266, 269, 272, 282, 284, 287).

6. Norris, notebook entries, Appendix F of Lars Åhnebrink, *The Beginnings of Naturalism in American Fiction: A Study of the Works of Hamlin Garland, Stephen Crane, and Frank Norris with Special Reference to Some European Influences, 1891–1903* (New York, 1961), 465.

7. Norris, *Moran of the Lady Letty* ([1898] New York, 1903) and *The Octopus: A Story of California* ([1901] New York, 1964).

8. Norris, "The Frontier Gone at Last," in *Responsibilities of the Novelist*, 221–27; Frederick Jackson Turner, "Contributions of the West to American Democracy," *Atlantic Monthly* 91 (January 1903): 83–95.

9. I. F. Marcosson, quoted in McElrath and Knight, *Frank Norris*, 130.

10. Norris, "Why Women Should Write the Best Novels," in *Responsibilities of the Novelist*, 286–89; Norris, notebook entries, Åhnebrink, *Beginnings*, 465. Christophe Charle has shown a similar displacement of poets by naturalists in his social history of literary groups in France in *La crise littéraire a l'époque du naturalisme, roman, théâtre et politique: Essai d'histoire sociale des groupes et des genres littéraires* (Paris, 1979).

11. See Robert A. Morace, "The Writer and His Middle-Class Audience: Frank Norris, A Case in Point," in Graham, *Critical Essays*, 60. For this information about Norris's relation to his publisher I am indebted to Oscar Cargill, Afterword to Norris, *The Octopus*; the characterization of *World's Work* is also Cargill's, Afterword, 464.

12. The quote about Carnegie is in Walker, *Frank Norris*, 293; Norris, *Responsibilities of the Novelist*, 198, 247. See also Joseph R. McElrath, Jr., "Frank Norris's *The Octopus*: The Christian Ethic as Pragmatic Response," 149: "His paternal model was the self-made businessman who undoubtedly contributed in large measure to Norris's achievement-oriented personality: 'success' is a major concept in every one of his seven novels."

13. See Howard, *Form and History*, 179. See also Amy Kaplan, *The Social Construction of American Realism* (Chicago, 1988), and Christopher Wilson, *The Labor of Words: Literary Professionalism in the Progressive Era* (Athens, Ga., 1985).

14. Norris, "The American Public and 'Popular' Fiction," in *Responsibilities of the Novelist*, 235.

15. Norris, "The True Reward of the Novelist," in *Responsibilities of the Novelist*, 200.

16. Franklin Walker, "Frank Norris at the University of California," *University of California Chronicle*, July 1931, 331.

17. See Alice Wexler, *Emma Goldman: An Intimate Life* (New York, 1984), 115, 119; Candace Falk, *Love, Anarchy, and Emma Goldman* (New York, 1984), 44–47; John Higham, *Strangers in the Land: Patterns of American Nativism 1860–1925* (New York, 1981), 111–12; David DeLeon, *The American as Anarchist: Reflections on Indigenous Radicalism* (Baltimore, Md., 1978); Margaret S. March, *Anarchist Women, 1870–1920* (Philadelphia, 1981), 12.

18. S. Weir Mitchell, *Doctor and Patient* ([1887] Philadelphia, 1904), 126.

19. George Santayana, "Emerson's Poems Proclaim the Divinity of Nature, with Freedom as His Profoundest Ideal," *Boston Daily Advertiser*, May 23, 1903, reprinted in James Ballowe, ed., *George Santayana's America* (Urbana, Ill., 1967); Liberty Hyde Bailey, *The Nature-Study Idea* (New York, 1903), 5. See also Stewart Edward White, *Conjurer's House* (New York, 1903) and *The Forest* (New York, 1903), and John Burroughs's seemingly innumerable publications.

20. Walker, *Frank Norris*, 144–48; John Muir, *Our National Parks* (New York, 1902), 1; the loafing narrator is in Norris, "A Bargain with Peg-Leg," in *A Deal in Wheat*, 334.

21. Norris, *A Deal in Wheat*, 324. Lockwood's degree also marks him as in the top two-tenths of one percent of his age cohort in terms of education. There were approximately one and a half million people in each of the college-level age-grades in America in 1903; some 70,000 graduated from high school in that year (5%). Fewer than 15,000 received bachelor's degrees (1%), and 2,783 received advanced degrees (0.2%) (*Report of the Commissioner of Education for the Year 1903* [Washington, D.C., 1905] 2:1507, 1813, 1816).

22. David Graham Phillips, *The Master Rogue* (New York, 1903).

23. For a discussion of Norris's Christian perspective in relation to James see McElrath, "Frank Norris's *The Octopus*" in Graham, ed., *Critical Essays*, 138–52.

24. Norris, *The Pit: A Story of Chicago* (New York, 1903).

25. Sigmund Freud, "The Uncanny" (1919), in *On Creativity and the Unconscious: Papers on the Psychology of Art, Literature, Love, and Religion*, trans. Joan Riviere (New York, 1958), 122–61.

26. George Ade, *In Babel: Stories of Chicago* (New York, 1903).

27. Henry Crosby Emery, *Speculation on the Stock and Produce Exchanges of the United States*, Columbia Studies in History, Economics, and Public Law 7 (New York, 1896), 294. See also pp. 289, 292, 295, 298, 322, 456–57. The change in usage from "panic" to "depression" as the primary emotion word in economics parallels changes in psychology—a move from the bodily panic of nerves to mental depression of neurosis.

28. Norris, *Vandover and the Brute* (Garden City, N.Y., 1914).

29. These observations play off the arguments of Walter Benn Michaels in several of the essays in *The Gold Standard and the Logic of Naturalism* (Berkeley, Calif., 1987).

30. For discussions of Norris's and the naturalists' use of the machine, see Leo Marx, *The Machine in the Garden* (New York, 1964); Åhnebrink, *The Beginnings of Naturalism*; Charles Child Walcutt, *American Literary Naturalism: A Divided Stream* (Minneapolis, Minn., 1956); W. F. Taylor, *The Economic Novel in America* (Chapel Hill, N.C., 1942); and Donald Pizer, "Synthetic Criticism and Frank Norris's *The Octopus*," in *Realism and Naturalism in Nineteenth-Century American Literature* (Carbondale, Ill., 1984), 154–65.

31. For views of the novel as flawed by the two plots, see Donald Pizer, *The Novels of Frank Norris* (Bloomington, Ind., 1966), 165–76; Ernest Marchand, *Frank Norris: A Study* (Stanford, Calif., 1942), 86. A reading of the two plots which sees the love plot as more interesting and central than the wheat plot is Larzer Ziff's in *The American 1890s: Life and Times of a Lost Generation* (Lincoln, Neb., 1966), 270–73.

32. Howard Horowitz, " 'To Find the Value of *X*': *The Pit* as Renunciation of Romance," in *American Realism: New Essays*, ed. Eric J. Sundquist (Baltimore, Md., 1982), 225–27.

33. Ziff, *The American 1890s*, 272.

34. Reproductions of Bouguereau's *Nymphs and Satyr* (1873) were "hung over the bars of men's saloons throughout the country" (John D'Emilio and Estelle B. Freedman, *Intimate Matters: A History of Sexuality in America* [New York, 1988], plate 23).

35. Quoted in Walker, *Frank Norris*, 278–79.

5. William Dean Howells: *Letters Home, Questionable Shapes,* and the American *Unheimlich*

1. Mark Twain, "Why Not Abolish It?" *Harper's Weekly*, May 2, 1903; Howells to Clemens, May 1, 1903, Howells to Aldrich, July 3, 1902, *Life in Letters of William Dean Howells*, ed. Mildred Howells, 2 vols. (Garden City, N.Y., 1928), 2:175, 158. The standard biographies of Howells, on which much of the following is based, are Edwin H. Cady's two volumes, *The Road to Realism: The Early Years, 1837–1885, of William Dean Howells* (Syracuse, N.Y., 1956) and *The Realist at War: The Mature Years, 1885–1920, of William Dean Howells* (Syracuse, N.Y., 1958), and Kenneth S. Lynn, *William Dean Howells: An American Life* (New York, 1971).

2. The Björnson quote is from Van Wyck Brooks, *Howells: His Life and World* (New York, 1959), 170. The neurotic Howells has been studied since Edwin H. Cady's 1946 essay "The Neuroticism of William Dean Howells," *PMLA* 61 (March 1946): 229–38. See also John W. Crowley, *The Black Heart's Truth: The Early Career of W. D. Howells* (Chapel Hill, N.C., 1985). The characterization of his childhood as morbid runs through most of Howells's autobiographical writings;

the quote is from *Years of My Youth* (1916) in *"Years of My Youth" and Three Essays*, ed. David J. Nordloh (Bloomington, Ind., 1975), 79. Kenneth E. Eble has argued that Elinor Howells is an example of Caroll Smith-Rosenberg's thesis about illness as a role option (*William Dean Howells* [Boston, 1982], 44).

3. Crowley, *Black Heart's Truth*, 117–18 (see also "Winifred Howells and the Economy of Pain," in his *The Mask of Fiction: Essays on William Dean Howells* [Amherst, Mass., 1989], 83–114); Howells, *Suburban Sketches* (New York, 1871), 96.

4. For Howells's breakdown, see Lynn, *William Dean Howells*, 254, Eble, *William Dean Howells*, 77; and Crowley, *Black Heart's Truth*, chap. 6. Cady, in an afterword to *A Modern Instance* (New York, 1984), claims that new evidence for a physiological cause of Howells's illness at this time invalidates his own previous thesis of a "nervous breakdown" (457–59). The distinction between "physiological" and "psychosomatic" which Cady makes, however, is simply irrelevant in the case of neurasthenia, which was, in the minds of medical practitioners and sufferers, a combination of both.

5. Richard H. Brodhead, "Hawthorne among the Realists: The Case of Howells," in *American Realism*, ed. Eric Sundquist (Baltimore, Md., 1982), 37, 39. Eric Cheyfitz argues for a more complex notion of the rhetorical work of Howells's endings in "*A Hazard of New Fortunes*: The Romance of Self-Realization," in the same volume, 42–65. Amy Kaplan's remarks are from *The Social Construction of American Realism* (Chicago, 1988), 37.

6. Howells, *A Modern Instance* (New York, 1984), 210.

7. Howells, "Editor's Easy Chair," *Harper's Monthly* 107 (June 1903): 149. See especially Howells to Clemens, February 12, 1903, April 26, 1903, and December 20, 1903. Clemens, also interested in psychic phenomena, was Howells's main correspondent on such matters. Also citing the passage from the June "Easy Chair," Martha Banta states: "It was not until 1903 . . . that Howells could fully record the 'swing of the pendulum' which took responsible fiction toward a mode that was 'unscientific' and yet not romantic in the pejorative sense; only then could he praise 'a whole order of literature' that was 'calling itself psychological, as realism called itself scientific, and dealing with life on its mystical side' " (Introduction to *The Shadow of a Dream*, in W. D. Howells, *The Shadow of a Dream and An Imperative Duty*, ed. Martha Banta, Ronald Gottesman, and David J. Nordloh [Bloomington, Ind., 1970], xxi). Crowley quotes parts of this passage in support of his argument that Howells moved from "psychologism" to "psychic romance" in the stories in *Questionable Shapes* (*The Mask of Fiction*, 133–55).

8. Howells, *Letters Home* (New York, 1903), 2.

9. Howells to Henry Blake Fuller, January 17, 1904, *Selected Letters*, ed. George Arms et al., 6 vols. (Boston, 1979–83), 5:71; Thomas Wentworth Higginson and Henry Walcott Boynson, *A Reader's History of American Literature* (Boston, 1903), 251; H. L. Mencken, *Prejudices, First Series* (New York, 1919), 52–54; Sinclair Lewis, Nobel Prize speech, 1930, quoted in Eble, *Howells: A Century of Criticism* (Dallas, Tex., 1962), 101.

10. James to Howells, 1904, quoted in Brooks, *Howells*, 195–96.

11. James to Radcliffe class, April 6, 1896, *Selected Letters of William James*, ed. Elizabeth Hardwick ([1961] Boston, 1980), 153. Howells also wrote such letters; see the thank-you note to Evelyn Garnaut Smalley: "I do not think that human tongue can utter / My grateful feelings for the paper cutter / You sent me at the Merry Christmas tide," January 13, 1903, *Selected Letters* 5:43.

12. Norton to Howells, October 4, 1903, and December 13, 1902, *Selected Letters* 5:67n, 41n.

13. Cady, "The Neuroticism of William Dean Howells," 229–38; Howells to Aurelia Howells, November 22, 1903, *Selected Letters* 5:69.

14. Howells, *Questionable Shapes* (New York, 1903).

15. "Fiction/*Questionable Shapes*," *Times Literary Supplement*, June 19, 1903, 193, quoted in Clayton L. Eichelberger, *Published Comment on William Dean Howells through 1920: A Research Bibliography* (Boston, 1976), 235.

16. See also Walter Benn Michaels, "Romance and Real Estate," in *The American Renaissance Reconsidered*, ed. Walter Benn Michaels and Donald Pease (Baltimore, Md., 1985): "Of course, haunted house stories (like *The House of the Seven Gables*) usually involve some form of anxiety about ownership" (157).

17. See Lars Åhnebrink on the relation of Ibsen to the naturalist writers in America (Åhnebrink, *The Beginnings of Naturalism in American Fiction* [New York, 1961]).

18. One could equally well argue that Howells prefigured later psychologies of the decentered subject in his description of the self as an onion: "Nothing but hulls, that you keep peeling off, one after another, till you think you have got down to the heart, at last, and then you have got down to nothing" (*A Boy's Town* [New York, 1890], 171).

19. Howells's irony pervades his work and is often missed by readers who find him a pious old maid. That Howells was a subtle humorist is a fact perhaps less appreciated today than at the turn of the century. Brander Matthews in 1902, for instance, called him "one of the most delicate of our humorists, with a reserve that recalls Hawthorne's" ("Mr. Howells as a Critic," *Forum* 32 [January 1902]: 629–38). Throughout "His Apparition" and his other ghost stories, a "delicate," reserved humor, like that of Henry James's as much as that of Hawthorne's, controls the narrative voice. The same is true for *Letters Home*, as many contemporary reviewers noted: Howells's humor "is part of the very fabric of his work," said *The Critic* 43 (December 1903): 578. See also the reviews of *The Son of Royal Langbrith* in *Times Literary Supplement*, December 2, 1904, 379, and *Reader* 5 (December 1904): 130–31.

20. See Graham Belcher Blackstock, "Howells's Opinions on the Religious Conflicts of His Age as Exhibited in Magazine Articles," *American Literature* 15 (November 1943): 262–78. Howells's comments were addressed to Howard Pyle, April 17, 1890, *Life in Letters of William Dean Howells*, ed. Mildred Howells, 2 vols. (Garden City, N.Y., 1928), 2:11—"The only peace is in giving up one's will."

21. Howells to Clemens (about Alfred Russell Wallace's *Man's Place in the Universe*), December 20, 1903, *Selected Letters* 5:70.

22. See Crowley, *The Black Heart's Truth*, 7; Cady, "The Neuroticism of William Dean Howells," 230; Howells, *A Boy's Town*, 216, 182, 189; Howells, "*Years of My Youth*," 19, 60, 80; Howells, *My Literary Passions* (New York, 1895), 51–52; Howells, *My Year in a Log Cabin* (New York, 1893), 38.

23. See Howells to S. Weir Mitchell, December 12, 1904 (*Selected Letters* 5:113–14), in which Howells claims that we are "entitled to an eternity in which we shall still have mighty questions to ponder, in which we shall have still to find out God."

24. Howells to Madison Cawein, January 11, 1903, *Selected Letters* 5:42; Howells to Pyle, April 17, 1890, *Life in Letters* 2:11.

25. Ormond reads Parnell's allegory as realism, a mistake preachers and editors warned readers to avoid. See the editor's introduction to [Thomas Parnell], *The Hermit and the Traveller* (Philadelphia, 1818). The critics' phrases all refer to Howells's *Their Wedding Journey* (1872): Kenneth Seib, "Uneasiness at Niagra: Howells' *Their Wedding Journey*," *Studies in American Fiction* 4 (Spring 1976): 24; Gary A. Hunt, " 'A Reality That Can't Be Quite Definitely Spoken': Sexuality in *Their Wedding Journey*," *Studies in the Novel* 9 (Spring 1977): 18; Marion W. Cumpiano, "The Dark Side of *Their Wedding Journey*," *American Literature* 40 (January 1969): 474. All are quoted in Crowley, *Black Heart's Truth*, 65.

26. Although she does not mention neurasthenia by name, this is Elizabeth Johns's analysis of Eakins's response to the wear and tear of everyday life. She also discusses Eakins's relations with Philadelphians and neurologists S. Weir

Mitchell and Horatio Wood (*Thomas Eakins: The Heroism of Modern Life* [Princeton, N.J., 1983], 159–62, 168).

27. In *Literature and Life: Studies* (New York, 1902), 1–35.

28. Howells to Mrs. James T. Fields, February 23, 1903, *Life in Letters* 2:169.

29. Freud had nevertheless noticed a correlation between syphilis in the male parent and "neuropathic constitution of children" (Sigmund Freud, *Dora: An Analysis of a Case of Hysteria* [New York, 1963], 35n–36n); Beard followed the lead of Acton, who thought that syphilis varied in severity from time to time and place to place (William Acton, *A Complete Practical Treatise on Venereal Diseases, and Their Immediate and Remote Consequences* [London, 1841], 17; Beard, *American Nervousness* [New York, 1881], 94). See also John S. Haller, Jr., and Robin Haller, *The Physician and Sexuality in Victorian America* (Urbana, Ill., 1974), 258.

30. Mitchell to Howells, November 27, 1904, and December 12, 1904, *Selected Letters* 5:114n, 113.

6. Local Color, Mary E. Wilkins Freeman, and the Limits of Propriety

1. Barbara H. Solomon, Introduction to *The Short Fiction of Sarah Orne Jewett and Mary Wilkins Freeman*, ed. Barbara H. Solomon (New York, 1979), 17.

2. Mary Austin, "How I Learned to Write," in *My First Publication*, ed. James D. Hart (San Francisco, Calif., 1961), 64.

3. Mary Austin, *The Land of Little Rain* (Boston, 1903).

4. Andy Adams, *The Log of the Cowboy* ([1903] Lincoln, Neb., 1964).

5. Horace Spencer Fiske, *Provincial Types in American Fiction* (Chatauqua, N.Y., 1903), iii, 3. Mary E. Wilkins was a well-known writer with a long history of publication by the time she married Dr. Freeman in 1902 and took his name. I concentrate on her texts from 1903 and use Freeman throughout to avoid confusion.

6. For a discussion of Freeman's "spinsterhood," see Michelle Clark's Afterword to Freeman's *The Revolt of Mother and Other Stories* (Brooklyn, N.Y., 1974), 184–89, which also discusses the possibilities of homosexuality. The evidence of homoeroticism in the texts and circumstances of her life seem more convincing than even Clark allows; homosexuality also would have created the kind of role and status anxiety so often expressed in neurasthenia.

7. Perry D. Westbrook, *Mary Wilkins Freeman* (New York, 1967), 176.

8. The reevaluation began with Clark's 1974 collection (see note 6), now out of print. This was followed by Solomon's 1979 collection (see note 1), *Selected Stories of Mary E. Wilkins Freeman*, ed. Marjorie Pryse (New York, 1983), and a reprint of *The Wind in the Rose-Bush* ([1903] Chicago, 1986).

9. Alice G. Brand, "Mary Wilkins Freeman: Misanthropy as Propaganda," *New England Quarterly* 50 (1977): 83–100; Ann D. Wood, "The Literature of Impoverishment: The Local Colorists in America, 1865–1914," *Women's Studies* 1 (1972): 3–45; Nan B. Maglin, "Visions of Defiance: Work, Political Commitment and Sisterhood in 21 Works of Fiction, 1895–1925," *Praxis* 3 (1976): 98–112.

10. Freeman, *Six Trees* (New York, 1903). There may be a reference as well to Sarah Orne Jewett's earlier story "Tom's Wife" (*Atlantic Monthly*, February 1882), about role reversal in the marriage of Mr. and Mrs. Tom Dunn.

11. Freeman, *The Wind in the Rose-Bush*.

12. Freeman, *The Portion of Labor* (New York, 1901).

13. Ida Tarbell, *All in the Day's Work: An Autobiography* (New York, 1939), 127. See also Alexander Berkman, *Prison Memoirs of an Anarchist* ([1912] New York, 1970); Prof. E. E. Slosson, "An Experiment in Anarchy," *Independent*, April

2, 1903, 779–85; Alice Wexler, *Emma Goldman: An Intimate Life* (New York, 1984).

14. [A. E. Horsley], *The Confessions and Autobiography of Harry Orchard* (New York, 1907), ix.

15. Freeman, "For the Girl Who Wants to Write: Things to Do and Avoid," *Harper's Bazaar* 47 (June 1913): 272.

16. G. Allen Foster, *Advertising: Ancient Marketplace to Television* (New York, 1967), chap. 2; Jennifer Wicke, *Advertising Fictions: Literature, Advertisement, and Social Reading* (New York, 1988), 92–93.

Neurasthenic Representation and the Economy of Cultural Change

7. Women and Economics in the Writings of Charlotte Perkins Gilman and Edith Wharton

1. Quoted in Laura Shapiro, *Perfection Salad: Women and Cooking at the Turn of the Century* (New York, 1986), 123.

2. Mabel Dodge Luhan tells the story of her breakdown in *Intimate Memories: Background* (New York, 1933), 289–96. The comment is by Christopher Lasch, *The New Radicalism in America* (New York, 1965), 128.

3. Addams's neurasthenia is described in *Twenty Years at Hull House* (New York, 1910), 70–78. The fit epitaph is from Addams, *Democracy and Social Ethics* (New York, 1902), 274.

4. Deland, *Dr. Lavender's People* (New York, 1903), 132. George Herbert Mead also argued that the self should be thought of in terms of "interest" and that a "larger self" is the result of identifying with the "interests of others." See Mead, *Mind, Self, and Society* ([1934] Chicago, 1972), 386. Although this collection of lecture notes and manuscript fragments was not published until 1934, Mead's ideas date from the turn of the century.

5. Information about St. Denis is from Elizabeth Kendall, *Where She Danced: The Birth of American Art-Dance* (Berkeley, Calif., 1979), 12–51.

6. *The Living of Charlotte Perkins Gilman: An Autobiography* (New York, 1935), 90.

7. Gilman, *The Yellow Wallpaper* ([1892] Old Westbury, N. Y., 1973) and "Why I Wrote the Yellow Wallpaper," *The Forerunner* (October 1913), reprinted in *The Charlotte Perkins Gilman Reader*, ed. Ann J. Lane (New York, 1980), 19–20.

8. Gilman, *Women and Economics* ([1898] New York, 1966). Gilman, *The Home: Its Work and Influence* ([1903] Urbana, Ill., 1972).

9. Gilman, *Herland* ([1915] New York, 1979), 20.

10. "If I Were a Girl Again: Advice from a Thinker," *Success Magazine* (1903): 5372.

11. Robert W. Edis, "Internal Decoration," in *Our Homes*, ed. Shirley F. Murphy (London, 1883), 313, 321.

12. Patricia Meyer Spacks, *The Female Imagination* (New York, 1975), 214, 208. This interpretation is seconded by Sheryl L. Meyering in her introduction to the volume of criticism she collected, *Charlotte Perkins Gilman: The Woman and Her Work* (Ann Arbor, Mich., 1989), 1–10.

13. Wharton, *The Decoration of Houses* ([1902] New York, 1978), 44.

14. Wharton, *A Backward Glance* ([1934] New York, 1990), 830.

15. Wharton, *Sanctuary* (New York, 1903), 60.

16. See Elizabeth Ammons, *Edith Wharton's Argument with America* (Athens, Ga., 1980), 30; Elaine Showalter, "The Death of the Lady (Novelist): Wharton's *House of Mirth*," *Representations* 9 (Winter 1985): 133–47. There is a counter-

argument, made by Joan Lidoff ("Another Sleeping Beauty: Narcissism in *The House of Mirth*," in *American Realism*, ed. Eric Sundquist [Baltimore, Md., 1982], 238–56); Spacks (*The Female Imagination*, 239–41); and even to some extent Cynthia Griffin Wolff (*A Feast of Words: The Triumph of Edith Wharton* [New York, 1977], 109–33); all argue for a more complex view of Wharton's ideological commitments.

17. Sandra M. Gilbert and Susan Gubar, "The Angel of Devastation," *No Man's Land: The Place of the Woman Writer in the Twentieth Century* (New Haven, Conn., 1988), vol. 2, *Sexchanges*.

18. R. W. B. Lewis, *Edith Wharton: A Biography* (New York, 1975), 76. Lewis points out that Wharton's primary physician in Philadelphia was one of Mitchell's associates, a Dr. McClellan. See also Wolff, *A Feast of Words*, 85–89. Joseph P. Lovering (*S. Weir Mitchell* [New York, 1971]) writes of Mitchell's "well-known vanity" (17) and its effect on the accuracy of his memory.

19. Mitchell's unpublished autobiography, quoted in Anna Robeson Burr, *Weir Mitchell: His Life and Letters* (New York, 1929), 31; Lovering, *S. Weir Mitchell*, 17. The *Backward Glance* manuscript fragment is published as a postscript to *The Ghost Stories of Edith Wharton* (New York, 1976), 320.

20. That "The Lady's Maid's Bell" is a story about incest would take some time to develop as an argument, but I briefly sketch the evidence here. The outline of "Beatrice Palmato," a novel about father-daughter incest which Wharton never wrote, has several similarities to "The Lady's Maid's Bell," including a wife with nervous illness, a servant who also has a nervous breakdown and dies, a new female servant that the father eventually marries, a separation between the couple with the wife in the country, and horrified recognition scenes. The maid in the ghost story wakes up at night with her bell ringing, a bell that is never supposed to ring, and the incest in "Beatrice Palmato" takes place entirely in the dark, we are told in the outline, until the explicit sexual scene described in the fragment Wharton did write. (The outline and the fragment are published in Lewis, *Edith Wharton*, 544–48, and in Wolff, *A Feast of Words*, 300–303.) The terror the maid experiences upon waking in the night with her bell ringing is similar to the experience described by incest victims, as are the splitting of the father into the good suitor and bad husband, the horrified denial on the part of the mother figure, and the schizophrenic doubling of the victim. "Beatrice Palmato" was "evidently designed as a kind of ghost story," Cynthia Griffin Wolff has written, and Wolff goes on to claim that Wharton's ghost stories tend to center on two themes, a "secret self or alter-ego who is the reflection of some evil or forbidden impulse," and "a jealous love triangle . . . there is a married couple and there is a rival—an intruder, an interloper." Wolff sees clear oedipal themes in this fiction but denies that there is any incest per se in "The Lady's Maid's Bell" or in Wharton's own experience. In a move akin to Freud's abandonment of the seduction theory, Wolff finds the experiences described to be the result of Wharton's or her protagonists' illicit desires and argues that incest is simply a convenient metaphor for Wharton's sexual fears. See *Words* (299–308). My own argument about surveillance is not meant to deny that the story is a representation of actual incest, which I think it is, but simply states that surveillance is a way to describe the power relations involved.

21. Sigmund Freud, *Standard Edition of the Complete Psychological Works of Sigmund Freud*, ed. James Strachey (London, 1955), 1:36; Lewis, *Edith Wharton*, 84. See also Frank Norris's "The Ship That Saw a Ghost," in which the climax is reached when the narrator finally says, "I could put a name to my uneasiness. I felt that we were being watched" (*A Deal in Wheat*, 397).

22. Wharton, *The House of Mirth* (New York, 1905).

23. Dolores Hayden, "Charlotte Perkins Gilman and the Kitchenless House," *Radical History Review* 21 (Fall 1979): 230.

24. Gilman, "The Women Do Not Want It," in *In This Our World* (Boston, 1899),

quoted in Carol Farley Kessler, "Bitter Jars and Bitter Jangles: Light Verse by Charlotte Perkins Gilman," in *Gilman: The Woman and Her Work*, Meyering, 140–41.

8. The Blues and the Double Consciousness of Henry James and W. E. B. Du Bois

1. *The Autobiography of W. E. B. Du Bois: A Soliloquy on Viewing My Life from the Last Decade of Its First Century* (New York, 1968), 61–73; James, *The Ambassadors*, Norton Critical Edition (New York, 1964), ed. S. P. Rosenbaum; W. E. B. Du Bois, *The Souls of Black Folk* (Greenwich, Conn., 1961). The use of "double consciousness" in James and Du Bois was first pointed out to me by Kenneth Warren.

2. Mary Austin, *The Land of Little Rain* (Boston, 1903), 12; James Lane Allen, *The Mettle of the Pasture* (New York, 1903), 23–25; Alfred Henry Lewis, *Peggy O'Neal* (New York, 1903), 491–93.

3. Sherwin Cody, *The Art of Writing and Speaking the English Language* (New York, 1903).

4. F. G. Gosling, *Before Freud: Neurasthenia and the American Medical Community, 1870–1910* (Urbana, Ill., 1987), 162.

5. James, "The Birthplace," in *The Better Sort* (New York, 1903), p. 246.

6. Charles Eliot Norton to Howells, August 29, 1903, *Selected Letters of William Dean Howells*, ed. George Arms et al. (Boston, 1979–83), 5:62.

7. *The Letters of Henry Adams (1892–1918)*, ed. Worthington Chauncey Ford (Boston, 1938), 2:622; *The Letters of Henry James*, ed. Percy Lubbock (New York, 1920), 2:360.

8. Ruth Bernard Yeazell, *The Death and Letters of Alice James* (Berkeley, Calif., 1981), 21; see also Jean Strouse, *Alice James: A Biography* (Boston, 1980).

9. James, *A Small Boy and Others* in James, *Autobiography: A Small Boy and Others, Notes of a Son and Brother, The Middle Years*, ed. Frederick W. Dupee (New York, 1956), 158–61, 395.

10. Howard Feinstein, *Becoming William James* (Ithaca, N.Y., 1984).

11. Wharton, *A Backward Glance* (New York, 1934), 190. Miranda Seymour, *A Ring of Conspirators: Henry James and His Literary Circle, 1895–1915* (Boston, 1989), describes James's letters about his distress at staying in Rye rather than visiting his friends in London and America: "Suiting his sentiments to his audience was a fault to which James was uncommonly prone" (69).

12. Ian Watt, "The First Paragraph of *The Ambassadors*: An Explication," in *The Ambassadors*, Norton Critical Edition, 465–84; William Veeder, *Henry James: The Lessons of the Master: Popular Fiction and Personal Style in the Nineteenth Century* (Chicago, 1975); John H. Raleigh, "Henry James: The Poetics of Empiricism," in *Henry James*, ed. Tony Tanner, *Modern Judgements* (London, 1969), 54.

13. James, Preface to *The Ambassadors*, in *The Art of the Novel* (New York, 1909), 314; E. M. Forster, *Aspects of the Novel* ([1927] New York, 1955), 160–61; William C. Brownell is quoted in *Of Making Many Books*, Roger Burlingame (New York, 1946), 36–37. According to Edith Wharton, Brownell was "the most discerning literary critic of our day," quoted in James L. W. West, III, *American Authors and the Literary Marketplace since 1900* (Philadelphia, 1988), 50–51.

14. Although he fails to mention Beard, see Wolfgang Schivelbusch, *The Railway Journey: The Industrialization of Time and Space in the Nineteenth Century* ([1977] Berkeley, Calif., 1986), 134–49. Schivelbusch argues that "railway spine" and other traumatic effects of railway accidents were the source of modern therapeutic views such as Freud's because of the various legal arguments about compensation for accident victims and the problematic nature of psychological

diagnoses or subclinical medical complaints. The changing perceptions of time and space Schivelbusch mentions were some of the many changes that neurasthenia mediated, since part of the "wear and tear" of modern life was the result of maintaining incommensurate conceptions of time and space.

15. James, "Project of Novel by Henry James," in *The Notebooks of Henry James*, ed. F. O. Matthiessen and Kenneth B. Murdock (New York, 1955), 372–415.

16. See Adeline R. Titner, "The Pop World of Henry James: From Fairy Tales to Science Fiction," *Studies in Modern Literature* 89 (Ann Arbor, Mich., 1989): 130–33.

17. Edward Atkinson, *The Industrial Progress of the Nation* (New York, 1890), quoted in Daniel T. Rogers, *The Work Ethic in Industrial America, 1850–1920* (Chicago, 1978), 101, 263n. For James's relation to the literary market, see Michael Anesko, *"Friction with the Market": Henry James and the Profession of Authorship* (New York, 1986), and Marcia Jacobson, *Henry James and the Mass Market* (Tuscaloosa, Ala., 1983).

18. "Type bourgeois-bostonien! A type quite as good as another, but more uniform. . . . God knows that we knew our want of knowledge! the self-distrust become introspection—nervous self-consciousness—irritable dislike of America, and antipathy of Boston. . . . So you have written not Story's life, but your own and mine,—pure autobiography,—the more keen for what is beneath, implied, intelligible only to me, and a half dozen other people still living. . . . You make me curl up, like a trodden on worm. Improvised Europeans we were, and—Lord God!—how thin! . . . You strip us, gently and kindly, like a surgeon, and I feel your knife in my ribs. No one else will ever know it. You have been extremely tactful. The essential superficiality of Story and all the rest, you have made painfully clear to us, but not, I think, to the family or the public" (November 18, 1903, *The Letters of Henry Adams*, vol. 5: 1899–1905, ed. J. C. Levenson et al. [Cambridge, Mass., 1988], 524).

19. James, "Émile Zola" (1903), in *Henry James: Literary Criticism*, ed. Leon Edel (New York, 1984), 875.

20. Quoted in Leon Edel, *Henry James, The Master: 1901–1916* (New York, 1972), 185–86, 188.

21. Julie Rivkin, "The Logic of Delegation in *The Ambassadors*," *PMLA* 101 (October 1986): 820, 830.

22. What most struck James's secretary at this time, according to her diary, was James's "nervousness" (Miranda Seymour, *Ring of Conspirators* [Boston, 1989], 57–58, 121–27). The most thorough study of James's relation to the language and values of advertising is Jennifer Wicke, *Advertising Fictions* (New York, 1988), 87–119. For James's attempts at advertising himself, see Jacobson, *Henry James and the Mass Market*, and Anesko, *"Friction with the Market."* For other takes on the relation of James to consumerism, see Jean-Christophe Agnew, "The Consuming Vision of Henry James," in *The Culture of Consumption* (New York, 1983), and Mark Seltzer, *Henry James and the Art of Power* (Ithaca, N.Y., 1984).

23. Du Bois, *Darkwater* (New York, 1920), 9.

24. See especially Richard A. Hocks, *Henry James and Pragmatistic Thought: A Study of the Relationship between the Philosophy of William James and the Literary Art of Henry James* (Chapel Hill, N.C., 1974), and the chapter on Henry James in Anthony Channell Hilfer, *The Ethics of Intensity in American Fiction* (Austin, Tex., 1981). The relation of the James brothers' writings has provoked many arguments, but to go into these is impossible here; my general remarks above are in tune with those of Hocks and Hilfer. No similar study of Du Bois is available, but we have his own brief remarks on his relation to James, his "friend and guide to clear thinking" who led him "out of the sterilities of scholastic philosophy to realist pragmatism" (*Autobiography of W. E. B. Du Bois*, 127, 133,

143). The Jubilee edition was published in 1953 by Blue Heron Press and reprinted in 1961 by Fawcett. The quote is from page xiv of the Fawcett edition; further references in the text are to this edition. Frantz Fanon, *Black Skin, White Masks* (New York, 1967), and *The Wretched of the Earth* (New York, 1969). In 1968, fifteen years after writing this Preface, Du Bois wrote his autobiography, in which he never mentions Freud.

25. Edward L. Thorndike, *Educational Psychology* (New York, 1903), 78.

26. See *Souls of Black Folk*, 20: "But alas! while sociologists gleefully count his bastards and his prostitutes, the very soul of the toiling, sweating black man is darkened by the shadow of a vast despair."

27. Rampersad also points out the use of the plural in the title, which observation I use in the sentence that follows (Arnold Rampersad, *The Art and Imagination of W. E. B. Du Bois* [Cambridge, Mass., 1976], 74–76).

28. Pauline Hopkins, *Of One Blood; or, The Hidden Self* (originally serialized in *Colored American Magazine*, November 1902–November 1903), in *The Magazine Novels of Pauline Hopkins*, ed. Hazel Carby (New York, 1988). In *Of One Blood*, the young doctor reanimates a young black woman's body that has been pronounced dead by several other medical examiners: "in some cases of seeming death—or even death in reality—consciousness may be restored" (467).

29. Charles Chesnutt, *The Marrow of Tradition* ([1901] Ann Arbor, Mich., 1969), 1–2, 267, 271, 325–29. The stories in Chesnutt's *Conjure Woman* (1899) also make reference to the relation of neurasthenia to the supernatural.

30. In *The Negro Problem*, ed. Charles Chesnutt (Cleveland, Ohio, 1903), 45.

31. August Meier, *Negro Thought in America, 1880–1915: Racial Ideologies in the Age of Booker T. Washington* (Ann Arbor, Mich., 1963), 206. See also Manning Marable, *W. E. B. Du Bois: Black Radical Democrat* (Boston, 1986), 1 and passim; Elliot Rudwick, "W. E. B. Du Bois: Protagonist of the Afro-American Protest," in *Black Leaders of the Twentieth Century*, ed. John Hope Franklin and August Meier (Urbana, Ill., 1982), 63–83.

32. Washington Gladden, "Some Impressions Gained during a Visit to the Southern United States," in *The Social Gospel: Religion and Reform in Changing America*, ed. Ronald C. White, Jr., and C. Howard Hopkins (Philadelphia, 1976), 104–7.

33. I assume that there is no pun intended in Du Bois's use of "foster land" here, although given Stephen Foster's use of black musical idioms, both musically and lyrically, and his importance as a popular composer, the pun would be appropriate. Elsewhere, Du Bois was less hesitant, as when he declared that blacks had created "the only real American music" ("The Negro in Literature and Art," [1913], in W. E. B. Du Bois, *Writings* [New York, 1986], 862–67).

34. Thomas P. Fenner, *Cabin and Plantation Songs of the Negro* (Hampton, Va., 1874), quoted in Paul Oliver, Max Harrison, and William Bolcom, *The New Grove: Gospel, Blues, and Jazz, with Spirituals and Ragtime* (New York, 1986), 15. Du Bois himself was introduced to black folk songs and spirituals while teaching summers in Tennessee in the mid-1880s, at the same time that he was singing in the Mozart Society at Fisk (Nathan Huggins, "Chronology," in Du Bois, *Writings*, 1283).

35. W. F. Gates, "Ethiopian Syncopation—The Decline of Ragtime," *Musician* 7 (October 1902): 341, cited in Edward A. Berlin, *Ragtime: A Musical and Cultural History* (Berkeley, Calif., 1980), 1; Al Rose, *Eubie Blake* (New York, 1979), 12–30; Harold Hubbs, "What Is Ragtime?" *Outlook*, February 27, 1918, 345; Edward Baxter Perry, "Ragging Good Music," *Etude* 36 (June 1918): 372; "Our Musical Condition," *Negro Music Journal* 1 (March 1903): 138; quoted in Berlin, *Ragtime*, 43–44.

36. James H. Dormon, "Shaping the Popular Image of Post-Reconstruction

N

Blacks: The 'Coon Song' Phenomenon of the Gilded Age," *American Quarterly* 40 (December 1988): 466.

37. Sam Dennison, *Scandalize My Name: Black Imagery in American Popular Music* (New York, 1982), 356–84.

38. W. C. Handy, *Father of the Blues: An Autobiography*, ed. Arna Bontemps (New York, 1941), 78; Oliver, Harrison, Bolcom, *The New Grove*, 53. See William Barlow, *"Lookin Up at Down": The Emergence of Blues Culture* (Philadelphia, 1989), 7–24. For the important relation of the blues to religious practice, see Albert Murray, *Stomping the Blues* (New York, 1976), 23–42.

39. Ben Sidran, *Black Talk*, 2d ed. (New York, 1981), 23.

40. See Charles Hamm, *Yesterdays: Popular Song in America* (New York, 1979), 305.

41. Martin Petrey, "Music as a Medicine in the Home," *Ladies' Home Journal* 20 (October 1903), 49; Albert Murray, *Stomping the Blues*, 45–48. See Bernard W. Bell, *The Afro-American Novel and Its Tradition* (Amherst, Mass., 1987), 6, 26; Houston A. Baker, Jr., *Blues, Ideology, and Afro-American Literature: A Vernacular Theory* (Chicago, 1984), 14.

9. Concluding Anecdotes: "The Death of the Strenuous Self"

1. James, in *Harvard College Class of 1903: Twenty-Fifth Anniversary Report* (private printing, 1928), 510.

2. Jack London, *The Kempton-Wace Letters* (New York, 1903).

3. *Q.E.D.* remained in manuscript for almost half a century and was first published as *Things as They Are* (Pawlet, Vt., 1950). Gertrude Stein, *The Making of Americans: Being a History of a Family's Progress* ([1925] New York, 1966).

4. See Ira B. Nadel, "Gertrude Stein and Henry James," in *Gertrude Stein and the Making of Literature*, ed. Shirley Neuman and Ira B. Nadel (Boston, 1988), 81–97. But see also Donald Sutherland on Stein's having "fundamentally the moral views of a lady of 1902," in "Gertrude Stein and the Twentieth Century," in *A Primer for the Gradual Understanding of Gertrude Stein*, ed. Robert Bartlett Haas (Los Angeles, 1971), 153. See also Anthony Channell Hilfer, *The Ethics of Intensity* (Austin, Tex., 1981), 162; Lisa Ruddick, "William James and the Modernism of Gertrude Stein," in *Modernism Reconsidered*, ed. Robert Kiely, Harvard English Studies 11 (Cambridge, Mass., 1983), and " 'Melanctha' and the Psychology of William James," *Modern Fiction Studies* 28 (Winter 1982–83): 545–56; and Harriet Scott Chessman, *The Public Is Invited to Dance: Representation, the Body, and Dialogue in Gertrude Stein* (Stanford, Calif., 1989), 156–60. Michael J. Hoffman discusses the relationship of *Q.E.D.* to Stein's later style in *The Development of Abstractionism in the Writings of Gertrude Stein* (Philadelphia, 1965), 31–61.

5. Richard Harding Davis, *About Paris* (New York, 1903), 177. Davis's scathing criticism of the "American colony" in Paris also offers an interesting counterpoint to *The Ambassadors*: "The only way by which they can justify their action [desertion] is either to belittle what they have given up, or to emphasize the benefits which they have received in exchange, and these benefits are hardly perceptible" (190). "The American colony is not wicked, but it would like to be thought so, which is much worse" (192). They like to pose as if they were involved in scandals, especially of young men with married women, writes Davis, but he claims that it is all just talk.

6. Horatio C. Wood, *Brain-Work and Overwork* (Philadelphia, 1880), 16; Elizabeth Johns, *Thomas Eakins: The Heroism of Modern Life* (Princeton, N.J., 1983), 159–62, 168, and passim. See also Gordon Hendricks, *The Life and Work of Thomas Eakins* (New York, 1974); Lloyd Goodrich, *Thomas Eakins* (Cambridge, Mass., 1982), esp. 2:59; Michael Fried, *Realism, Writing, Disfiguration:*

On Thomas Eakins and Stephen Crane (Chicago, 1987). Fried's reading of *The Gross Clinic* in terms of writing, "disfiguration," and the changing ground of representation at the end of the century could be further historicized by reference to this account of the relation of neurasthenia to changing notions of social life and the self; the older face of the portrait has more written on it, as if disfigured by time, than the younger face of the sitter. See also Eakins's portraits of Mrs. Thomas Eakins (1899), Mary Adeline Williams (1900), himself (1902), and Edith Mahon (1904). See also David Lubin, *The Act of Portrayal: Eakins, Sargent, James* (New Haven, Conn., 1985). Lubin's emphasis on the doubleness of the act of portrayal in the work of Eakins and James is well taken, but this doubleness is not, for James or Eakins, a psychological notion (14) but one dependent on a series of attitudes toward the body and consciousness which I have tried to tease out in the case of James, and one that, given Eakins's lifelong relation to medical theory, would seem to be even more true for the painter. For the "nonpsychological" nature of James's representation of consciousness, see Sharon Cameron, *Thinking in Henry James* (Chicago, 1989), 1–13, 42–45.

7. S. Weir Mitchell, *A Comedy of Conscience* (New York, 1903), 66.

8. A. T. Mahan, "The Writing of History," *Atlantic Monthly* 91(March 1903), 289–98.

9. On the democratization of neurasthenia see F. G. Gosling, *Before Freud* (Urbana, Ill., 1987). See Sigmund Freud, "On the Grounds for Detaching a Particular Syndrome from Neurasthenia under the Description 'Anxiety-Neurosis,' " *Standard Edition of the Complete Psychological Works of Sigmund Freud* (hereafter *S.E.*) 3:87–139; review of S. Weir Mitchell's *Neurasthenie und Hysterie* [translation of *Fat and Blood*] *S.E.* 1:36; review of Averbeck's "Die akute Neurasthenie," *S.E.* 1:35; "Hysteria," *S.E.* 1:39–57; *Studies on Hysteria, S.E.* 2:267; reviews of Baumgarten's *Neurasthenie* and Wichmann's *Lebensreglen für Neurastheniker*, trans. Mark Solms, "Three Previously Untranslated Reviews by Freud from the *Neue Freie Presse*," *International Journal of Psycho-Analysis* 70 (1989): 397–400.

10. Ida Macalpine and Richard A. Hunter, quoted in Samuel M. Weber's Introduction to Daniel Paul Schreber, *Memoirs of My Nervous Illness*, trans. Ida Macalpine and Richard A. Hunter (Cambridge, Mass., 1988), xii. The information about Schreber which follows is from Weber's Introduction.

11. Simon Nelson Patten, *The New Basis of Civilization* (New York, 1907), 11, 215, 149, 215, 150, 164. Originally given as the Kennedy Lectures, New York, 1905; *Culture of Consumption*, ed. Richard Wightman Fox and T. J. Jackson Lears (New York, 1983), ix–xvii; Lears, *No Place of Grace* (New York, 1981), xiii–xvii, 37, 54–56, 301–6; Christopher Lasch, *The Culture of Narcissism: American Life in an Age of Diminishing Expectations* (New York, 1978), 7, 32, 48, 68–74; Philip Rieff, *The Triumph of the Therapeutic: Uses of Faith after Freud* (New York, 1966), 2–27, 49–50, 54, 236–49.

12. Woodrow Wilson, *The New Freedom: A Call for the Emancipation of the Generous Energies of a People* (New York, 1913), 277–94; Adams to Elizabeth Cameron, March 1, 1903, *The Letters of Henry Adams*, ed. Worthington Chauncey Ford (Boston, 1938), 464.

13. See the special issue of *Culture, Medicine, and Psychiatry* 13 (1989): 105–241.

14. Adams to Brooks Adams, January 9, 1903, *Letters*, 435; to Elizabeth Cameron, February 15, 1903, *Letters*, 456–57; to Elizabeth Cameron, March 29, 1903, *Letters*, 477; to Charles Francis Adams, Jr., December 8, 1903, *Letters*, 529; to Elizabeth Cameron, April 26, 1903, *Letters*, 493.

Index

Abrams, Albert
  The Blues: Its Causes and Cures,
    273
Abrams, M. H.
  Natural Supernaturalism, 123
activity, 34, 78, 93, 132, 143, 171,
    202, 224
Adams, Andy, 19, 88, 200, 202, 250
  The Log of the Cowboy, 201
  The Texas Matchmaker, 201
Adams, Brooks, 19, 43, 55, 81, 97,
    289
Adams, Henry, 14–16, 50, 94, 97,
    248, 257, 277
  The Education of Henry Adams, 3,
    127
    "The Virgin and the Dynamo," 4,
      156
  the multiverse, 24, 86
Addams, Jane, 19, 28, 102, 202, 222,
    223
Ade, George, 129
  In Babel, 151
adultery, 168, 179, 233
advertising, 9, 29, 47, 100, 159, 216–
    18, 239, 245–46, 272
  in *The Ambassadors*, 28, 256–61
aestheticism, 53, 103, 116, 123, 163,
    275
Agassiz, Louis, 66
Aldrich, Thomas Bailey, 166
Allen, James Lane, 19
  The Mettle of the Pasture, 40, 244

Allen, Maud, 223
American Kitchen Magazine, 215
American Psychiatric Association
  Diagnostic and Statistical Manual,
    23
anarchy, 35, 131, 136, 139, 142,
    212–14, 256
Armour, Philip, 126
asceticism, 34, 76–77, 223
Atkinson, Edward
  *The Industrial Progress of the Na-
    tion*, 256
Austin, Mary
  The Land of Little Rain, 200–201,
    244
automobiles, 9, 172

Baer, Robert, 7
Bailey, Liberty Hyde, 143
Baker, Ray Stannard, 71
Bakhtin, M. M., 278
Barthes, Roland, 23
Beach, Rex E., 129
  "The Mule Driver and the Garrulous
    Mute," 110
Beard, George M., 3–12, 19, 24, 50,
    63, 69, 101, 186, 196, 280
  American Nervousness, 3–7, 47, 83
  and Freud, 246, 285–86
  Nervous Exhaustion, 130
  and Norris, 131, 134, 145, 152
  on refinement, 16, 28, 53, 93, 108,
    264

110, 131, 198, 200, 204, 208, 216
medical discourse, 2, 4, 6, 12, 23, 24, 129, 230, 268, 285, 288
medical doctors, 3, 14, 35, 49, 64, 66, 126, 130, 224, 234, 249–50, 253, 281, 284–87
Meier, August, 266
Mencken, H. L., 105, 171, 177
Merriman, Charles Eustace, 11
Metaphysical Club, 73
Michaels, Walter Benn, 51
militarism, 8, 35, 39, 40, 45, 61, 64, 94
Miller, Perry, 71
miners, 8, 56, 100, 109–14, 145
Mitchell, John, 112
Mitchell, Langdon, 79
Mitchell, S. Weir, 6, 20, 32–34, 46, 69, 131, 280–88
A Comedy of Conscience, 281
Doctor and Patient, 32, 34, 142, 198, 209
exercise and, 79–80
Fat and Blood, 32
Gilman and, 231–34
Howells and, 168, 196
priestly medicine and, 66–67, 125
rest cure and, 32, 125
Wharton and, 231–34
modernism, 20, 207
modernity, 18, 27, 54, 84, 248, 275
Moody, Dwight L, 159
moral energy, 288
moral philosophy, 74, 143
moral tension, 170, 171
morbidity, 67–72, 102, 108, 124, 136–38, 184, 191, 203, 209, 214–17, 228, 250, 267
Muir, John, 19, 90, 143, 201
Our National Parks, 90, 144
Muldoon, William, 32, 45, 141
Murray, Albert, 273
music, 267, 272
blues, 272–75
"coon songs," 267, 269, 273
ragtime, 267–69, 272–73
spirituals, 272
Myers, F. H., 70, 212
Journal of the Society for Psychical Research, 70
mysticism, 60, 69, 127, 142, 170, 187, 194, 205, 212, 213, 223

Native Americans, 117
naturalism, 57–59, 65–66, 77, 87–92, 100, 108, 115, 118, 187, 201–6, 215, 257, 277
Norris and, 124–39, 156, 161, 164
nature, 40, 115, 133, 134, 143, 161, 187, 201, 206, 229
natural philosophy, 123
natural science, 79
Negro Music Journal, 268
nerve force, 2, 3, 12, 47, 96, 136, 151, 166, 209, 229, 246
nerves, 152, 186
nerve strength, 168
nervous illnesses, 132, 209
breakdown, 13, 75, 79, 154, 158, 222, 273
dyspepsia, 4, 12, 116, 170, 216, 264, 277, 278
prostration, 166, 168, 184
psychic sources, 168, 169
sickness, 186, 188
syphilis, 196
neurasthenia
history of, 2, 4–19
medical definition of, 20, 21, 23
neuroticism, 166, 177
Newcomb, Simon
"The End of the World," 124
New England, 200, 203, 205, 216
New York, 18, 106, 170, 171, 172, 173, 175, 248
newspapers in, 7–13, 38, 79, 239, 287
New York State Assembly, 78
Nietzsche, Friedrich, 23, 60, 97, 124–26, 194, 285–86
The Genealogy of Morals, 124
Norris, Frank, 28, 55, 105, 118–20, 131–65, 200–203, 216
Blix, 132, 134, 136, 144, 160, 164
A Deal in Wheat, 144, 147
"The Frontier Gone at Last," 141
and *McClure's Magazine*, 139
McTeague, 59, 118, 134, 144
A Man's Woman, 134, 160, 164
Moran of the Lady Letty, 134, 136, 164
"The Need of a Literary Conscience," 132, 133, 141
The Octopus, 114, 118, 131, 134, 135, 137, 139, 164
The Pit, 6, 42, 103, 108, 118, 134,

Library of Congress Cataloging-in-Publication Data

Lutz, Tom.
   American nervousness, 1903: an anecdotal history / Tom Lutz.
      p.   cm.
   Includes bibliographical references and index.
   ISBN 0-8014-2581-6 (cloth: alk. paper).—ISBN 0-8014-9901-1 (pbk.: alk. paper)
      1. United States—Civilization—1865–1918—Psychological aspects.
2. Neurasthenia—Social aspects—United States—History—20th century.
I. Title.   II. Title: 1903.
E169.1.L88   1991
973.91—dc20   90-55737